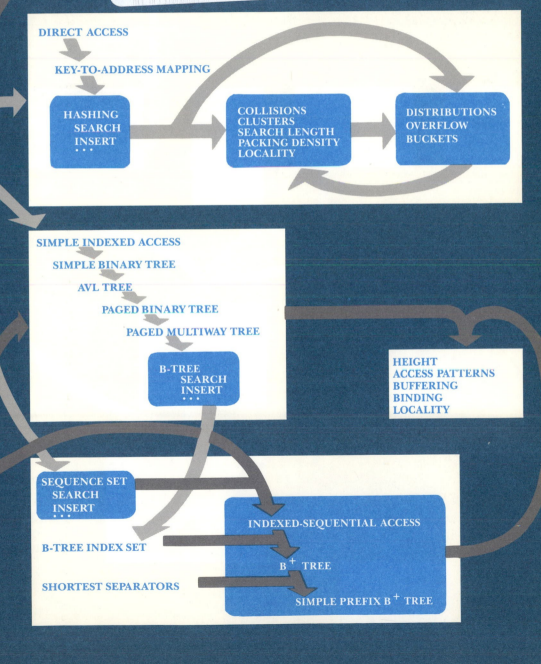

COSEQUENTIAL PROCESSING
MATCH/MERGE
REPLACEMENT SELECTION
MERGE SORTS

D0073003

DIRECT ACCESS

KEY-TO-ADDRESS MAPPING

HASHING
SEARCH
INSERT
· · ·

COLLISIONS
CLUSTERS
SEARCH LENGTH
PACKING DENSITY
LOCALITY

DISTRIBUTIONS
OVERFLOW
BUCKETS

SIMPLE INDEXED ACCESS

SIMPLE BINARY TREE

AVL TREE

PAGED BINARY TREE

PAGED MULTIWAY TREE

B-TREE
SEARCH
INSERT
· · ·

HEIGHT
ACCESS PATTERNS
BUFFERING
BINDING
LOCALITY

SEQUENCE SET
SEARCH
INSERT
· · ·

B-TREE INDEX SET

SHORTEST SEPARATORS

INDEXED-SEQUENTIAL ACCESS

B$^+$ TREE

SIMPLE PREFIX B$^+$ TREE

FILE STRUCTURES
A CONCEPTUAL TOOLKIT

MICHAEL J. FOLK
Oklahoma State University

BILL ZOELLICK

FILE
STRUCTURES
A CONCEPTUAL TOOLKIT

 **Addison-Wesley
Publishing Company**

Reading, Massachusetts ▪ Menlo Park, California
Don Mills, Ontario ▪ Wokingham, England
Amsterdam ▪ Sydney ▪ Singapore ▪ Tokyo
Madrid ▪ Bogotá ▪ Santiago ▪ San Juan

Sponsoring Editor ▪ Mark S. Dalton
Production Supervisor ▪ Laura Skinger
Packager ▪ Sherry Berg
Designer ▪ Melinda Grosser
Manufacturing Supervisor ▪ Hugh Crawford
Cover Designer ▪ Marshall Henrichs

Reprinted with corrections December, 1987

Library of Congress Cataloging-in-Publication Data

Folk, Michael J.
    File structures.

    1. File organization (Computer science)   I. Zoellick,
Bill.   II. Title.
QA76.9.F5F65   1987   005.74   86–25890
ISBN 0–201–12003–8

5-31-88

TO THE MEMORY OF
MARTHA LIVERIGHT FOLK

Designing fast, flexible file structures is one of the most interesting and satisfying activities in computer science. This book instructs the reader in the elements of this design process. As in any text on the subject of design, we focus on design *concepts* and *constraints*.

We think of design *concepts* as *conceptual tools*. There are a handful of these tools that all file structure designers must be able to use with facility. For example, the designer must be comfortable with a wide range of options for organizing a file into records. Similarly, one must have a *toolkit* of approaches to *retrieving* these records. This toolkit should include, for example, hashed access, simple indexes, paged indexes such as B-trees, and variations on paged indexes such as B^+ trees, and B* trees. The designer must know more than the names of these tools and how to use them; he or she must know *why* and *when* to use them.

The why and when is associated with the matter of *constraints*. The file structure designer must understand the design medium, which is to say that he or she must understand the strengths and weaknesses of the storage devices used to hold files. The designer must be able to relate these media constraints to the capabilities of the tools and, of course, to the design *objectives* of the system that he or she is building. The goal of this book is to help the reader develop such *design judgment*.

This book is structured as a text for use in undergraduate coursework, but it is also intended for computer science professionals who want to learn more about file structure design. We have tried to make this

PREFACE

book *readable*; this is not a reference manual that must be explained through a set of accompanying lectures, but a book that a student or professional programmer can sit down and read cover to cover.

THE USE OF C AND PASCAL

Pseudocode is a wonderful instructional tool that focuses on the essential aspects of an algorithm by setting aside all of the details that must be present in a real program. We use pseudocode extensively in this book, particularly in the later chapters where the procedures are complex and where it is therefore important to avoid the distractions inherent in actual, compilable code. However, there are also times when looking at the details is important. This is particularly true in the early chapters of the book where we explore matters such as the many ways of expressing the concept of a *record* in a file structure. For this reason we need to be able to present real programs in addition to the pseudocode, and therefore need to choose a programming language for use in the text.

We actually use two languages: C and Pascal. C is an excellent language for implementing new, innovative file structures and is used by a rapidly increasing number of professional programmers. Pascal, on the other hand, is a more familiar language for many university students. One of our initial motivations for using both languages was to make the book more readily accessible to a larger number of readers. As we developed the sample programs in both languages, however, a second benefit emerged: Insofar as the most "natural" approach to a problem in C sometimes differs from the "natural" Pascal solution, the use of both languages helps us underscore the fact that file structure design is a matter of *judgment*. The "right" solution to a file structure problem depends on many factors, including the language used to implement the design.

USING THIS BOOK IN TEACHING
A COURSE

For the past two years early drafts of this book have been used as the main text for a course in file structures at Oklahoma State University. This is a one-semester course that treats material outlined as Course

CS-5 in the *ACM Curriculum '78*, and provides a foundation for the study of database design. Enrollment for the course consists primarily of juniors and seniors; a large percentage of incoming graduate students also take the course. The course includes three lectures a week and a one hour and a half laboratory session.

Because the book is quite readable, we have found that it is reasonable to expect the students to read the entire book over the course of the semester. The text covers the basics; class lectures extend and supplement the base of material presented in the text. This leaves the lecturer free to explore more complex questions and possibilities. We have found that, given the time constraints of a single semester, we cannot focus in detail on both hashing and B-trees. Although we always lecture on both topics, in any given semester we concentrate our problem assignments on either hashing or B-trees.

A word of caution: It is easy to spend too much time on the low-level issues presented in the first seven chapters. Move quickly through this material. The relatively large number of pages devoted to these matters is not a reflection of the percentage of the course that should be spent on them. The intent, instead, is to cover them very thoroughly in the text so that the instructor can simply assign these chapters as background reading, saving precious lecture time for more important topics.

We have found that it is important to get students involved in writing file processing programs early in the semester. We start with a simple file reading and writing assignment that is due after the first week of class. The text's inclusion of sample programs in both C and Pascal makes it easier to work in this hands-on style. We recommend that, by the time the students encounter the B-tree chapter, they should have already written programs that access a data set through a simple index structure. Since the students will already have first-hand experience with the fundamental organizational issues, it is possible for lectures to focus on the *conceptual* issues involved in B-tree design.

Finally, we suggest that instructors adhere to a close approximation of the sequence of topics used in the book, especially the first seven chapters. We have already stressed that we wrote the book so that it can be read cover to cover. It is not a reference work. For that reason, we *develop* ideas as we proceed from chapter to chapter. Skipping around in the book makes it difficult for students to follow this development. The one notable exception to this guideline involves the B-tree chapters and the hashing chapter. The text is written to accommodate instructors who want to treat hashing before looking at B-trees and B^+ trees.

═══ ORGANIZATION OF THE BOOK

Here is a skeletal summary of the sequence of topics discussed in the text:

INTRODUCTION

Chapter 1: How file structures differ from data structures that are contained in electronic memory. The key issues of file structure design.

FUNDAMENTALS

Chapter 2: Fundamental file processes: creating, opening, reading, writing, and seeking.

Chapter 3: Secondary storage devices: the physical constraints and capabilities that shape file structure design.

Chapter 4: Fundamental concepts: fields, records, sequential and direct access, and sequential searching.

Chapter 5: File maintenance and record deletion: reusing the space in a file, storage fragmentation, and storage management.

SIMPLE RETRIEVAL STRATEGIES

Chapter 6: Sorting and searching: sorting in RAM and access through binary searching.

Chapter 7: Indexing: simple index structures, retrieval on secondary keys, and inverted list structures.

COSEQUENTIAL PROCESSING

Chapter 8: Cosequential processing and sorting large files: a general model for two-way matching and merging, K-way merging, sorting large files on disk, replacement selection, and tape sorting.

TREE ACCESS METHODS

Chapter 9:   B-trees and other tree-structured file organizations: the
               history of B-tree development, other paged tree
               structures and balanced tree structures, fundamental
               B-tree operations, virtual B-trees, B* trees, and other
               variants.

Chapter 10:   B$^+$ trees and indexed sequential file access: an
               introduction to indexed sequential access, simple prefix
               B$^+$ trees, loading trees, and a comparison of tree-
               structured methods.

HASHING

Chapter 11:   Hashing: fundamental concepts, simple approaches to
               collision reduction and resolution, tools for analyzing and
               predicting performance, file deterioration, advanced
               hashing structures, and patterns of record access.

ACKNOWLEDGMENTS

It is impossible to acknowledge all the individuals who helped us prepare this book. A major expression of thanks must go to our colleague
Jim VanDoren, whose views of file structures strongly influenced our
original approach to the subject. We would like to express special
thanks to Gail Smith for help in implementing many of the programs
that appear at the ends of chapters throughout the text. We would like
to thank TMS, Inc., for providing the flexible work schedule required
to accommodate the writing of a book.

The 200-plus students who used the evolving manuscript during
the past two years made important contributions by questioning the
material, by finding errors in the text and the exercises, and by generally supporting our efforts. Thanks especially to students Huey Liu and
Marilyn Aiken, and colleagues Art Crotzer and Don Fisher, for their
helpful comments and suggestions.

Mark Dalton, our editor at Addison-Wesley, gave unflagging support from the very first tentative chapters to final publication. We
thank Sherry Berg and Sarah Meyer for polishing the book's format
and tightening the prose. Thanks also to Addison-Wesley's reviewers,

who provided constructive comments and suggestions throughout the development of the book: Laurian M. Chirica, California Polytechnic State University; Charles W. Reynolds, James Madison University; Billy G. Claybrook, Wang Institute; Henry A. Etlinger, Rochester Institute of Technology; Paul W. Ross, Millersville University; Sharon Salveter, Boston University; Ronald L. Lancaster, Bowling Green State University; and Karen A. Lemone, Worcester Polytech Institute.

We should also note the contribution of two Stillwater restaurants, the Hideaway and Mom's Place, for fueling this project and providing the location for countless meetings.

Finally, our sincere thanks to those who put up with shortened days and weekends for two years, and returned the favor with encouragement and support: Ruthann, Rachel, Martha, Joshua, and Peter.

Stillwater, Oklahoma   M.F.
                                                                         B.Z.

CONTENTS

3   SECONDARY STORAGE DEVICES AND SYSTEM SOFTWARE: PERFORMANCE CONSIDERATIONS

4 FUNDAMENTAL FILE STRUCTURE CONCEPTS

7 INDEXING

8 COSEQUENTIAL PROCESSING AND SORTING LARGE FILES

9 B-TREES AND OTHER TREE-STRUCTURED FILE ORGANIZATIONS

10 THE B⁺ TREE FAMILY AND INDEXED SEQUENTIAL FILE ACCESS

11 HASHING

CHAPTER

OBJECTIVES

Enumerate the reasons for using secondary
storage devices.

Assess the large cost of using secondary storage.

Define the term *file*.

Describe the difference between the study of *file structures*
and the more general study of *data structures,* and show
that the design of efficient secondary storage systems
requires a knowledge of file structure fundamentals.

Introduce the notion of a *conceptual toolkit.*

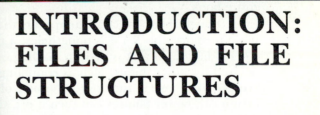

1 INTRODUCTION: FILES AND FILE STRUCTURES

CHAPTER OUTLINE

1.1
PRIMARY AND SECONDARY STORAGE

In 1986, 64 kilobytes (64K) of moderately fast random access memory (RAM) for a computer costs about ten dollars. This 64K of RAM, which is the computer's *primary storage,* has enough capacity to hold approximately 25 typewritten pages of text; the storage cost for a typewritten page of manuscript, such as the one we are typing now, is about 40 cents.

By the time we finish this book we will have written about 700 pages of manuscript, so there are at least three good reasons why we are not interested in storing the entire book in the electronic memory inside a computer:

☐ There is a limit to how much RAM a given computer can address. The computer we are using to write this book can address only 640K of RAM, or only about a third of what we need to hold the entire book.

☐ Even though there are large computers that can address much more memory, this RAM is nonetheless a relatively expensive commodity. RAM that is tied up holding our manuscript cannot be used for other things, such as compiling programs.

☐ We like to be able to turn our computer off. Even if we did not turn it off, power failures can turn it off. Once the computer is off, even for a few seconds, everything stored in RAM is gone. That is no way to treat a manuscript.

The term *secondary storage* refers to storage media that are outside of the primary RAM storage inside the computer. Examples of secondary storage media are magnetic tapes, disk packs, floppy disks, and optical storage discs. More information can be stored on these media than can normally be stored in RAM. These media also store the information more cheaply and remember what has been stored without continual power input. For example, we use a fixed disk to store our manuscript pages in our personal computer. This fixed disk holds about 20,000K, or 7,800 typewritten manuscript pages. Since this kind of disk costs about $600, using a fixed disk rather than RAM brings the storage cost per page down from 40 cents to 8 cents. That is a substantial, nearly order-of-magnitude, improvement.

We could also use floppy disks to store our manuscript. The disks that would fit in our computer can hold about 360K, or 150 manuscript pages. Since a floppy disk costs about $1.50, our storage costs would drop to under one cent per page. That is almost another order of magnitude of improvement in cost savings.

We could store and distribute the finished manuscript on $5\frac{1}{4}$ inch, CD-ROM digital laser discs. Each of these discs can hold 540,000K, which means that a laser disc can hold over 210,000 pages of manuscript. It could store this book and over 300 others. If the discs were produced in quantity, the cost of a single disc containing all of this information would be less than 20 dollars. That brings the cost per page down to one hundredth of a cent per page. We have come a long way from the 40 cents per page cost of using RAM.

1.2 NO FREE LUNCH

One cannot achieve such savings without giving up something. Accessing information from secondary storage takes more time than accessing it from RAM. A lot more time. Retrieving a single character from the memory of our personal computer takes about 150 nanoseconds, which is 150 billionths of a second. If that character is stored on our fixed disk, we have to bring it from the disk into RAM before the computer can do anything with it. The average time required to access a character on our disk is somewhat longer than 75 milliseconds (msec), or 75 thousandths of a second.

Now, 75 msec does not sound like a very long time, but the cost of expending this time for a disk access must be viewed relative to the time needed to access the same byte if it is already in RAM. To put this cost in perspective, let's make up a retrieval problem that uses you rather than a computer as the retrieval device.

Suppose we ask you to retrieve a definition of the term *record* by accessing the book you have in your hands. You might want to try it and time yourself. Our guess is that if you work rapidly, using the index at the back of the book, it might take you about 20 seconds to retrieve this definition. We take this to be your RAM retrieval time.

Now we need to calculate how long it would take you to find this definition if you were retrieving it from secondary storage. To follow the computer model, we need to keep your RAM access/secondary store access ratio equal to the ratio that really exists between a computer accessing RAM and accessing a fixed disk.

If you do the arithmetic, you can see that 75 msec is 500,000 times longer than 150 nanoseconds. So, since your RAM access took 20 seconds, your secondary storage access would take 10,000,000 seconds. That is 2778 hours, or almost 116 days!

Using a large computer with a fast, expensive disk drive can help reduce the ratio between a memory access and a disk access, but the reduction is not substantial. A larger computer has an average disk access time that is about one third that of our small computer, but access to RAM is also quicker. Even with a large computer, the fact remains that disk accesses are *enormously* more expensive than are accesses to electronic memory.

As you can see, when you decide to store something out on a disk rather than in RAM, you make a costly decision. When you start making such costly decisions, you need to make them carefully.

1.3　FILES

Data that are placed off on secondary storage are collected into *files*. A file is usually defined as a collection of related information. Witness the following definitions:

> A collection of records involving a set of entities with certain aspects in common and organized for some particular purpose
>
> *Tremblay and Sorenson [1984]*

> A collection of similar records kept on secondary computer storage devices
>
> *Wiederhold [1983]*

One of the reviewers of an early version of this manuscript turned this "collection of related information" definition around to make an important, interesting point:

> I have always maintained that the information is related because it is in the same file.
>
> *Lemone [1984]*

We like this view because it emphasizes that the data in a file does not somehow organize itself. The decisions related to structuring a file are among the most critical decisions made by the designer of a file system.

Let's return for a moment to our two sources of information, one of which was accessible within 20 seconds, the other requiring a 116 day wait. Suppose that we knew that we had to go ahead and send off for the information from secondary storage; we are resigned to waiting 116 days for it to be sent to us. Having committed ourselves to the use of secondary storage, what sorts of characteristics would we want our interaction with secondary storage to have? Our guess is that we would want to try to meet the following conditions:

☐ We will get exactly what we need as a result of our first try. We do not want to end up waiting 116 days only to discover that we received the wrong information.

☐ If it is absolutely impossible to know what to ask for on our first try, we want the information in that distant source to be organized so that we can, at the very least, get some initial information that will minimize the number of other requests that we must submit.

☐ We want to get *everything* we need at once. If we know we need four different pieces of information, we would certainly hope to be able to request them all at once, rather than at the rate of one data item per 116-day interval.

These are exactly the kinds of considerations that go into the design of a file structure. We are resigned to the use of secondary storage, but want to minimize that use. When we request data from a file, we want to be able to go directly to it, if at all possible. And, at best, we want to be able to get everything that we need in a single access. Whether or not we can meet these objectives is determined by the file structure. The formal study of file structures is motivated by the requirement that, given the relatively large cost of accessing secondary storage, a designer of file structures must begin work from a solid conceptual framework.

1.4   FILE STRUCTURES VERSUS DATA STRUCTURES

We assume that most readers of this book are familiar with simple fundamental data structures such as linked lists and binary trees. The study of file structures is essentially an application of data structure techniques to the special problems associated with storage and retrieval of data on secondary storage devices.

A few months ago one of us was interviewing an applicant for a position that involved working on a large information retrieval problem. Over lunch we told the applicant about the difficulties we had finding a sort package suitable for sorting the hundreds of millions of records involved in the index structures for the system we were working on. The applicant asked, "I suppose you use Quicksort for that?"

His question can serve as a nice illustration of the difference between a typical *data structure* course and the study of *file structures*. The study of data structures usually assumes that the data are stored in RAM. The term *random access*, as in Random Access Memory, means that the cost of getting one piece of information is the same as the cost of getting any other. Moreover, in RAM the cost of accessing information is actually less than the cost of many other operations, such as comparing two quantities. Given this traditional, pure data structure perspective, it is possible to show that Quicksort is, on the average, faster than other sorting algorithms. So, when the applicant asked about Quicksort, he was demonstrating knowledge gained from a data structure course.

Unfortunately, he was also showing us that he had not had the opportunity to take a file structure course. A file consisting of hundreds of millions of records is much too big to load into RAM for sorting. The sorting must involve use of secondary storage. That means that we are no longer in a *random access* environment; the cost of getting some pieces of information is now enormously more expensive than the cost of getting other information. An approach to sorting that is oriented to file structure design would recognize this. It would minimize the number of disk accesses and, moreover, try to arrange the pattern of access so that, when we need another piece of information, it is located in a place that is relatively inexpensive to access.

Quicksort does not take these differences into account at all. Applying Quicksort to the entire file results in a great many disk accesses without regard to the relative cost of each access, and consequently results in very slow performance. A later chapter gives careful consideration to the limitations of secondary storage devices in the construction of a sorting algorithm that is very different than Quicksort.

1.5 ⬛ A CONCEPTUAL TOOLKIT

The study of file structures, then, involves taking advantage of a medium that provides vast, inexpensive, nonvolatile storage. It also involves confronting the limitations of the medium, such as the 20-second/116-day ratio between primary memory access time and secondary memory access. The solution emerges in the form of file structures that minimize secondary storage accesses and maximize the amount of information returned in a single access.

One of the attractive aspects of working with file structures is that designing them involves consideration of only a handful of basic concepts, yet there seems to be an almost infinite number of ways to combine and vary these concepts. Working on a storage and retrieval problem is always an opportunity to make something new. Along with the excitement of making new things, however, there is the pleasure that comes from working with fundamental conceptual tools that you understand well and have used many times before.

Our purpose throughout this book is to provide the conceptual toolkit needed to build useful file structures in response to a variety of problems.

SUMMARY

Even though the primary computer memory (RAM) provides the fastest and simplest form of memory, there are several reasons why we need to keep information on secondary storage devices rather than in RAM:

- The amount of available RAM is usually quite limited compared to available secondary storage space;
- RAM is more expensive than secondary storage; and
- RAM is volatile; secondary storage is not.

The problem with secondary storage is that much more time is needed to access data on secondary storage than in RAM. The decision to access data from secondary storage is so costly that it becomes very important to send and retrieve data as intelligently as possible. When we search for data, we want to find it on our first try, or at least just a few tries, rather than having to look through an entire file for it. Or, if we want several pieces of data, we would like to get them all at once, rather than perform separate accesses for each of them.

Another important difference between secondary storage and RAM is that, on secondary storage, the cost of getting some pieces of information is much greater than the cost of getting other pieces of information. In RAM all access is equally costly. When there is a pattern to the way information is accessed, good file structure design attempts to organize the information to minimize the cost of access.

The information on secondary devices is organized into files. A file is just a collection of bytes representing information, but the bytes that make up a file can be organized hierarchically into structures that can have an enormous effect on how easily and efficiently we can carry out operations on files.

As you learn about files, you will find that several basic concepts are the key to working intelligently with files. These concepts have to do with the ways we can organize files to accommodate the different space and time costs when working with data on secondary storage instead of in RAM.

KEY TERMS

File. A collection of bytes that represent information and are typically kept on secondary storage. Some or all of the contents of a file are usually loaded into RAM for processing.

File structure. The organization imposed on a file to facilitate file processing. File structures we encounter in this book include fields, records, blocks, trees, indexes, sequences, and other conceptual constructs.

RAM. Random access memory. As we use the term, it is synonymous with *primary memory*. The word *random* is used because it provides immediate access to any storage location, no matter what its address. In the text, we contrast RAM with secondary memory, which typically takes much longer to access any location, and on which different amounts of time are required to access different locations.

OBJECTIVES

Describe the process of linking a *logical file* within a program to an actual *physical file* or device.

Describe the procedures used to create, open, and close files.

Provide examples of reading from and writing to files.

Introduce the concept of *position* within a file and describe procedures for *seeking* different positions.

FUNDAMENTAL FILE PROCESSING OPERATIONS

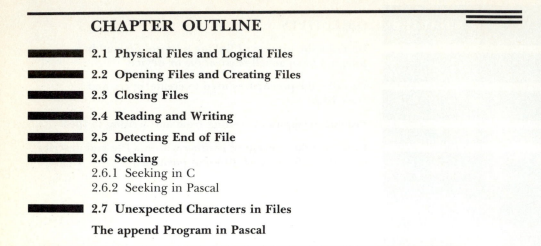

CHAPTER OUTLINE

2.1
PHYSICAL FILES AND LOGICAL FILES

When we talk about a file on a disk or tape, we refer to a particular collection of bytes stored there. A file, when the word is used in this sense, physically exists. A disk drive might contain hundreds, even thousands, of these *physical files*.

From the standpoint of an application program, the notion of a file is different. To the program, a file is somewhat like a telephone line connected to a telephone network. The program can receive bytes through this phone line, or send bytes down it, but knows nothing about where these bytes actually come from or where they go. The program knows only about its own end of the phone line. Moreover, even though there may be thousands of physical files on a disk, a single program is usually limited to the use of only about 20 telephone hookups.

The application program relies on the operating system to take care of the details of the telephone switching system, as illustrated in Fig. 2.1. It could be that bytes coming down the line into the program originate from an actual physical file, or they might come from the keyboard or some other input device. Similarly, the bytes that the program sends down the line might end up in a file, or they could appear on the terminal screen. Although the program often doesn't know where bytes are coming from or where they are going, it does know which line it is using. This line is usually referred to as the *logical file* to distinguish this view from the *physical files* on the disk or tape.

Before the program can open a file for use, the operating system must receive instructions about making a hookup between a logical file (e.g., a phone line) and some physical file or device. When using operating systems such as IBM's OS/MVS, these instructions are provided through job control language (JCL). On minicomputers and microcomputers, more modern operating systems such as UNIX, MS-DOS, and VMS provide the instructions within the program. For example, in Turbo Pascal† the association between a logical file called *inp_file* and a physical file called *myfile.dat* is made with the following statement:

```
assign(inp_file,'myfile.dat')
```

This statement asks the operating system to find the physical file named *myfile.dat* and then to make the hookup by assigning a logical file (phone line) to it. The number identifying the particular phone line that is assigned is returned through the FILE variable *inpfile*, which is the file's *logical name*. This logical name is what we use to refer to the file inside the program. Again, the telephone analogy applies: my office phone is connected to six telephone lines. When I receive a call I get an intercom message such as, "You have a call on line three." The receptionist does not say, "You have a call from 918-123-4567." I need to have the call identified *logically*, not *physically*.

2.2   OPENING FILES AND CREATING FILES

Once we have a logical file identifier hooked up to a physical file or device, we need to declare what we intend to do with the file. In general, we have two options:

1. OPEN an existing file; or

2. CREATE a new file, deleting any existing contents in the physical file.

Opening a file makes it ready for use by the program. We are positioned at the beginning of the file and are ready to start reading or writing. The file contents are not disturbed by the OPEN statement.

Creating a file also opens the file in the sense that it is ready for use after creation. Since a newly created file has no content, writing is initially the only use that makes sense.

---

†Different Pascal compilers vary widely with regard to I/O procedures, since standard Pascal contains little in the way of an I/O definition. Throughout this book we use the term *Pascal* when discussing features common to most Pascal implementations. When we refer to the features of a specific implementation, such as Turbo Pascal, we say so.

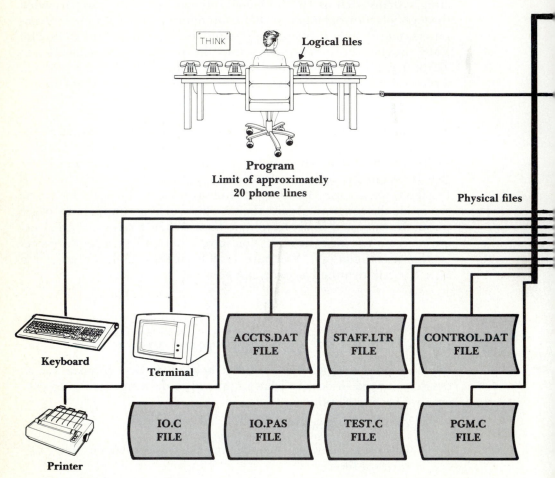

FIGURE 2.1 ▪ The program relies on the operating system to make connections between logical files and physical files and devices.

In Pascal, the *reset()* statement is used to open files and the *rewrite()* statement is used to create them. For example, to open a file in Turbo Pascal, we might use a sequence of statements such as:

```
assign(inp_file, 'myfile.dat');
reset(inp_file)
```

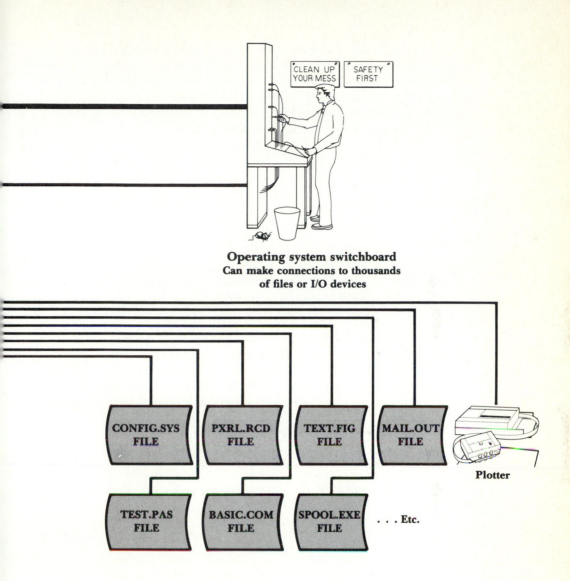

Operating system switchboard
Can make connections to thousands
of files or I/O devices

Note how we use the logical file name, not the physical one, in the *reset()* statement. To create a file in Turbo Pascal, the statements might read:

```
assign(out_file, 'myfile.dat');
rewrite(out_file)
```

In Turbo Pascal, the separation of the logical/physical name *assignment* from the actual file opening has the nice property of making the steps in the process clear, but this is atypical. The approach used in the C language is like that used in most other languages: name assignment and file opening are handled in a single call to the operating system. In C, the *open()* function takes the following form:

```
fd = open(filename, RWMODE);
```

where fd, filename, and RWMODE have the following meanings:

fd	The *file descriptor*. This is the number of the phone line used to refer to the file within the program. As you can see, it is an integer value returned by *open()* rather than something set up with a separate statement.
filename	The physical file name.
RWMODE	The access mode for the file. It is specified as an integer equal to 0 if the file is opened for reading only, 1 for writing only, and 2 for both reading and writing.

Besides the combination of name assignment and file opening into a single call, the other notion that we encounter here is that of an *access mode*. Numerous Pascal implementations have extended standard Pascal to provide this same capability. Controlling access to a file, restricting it to read-only use, can be particularly important when several programs share access to a file.

We can use C to create a new file, as follows:

```
fd = creat(filename, PMODE);
```

where *fd* and *filename* have the same meaning as for the *open()* function. The new, different argument for *creat()* is:

PMODE	The protection mode established for the file, indicating who can read to, write from, and execute the file.

Different operating systems offer different kinds of file protection; some offer none at all. In the UNIX operating system, for example, the PMODE is a three-digit octal number that indicates how the file can be used by the owner (first digit), members of the owner's group (second digit), and everybody else. The first bit of each octal number indicates read permission, the second bit write permission, and the third bit execute permission. So, if PMODE is the octal number 0751, the file's owner would have read, write, and execute permission for the file, the owner's group would have read and execute permission, and everyone else would have permission only to execute it.

```
                              r w e    r w e    r w e
        PMODE  =  0751  =>    1 1 1    1 0 1    0 0 1
                              owner    group    world
```

File protection is tied more to the host operating system than to a specific language. For example, implementations of Pascal running on systems that support file protection, such as VAX/VMS, often include extensions to standard Pascal that let you associate a protection status with a file when you create it.

2.3 CLOSING FILES

In terms of our telephone line analogy, closing a file is like hanging up the phone. When you hang up the phone, the phone line is available for taking or placing another call; when you close a file, the logical file name or file descriptor is available for use with another file. Closing a file that has been used for output also ensures that everything has been written to the file. As you will learn in a later chapter, it is more efficient to move data to and from secondary storage in blocks than it is to move data one byte at a time. Consequently, the operating system does not immediately send off the bytes we write, but saves them up in a buffer for transfer as a block of data. Closing a file makes sure that the buffer for that file has been flushed of data and that everything we have written has actually been sent to the file.

Files are usually closed automatically by the operating system when a program terminates normally. Consequently, the explicit use of a CLOSE statement is needed only as protection against data loss in the event of program interruption and to free up logical file names for reuse. Some languages, including some implementations of Pascal, do not even provide a CLOSE statement. However, explicit file closing is possible in the C language, Turbo Pascal, VAX Pascal, PL/I, and in most other languages used for serious file processing work.

Now that you know how to connect and disconnect programs to and from physical files and how to open the files, you are ready to start sending and receiving data.

2.4 READING AND WRITING

Reading and *writing* are fundamental to file processing; they are the actions that make file processing an *input/output* (I/O) operation. The actual form of the read and write statements used in different languages varies. Some languages provide very high-level access to reading and writing, and automatically take care of details for the programmer. Other languages provide access at a much lower level. Our use of Pascal and C allows us to explore some of these differences.†

We begin here with reading and writing at a relatively low level. It is useful to have a kind of systems-level understanding of what happens when we send and receive information to and from a file.

A low-level read call requires three pieces of information, expressed here as arguments to a generic READ() function.

READ(Source_file, Destination_addr, Size)

Source_file. The READ() call must know from where it is to read. We specify the source by logical file name (phone line) through which data is received. (Remember, before we do any reading we have already opened the file, so the connection between a logical file and a specific physical file or device already exists.)

Destination_addr. READ() must know where to place the information it reads from the input file. In this generic function we specify the destination by giving the address of the memory location where we want to store the data.

Size. Finally, READ() must know how much information to bring in from the file. Here the argument is supplied as a byte count.

A *WRITE* statement is similar; the only difference is that the data moves in the other direction:

WRITE(Destination_file, Source_addr, Size)

Destination_file. The logical file name (phone line) we use for sending the data.

Source_addr. WRITE() must know where to find the information that it will send. We provide this specification as a memory address.

Size. The number of bytes to be written must be supplied.

Let's do some reading and writing to see how these functions are used. This first simple file processing program, which we call LIST, opens a file for input and reads it, character by character, sending each character to the screen after it is read from the file. LIST includes the following steps.

---

†To accentuate these differences and provide a look at I/O operations at something closer to a systems level, we use the *read()* and *write()* system calls in C rather than higher-level functions such as *fgetc()*, *fgets()*, and so on.

1. Display a prompt for the name of the input file.

2. Read the user's response from the keyboard into a variable called *filename*.

3. OPEN the file for input.

4. WHILE there are still characters to be read from the input file:
   a) READ a character from the file;
   b) WRITE the character to the terminal screen.

5. CLOSE the input file.

Figures 2.2 and 2.3 are, respectively, C and Pascal language implementations of this program. It is instructive to compare the differences between these implementations.

Steps 1 and 2 of the program involve writing and reading, but in each of the implementations this is accomplished through the usual functions for handling the screen and keyboard. Step 4a, where we read from the input file, is the first instance of actual file I/O. Note that the *read()* call in the C language parallels the low-level, generic *READ()* statement we described earlier; in truth, we used the *read()* system call in C as the model for our low-level *READ()*. The function's first argument gives the file descriptor (C's version of a logical file name) as the *source* for the input, the second argument gives the *address* of a charac-

```
/* list.c -- program to read characters from a file and
             write them to the terminal screen
*/
#define READONLY 0

main() {

    char c;
    int  fd;    /* file descriptor */
    char filename[20];

    printf("Enter the name of the file: ");      /* Step 1 */
    gets(filename);                              /* Step 2 */
    fd = open(filename, READONLY);               /* Step 3 */

    while (read(fd, &c, 1) > 0)                   /* Step 4a */
        write(1, &c, 1);                         /* Step 4b */

    close(fd);                                   /* Step 5 */
}
```

FIGURE 2.2 ▪ The LIST program in C

```
PROGRAM list (INPUT, OUTPUT);
{
    reads input from a file and writes it to the terminal screen
}
VAR
    c        : char;
    infile   : file of char;                { logical file name  }
    filename : packed array [1..20] of char;  { physical file name }

BEGIN {main}

    write('Enter the name of the file: ');   { Step 1 }
    readln(filename);                        { Step 2 }
    assign(infile,filename);                 { Step 3 }
    reset(infile);

    while not (eof(infile)) DO
    BEGIN
        read(infile,c);                      { Step 4a }
        write(c)                             { Step 4b }
    END;
    close(infile)                            { Step 5 }
END.
```

FIGURE 2.3 ▪ The LIST program in Pascal.

ter variable used as the *destination* for the data, and the third argument specifies that only one byte will be read.

The arguments for the Pascal *read()* call communicate the same information at a higher level. Once again, the first argument is the logical file name for the input source. The second argument gives the *name* of a character variable used as a destination; given the name, Pascal can find the address. Because of Pascal's strong emphasis on variable types, the third argument of the generic READ() function is not required. Pascal assumes that since we are reading data into a variable of type *char*, we must want to read only one byte.

After a character is read, we write it out to the screen in Step 4b. Once again the differences between C and Pascal are indicative of the range of approaches to I/O used in different languages. Everything must be stated explicitly in the C *write()* call: using the special, assigned file descriptor of 1 to identify the terminal screen as the destination for our writing,

```
write( 1, &c, 1);
```

means: "Write to the screen the contents from memory starting at the address &c. Write only one byte." Beginning C programmers should pay special attention to the use of the & symbol in the *write()* call here; this particular C call, as a very low-level call, requires that the programmer provide the starting *address* in RAM of the bytes to be transferred.

Again Pascal works at a higher level. When no logical file name is specified in a *write()* statement, Pascal assumes that we are writing to the terminal screen. Since the variable *c* is of type *char*, Pascal assumes we are writing a single byte. The statement becomes simply

```
write(c)
```

As in the *read()* statement, Pascal takes care of finding the *address* of the bytes; the programmer need specify only the name of the variable *c* that is associated with that address.

2.5 DETECTING END OF FILE

The programs in Figs. 2.2 and 2.3 have to know when to end the *while* loop and stop reading characters. Pascal and C signal the end-of-file condition differently, illustrating two of the most commonly used approaches to end-of-file detection.

Pascal supplies a Boolean function, *eof()*, that can be used to test for end of file. As we read from a file, the operating system keeps track of our location in the file with something we call the *read/write pointer*. This is necessary so that when we go to read the next byte, the system knows where to get it. The *eof()* function queries the system to see whether the read/write pointer has moved past the last element in the file. If it has, *eof()* returns *true*; otherwise it returns *false*. As Fig. 2.3 illustrates, we use the *eof()* call before trying to read the next byte. For an empty file, *eof()* immediately returns *true* and no bytes are read.

In the C language, the *read()* call returns the number of bytes read. If *read()* returns a value of zero, then the program has reached the end of the file. So, rather than using an *eof()* function, we construct the *while* loop so that it runs for as long as the *read()* call finds something to read.

2.6 SEEKING

In the preceding sample programs we read through the file *sequentially*, reading one byte after another until we reach the end of the file. Every time a byte is read, the operating system moves the read/write pointer ahead, and we are ready to read the next byte.

Sometimes we want to read or write without taking the time to go through every byte sequentially. Perhaps we know that the next piece of information we need is 10,000 bytes away, and so we want to jump there to begin reading. Or perhaps we need to jump to the end of the file so we can add new information there. To satisfy these needs we must be able to control the movement of the read/write pointer.

The action of moving directly to a certain position in a file is often called *seeking*. A *seek* requires at least two pieces of information, expressed here as arguments to the function SEEK():

SEEK(Source_file, Offset)

where the variables have the following meanings:

Source_file. The logical file name in which the seek will occur.
Offset. The number of positions in the file the pointer is to be moved
    from the start of the file.

Now, if we want to move directly from the origin to the 373rd position in a file called *data*, we don't have to move sequentially through the first 372 positions first. Instead, we can say

    SEEK(data, 373)

2.6.1 SEEKING IN C

One of the features of the UNIX operating system that has been incorporated into many implementations of the C language is the ability to view a file as a potentially very large *array of bytes* that just happens to be kept on secondary storage. In an array of bytes in RAM, we can move to any particular byte through the use of a subscript. The C language seek function, called *lseek()*, provides a similar capability for files. It lets us set the read/write pointer to any byte in a file.

The *lseek()* function has the following form:

    cpos = lseek(fd,byte_offset,origin)

where the variables have the following meanings:

cpos	A long integer value returned by *lseek()* equal to the position (in bytes) of the read/write pointer after it has been moved. *lseek()* returns a value of $-1L$ if you try to seek beyond the bounds of the file.
fd	The file descriptor of the file to which the *lseek()* is to be applied.
byte_offset	The number of bytes to be moved from some *origin* in the file. The byte offset must be specified as a long integer, hence the name *lseek* for long seek. When appropriate, the *byte_offset* can be negative.

    origin   An integer that specifies the starting position from which the *byte_offset* is to be taken. The *origin* can have the value 0, 1, or 2:

0 – *lseek()* from the beginning of the file;

1 – *lseek()* from the current position;

2 – *lseek()* from the end of the file.

The following program fragment shows how you could use *lseek()* to move to a position that is 373 bytes into a file.

```
long cpos,lseek();
int fd;
        .
        .
        .
cpos = lseek(fd, 373L, 0);
if (cpos == -1L)
      printf("Attempt to seek beyond end of file\n");
```

Figure 2.4 shows a C program that gets an input string from the keyboard and then seeks to the end of the file to write the string there.

```
/* append.c -- accepts an input string and adds it to the end of a file.
          The file is either opened or created.
*/
#define READWRITE 2
#define PMODE     0644   /* owner can read and write; everyone else
                             is read-only */
main() {

    char c;
    int  fd;                    /* file descriptor */
    char filename[20];
    char new_string[80];        /* input string    */
    long lseek();

    printf("Enter the name of the file: ");
    gets(filename);
    if (( fd = open(filename, READWRITE)) < 0)  /* if OPEN fails   */
        fd = creat(filename, PMODE);            /*    then CREAT   */

    printf("String that is to be appended: ");
    gets(new_string);
    lseek(fd, 0L, 2);                           /* jump to end     */
    write(fd,new_string,strlen(new_string));    /* write the data  */
    close(fd);
}
```

FIGURE 2.4 ▪ The APPEND program in C.

The program also illustrates how we can combine the *open()* and *creat()* statements to reuse an existing file or create a new one.

2.6.2 SEEKING IN PASCAL

The view of a file as presented in Pascal differs from the UNIX and C view in at least two important respects:

☐   In C a file is a sequence of bytes, so addressing within the file is on a byte-by-byte basis. When we seek to a position we express the address in terms of bytes. In Pascal a file is a sequence of elements of some particular type. A file can be a sequence of characters, a sequence of integers, a sequence of records, and so on. Addressing within a file in Pascal is in terms of these elements. For example, if a file is made up of 100-byte records, and we want to refer to the fourth record, we would do so in Pascal simply by referencing record number 4. In C, where the view is solely and always in terms of bytes, we would have to address the fourth record as byte address 400.

☐   Standard Pascal actually does not provide for seeking, since the model for I/O for standard Pascal is magnetic tape, which must be read sequentially. In standard Pascal, adding data to the end of a file requires reading the entire file from beginning to end, writing out the data from the input file to a second, output file, and then adding the new data to the end of the output file. However, many implementations of Pascal such as VAX Pascal and Turbo Pascal have extended the standard and do support seeking.

An extension to Pascal proposed by The Joint ANSI/IEEE Pascal Standards Committee [1984] that may be included in the Pascal standard in the future includes the following procedures and functions that permit seeking.

SeekWrite(f,n).   A procedure that positions the file *f* on the element with index *n* and places the file in write mode, so that the selected and following elements may be modified.

SeekRead(f,n).   A procedure that positions the file *f* on the element with index *n* and places the file in read mode, so that the selected and following elements may be examined. If SeekRead() attempts to position beyond the end of the file, then the file is positioned at the end of the file.

Position(f).   A function that returns the index value representing the position of the current file element.

EndPosition(f).   A function that returns the index value representing the position of the last file element.

Unfortunately, many Pascal implementations, recognizing the need to provide seeking capabilities, had already implemented seeking functions before these proposals were set forth. Consequently, the mechanisms for handling seeking vary widely between implementations. We note some of these variations in subsequent chapters as we develop programs that require seeking. A program called *append.pas*, listed at the end of this chapter, is functionally similar to the C program in Fig. 2.4 and illustrates how seeking is implemented in Turbo Pascal.

2.7 UNEXPECTED CHARACTERS IN FILES

As you create the file structures described in this text you may encounter some difficulty with extra, unexpected characters that turn up in your files, with characters that disappear, and with numeric counts that are inserted into your files. Here are some examples of the kinds of things you might encounter:

☐ On many small computers you may find that a Control-Z (ASCII value of 26) is appended at the end of your files. Many systems use this to indicate end of file even if you have not placed it there. This is most likely to happen on MS-DOS or CP/M based systems.

☐ Some systems adopt a convention of indicating end of line in a text file as a pair of characters consisting of a carriage return (CR: ASCII value of 13) and a line feed (LF: ASCII value of 10). Sometimes I/O procedures written for such systems automatically expand single CR characters or LF characters into CR-LF pairs. This unrequested addition of characters can cause a great deal of difficulty. Again, you are most likely to encounter this phenomenon on MS-DOS or CP/M systems.

☐ Users of larger systems, such as VMS, may find that they have just the opposite problem. Certain file formats under VMS *remove* carriage return characters from your file without asking you, replacing them with a *count* of the characters in what the system has perceived as a line of text.

These are just a few examples of the kinds of uninvited modifications that record management systems or I/O support packages might make to your files. You will find that they are usually associated with the concepts of a line of text or end of file. In general, these modifications to your files are an attempt to make your life easier by doing things for you automatically. This might, in fact, actually work out for users who want to do nothing more than store some text in a file. But, unfortunately, programmers building sophisticated file structures must sometimes spend a lot of time finding ways to disable this automatic assistance so that they can have complete control over what they are building. Forewarned is forearmed; readers who encounter these kinds of difficulties as they build the file structures described in this text can take some comfort from the knowledge that the experience they gain in disabling automatic assistance will serve them well, over and over, in the future.

SUMMARY

This chapter introduced the fundamental operations of file systems: OPEN(), CREATE(), CLOSE(), READ(), WRITE(), and SEEK(). Each of these operations involves the creation or use of a link between a *physical file* stored on a secondary device and a *logical file* that represents a program's more abstract view of the same file. When the program describes an operation using the *logical file name,* the equivalent physical operation is performed on the corresponding physical file.

The five operations appear in programming languages in many different forms. Sometimes they are built-in commands, sometimes they are functions, and sometimes they are direct calls to an operating system. Not all languages provide the user with all five operations. The operation SEEK(), for instance, is not available in standard Pascal.

Before we can use a physical file, we must link it to a logical file. In some programming environments we do this with a statement (e.g., *assign* in Turbo Pascal) or with instructions outside of the program (e.g., job control language (JCL) instructions). In other languages the link between the physical file and a logical file is made with OPEN() or CREATE().

The operations CREATE() and OPEN() make files ready for reading or writing. CREATE() causes a new physical file to be created. OPEN() operates on an already existing physical file, usually setting the read/write pointer to the beginning of the file.

The CLOSE() operation breaks the link between a logical file and its corresponding physical file. It also makes sure that the file buffer is flushed so that everything that was written is actually sent to the file.

The I/O operations READ() and WRITE(), when viewed at a low, systems level, require three items of information:

- The *logical name* of the file to be read from or written to;
- An *address* of a memory area to be used for the "inside of the computer" part of the exchange; and

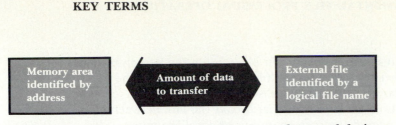

FIGURE 2.5 ▪ The exchange between memory and external device.

- An indication of *how much data* is to be read or written.

These three fundamental elements of the exchange are illustrated in Fig. 2.5.

READ() and WRITE() are sufficient for moving sequentially through a file to any desired position, but this form of access is often very inefficient. Some languages provide seek operations that let a program move directly to a certain position in a file. C provides direct access by means of the *lseek()* operation. The *lseek()* operation lets us view a file as a kind of large array, giving us a great deal of freedom in deciding how to organize a file. Standard Pascal does not support direct file access, but many dialects of Pascal do.

One other useful file operation involves knowing when the end of a file has been reached. End-of-file detection is handled in different ways by different languages.

Much effort goes into shielding programmers from a need to deal with the physical characteristics of files, but inevitably there are little details about the physical organization of files that programmers need to know. When we try to have our program operate on files at a very low level (as we do a great deal in this text), we must be constantly on the lookout for little surprises inserted in our file by the part of our operating system that organizes files.

KEY TERMS

Access mode. Type of file access allowed. The variety of access modes permitted varies from operating system to operating system.

Buffering. When input or output is saved up rather than sent off to its destination immediately, we say that it is *buffered*. In later chapters, we find that we can dramatically improve the performance of programs that read and write data if we buffer the I/O.

Byte offset. The distance, measured in bytes, from the beginning of the file. The very first byte in the file has an offset of 0, the second byte has an offset of 1, and so on.

CLOSE(). A function or system call that breaks the link between a logical file name and the corresponding physical file name.

CREATE(). A function or system call that causes a file to be created on secondary storage, and may also bind a logical name to the file's physical name (see OPEN()). A call to CREATE() also results in the generation of information used by the system to manage the file, such as time of creation, physical location, and access privileges for anticipated users of the file.

Logical file. The file as seen by the program. The use of logical files allows a program to describe operations to be performed on a file without knowing what actual physical file will be used. The program may then be used to process any one of a number of different files that share the same structure.

OPEN(). A function or system call that makes a file ready for use. It may also bind a logical file name to a physical file. Its arguments include the logical file name and the physical file name, and may also include information on how the file is expected to be accessed.

Physical file. A file that actually exists on secondary storage. It is the file as known by the computer operating system and which appears in its file directory.

READ(). A function or system call used to obtain input from a file or device. When viewed at the lowest level, it requires three arguments: 1) a Source_file logical name corresponding to an open file; 2) the Destination_address for the bytes that are to be read; and 3) the Size or amount of data to be read.

SEEK(). A function or system call that sets the read/write pointer to a specified position in the file. Languages that provide seeking functions allow programs to access specific elements of a file *directly*, rather than having to read through a file from the beginning (*sequentially*) each time a specific item is desired. In C, the *lseek()* system call provides this capability. Standard Pascal does not have a seeking capability, but many nonstandard dialects of Pascal do.

WRITE(). A function or system call used to provide output capabilities. When viewed at the lowest level, it requires three arguments: 1) a Destination_file name corresponding to an open file; 2) the Source_address of the bytes that are to be written; and 3) the Size or amount of the data to be written.

EXERCISES

1. Look up operations equivalent to *OPEN()*, *CLOSE()*, *CREATE()*, *READ()*, *WRITE()*, and *SEEK* in other high-level languages, such as PL/I, COBOL, and Fortran. Compare them with the C or Pascal versions.

2. If you use C:
a) Make a list of the different ways to perform the file operations CREATE(), OPEN(), CLOSE(), READ(), and WRITE(). Why is there more than one way to do each operation?
b) How would you use *lseek()* to find the current position in a file?
c) Describe a situation in which a PMODE of 0644 might be used. Assume a UNIX operating system.
d) What is the difference between PMODE and RWMODE? What PMODEs and RWMODEs are available on your system?
e) In some typical C environments, such as UNIX and MS-DOS, all of the following represent ways to move data from one place to another:

```
scanf()     fgetc()     read()     cat (or type)
fscanf()    gets()      <          main (argc,argv)
getc()      fgets()     ¦
```

Describe as many of these as you can, and indicate how they might be useful. Which belong to the C language, and which belong to the operating system?

3. If you use Pascal:
a) What ways are provided in your version of Pascal to perform the file operations CREATE(), OPEN(), CLOSE(), READ(), and WRITE()? If there is more than one way to do a certain operation, tell why. If an operation is missing, how are its functions carried out?
b) Implement a SEEK() function in your Pascal, if it does not already have one.

4. A couple of years ago a company we know of bought a new COBOL compiler. One difference between the new compiler and their old one was that the new compiler did not automatically close files when execution of a program terminated, whereas the old compiler did. What sorts of problems did this cause when some of the old software was executed after having been recompiled with the new compiler?

5. Look at the two LIST programs in the text. Each has a *while* loop. In Pascal the sequence of steps in the loop is test, read, write. In C it is read, test, write. Why the difference? What would happen in Pascal if we used the loop construction used for C? What would happen in C if we used the Pascal loop construction?

PROGRAMMING EXERCISES

6. Make the LIST program we provide in this chapter work with your compiler on your operating system.

7. Write a program to create a file and store a string in it. Write another program to open the file and read the string.

8. Try setting the *protection mode* on a file to read-only, then opening the file with an access mode of read/write. What happens?

9. Implement the *append.c* program in the text, or write a Pascal program that accomplishes the same thing.

10. Write a function *tail()* that prints on the screen the last part of a file starting at the byte offset *n*, where *n* is relative to the beginning of the file. Write a driver program that prompts the user for the file name and a value for *n*. (In C, you might write *tail()* as a main program that takes the file name and *n* as command line arguments.)

FURTHER READINGS

Introductory textbooks on C and Pascal tend to treat the fundamental file operations only briefly, if at all. This is particularly true with regard to C, since there are higher-level standard I/O functions in C, such as the read operations *fgets()* and *fgetc()*, which are thought by some to be easier to use.

Some books on C that do provide full (though brief) treatment of the fundamental file operations are Bourne [1984], Kelly and Pohl [1984], Kernighan and Pike [1984], and Kernighan and Ritchie [1978]. These books also provide discussions of higher-level I/O functions that we omitted from our text.

As for Pascal, these operations vary so greatly from one implementation to another that it is probably best to consult user manuals and literature relating to your specific implementation. Cooper [1983] covers the ISO standard Pascal, as well as some extensions. Jensen and Wirth [1974] is the definition of Pascal on which all others are based. Wirth [1975] discusses some difficulties with standard Pascal and file operations in the section, "An Important Concept and a Persistent Source of Problems: Files."

THE append PROGRAM IN PASCAL

REMARKS: *append.pas*

The Turbo Pascal program named *append.pas* is functionally similar to the *append.c* program provided in Chapter 2. It illustrates the use of the *seek()* statement in Turbo Pascal. Some things to note about the program:

☐   Turbo Pascal actually supports a special string type. We choose not to use that type here so we can come closer to conforming to standard Pascal.

☐   We use a WHILE loop to get the contents of the string to be appended one character at a time. We need to do this to count the characters in the string. Note that the EOLN() function behaves in the same way as the EOF() function described in Chapter 2: EOLN() is true as soon as the last character is input; consequently the *read()* statement must be at the top of the loop. Stated another way, the EOLN() and EOF() functions behave in the same way for keyboard input as they do for files. In future Pascal programs we incorporate this keyboard input loop into a function called *read_str()*.

☐   The comment {$B −} is actually a directive to the Turbo Pascal compiler, instructing it to handle keyboard input as a standard Pascal file. Without this directive we would not be able to handle the EOLN() function properly in the WHILE loop that receives input from the keyboard.

☐   We note in the chapter that the *assign()* statement is not a part of standard Pascal, but is instead a feature of Turbo Pascal. The binding of logical file to physical file name is done in different ways in different Pascal environments. Similarly, the *seek()* statement and *FileSize()* function are not standard; they are, once again, features of Turbo Pascal. When other versions of Pascal provide such functions, they often have different names.

```pascal
PROGRAM append (INPUT, OUTPUT);
{
    accepts an input string to add to the end of a file, using the
    seek() statement to jump to the end.
}
{$B-}  { this is a special directive to the Turbo Pascal compiler to
          make it handle keyboard input in a standard way -- see the
          associated program remarks }
VAR
    ch               : char;
    i, data_length : integer;
    resp             : char;
    filename         : packed array [1..20] of char;
    new_data         : packed array [1..80] of char;
    outfile          : file of char;

BEGIN {main}
    write('Enter the name of the file: ');
    readln(filename);
    assign(outfile,filename);

    write('Does this file already exist? (respond Y or N): ');
    readln(resp);
    if (resp = 'Y') or (resp = 'y') then
        reset(outfile)
    else
        rewrite(outfile);

    { get the new data from the keyboard, keeping track of
      the number of characters entered                        }

    write('String that is to be appended: ');
    data_length := 0;
    while (not EOLN) and (data_length < 80) DO
    BEGIN
        read(ch);
        data_length := data_length + 1;
        new_data[data_length] := ch
    END;

    {seek to the end of the file and write the data there }
    seek(outfile, FileSize(outfile));
    for i := 1 to data_length DO
        write(outfile,new_data[i]);

    close(outfile)
END.
```

CHAPTER

OBJECTIVES

Describe the organization of typical disk drives, including basic units of organization (sectors, blocks, tracks, and cylinders) and their relationships.

Identify and describe the factors affecting disk access time, and describe methods for estimating access times and space requirements.

Describe magnetic tapes, identify some tape applications, and investigate the implications of differing block sizes on space requirements and transmission speeds.

Identify other secondary media and indicate the roles they play in the hierarchy of memory systems.

Describe in general terms the events that occur when data is transmitted between a program's data area and a secondary device.

Introduce concepts and techniques of buffer management.

3

SECONDARY STORAGE DEVICES AND SYSTEM SOFTWARE: PERFORMANCE CONSIDERATIONS

CHAPTER OUTLINE

Good design is always responsive to the constraints of the medium and to the environment. This is as true for file structure design as it is for designs to be constructed in wood and stone. Given the ability to create, open, and close files, and to seek, read, and write, we can perform the fundamental operations of file *construction*. Now we need to look at the nature and limitations of the devices and systems used to store and retrieve files, preparing ourselves for file *design*.

If files were stored just in RAM, there would be no separate discipline called file structures. The general study of data structures would give us all the tools we would need to build file applications. But secondary storage devices are very different from RAM. One difference, as already noted, is that accesses to secondary storage take much more time than do accesses to RAM. An even more important difference, measured in terms of design impact, is that not all accesses are equal. Good file structure design uses knowledge of disk and tape performance to arrange data in ways that minimize access costs.

In this chapter we examine the characteristics of secondary storage devices, focusing on the constraints that shape our design work in the chapters that follow. We begin with a look at the major media used in the storage and processing of files, magnetic disks, and tapes. This is followed by an overview of the range of other devices and media used for secondary storage. Next, by following the journey of a byte we take a brief look at the many pieces of hardware and software that become involved when a byte is sent by a program to a file on a disk. Finally, we take a closer look at one of the most important aspects of file management—buffering.

3.1 DISKS

Compared to the time it takes to access an item in RAM, disk accesses are always expensive. However, not all disk accesses are *equally* expensive. The reason for this has to do with the way a disk drive works. Disk drives† belong to a class of devices known as *direct access storage devices* (DASDs) because they make it possible to access data *directly*. DASDs are contrasted with *serial devices,* the other major class of secondary storage devices. Serial devices use media such as magnetic tape that permit only serial access—a particular data item cannot be read or written until all of the data preceding it on the tape have been read or written in order.

3.1.1 THE ORGANIZATION OF DISKS

The information stored on a disk is stored on the surface of one or more platters (Fig. 3.1). The arrangement is such that the information is stored in successive *tracks* on the surface of the disk (Fig. 3.2). Each track is often divided into a number of *sectors*. A sector is the smallest addressable portion of a disk. When a *READ()* statement calls for a

---

†When we use the terms disks or disk drives we are referring to *magnetic* disk media. Nonmagnetic disk media, especially optical discs, are becoming increasingly important for secondary storage.

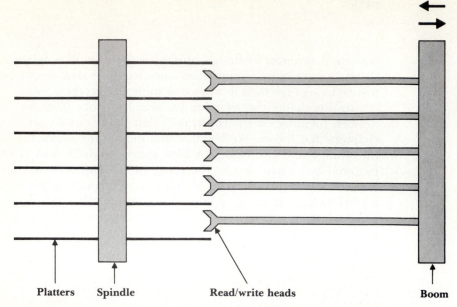

Platters   Spindle   Read/write heads   Boom

FIGURE 3.1 ▪ Schematic illustration of a disk drive with six platters on
one spindle and five movable access arms with read/write heads. There are
ten read/write heads, one head per surface, so that ten different tracks may
be read without moving the access arm. These ten tracks constitute a cylinder (see Fig. 3.3). (From Harvey Deitel, *An Introduction to Operating
Systems*, © 1984, Addison-Wesley, Reading, Mass. Page 303, Fig. 12.1.
Reprinted with permission.)

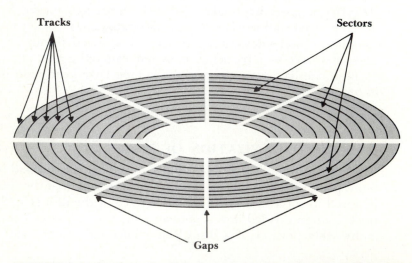

FIGURE 3.2 ▪ Surface of a disk showing tracks and sectors. This disk has 12
tracks, with eight sectors per track. Usually each sector contains the same
amount of data, so the inner tracks contain more bits per inch than the
outer tracks. The gaps between sectors help the disk reading device
distinguish between sectors.

particular byte from a disk file, the computer operating system finds the correct surface, track, and sector, reads the entire sector into a special area in RAM called a *buffer*, then finds the requested byte within that buffer.

If a disk drive uses a number of platters, it may be called a *disk pack*. The tracks that are directly above and below one another form a *cylinder* (Fig. 3.3). The significance of the cylinder is that all of the information on a single cylinder can be accessed without moving the arm that holds the read/write heads. Moving this arm is called *seeking*. This arm movement is usually the slowest part of reading information from a disk.

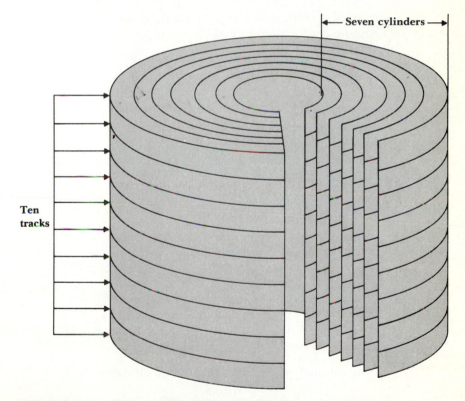

FIGURE 3.3 ▪ **Schematic illustration of a disk drive viewed as a set of seven cylinders, ten tracks per cylinder. A cylinder is a set of tracks, all of which can be accessed without moving the arm that holds the read/write heads. Physically, each of the tracks that makes up a cylinder is on a different surface.**

3.1.2 ESTIMATING CAPACITIES AND SPACE NEEDS

Disks range in width from 3 to about 14 inches. They range in storage capacity from less than 100,000 bytes to billions of bytes. In a typical disk pack, the top and bottom platter each contribute one surface, and all other platters contribute two surfaces to the pack, so the number of tracks per cylinder is a function of the number of platters.

The amount of data that can be held on a track depends on how densely bits can be stored on the disk surface. (This in turn depends on the quality of the recording medium and the size of the read/write heads.) An inexpensive, low-density disk can hold about 4 kilobytes on a track, and 35 tracks on a surface. A top-of-the-line disk can hold about 50 kilobytes on a track, and more than 1,000 tracks on a surface.

Since a cylinder consists of a group of tracks, a track consists of a group of sectors, and a sector consists of a group of bytes, it is easy to compute track, cylinder, and drive capacities:

$$\text{Track capacity} = \text{Number of sectors per track} \times \text{Bytes per sector}$$
$$\text{Cylinder capacity} = \text{Number of tracks per cylinder} \times \text{Track capacity}$$
$$\text{Drive capacity} = \text{Number of cylinders} \times \text{Cylinder capacity}$$

If we know the number of bytes in a file, we can use these relationships to compute the amount of disk space the file is likely to require. Suppose, for instance, that we want to store a file with 20,000 fixed length data records on a disk with the following characteristics.

$$\text{Number of bytes per sector} = 512$$
$$\text{Number of sectors per track} = 40$$
$$\text{Number of tracks per cylinder} = 11$$

How many cylinders does the file require if each data record requires 256 bytes? Since each sector can hold two records, the file requires

$$\frac{20,000}{2} = 10,000 \text{ sectors.}$$

One cylinder can hold

$$40 \times 11 = 440 \text{ sectors}$$

so the number of cylinders required is approximately

$$\frac{10,000}{440} = 22.7 \text{ cylinders.}$$

Of course, it may be that a disk drive with 22.7 cylinders of available space does not have 22.7 *physically contiguous* cylinders available. In this very likely case, the file might in fact have to be spread out over hundreds of cylinders.

3.1.3 SECTOR ORGANIZATION

There are two basic ways to organize data on a disk: by sector and by user-defined block. So far, we have only mentioned sector organizations. In this section we examine sector organizations more closely. In the next section we look at block organizations.

THE PHYSICAL PLACEMENT OF SECTORS. There are several views that one can have of the organization of sectors on a track. The simplest view, one that suffices for most users most of the time, is that sectors are adjacent, fixed-sized segments of a track that happen to hold a file (Fig. 3.4a). This is often a perfectly adequate way to view a file *logically*, but it is not a good way to store sectors *physically*.

It turns out that when you want to read a series of sectors that are all in the same track, one right after the other, you cannot generally

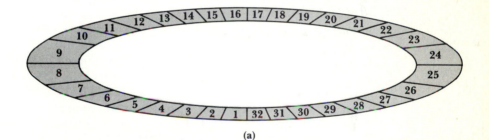

(a)

(b)

FIGURE 3.4 ▪ Two views of the organization of sectors on a 32-sector track.
(a) Simplest view of the organization of sectors on a track. Sectors are seen as fixed sized adjacent segments of a track that happen to hold a file.
(b) Sector interleaving, with an interleaving factor of 5. Logically adjacent sectors occur at intervals of five physical sectors.

read *adjacent* sectors. That is because, after reading the data, it takes the computer a certain amount of time to process the received information before it is ready to accept more. So, if *logically* adjacent sectors were placed on the disk so that they were also *physically* adjacent, we would miss the start of the following sector while we were processing the one we had just read in. Consequently, we would be able to read only one sector per revolution of the disk.

I/O system designers usually approach this problem by *interleaving* the sectors, leaving an interval of several physical sectors between logically adjacent sectors. Suppose our disk had an *interleaving factor* of 5. The assignment of logical sector content to the 32 physical sectors in a track is illustrated in Fig. 3.4(b). If you study this picture you can see that it takes five revolutions to read the entire 32 sectors of a track. That is a big improvement over having to wait 32 revolutions.

CLUSTERS.   A third view of sector organization, also designed to improve performance, is the view maintained by that part of a computer's operating system that we call the *file manager*. When a program accesses a file, it is the file manager's job to map the logical parts of the file to their corresponding physical locations. It does this by viewing the file as a series of *clusters* of sectors. A cluster is a fixed number of contiguous sectors,† so all clusters on a disk are the same size, and once a given cluster has been found on a disk, all sectors in that cluster can be accessed without requiring an additional seek.

To view a file as a series of clusters and still maintain the sectored view, the file manager ties logical sectors to the physical clusters that they belong to by using a *file allocation table* (FAT). The FAT contains a linked list of all the clusters in a file, ordered according to the logical order of the sectors they contain. With each cluster entry in the FAT is an entry giving the physical location of the cluster (Fig. 3.5).

On many systems, the system administrator can decide how many sectors there should be in a cluster. For instance, in the standard physical disk structure used by VAX systems, the system administrator sets the cluster size to be used on a disk when the disk is initialized. The default value is three 512-byte sectors per clusters, but the cluster size may be set to any value between 1 and 65535 sectors. Since clusters represent physically contiguous groups of sectors, larger clusters guarantee the ability to read more sectors without seeking, so the use of

---

†It is not quite *physically* contiguous; the degree of physical contiguity is determined by the interleaving factor.

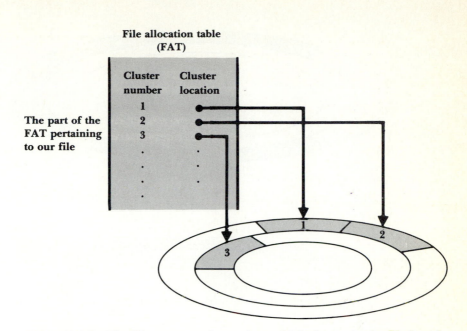

FIGURE 3.5 ▪ **The file manager determines which cluster in the file has the sector that is to be accessed. The FAT tells the file manager where that cluster is physically located on the disk. The FAT can have entries for many files, but only one is shown here.**

large clusters can lead to substantial performance gains when a file is being processed sequentially.

EXTENTS. Our final view of sector organization represents a further attempt to emphasize physical contiguity of sectors in a file, hence minimizing seeking even more. (If you are getting the idea that the avoidance of seeking is an important part of file design, you are right.) If there is a lot of free room on a disk, it may be possible to make a file consist entirely of contiguous clusters. When this is the case, we say that the file consists of one *extent:* all of its sectors, tracks, and (if it is large enough) cylinders form one contiguous whole (Fig. 3.6a). This is a good situation, especially if the file is to be processed sequentially, because it means that the whole file can be accessed with a minimum amount of seeking.

If there is not enough contiguous space available to contain an entire file, the file is divided into two or more noncontiguous parts. Each part is an extent. When new clusters are added to a file, the file man-

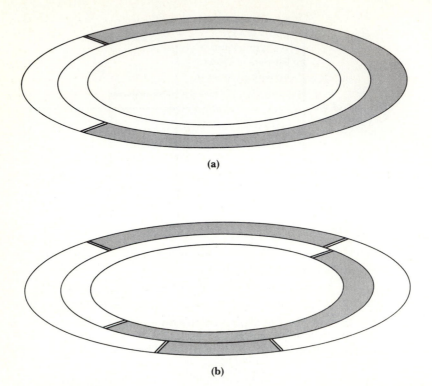

(a)

(b)

FIGURE 3.6 ● File extents (shaded area represents space on disk used by a single file). (a) Entire file stored as one extent. (b) File divided into several extents.

ager tries to make them physically contiguous to the previous end of the file, but if space is unavailable for this, it must add one or more extents (Fig. 3.6b). The most important thing to understand about extents is that as the number of extents in a file increases, the file becomes more spread out on the disk, and the amount of seeking required to process the file increases.

FRAGMENTATION.   Generally, all sectors on a given drive must contain the same number of bytes. If, for example, the size of a sector is 512 bytes and the size of all records in a file is 300 bytes, there is no convenient fit between records and sectors. There are two ways to deal with this situation: store only one record per sector, or allow records to *span* sectors, so that the beginning of a record might be found in one sector and the end of it in another (Fig. 3.7).

The first option has the advantage that any record can be retrieved by retrieving just one sector, but it has the disadvantage that it might leave an enormous amount of unused space within each sector. This loss of space within a sector is called *internal fragmentation*. The second option has the advantage that it loses no space from internal fragmentation, but it has the disadvantage that some records may be retrieved only by accessing two sectors.

Another potential source of internal fragmentation results from the use of clusters. Recall that a cluster is the smallest unit of space that can be allocated for a file. When the number of bytes in a file is not an exact multiple of the cluster size, there will be internal fragmentation in the last extent of the file. For instance, if a cluster consists of three 512-byte sectors, a file containing one byte would use up 1536 bytes on the disk. 1535 bytes would be wasted due to internal fragmentation.

Clearly, there are important trade-offs in the use of large cluster sizes. A disk that is expected to have mainly large files that will often be processed sequentially would usually be given a large cluster size since internal fragmentation would not be a big problem, and the performance gains might be great. A disk holding smaller files or

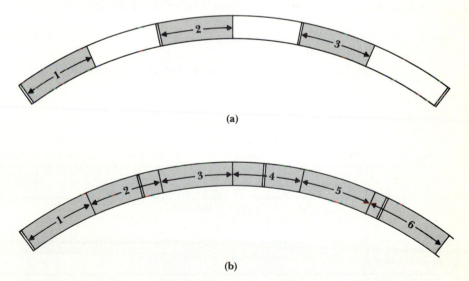

(a)

(b)

FIGURE 3.7 ▪ Alternate record organization within sectors (shaded areas represent data records, and unshaded areas represent unused space).
(a) One record stored per sector, causing *fragmentation*. (b) Records span sectors, eliminating fragmentation, but perhaps requiring more than one access for a record.

files that are usually accessed only randomly would normally be given small clusters.

3.1.4 BLOCK ORGANIZATION

Sometimes disk tracks are *not* divided into sectors, but into integral numbers of user-defined *blocks* whose size can vary. When the data on a track is organized by block, this usually is taken to mean that the amount of data transferred in a single I/O operation can vary depending on the needs of the software designer, not the hardware. Blocks can normally be either fixed or variable in length, depending on the requirements of the file designer. As with sectors, blocks are often referred to as physical records. (Sometimes the word block is used as a synonym for a sector or group of sectors. To avoid confusion, we do not use it in that way here.) Figure 3.8 illustrates the difference between one view of data on a sectored track and that of a blocked track.

A *block* organization does not present the sector-spanning and fragmentation problems of sectors because blocks can vary in size to fit the logical organization of the data. A block is usually organized to hold an integral number of logical records. The term *blocking factor* is used to indicate the number of records that are to be stored in each block in a file. Hence, if we had a file with 300-byte records, a block-addressing scheme would let us define a block to be some convenient multiple of 300 bytes, depending on the needs of the program. No space would be lost to internal fragmentation, and there would be no need to load two blocks to retrieve one record.

Sector 1	Sector 2	Sector 3	Sector 4	Sector 5	Sector 6
1111111111	1111111111	111¦222222	22¦333¦444	4444444444	44¦555 . . .

(a)

| 1111111111 . . . 11111111¦222 . . . 22¦333¦444444 . . . 4444 44¦555 . . . |

(b)

FIGURE 3.8 ▪ Sector organization versus block organization. (a) Sector organization: regardless of the size of a record or other logical grouping of data, the data is grouped physically in sectors. Every access involves transmission of an integral number of sectors. (b) Block organization: the amount of data transmitted in an access depends on the block size.

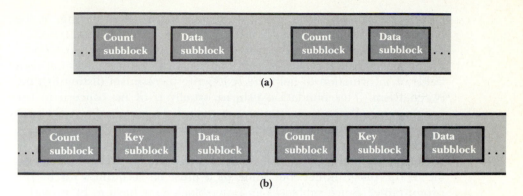

FIGURE 3.9 ▪ Block-addressing requires that each physical data block be accompanied by one or more subblocks containing information about its contents. *Count subblocks* tell how many bytes of data there are in the corresponding data block. *Key subblocks* indicate the key to the last record in the corresponding data block. (a) Blocking with count and data subblocks. (b) Blocking with count, key, and data subblocks.

    Generally speaking, blocks are superior to sectors when it is desirable to have the physical allocation of space for records correspond to their logical organization. (There are disk drives that allow both sector-addressing and block-addressing, but we do not describe them here. See Bohl [1981].)

    In block-addressing schemes, each block of data is usually accompanied by one or more extra *subblocks* containing extra information about the data block. Typically there is a *count subblock* that contains (among other things) the number of bytes in the accompanying data block (Fig. 3.9a). There may also be a *key subblock* containing the key for the last record in the data block (Fig. 3.9b). When *key* subblocks are used, a track can be searched by the disk controller for a block or record identified by a given key. This means that a program can ask its disk drive to search among all of the blocks on a track for a block with a desired key. This approach can result in much more efficient searches than are normally possible with sector-addressable schemes, where keys cannot generally be interpreted without first loading them into primary memory.

3.1.5 NONDATA OVERHEAD

Both blocks and sectors require that a certain amount of space be taken up on the disk in the form of *nondata overhead*. Some of the overhead consists of information that is stored on the disk during *preformatting*, which is done before the disk can be used.

On sector-addressable disks, preformatting involves storing, at the beginning of each sector, such information as sector address, track address, and condition (whether the sector is usable or defective). Preformatting also involves placing gaps and synchronization marks between fields of information to help the read/write mechanism distinguish between them. This nondata overhead usually is of no concern to the programmer. When the sector size is given for a certain drive, the programmer can assume that this is the amount of actual data that can be stored in a sector.

On a block-organized disk, some of the nondata overhead is invisible to the programmer, but some of it must be accounted for by the programmer. Since subblocks and interblock gaps have to be provided with every block, there is generally more nondata information provided with blocks than with sectors. Also, since the number and sizes of blocks can vary from one application to another, the relative amount of space taken up by overhead can vary when block-addressing is used. This is illustrated in the following example.

Suppose we have a block-addressable disk drive with 20,000 bytes per track, and the amount of space taken up by subblocks and interblock gaps is equivalent to 300 bytes per block. We want to store a file containing 100-byte records on the disk. How many records can be stored per track if the blocking factor is 10, or if it is 60?

1. If there are 10 100-byte records per block, each block holds 1,000 bytes of data, and uses $300 + 1,000$, or $1,300$, bytes of track space when overhead is taken into account. The number of blocks which can fit on a 20,000-byte track can be expressed as

$$\left\lfloor \frac{20,000}{1,300} \right\rfloor = \lfloor 15.38 \rfloor = 15$$

So 15 blocks, or 150 records, can be stored per track. (Note that we have to take the *floor* of the result because a block cannot span two tracks.)

2. If there are 60 100-byte records per block, each block holds 6,000 bytes of data and uses 6,300 bytes of track space. The number of blocks per track can be expressed as

$$\left\lfloor \frac{20,000}{6,300} \right\rfloor = 3$$

So 3 blocks, or 180 records, can be stored per track.

Clearly, the larger blocking factor can lead to more efficient use of storage. When blocks are larger, fewer blocks are required to hold a file, so there is less space consumed by the 300 bytes of overhead that accompany each block.

Can we conclude from this example that larger blocking factors always lead to more efficient storage utilization? Not necessarily. Since we can put only an integral number of blocks on a track, and since tracks are fixed in length, we almost always lose some space at the end of a track. Here we have the internal fragmentation problem again, but this time it applies to fragmentation within a *track*. The greater the block size, the greater potential amount of internal track fragmentation. What would have happened if we had chosen a blocking factor of 98 in the preceding example? What about 97?

The flexibility introduced by the use of blocks, rather than sectors, can result in savings in time and efficiency, since it lets the programmer determine to a large extent how data are to be organized physically on a disk. On the negative side, blocking schemes *require* the programmer and/or operating system to do the extra work of determining the data organization. Also, the very flexibility introduced by the use of blocking schemes precludes the synchronization of I/O operations with the physical movement of the disk, which sectoring permits. This means that strategies such as sector interleaving cannot be used to improve performance.

3.1.6 THE COST OF A DISK ACCESS

To give you a feel for the factors contributing to the total amount of time needed to access a file on a fixed disk, we will calculate some access times. A disk access can be divided into three distinct physical operations, each with its own cost: *seek time, rotational delay* and *transfer time*.

SEEK TIME. Seek time is the time required to move the access arm to the correct cylinder. The amount of time spent seeking during a disk access depends, of course, on how far the arm has to move. If we are accessing a file sequentially and the file is packed into several consecutive cylinders, seeking needs to be done only after all of the tracks on a cylinder have been processed, and even then the read/write head needs to move the width of only one track. At the other extreme, if we are alternately accessing sectors from two files that are stored at opposite extremes on a disk (one at the innermost cylinder, one at the outermost cylinder), seeking is very expensive.

Seeking is likely to be more costly in a multiuser environment, where several processes are contending for use of the disk at one time, than in a single user environment, where disk usage is dedicated to one process. Since seeking can be very costly, system designers often go to great extremes to minimize seeking. In an application that merges three files, for example, it is not unusual to see the three input files stored on three different drives and the output file stored on a fourth drive, so that no seeking need be done as I/O operations jump from file to file.

Seeking involves several operations that take time, the most important of which are the initial startup time (*s*) and the time taken to traverse the cylinders that have to be crossed once the access arm is up to speed. If we let *n* stand for the number of cylinders traversed, then the contributions of these two values can be approximated with a linear function of the form

$$f(n) = m \times n + s$$

where *m* is a constant that depends on the drive itself. For example, the seek time on an inexpensive (circa 1985) 20-megabyte fixed disk used with personal computers might be approximated by

$$f(n) = 0.3 \times n + 20 \text{ msec.}$$

A large, more expensive disk drive might have a seek time approximated by

$$f(n) = 0.1 \times n + 3 \text{ msec.}$$

The larger drive starts faster (*s* = 3 msec versus *s* = 20 msec) and traverses tracks faster (*m* = 0.1 versus *m* = 0.3).

Since it is usually impossible to know exactly how many tracks will be traversed in every seek, we usually try to determine the *average seek time* required for a particular file operation. If the starting and ending positions for each access are random, it turns out that the average seek traverses one third of the total number of tracks.†

ROTATIONAL DELAY.   Rotational delay refers to the time it takes for the disk to rotate so that the sector we want is under the read/write head. Disks usually rotate at about 3600 rpm,‡ which is one revolution per 16.7 msec. On the average the rotational delay is half a revolution, or about 8.3 msec.

---

†Derivations of this result, as well as more detailed and refined models, can be found in Wiederhold [1983], Knuth [1973b], and Teory and Fry [1982]. Pechora and Schoeffler [1983] show that a very different set of assumptions applies for floppy disks.

‡Floppy disks rotate much more slowly—typically between 300 and 600 rpm.

TRANSFER TIME. Once the data we want is under the read/write head, it can be transferred. The transfer time is given by the formula

$$\text{Transfer time} = \frac{\text{Number of bytes transferred}}{\text{Number of bytes on a track}} \times \text{Rotation time.}$$

If a drive is sectored, the transfer time for one sector depends on the number of sectors on a track. For example, if there are 32 sectors per track, the time required to transfer one sector would be 1/32nd of a revolution, or 0.5 msec.

SOME TIMING COMPUTATIONS. Let's look at two different file processing situations that show how different types of file access can affect access times. The basis for our calculations is the typical 20-megabyte fixed disk mentioned earlier. Although this particular disk is typical of inexpensive fixed disks used with personal computers, the observations we draw as we perform these calculations are quite general. The disks used with larger, more expensive computers are bigger and faster than this disk, but the nature and relative costs of the factors contributing to total access times are essentially the same.

Our disk drive has four surfaces (two platters), with one read/write head per surface. There are 612 tracks per surface, 16 sectors per track, and 512 bytes per sector. The drive uses a cluster size of 16 sectors (8K bytes) and an extent size of one cluster, so space is allocated for storing files in one-track units. Sectors are interleaved with an interleaving factor of 5, so a track can be transferred in five revolutions. Since one revolution takes 16.7 msec, one track can be transferred in 83.5 msec.

Let's suppose that, given this disk, we want to know how long it will take to read a 128K byte file that is divided into 256 sector-sized records. We first need to know how the file is distributed on the disk. Since each cluster is one track, our file will be stored as a sequence of tracks. Since each track of the disk holds 8K, the disk needs 16 tracks to hold the entire 128K bytes that we want to read. We assume a situation in which the 16 clusters are randomly dispersed over the surface of the disk. (This is an extreme situation chosen to dramatize the point we want to make. Still, it is not so extreme that it could not easily occur on a typical overloaded personal computer disk that has a large number of small files.)

An average seek in this environment traverses one third of the 612 cylinders, so using the preceding formula, an

$$\text{Average seek} = f(612/3) = 0.3 \times (612/3) + 20 \text{ msec} = 81.2 \text{ msec.}$$

Now we are ready to calculate the time it would take to read the 128K bytes from the disk. We first estimate the time it takes to read the file sector by sector *in sequence*. This process involves the following operations for each cluster.

Average seek	81.2 msec
Rotational delay	8.3 msec
Read 16 sectors (5 × 16.7 msec)	83.5 msec
	173.0 msec

We want to find and read 16 tracks, so the

Total time = 16 × 173 msec = 2768 msec = 2.8 seconds.

Now let's calculate the time it would take to read in the same data using *random access* rather than sequential access. In other words, rather than being able to read one sector right after another, we assume that we have to access the sectors in some order that requires a lot of jumping from track to track every time we read a new sector. This process involves the following operations for each sector.

Average seek	81.2 msec
Rotational delay	8.3 msec
Read one sector (1/16 × 16.7)	1.0 msec
	90.5 msec

Total time = 256 × 90.5 msec = 23168 msec = 23.2 seconds.

This difference in performance between sequential access and random access is very important. If we can get out to the right location on the disk and read a lot of information sequentially, we are clearly much better off than we are if we have to jump around, *seeking* every time we need a new sector. Remember that seek time is very expensive; when we are performing disk operations we should try to minimize seeking.

3.2 MAGNETIC TAPE

When a file is usually accessed sequentially, there may be no need to store it on a disk if a less expensive device can be used. Consider a sorted mailing list, for example. When it is used to generate mailing labels, its records can be accessed in the order in which they occur in the file. It can be merged with a second mailing list by sorting the second list, then processing the two files together sequentially. Updating can be done in a similar serial manner. The need to access only one record in a mailing list is likely to happen so seldom that the extra cost of doing so would normally not be worth the cost of keeping it on a disk.

Magnetic tape units belong to a class of devices that provide no direct accessing facility, but that are very good for sequential processing of data. When it is known that a large file does not normally require direct access, there are a number of advantages to storing it on tape. Tapes are compact, stand up well under different environmental conditions, and are easy to store and transport. Also, tape space is generally less expensive than is disk space.

3.2.1 ORGANIZATION OF DATA ON TAPES

Since tapes are accessed sequentially, there is no need for addresses to identify the locations of data on a tape. On a tape, the logical position of a byte within a file corresponds directly to its physical position relative to the start of the file. We may envision the surface of a typical tape as a set of parallel tracks, each of which is a sequence of bits. If there are eight tracks, the eight bits that are at corresponding positions, in the eight respective tracks are taken to constitute one byte. So a byte can be thought of as a one-bit-wide slice of tape. Such a slice is called a *frame*.

A typical tape has nine tracks (Fig. 3.10), with one of the tracks used for *parity*. The *parity bit* is not part of the data, but is used to check the validity of the data. If *odd parity* is in effect, this bit is set to make

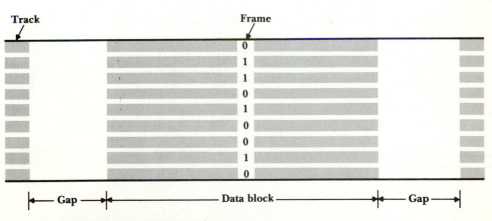

FIGURE 3.10 ▪ Nine-track tape.

the number of 1 bits in the frame *odd*. Even parity works similarly, but is rarely used with tapes.

Frames (bytes) are grouped into data blocks whose size can vary from a few bytes to many kilobytes, depending on the needs of the user. Since tapes are often read one block at a time, and since tapes cannot stop or start instantaneously, blocks are separated by *interblock gaps*, which contain no information and which are long enough to permit stopping and starting. When tapes use odd parity, no valid frame can contain all 0 bits, so a large number of consecutive 0 frames is used to fill the interrecord gap.

Tape drives come in many shapes, sizes, and speeds. Performance differences among drives can usually be measured in terms of three quantities:

☐ Tape density—commonly 800, 1,600, or 6,250 bits per inch (bpi) per track, but recently as much as 30,000 bpi;
☐ Tape speed—commonly 30–200 inches per second (ips); and
☐ Size of interblock gap—commonly between 0.3 inch and 0.75 inch.

3.2.2 ESTIMATING TAPE LENGTH REQUIREMENTS

It is common to back up collections of disk files to guard against loss of information due to hardware or software errors. Tapes provide a good medium for doing this. For example, suppose we want to store a backup copy of a large mailing list file, and we need to know how much tape it will require. Suppose the file has one million addresses, and each address is stored in a 100-byte record. If we want to store the file on a 6,250-bpi tape that has an interblock gap of 0.3 inches, how much tape is needed?

To answer this question we first need to determine what takes up space on the tape. There are two primary contributors: interblock gaps and data blocks. For every data block there is an interblock gap. If we let

$$b = \text{the physical length of a data block,}$$
$$g = \text{the length of an interblock gap, and}$$
$$n = \text{the number of data blocks,}$$

then the space requirement s for storing the file is

$$s = n \times (b + g).$$

We know that g is 0.3 inch, but we do not know what b and n are. In fact, b is whatever we want it to be, and n depends on our choice of b.

Suppose we choose each data block to contain one 100-byte record. Then b, the length of each block, is given by

$$b = \frac{\text{Block size (bytes per block)}}{\text{Tape density (bytes per inch)}} = \frac{100}{6,250} = 0.016 \text{ inch},$$

and n, the number of blocks, is one million (one per record).

The number of records stored in a physical block is called the *blocking factor*. It has the same meaning that it had when it was applied to the use of blocks for disk storage. The blocking factor we have chosen here is 1 because each block has only one record. Hence, the space requirement for the file is

$$\begin{aligned}
s &= 1,000,000 \times (0.016 + 0.3) \text{ inch} \\
&= 1,000,000 \times 0.316 \text{ inch} \\
&= 316,000 \text{ inches} \\
&= 26,333 \text{ feet.}
\end{aligned}$$

Magnetic tapes range in length from 300 feet to 3,600 feet, with 2,400 feet being the most common length. Clearly, we need quite a few 2,400-foot tapes to store the file. Or do we? You may have noticed that our choice of block size was not a very smart one from the standpoint of space utilization. The interblock gaps in the physical representation of the file take up about *nineteen times* as much space as the data blocks do. If we were to take a snapshot of our tape, it would look something like this:

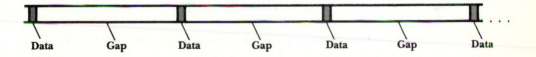

Data   **Gap**   **Data**   **Gap**   **Data**   **Gap**   **Data**

Most of the space on the tape is not used!

Clearly we should consider increasing the relative amount of space used for actual data if we want to try to squeeze the file onto one 2,400-foot tape. If we increase the blocking factor, we can *decrease* the number of blocks, which decreases the number of interblock gaps, which in turn decreases the amount of space consumed by interblock gaps. For example, if we increase the blocking factor from 1 to 50, the number of blocks becomes

$$n = \frac{1,000,000}{50} = 20,000,$$

and the space requirement for interblock gaps decreases from 300,000 inches to 6,000 inches. The space requirement for the data is of course the same as it was previously. What has changed is the *relative* amount of space occupied by the gaps, as compared to the data. Now a snapshot of the tape would look much different:

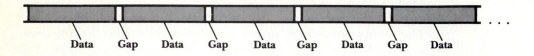

We leave it to you to show that the file can fit easily on one 2,400-foot tape when a blocking factor of 50 is used.

When we compute the space requirements for our file, we produce numbers that are quite specific to our file. A more general measure of the effect of choosing different block sizes is *effective recording density*. The effective recording density is supposed to reflect the amount of actual data that can be stored per inch of tape. Since this depends exclusively on the relative sizes of the interblock gap and the data block, it can be defined as

$$\frac{\text{Number of bytes per block}}{\text{Number of inches required to store a block}}.$$

When a blocking factor of 1 is used in our example, the number of bytes per block is 100, and the number of inches required to store a block is 0.316. Hence, the effective recording density is

$$\frac{100 \text{ bytes}}{0.316 \text{ inches}} = 316.4 \text{ bpi},$$

which is a far cry from the *nominal* recording density of 6,250 bpi.

Either way you look at it, space utilization is sensitive to the relative sizes of data blocks and interblock gaps. Let us now see how they affect the amount of *time* it takes to transmit tape data.

3.2.3 ESTIMATING DATA TRANSMISSION TIMES

If you understand the role of interblock gaps and data block sizes in determining effective recording density, you can probably see immediately that these two factors also affect the rate of data transmission. Two other factors that affect the rate of data transmission to or from tape are the nominal recording density and the speed with which the tape passes the read/write head. If we know these two values, we can compute the *nominal data transmission rate*:

Nominal rate = Tape density (bpi) × Tape speed (ips).

Hence, our 6,250-bpi, 200-ips tape has a nominal transmission rate of

$$6{,}250 \times 200 = 1{,}250{,}000 \text{ bytes/sec}$$
$$= 1{,}250 \text{ kilobytes/sec.}$$

This rate is competitive with most disk drives.

But what about those interblock gaps? Once our data gets dispersed by interblock gaps, the *effective transmission rate* certainly suffers. Suppose, for example, that we use our blocking factor of 1 with the same file and tape drive discussed in the preceding section (1,000,000 100-byte records, 0.3 inch gap). We saw that the effective recording density for this tape organization is 316.4 bpi. If the tape is moving at a rate of 200 ips, then its effective transmission rate is

$$316.4 \times 200 = 63{,}280 \text{ bytes/sec}$$
$$= 63.3 \text{ kilobytes/sec,}$$

a rate that is about *one twentieth* of the nominal rate!

It should be clear that a blocking factor larger than 1 improves on this result, and that a substantially larger blocking factor improves on it substantially.

Although there are other factors that can influence performance, block size is generally considered to be the one variable with the greatest influence on space utilization and data transmission rate. The other factors we have included—gap size, tape speed, and recording density—are often beyond the control of the user. Another factor that can sometimes be important is the time it takes to start and stop the tape. We consider start/stop time in the exercises at the end of the chapter.

3.2.4 TAPE APPLICATIONS

Magnetic tape is an appropriate medium for sequential processing applications *if* the files being processed are not likely also to be used in applications that require direct access. For example, consider the problem of updating a mailing list for a monthly periodical. Is it essential that the list be kept absolutely current, or is a monthly update of the list sufficient?

If information must be up-to-the-minute, then the medium must permit direct access so that individual updates can be made immediately. But if the mailing list needs to be current only when mailing labels are printed, all of the changes that occur during the course of a month can be collected in one batch and put into a transaction file that is sorted in the same way that the mailing list is sorted. Then a program that reads through the two files simultaneously can be executed, making all the required changes in one pass through the data.

Since tape is relatively inexpensive, it is also a good medium for storing data offline. At current prices a removable disk pack that holds 150 megabytes costs about 30 times as much as a reel of tape that, properly blocked, can hold the same amount. Tape is a good medium for archival storage and for transporting data, as long as the data do not have to be available on short notice for direct processing.

3.3
OTHER KINDS OF STORAGE

When computing systems become large and complex or very specialized, tapes and disks alone may not satisfy all secondary storage requirements. There are other media and devices less common than disks and tape, but that nevertheless have important uses for certain file applications. Here are some of the most important other secondary media.

PUNCHED CARDS. Punched cards are expensive, slow, and error-prone. Despite their drawbacks, however, there are at least two reasons why punched cards are still around:

☐ Their size and durability makes them easy to handle individually by people in uncontrolled environments, such as shop floors, the mail, and turnpikes; and

☐ There is a lot of old hardware and software still around that work only with punched cards and that are not easily replaced by newer, cheaper, and faster hardware and software.

BACKUP AND ARCHIVAL STORAGE. Normally backup and archival files are kept offline and must be loaded into RAM or onto a disk drive before they can be accessed. Some devices and media that are commonly used for backup and archival storage include the following.

Streaming tape drives. These drives are especially designed for nonstop, high-speed dumping of data from disks. Generally less expensive than general purpose tape drives, they are also less suited for processing that involves much starting and stopping.

Floppy disk drives. Floppy disk units are inexpensive, but they are slow and hold relatively little data. Floppies are good for backing up individual files or other floppies and for transporting small amounts of data.

Removable disk packs. Sometimes different disk packs can be mounted on the same drive at different times. This provides a convenient form of backup storage that also makes it possible to access data directly.

Mass storage systems. These systems can access any of a large number of specially designed tape cartridges from a cartridge library in a few seconds, without human intervention. Mass storage systems have extremely large capacities (hundreds of billions of bytes) and provide access times of less than 15 seconds. They are inexpensive in terms of cost-per-bit, but they are economical only in places where large amounts of offline data are used. Strictly speaking, mass storage systems are not really backup devices since they generally hold the only copy of a given piece of data. For this reason some mass storage systems keep two identical copies of every cartridge.

Redundant online storage. If the cost of losing access to data even for a very short time is extremely high, two identical copies of all data might be kept on two identical devices. This approach has the added advantage that if only one of two identical devices is busy when a certain piece of data is needed, the data may be accessed from the other device without delay. A disadvantage of redundant storage is that it is not easy to ensure that both copies are truly identical at all times. During a write operation, for instance, it is likely that new data will arrive at one device at a slightly different time than it will at the other.

Optical discs. Optical disc storage is emerging as a major secondary storage medium. It is proving to be very competitive with all other backup and archival storage media in terms of capacity, speed, and cost.

FASTER-THAN-DISK STORAGE. As the cost of RAM steadily decreases, more and more users are using RAM to hold data that a few years ago had to been kept on a disk. Two effective ways in which RAM can be used to replace secondary storage are *RAM disks* and *disk caches*.

A *RAM disk* is a large part of RAM configured to simulate the behavior of a mechanical disk in every respect except speed and volatility. Since data can be located in RAM without a seek or rotational delay, RAM disks can provide much faster access than mechanical disks provide. Since RAM is normally volatile, the contents of a RAM disk are lost when the computer is turned off. RAM disks are often used in place of floppy disks because they are much faster than floppies and because relatively little RAM is needed to simulate a typical floppy disk.

A *disk cache*† is a large block of RAM configured to contain *pages* of data from a disk. A typical disk caching scheme might use a 256K cache with a disk. When data is requested from secondary memory, the file manager first looks into the disk cache to see if it contains the page with the requested data. If it does, the data can be processed immediately. Otherwise, the file manager reads the page containing the data from disk, replacing some page already in the disk cache. When a program's data access patterns exhibit a high degree of locality, a cache memory can provide substantial improvements in performance.

3.4   STORAGE AS A HIERARCHY

Although the best mixture of devices for a computing system depends very much on the needs of the system's users, we can imagine any computing system as a hierarchy of storage devices of different speed, capacity, and cost. Figure 3.11 summarizes the different types of storage found at different levels in such hierarchies and shows approximately how they compare in terms of access time, capacity, and cost.

3.5   A JOURNEY OF A BYTE

What happens when a program writes a byte to a file on a disk? We know what the program does (it says WRITE(...)), and we now know something about how the byte is stored on a disk, but we haven't looked at what happens *between* the program and the disk. The whole story of what happens to data between program and disk is not one we can tell here (you need to learn about operating systems and data communications to fill it all in), but we can give you an idea of the many different pieces of hardware and software involved, and the many jobs that have to be done, by looking at one example of a journey of one byte.

Suppose we want to append a byte representing the character 'P' stored in a character variable c to a file called TEXT stored somewhere

---

†The term *cache* (as opposed to *disk cache*) generally refers to a very high-speed block of primary memory that performs the same types of performance-enhancing operations with respect to RAM that a disk cache does with respect to secondary memory.

Types of memory	Devices and media	Access times (sec)	Capacities (bytes)	Cost (cents/bit)
Primary Registers RAM RAM disk and disk cache	Core and semiconductors	10^{-8}–10^{-5}	10^0–10^7	10^0–10^{-2}
Secondary Direct-access	Magnetic disks	10^{-3}–10^{-1}	10^4–10^9	10^{-2}–10^{-5}
Serial	Tape and mass storage	10^1–10^2	10^0–10^{11}	10^{-5}–10^{-7}
Offline Archival and backup	Removable magnetic disks, optical discs, and tapes	10^0–10^2	10^4–10^9	10^{-5}–10^{-7}

FIGURE 3.11 ▪ Approximate comparisons of types of storage, circa 1985.

on a disk. From the program's point of view, the entire journey that the byte will take might be represented by the statement

```
WRITE(TEXT, c, 1)
```

but the journey is much longer than this simple statement suggests. It is a journey that is marked by obstructions, delays, and possibly even accidents. The byte has to use several different means of transportation, some slow, some fast. Occasionally it has to sit waiting for a bus or other vehicle to become available. Some of the time it travels with a group, some of the time by itself. It passes many checkpoints, each time having to reestablish its credentials.

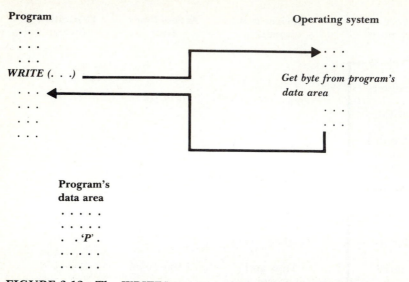

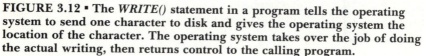

FIGURE 3.12 ▪ The *WRITE()* statement in a program tells the operating system to send one character to disk and gives the operating system the location of the character. The operating system takes over the job of doing the actual writing, then returns control to the calling program.

Our byte begins in RAM somewhere, as the contents of the character variable *c*. The *WRITE()* statement results in a call to the computer's operating system, which has the task of seeing that the rest of the journey is completed successfully (Fig. 3.12). Often our program can provide the operating system with information that helps it carry out this task more effectively, but once the operating system has taken over, the job of overseeing the rest of the journey is largely out of our program's hands.

3.5.1 THE FILE MANAGER

An operating system is not a single program, but a collection of programs, each one designed to manage a different part of the computer's resources. Among these programs are ones that deal with file-related matters and I/O devices. We call this subset of programs the operating system's *file manager*. The file manager may be thought of as several layers of procedures (Fig. 3.13), with the upper layers dealing mostly with symbolic, or *logical*, aspects of file management, and the lower layers dealing more with the *physical* aspects. The journey of our byte begins with a call to the uppermost layer. Each layer calls the one below it, until, at the lowest level, the byte is actually written to the disk.

The file manager begins by finding out whether the logical characteristics of the file are consistent with what we are asking it to do with the file. It may look up the requested file in a table, where it finds out

Logical

1. The program asks the operating system to write the contents of the variable c to the next available position in TEXT.

2. The operating system passes the job on to the file manager.

3. The file manager looks up TEXT in a table containing information about it, such as whether the file is open and available for use, what types of access are allowed, if any, and what physical file the logical name TEXT corresponds to.

4. The file manager searches a file allocation table for the physical location of the sector that is to contain the byte.

5. The file manager makes sure that the last sector in the file has been stored in a system I/O buffer in RAM, then deposits the 'P' into its proper position in the buffer.

6. The file manager gives instructions to the I/O processor about where the byte is stored in RAM and where it needs to be sent on the disk.

7. The I/O processor finds a time when the drive is available to receive the data and puts the data in proper format for the disk. It may also buffer the data to send it out in chunks of the proper size for the disk.

8. The I/O processor sends the data to the disk controller.

9. The controller instructs the drive to move the read/write head to the proper track, waits for the desired sector to come under the read/write head, then sends the byte to the drive to be deposited, bit-by-bit, on the surface of the disk.

Physical

FIGURE 3.13 ▪ Layers of procedures involved in transmitting a byte from a program's data area to a file called TEXT on disk.

such things as whether the file has been opened, what type of file the byte is being sent to (a binary file, a text file, some other organization), who the file's owner is, and whether WRITE() access is allowed for this particular user of the file (Fig. 3.14).

Having identified the desired file and verified that the requested access is legal, the file manager must now figure out where in the file TEXT the 'P' is to be deposited. Since the 'P' is to be appended to the file, the file manager needs to know where the end of the file is—the physical location of the last sector in the file. This information is obtained from the file allocation table (FAT) described earlier. From the FAT, the file manager locates the drive, cylinder, track, and sector where the byte is to be stored.

3.5.2 THE I/O BUFFER

Next, the file manager determines whether the sector that is to contain the 'P' is already in RAM or needs to be loaded into RAM. If the sector needs to be loaded, the file manager must find an available *system I/O buffer* space for it, then read it from the disk. Once it has the sector in a buffer in RAM, the file manager can deposit the 'P' into its proper position in the buffer (Fig. 3.15).

The system I/O buffer allows the file manager to read and write data in sector-sized or block-sized units. In other words, it enables the

Name	Opened by	Type of access opened for	Owner	Protection modes	. . .
AFILE	Smith	read only	Smith	Owner: read/write Others: read only	. . .
PROGRAM1	Jones	read/write	Smith	Owner: read/write Others: read/write	. . .
TEXT	Reader	write only	Reader	Owner: read/write Others: no access	. . .
.	.	.	.	.	. . .
.	.	.	.	.	
.	.	.	.	.	

FIGURE 3.14 ▪ Table of information about logical aspects of a file. The ellipses (. . .) indicate that other information might also be included, such as where information about physical aspects of the file might be found in the FAT.

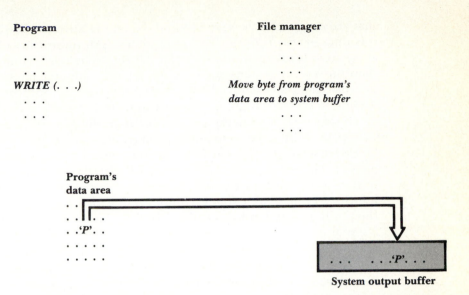

Program

. . .

. . .

. . .

WRITE (. . .)

. . .

. . .

File manager

. . .

. . .

. . .

Move byte from program's
data area to system buffer

. . .

. . .

Program's
data area

. . .

. . .

. . .'P'. .

. . . . .

. . . . .

System output buffer

. . .   . . .'P'. . .

FIGURE 3.15 ▪ The file manager moves 'P' from the program's data area to a system output buffer, where it may join other bytes headed for the same place on the disk.

file manager to ensure that the organization of data in RAM conforms to the organization it will have on the disk.

Instead of sending the sector immediately to the disk, the file manager usually waits to see if it can accumulate more bytes going to the same sector before actually transmitting anything. Even though the statement WRITE(TEXT,c,1) seems to imply that our character is being sent immediately to the disk, it may in fact be kept in RAM for some time before it is actually sent. (There are many situations when the file manager cannot wait until a buffer is filled before transmitting it. For instance, if TEXT were closed, it would have to *flush* all output buffers holding data waiting to be written to TEXT so that the data would not be lost.)

3.5.3 THE BYTE LEAVES RAM— THE I/O PROCESSOR

So far, all of our byte's activities have occurred within the computer's primary memory and have probably been carried out by the computer's central processing unit (CPU). The byte has travelled along data paths that are designed to be very fast and that are relatively expensive. Now it is time for the byte to travel outside of RAM, toward the disk drive. It has to travel along a data path that is likely to be slower and narrower than the one in primary memory. (A typical computer might have an internal data path width of four bytes, whereas the width of the path leading to the disk might be one or two bytes.)

Because of bottlenecks created by these differences in speed and data path widths, our byte and its companions might have to wait for an external data path to become available, and even when they do enter an available path, they travel more slowly than they would in RAM.† It also means that the CPU has extra time on its hands as it deals out information in small enough chunks and at slow enough speeds that the world outside can handle them. In fact, the differences between the internal and external speeds for transmitting data are often so great that the CPU can transmit to several external devices simultaneously.

The processes of disassembling and assembling groups of bytes for transmission to and from external devices are so specialized that it is unreasonable to ask an expensive, general purpose CPU to spend its valuable time doing I/O when a simpler device could do the job as well, freeing the CPU to do the work that it is most suited for. Such a special purpose device is called an *I/O processor*.

An I/O processor may be anything from a simple chip capable of taking a byte and, on cue, just passing it on, to a powerful small computer capable of executing very sophisticated programs and communicating with many devices simultaneously. The I/O processor takes its instructions from the operating system, but once it begins processing I/O, it runs independently, relieving the operating system (and the CPU) of the task of communicating with secondary storage devices. This allows I/O processes and internal computing to overlap.‡

In a typical computer the file manager might now tell the I/O processor that there is data in the buffer that is to be transmitted to the disk, how much data there is, and where it is to go on the disk. This information might come in the form of a little program that the operating system constructs and the I/O processor executes (Fig. 3.16).

Because it must be capable of dealing with a number of different kinds of devices, the I/O processor is usually not designed to control

---

†On many computers, the data path is referred to as a *data bus*, so we can say that our byte's journey might be stalled while it "waits for the bus."

‡On many systems the I/O processor can take data directly from RAM, without further involvement from the CPU. This process is called *direct memory access* (DMA). On other systems, the CPU must place the data in special I/O registers before the I/O processor can have access to it.

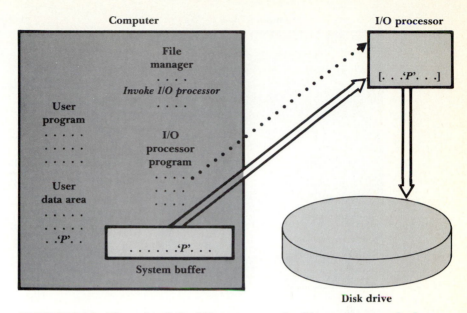

FIGURE 3.16 ▪ **The role of the I/O processor: the file manager sends the I/O processor instructions in the form of an I/O processor program. The I/O processor gets the data from the system buffer, prepares it for storing on the disk, then sends it to the disk.**

specific devices. Instead, its job is primarily to put data in a form that is acceptable to any device, and to pass on other information that a particular device might need in order to do the rest.

3.5.4 THE BYTE IS PUT ON THE DISK—THE DISK CONTROLLER

The job of actually controlling the operation of the disk is done by another device, called a *disk controller*. In the case of our byte, the I/O processor probably asks the disk controller if the disk drive is available for writing. If there is much I/O processing, there is a good chance that the drive will not be available and that our byte will have to wait in its buffer until the drive becomes available.

The next thing that happens often makes the time spent so far seem insignificant in comparison: the disk drive is instructed to move its read/write head to the track and sector on the drive where our byte and its companions are to be stored. For the first time, a device is being asked to do something mechanical! The read/write head must seek to

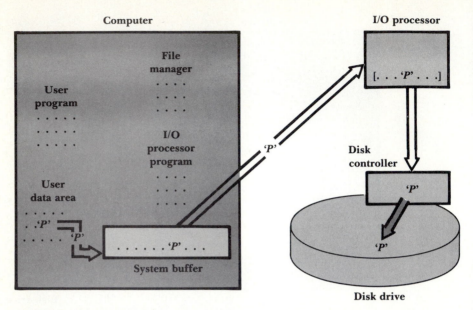

FIGURE 3.17 ▪ **Typical journey of a byte: from the program's data area to the system buffer, to the I/O processor, to the disk controller, to the disk.**

the proper track (unless it is already there), then wait until the disk has spun around so that the desired sector is under the head. Once the track and sector are located, the I/O processor (or perhaps the controller) can send out bytes, one at a time, to the drive. Our byte waits until its turn comes, then travels, alone, to the drive, where it probably is stored in a little one-byte buffer while it waits to be deposited on the disk.

Finally, as the disk spins under the read/write head, the eight bits of our byte are deposited, one at a time, on the surface of the disk (Fig. 3.17). There the 'P' remains, at the end of its journey, spinning about at a leisurely 50–100 miles per hour.

3.6 ▬ BUFFER MANAGEMENT

Any user of files can benefit from some knowledge of what happens to data travelling between a program's data area and secondary storage. One aspect of this process that is particularly important is the use of buffers. Buffering involves working with large chunks of data in RAM so that the number of accesses to secondary storage can be reduced. We concentrate on the operation of system I/O buffers, but be aware that the use of program buffers can also substantially affect performance.

THE ONE-BUFFER BOTTLENECK. We know that a file manager allocates I/O buffers that are big enough to hold incoming data, but we have said nothing so far about *how many* buffers are used. In fact, it is common for file managers to allocate several buffers for performing I/O.

To understand the need for several system buffers, consider what happens if a program is performing both input and output one character at a time, and only one I/O buffer is available. When the program asks for its first character, the I/O buffer is loaded with the sector containing the character, and the character is transmitted to the program. If the program then decides to output a character, the I/O buffer is filled with the sector into which the output character needs to go, destroying its original contents. Then when the next input character is needed, the buffer contents have to be written to disk to make room for the (original) sector containing the second input character. And so on.

Fortunately, there is a simple and generally very effective solution to this ridiculous state of affairs, and that is to use more than one system buffer. For this reason, I/O systems almost always use at least two buffers—one for input and one for output.

Even if a program transmits data in only one direction, the use of a single system I/O buffer can slow it down considerably. We know, for instance, that the operation of reading a sector from a disk is extremely slow compared to the amount of time it takes to move data in RAM, so we can guess that a program that reads many sectors from a file might have to spend much of its time waiting for the I/O system to fill its buffer every time a read operation is performed before it can begin processing. When this happens, the program that is running is said to be *I/O bound*—the CPU spends much of its time just waiting for I/O to be performed. The solution to this problem is to use more than one buffer, and to have the I/O system be filling the next sector or block of data while it is processing the current one.

BUFFERING STRATEGIES. Suppose that a program is only writing to a disk and that it is I/O bound. The CPU wants to be filling a buffer at the same time that I/O is being performed. If *two* buffers are used and I/O-CPU overlapping is permitted, the CPU can be filling one buffer while the contents of the other are being transmitted to disk. When both tasks are finished, the roles of the buffers can be exchanged. This technique of swapping the roles of two buffers after each output (or input) operation is called *double buffering*. Double buffering allows the operating system to be operating on one buffer while the other buffer is being loaded or emptied (Fig. 3.18).

The idea of swapping system buffers to allow processing and I/O to overlap need not be restricted to two buffers. In theory, any number of buffers can be used, and they can be organized in a variety of ways. The actual management of system buffers is usually done by the operating system and can rarely be controlled by programmers who do not work at the systems level. It is common, however, for users to be able to control the *number* of system buffers assigned to jobs.

Some file systems use a buffering scheme called *buffer pooling*: when a system buffer is needed, it is taken from a pool of available buffers and used. When the system receives a request to read a certain sector or block, it looks to see if one of its buffers already contains that sector or block. If no buffer contains it, then the system finds from its pool of buffers one that is not currently in use and loads the sector or block into it.

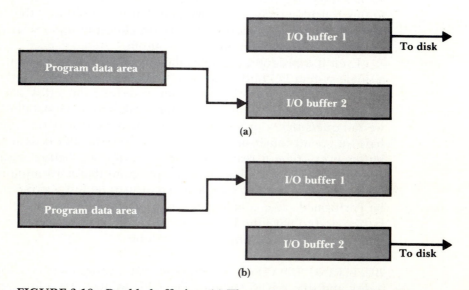

FIGURE 3.18 ▪ **Double buffering. (a) The contents of system I/O buffer 1 are sent to disk while I/O buffer 2 is being filled. (b) The contents of buffer 2 are sent to disk while I/O buffer 1 is being filled.**

Several different schemes are used to decide which buffer to take from a buffer pool. One generally effective strategy is to take from the pool that buffer that is least recently used. When a buffer is accessed, it is put on a least-recently used queue, so that it is allowed to retain its data until all other less-recently used buffers have been accessed. The least-recently used (LRU) strategy for replacing old data with new data has many applications in computing. It is based on the assumption that a block of data that has been used recently is more likely to be needed in the near future than one that has been used less recently. We encounter LRU again in later chapters.

It is difficult to predict the point at which the addition of extra buffers ceases to contribute to improved performance. Buffers take up valuable RAM space, and the more buffers there are, the more time the file manager must take to manage them. When in doubt, consider experimenting with different numbers of buffers.

MOVE MODE AND LOCATE MODE. Sometimes it is not necessary to distinguish between a program's data area and system buffers. When data must always be copied from a system buffer to a program buffer (or vice versa), the amount of time taken to perform the move can be substantial. This way of handling buffered data is called *move mode*, since it involves moving chunks of data from one place in RAM to another before they can be accessed.

There are two ways that move mode can be avoided. If the file manager can perform I/O directly between secondary storage and the program's data area, no extra move is necessary. Alternatively, the file manager could use system buffers to handle all I/O, but provide the program with the *locations*, through the use of pointer variables, of the system buffers. Both techniques are examples of a general approach to buffering called *locate mode*. When locate mode is used, a program is able to operate directly on data in the I/O buffer, eliminating the need to transfer data between an I/O buffer and a program buffer.

It is not always obvious when features like locate mode and buffer pooling are available in an operating system. You often have to go looking for them. Sometimes you can invoke them by communicating with your operating system, and sometimes you can cause them to be invoked by organizing your program in ways that are compatible with the way the operating system does I/O. In the rest of the text we return many times to the issue of how to enhance performance by thinking about how buffers work and adapting programs and file structures accordingly.

SUMMARY

In this chapter we look at the software environment in which file processing programs must operate and at some of the hardware devices on which files are commonly stored, hoping to understand how they influence the ways we design and process files.

We begin by looking at the two most important storage media: magnetic disks and tapes.

Disk drives consist of a set of read/write heads that are interspersed among one or more platters. Each platter contributes one or two surfaces, each surface contains a set of concentric tracks, and each track is divided into sectors or blocks. The set of tracks that can be read without moving the read/write heads is called a cylinder.

There are two basic ways to address data on disks: by sector and by block. Used in this context, the term *block* refers to a group of records that are stored together on a disk and treated as a unit for I/O purposes. When blocks are used, the user is better able to make the physical organization of data correspond to its logical organization, and hence can sometimes improve performance. Block-organized drives also sometimes make it possible for the disk drive to search among blocks on a track for a record with a certain key without first having to transmit the unwanted blocks into RAM.

Three possible disadvantages of block-organized devices are the danger of internal track fragmentation, the burden of dealing with the extra complexity that the user has to bear, and the loss of opportunities to do some of the kinds of synchronization (such as sector interleaving) that sector-addressing devices provide.

The cost of a disk access can be measured in terms of the time it takes for seeking, rotational delay, and transfer time. If sector interleaving is used, it is possible to access logically adjacent sectors by separating them physically by one or more sectors. Although it takes much less time to access a single record directly than sequentially, the extra seek time required for doing direct accesses makes it much slower than sequential access when a series of records is to be accessed.

Though not as important as disks, magnetic tape has an important niche in file processing. Tapes are inexpensive, reasonably fast for sequential processing, compact, robust, and easy to store and transport. Data are usually organized on tapes in one-bit-wide parallel tracks, with a bit-wide cross section of tracks interpreted as one or more bytes. When estimating processing speed and space utilization, it is important to recognize the role played by the interblock gap. Effective recording density and effective transmission rate are useful measurements of the performance one can expect to achieve for a given physical file organization.

We look at a variety of other media used to store files. Different applications call for widely varying devices and media, and mixing them according to the demands of specific problems can pay dividends in terms of cost and performance.

The chapter follows a journey of a byte as it is sent from RAM to disk. The journey involves the participation of many different programs and devices, including:

- A user's program, which makes the initial call to the operating system;
- The operating system's file manager, which maintains and accesses tables with information that it uses to translate between the program's logical view of the file and the physical file where the byte is to be stored;
- An I/O processor and its software, which transmit the byte, synchronizing the transmission of the byte between an I/O buffer in RAM and the disk;
- The disk controller and its software, which instruct the drive about how to find the proper track and sector, then send the byte; and
- The disk drive, which accepts the byte and deposits it on the disk surface.

We conclude with a closer look at buffering, focusing mainly on techniques for managing buffers to improve performance. Some techniques include double buffering, buffer pooling, and locate-mode buffering.

KEY TERMS

Bpi. Bits per inch per track. On a disk, data are recorded serially on tracks. On a tape, data are recorded in parallel on several tracks, so a 6,250-bpi 9-track tape contains 6,250 *bytes* per inch, when all nine tracks are taken into account (one track being used for parity).

Block. Unit of data organization corresponding to the amount of data transferred in a single access. Often block refers to a collection of records, but it may be a collection of sectors (see *cluster*) whose size has no correspondence to the organization of the data. A block is sometimes called a *physical record*. Sometimes a *sector* is called a block.

Block organization. Disk drive organization that allows the user to define the size and organization of blocks, then access a block by giving its block address or the key of one of its records. See *Sector organization*.

Blocking factor. The number of records stored in one block.

Cluster. Minimum unit of *space allocation* on a sectored disk, consisting of one or more contiguous sectors. The use of large clusters can improve sequential access times by guaranteeing the ability to read longer spans of data without seeking. Small clusters tend to decrease internal fragmentation.

Controller. Device that directly controls the operation of one or more secondary storage devices, such as disk drives and magnetic tape units.

Count subblock. On block-organized drives, a small block that precedes each data block and contains information about the data block, such as its byte count and its address.

Cylinder. The set of tracks on a disk that are directly above and below each other. All of the tracks in a given cylinder can be accessed without having to move the access arm, which is to say that they can be accessed without the expense of *seek time*.

Direct access storage device (DASD). Disk or other secondary storage device that permits access to a specific sector or block of data without first requiring the reading of the blocks that precede it.

Direct memory access (DMA). Transfer of data directly between RAM and peripheral devices, without significant involvement by the CPU.

Disk cache. A segment of RAM configured to contain pages of data from a disk. Disk caches can lead to substantial improvements in access time when access requests exhibit a high degree of locality.

Disk pack. An assemblage of magnetic disks mounted on the same vertical shaft. A pack of disks is treated as a single unit consisting of a number of cylinders equivalent to the number of tracks per surface. If disk packs are *removable*, different packs can be mounted on the same drive at different times, providing a convenient form of offline storage for data that can be accessed directly.

Effective recording density. Recording density after taking into account the space used by interblock gaps, nondata subblocks, and other space-consuming items that accompany data.

Effective transmission rate. Transmission rate after taking into account the time used to locate and transmit the block of data in which a desired record occurs.

Extent. One or more adjacent clusters allocated as part (or all) of a file. The number of extents in a file reflects how dispersed the file is over the disk. The more dispersed a file, the more seeking must be done in moving from one part of the file to another.

File allocation table (FAT). A table that contains mappings of the physical locations of all of the clusters in all files on disk storage.

File manager. The part of an operating system that is responsible for managing files, including a collection of programs whose responsibilities range from keeping track of files to invoking I/O processes that transmit information between primary and secondary storage.

Fixed disk. A disk drive with platters that may not be removed.

Formatting. The process of preparing a disk for data storage, involving such things as laying out sectors, setting up the disk's file allocation table, and checking for damage to the recording medium.

Fragmentation. Space that goes unused within a cluster, block, track, or other unit of physical storage. For instance, *track* fragmentation occurs when space on a track goes unused because there is not enough space left to accommodate a complete block.

Frame. A one-bit-wide slice of tape, usually representing a single byte.

Interblock gap. An interval of blank space that separates sectors, blocks, or subblocks on tape or disk. In the case of tape, the gap provides sufficient space for the tape to accelerate or decelerate when starting or stopping. On both tapes and disks the gaps enable the read/write heads to tell accurately when one sector (or blocks or subblock) ends and another begins.

Interleaving factor. Since it is often not possible to read physically adjacent sectors of a disk, *logically* adjacent sectors are sometimes arranged so that they are not *physically* adjacent. This is called interleaving. The *interleaving factor* refers to the number of physical sectors the next logically adjacent sector is from the current sector being read or written.

I/O processor. A device that carries out I/O tasks, allowing the CPU to work on non-I/O tasks.

Key subblock. On block-addressable drives, a block that contains the key of the last record in the data block that follows it, allowing the drive to search among the blocks on a track for a block containing a certain key, without having to load the blocks into primary memory.

Mass storage system. General term applied to storage units with large capacity. Also applied to very high capacity secondary storage systems that are capable of transmitting data between a disk and any of several thousand tape cartridges within a few seconds.

Nominal recording density. Recording density on a disk track or magnetic tape without taking into account the effects of gaps or nondata subblocks.

Nominal transmission rate. Transmission rate of a disk or tape unit without taking into account the effects of such extra operations as seek time for disks and interblock gap traversal time for tapes.

Parity. An error-checking technique in which an extra parity bit accompanies each byte and is set in such a way that the total number of 1 bits is even (even parity) or odd (odd parity).

Platter. One disk in the stack of disks on a disk drive.

RAM disk. Block of RAM configured to simulate a disk.

Rotational delay. The time it takes for the disk to rotate so that the desired sector is under the read/write head.

Sector. The fixed-sized data blocks that together make up the tracks on certain disk drives. Sectors are the smallest addressable unit on a disk whose tracks are made up of sectors.

Sector organization. Disk drive organization that uses sectors.

Seek time. The time required to move the access arm to the correct cylinder on a disk drive.

Sequential access device. A device, such as a magnetic tape unit or card reader, in which the medium (e.g., tape) must be accessed from the beginning. Sometimes called a *serial* device.

Streaming tape drive. A tape drive whose primary purpose is dumping large amounts of data from disk to tape or from tape to disk.

Subblock. When blocking is used, there are often separate groupings of information concerned with each individual block. For example, a count subblock, a key subblock, and a data subblock might all be present.

Track. The set of bytes on a single surface of a disk that can be accessed without seeking (without moving the access arm). The surface of a disk can be thought of as a series of concentric circles, with each circle corresponding to a particular position of the access arm and read/write heads. Each of these circles is a track.

Transfer time. Once the data we want is under the read/write head, we have to wait for it to pass under the head as we read it. The amount of time required for this motion and reading is the transfer time.

EXERCISES

1. Try to determine as well as you can what the journey of a byte would be like on your system. You may have to consult technical reference manuals that describe your computer's file management system, operating system, and peripheral devices. You may also want to talk to local gurus who have experience using your system.

2. Find out what utility routines are available on your computer system for monitoring I/O performance and disk utilization. If you have a large computing system, there are different routines available for different kinds of users, depending on what privileges and responsibilities they have.

3. When you create or open a file in C or Pascal, you must provide certain information to your computer's file manager so that it can handle your file properly. Compared to certain languages, such as PL/I or COBOL, the amount of information you must provide in C or Pascal is very small. Find a text or manual on PL/I or COBOL, and look up the ENVIRONMENT file description attribute, which can be used to tell the file manager a great deal about how you expect a file to be organized and used. Compare PL/I or COBOL with C or Pascal in terms of the types of file specifications available to the programmer.

4. A disk drive uses 512-byte sectors. If a program requests that a 128-byte record be written to disk, the file manager may have to *read* a sector from the disk before it can write the record. Why? What could you do to decrease the number of times such an extra read is likely to occur?

5. We have seen that some disk operating systems allocate storage space on disks in clusters and/or extents, rather than sectors, so that the size of any file must be a multiple of a cluster or extent.
   a) What are some advantages and potential disadvantages of this method of allocating disk space?
   b) How appropriate would the use of large extents be for an application that mostly involves sequential access of very large files?
   c) How appropriate would large extents be for a computing system that serves a large number of C programmers? (C programs tend to be small, so there are likely to be many small files that contain C programs.)
   d) The VAX record management system uses a default cluster size of three 512-byte sectors, but lets a user reformat a drive with any

cluster size from 1–65535 sectors. When might a cluster size larger than three sectors be desirable? When might a smaller cluster size be desirable?

6. The IBM 3350 disk drive uses block-addressing. The two subblock organizations described in the text are available:

Count-data, where the extra space used by count subblock and interblock gaps is equivalent to 185 bytes; and

Count-key-data, where the extra space used by the count and key subblocks and accompanying gaps is equivalent to 267 bytes, plus the key size.

An IBM 3350 has 19,069 usable bytes available per track, 30 tracks per cylinder, and 555 cylinders per drive. Suppose you have a file with 350,000 80-byte records that you want to store on a 3350 drive. Answer the following questions. Unless otherwise directed, assume that the blocking factor is 10, and that the count-data subblock organization is used.

a) How many blocks can be stored on one track? How many records?
b) How many blocks can be stored on one track if the count-key-data subblock organization is used?
c) Make a graph that shows the effect of block size on storage utilization, assuming count-data subblocks. Use the graph to help predict the best and worst possible blocking factor in terms of storage utilization.
d) Assuming that access to the file is always sequential, use the graph from the preceding question to predict the best and worst blocking factor. Justify your answer in terms of efficiency of storage utilization and processing time.
e) How many cylinders are required to hold the file (blocking factor 10 and count-data format)? How much space will go unused due to internal track fragmentation?
f) If the file were stored on contiguous cylinders and if there were no interference from other processes using the disk drive, the average seek time for a random access of the file would be about 12 msec. Use this to compute the average time needed to access one record randomly.
g) Explain how retrieval time for random accesses of records is affected by increasing block size. Discuss trade-offs between storage efficiency and retrieval when different block sizes are used. Make a table with different block sizes to illustrate your explanations.
h) Suppose the file is to be sorted, and a shell sort is to be used to sort the file. Since the file is too large to read into memory, it will

be sorted in place, on the disk. It is estimated (Knuth, 1973b, p. 380) that this requires about $15N^{1.25}$ moves of records, where N represents the total number of records in the file. Each move requires a random access. If all of the preceding is true, how long does it take to sort the file? (As you will see, this is not a very good solution. We provide much better solutions in the chapter on cosequential processing.)

7. A sectored disk drive differs from one with a block organization in that there is less of a correspondence between the logical and physical organization of data records or blocks.

For example, consider the Digital RM05 disk drive, which uses sector addressing. It has 32 512-byte sectors per track, 19 tracks per cylinder, and 823 cylinders per drive. From the drive's (and drive controller's) point of view, a file is just a vector of bytes divided into 512-byte sectors. Since the drive knows nothing about where one record ends and another begins, a record can span two or more sectors, or tracks, or cylinders.

One common way that records are formatted on the RM05 is to place a two-byte field at the beginning of each block, giving the number of bytes of data, followed by the data itself. There is no extra gap, and no other overhead. Assuming that this organization is used, that you want to store a file with 350,000 80-byte records, answer the following questions.

 a) How many records can be stored on one track if one record is stored per block?
 b) How many cylinders are required to hold the file?
 c) How might you block records so that each physical record access results in ten actual records being accessed? What are the benefits of doing this?

8. Consider the 1,000,000-record mailing list file discussed in the text. The file is to be backed up on 2,400 foot reels of 6,250-bpi tape with 0.3 inch interblock gaps. Tape speed is 200 inches per second.

 a) Show that only one tape would be required to back up the file if a blocking factor of 50 is used.
 b) If a blocking factor of 50 is used, how many extra records could be accommodated on a 2,400-foot tape?
 c) What is the effective recording density when a blocking factor of 50 is used?
 d) How large does the blocking factor have to be to achieve the maximum effective recording density? What negative results can result from increasing the blocking factor? (Note: an I/O buffer large enough to hold a block must be allocated.)

e) What would be the *minimum* blocking factor required to fit the file onto the tape?

f) If a blocking factor of 50 is used, how long would it take to read one block, including the gap? What would the effective transmission rate be? How long would it take to read the entire file?

g) How long would it take to perform a binary search for one record in the file, assuming that it is not possible to read backwards on the tape? (Assume that it takes 60 seconds to rewind the tape from end to beginning.) Compare this with the expected average time it would take for a sequential search for one record.

h) We implicitly assume in our discussions of tape performance that the tape drive is always reading or writing at full speed, so that no time is lost by starting and stopping. This is not necessarily the case. For example, some drives automatically stop after writing each block.

    Suppose that the extra time it takes to start before reading a block and to stop after reading the block totals 1 msec, and that the drive must start before and stop after reading each block. How much will the effective transmission rate be decreased due to starting and stopping if the blocking factor is 1? What if it is 50?

9. The use of large blocks can lead to severe internal fragmentation of tracks on disks. Does this occur when tapes are used? Explain.

FURTHER READINGS

Many textbooks contain more detailed information on the material covered in this chapter. In the area of operating systems and file management systems, we have found the operating system texts by Deitel [1984], Peterson and Silberschatz [1985], and Madnick and Donovan [1974] useful. Hanson [1982] has a great deal of material on blocking and buffering, secondary storage devices, and performance. Flores' book [1973] on peripheral devices may be a bit dated, but it contains a comprehensive treatment of the subject.

    Bohl [1981] provides a thorough treatment of mainframe-oriented IBM DASDs. Chaney and Johnson [1984] is a good article on maximizing hard disk performance on small computers. Ritchie and Thompson [1974], Kernighan and Ritchie [1978], Deitel [1984], and McKusick et al. [1984] provide information on how file I/O is handled in the UNIX operating system. The latter provides a good case study of ways in which a file system can be altered to provide substantially faster throughput for certain applications.

Information on specific systems and devices can often be found in manuals and documentation published by manufacturers. (Unfortunately, information about how software actually works is often proprietary and therefore not available.) If you use a VAX, we recommend the manuals *Introduction to the VAX Record Management Services* (Digital, 1978), *VAX Software Handbook* (Digital, 1982), and *Peripherals Handbook* (Digital, 1981). UNIX users will find it useful to look at the Bell Laboratories' monograph *The UNIX I/O System* by Dennis Ritchie [1978]. Users of IBM PCs will find the *Disk Operating System* (Microsoft, 1983 or later) and *Technical Reference* (IBM, 1983 or later) manuals from IBM useful.

CHAPTER

OBJECTIVES

To introduce file structure concepts dealing with:

Stream files;

Field and record boundaries;

Fixed length and variable length fields and records;

Search keys and canonical forms;

Sequential search;

Direct access; and

File access and file organization.

4 FUNDAMENTAL FILE STRUCTURE CONCEPTS

CHAPTER OUTLINE

4.1
A STREAM FILE

When we build file structures we are imposing order on data. In this chapter we are going to investigate the many forms that this ordering can take. We begin by looking at the base case: a file organized as a stream of bytes.

Suppose the file we are building contains name and address information. A program to accept names and addresses from the keyboard, writing them out as a stream of consecutive bytes to a file with the logical name OUTPUT, is described in the pseudocode shown in Fig. 4.1.

Implementations of this program in both C and Turbo Pascal, called *writstrm.c* and *writstrm.pas,* are provided in the collection of programs at the end of this chapter. You should type in this program, working in either C or Pascal, compile it, and run it. We use it as the basis for a number of experiments, and you can get a better feel for the differences between the file structures we are discussing if you perform the experiments yourself.

The following names and addresses are used as input to the program:

John Ames	Alan Mason
123 Maple	90 Eastgate
Stillwater, OK 74075	Ada, OK 74820

When we list the output file on our terminal screen, here is what we see:

```
AmesJohn123 MapleStillwaterOK74075MasonAlan90 EastgateAdaOK74820
```

```
PROGRAM: writstrm

    get output file name and open it with the logical name OUTPUT

    get LAST name as input
    while ( LAST name has a length > 0)
        get FIRST name, ADDRESS, CITY, STATE and ZIP as input

        write LAST    to the file OUTPUT
        write FIRST   to the file OUTPUT
        write ADDRESS to the file OUTPUT
        write CITY    to the file OUTPUT
        write STATE   to the file OUTPUT
        write ZIP     to the file OUTPUT

        get LAST name as input
    endwhile

    close OUTPUT

end PROGRAM
```

FIGURE 4.1 ▪ Program to write out a name and address file as a stream of bytes.

The program writes the information out to the file precisely as specified: as a stream of bytes containing no added information. But in meeting our specifications, the program creates a kind of "reverse Humpty-Dumpty" problem. Once we put all that information together as a single byte stream, there is no way to get it apart again.

What has happened is that we have lost the integrity of the fundamental organizational units of our input data; these fundamental units are not the individual characters, but meaningful aggregates of characters, such as "John Ames" or "123 Maple". When we are working with files, we call these fundamental aggregates *fields*. A field is *the smallest logically meaningful unit of information in a file.*†

A field is a logical notion; it is a *conceptual tool*. A field does not necessarily exist in any physical sense, yet it is important to the file's structure. When we write out our name and address information as a stream of undifferentiated bytes, we lose track of the fields that make the information meaningful. We need to organize the file in some way that lets us keep the information divided into fields.

4.2   FIELD STRUCTURES

There are many ways of adding structure to files to maintain the identity of fields. Three of the most common methods are:

- ☐   Force the fields into a predictable length;
- ☐   Begin each field with a length indicator; and
- ☐   Place a *delimiter* at the end of each field to separate it from the next field.

4.2.1 METHOD 1: FIXING THE LENGTH OF FIELDS

The fields in our sample file vary in their length. If we force the fields into predictable lengths, then we can pull them back out of the file by simply counting our way to the end of the field. We can define a struc-

---

†Readers should not confuse the term *field* and *record* with the meanings given them by some programming languages, including Pascal. In Pascal, a record is an aggregate data structure that can contain members of different types, where each member is referred to as a field. As we shall see, there is often a direct correspondence between these definitions of the terms and the fields and records that are used in files. However, the terms field and record as we use them have much more general meanings than they do in Pascal.

In C:

```
struct {
    char last[10];
    char first[10];
    char address[15];
    char city[15];
    char state[2];
    char zip[9];
} set_of_fields;
```

In Pascal:

```
TYPE
  set_of_fields = RECORD
    last    : packed array [1..10] of char;
    first   : packed array [1..10] of char;
    address : packed array [1..15] of char;
    city    : packed array [1..15] of char;
    state   : packed array [1..2]  of char;
    zip     : packed array [1..9]  of char;
  END;
```

FIGURE 4.2 ▪ Fixed length fields.

ture in C or a record in Pascal to hold these fixed length fields, as shown in Fig. 4.2.

Using this kind of fixed field length structure changes our output so that it looks like that shown in Fig. 4.3(a). Simple arithmetic is sufficient to let us recover the data in terms of the original fields.

One obvious disadvantage of this approach is that adding all the padding required to bring the fields up to a fixed length makes the file much larger. Rather than using four bytes to store the last name Ames, we use ten. We can also encounter problems with data that are too long to fit into the allocated amount of space. We could solve this second problem by fixing all the fields at lengths that are large enough to cover all cases, but this would just make the first problem of wasted space in the file even worse.

Because of these difficulties, the fixed field approach to structuring data is often inappropriate for data that inherently contain a large amount of variability in the length of fields, such as names and addresses. But there are kinds of data for which fixed length fields are highly appropriate. If every field is already fixed in length, or if there is very little variation in field lengths, using a file structure consisting of a continuous stream of bytes organized into fixed length fields is often a very good solution.

4.2.2 METHOD 2: BEGINNING EACH FIELD WITH A LENGTH INDICATOR

Another way to make it possible to count to the end of a field involves storing the field length just ahead of the field, as illustrated in Fig. 4.3(b). If the fields are not too long (length less than 256 bytes), it is possible to store the length in a single byte at the start of each field.

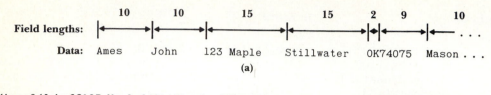

FIGURE 4.3 ▪ Three methods for organizing field structures. (a) Fixed length fields. (b) Beginning each field with a length indicator. (c) Separating the fields with delimiters.

4.2.3 METHOD 3: SEPARATING THE FIELDS WITH DELIMITERS

We can also preserve the identity of fields by separating them with delimiters. All we need to do is choose some special character that will not appear as a legitimate character within a field and then *insert* that character into the file after writing each field.

The choice of a delimiter character can be very important since it must be a character that does not get in the way of processing. The comma character, for example, would be a poor choice for this file since commas often occur as legitimate characters within an address field. We use the vertical bar character as our delimiter, so that our file appears as in Fig. 4.3(c). Readers should modify the original stream-of-bytes programs, *writstrm.c* and *writstrm.pas* (found at the end of the chapter), changing them so that they place a delimiter after each field. We use this delimited field format in the next few sample programs.

4.3
READING A STREAM OF FIELDS

Given modified versions of *writstrm.c* and *writstrm.pas* that use delimiters to separate fields, we can write a program called *readstrm* that reads the stream of bytes back in, breaking the stream into fields. It is convenient to conceive of the program in two levels, as shown in the pseudocode description provided in Fig. 4.4. The outer level of the program opens the file and then calls the function *readfield()* until *readfield()* returns a field length of zero, indicating that there are no more fields to read.

The *readfield()* function, in turn, works through the file, character by character, collecting characters into a field until the function encounters a delimiter or the end of the file. The function returns a count of the characters that are found in the field. Implementations of *readstrm* in both C and Pascal are included with the programs at the end of the chapter.

```
Define Constant: DELIMITER = '¦'

PROGRAM: readstrm

    get input file name and open as INPUT
    initialize FIELD_COUNT

    FIELD_LENGTH := readfield (INPUT, FIELD_CONTENT)
    while ( FIELD_LENGTH > 0 )

        increment the FIELD_COUNT
        write FIELD_COUNT and FIELD_CONTENT to the screen
        FIELD_LENGTH := readfield (INPUT, FIELD_CONTENT)

    endwhile

    close INPUT
end PROGRAM


FUNCTION: readfield (INPUT, FIELD_CONTENT)

    initialize I
    initialize CH

    while (not EOF (INPUT) and CH does not equal DELIMITER)

        read a character from INPUT into CH
        increment I
        FIELD_CONTENT [I] := CH

    endwhile
    return (length of field that was read)

end FUNCTION
```

FIGURE 4.4 ▪ **Program to read fields from a file and display them on the screen.**

When this program is run using our delimited-field version of the file containing data for John Ames and Alan Mason, the output looks like this:

```
Field #  1:  Ames
Field #  2:  John
Field #  3:  123 Maple
Field #  4:  Stillwater
Field #  5:  OK
Field #  6:  74075
Field #  7:  Mason
Field #  8:  Alan
Field #  9:  90 Eastgate
Field # 10:  Ada
Field # 11:  OK
Field # 12:  74820
```

Clearly we now preserve the notion of a field as we store and retrieve these data. But something is still missing. We do not really think of this file as a stream of fields. In fact, the fields need to be grouped into sets. The first six fields are a set associated with someone named John Ames. The next six are a set of fields associated with Alan Mason. We call these sets of fields *records*.

4.4
RECORD STRUCTURES

A *record* can be defined as *a set of fields that belong together when the file is viewed in terms of a higher level of organization.* Like the notion of a field, a record is another conceptual tool. It is another level of organization that we impose on the data to preserve meaning. Records do not necessarily exist in the file in any physical sense, yet they are an important logical notion included in the file's structure.

Here are some of the most often used methods for organizing a file into records:

☐ Require that the records be a predictable length. This length can be measured either in terms of bytes or in terms of the number of fields.

☐ Begin each record with a length indicator consisting of a count of the number of bytes that the record contains.

☐ Use a second file to keep track of the beginning byte address for each record.

☐ Place a delimiter at the end of each record to separate it from the next record.

4.4.1 METHOD 1: MAKING RECORDS A PREDICTABLE LENGTH

Making a record a predictable length lets us count our way through a record. When our counting reaches some predetermined quantity, we know we have read in all of the record; any more reading would take us into the next record. This method of recognizing records is analogous to the first method we discussed for making fields recognizable, which involved fixing the field length. The important difference is that when we are counting our way through a record we have a choice of units to use in our counting. We can either count bytes or we can count fields.

COUNTING BYTES: FIXED LENGTH RECORDS. A *fixed length record file* is one in which each record contains the same number of bytes. As we will see in the chapters that follow, fixed length record structures are among the most commonly used methods for organizing files.

The C structure *set_of_fields* (or the Pascal RECORD of the same name) that we define in our discussion of fixed length fields is actually an example of a fixed length *record* as well as an example of fixed length fields. We have a fixed number of fields, each with a predetermined length, which combine to make a fixed length record. This kind of field and record structure is illustrated in Fig. 4.5(a).

It is important to realize, however, that fixing the number of bytes in a record does not by any means imply that the sizes or number of fields in the record must be fixed. Fixed length records are very frequently used as containers to hold variable numbers of variable length fields. It is also possible to mix fixed and variable length fields within a record. Figure 4.5(b) illustrates how variable length fields might be placed in a fixed length record.

COUNTING FIELDS. Rather than specifying that each record in a file contain some fixed number of bytes, we can specify that it will contain a fixed number of fields. This is the simplest way to organize the records in the name and address file we have been looking at. The *writstrm* program asks for six pieces of information for every person, so there are six contiguous fields in the file for each record (Fig. 4.5c). We could modify *readstrm* to recognize fields by simply counting the fields *modulo*

Ames	John	123 Maple	Stillwater	OK74075
Mason	Alan	90 Eastgate	Ada	OK74820

(a)

Ames ¦ John ¦ 123 Maple ¦ Stillwater ¦ OK ¦ 74075 ¦ ◄———— Unused space ————►

Mason ¦ Alan ¦ 90 Eastgate ¦ Ada ¦ OK ¦ 74820 ¦ ◄———— Unused space ————►

(b)

Ames ¦ John ¦ 123 Maple ¦ Stillwater ¦ OK ¦ 74075 ¦ Mason ¦ Alan ¦ 90 Eastgate ¦ Ada ¦ OK . . .

(c)

FIGURE 4.5 ▪ **Three ways of making the lengths of records constant and predictable. (a) Counting bytes: fixed length records with fixed length fields. (b) Counting bytes: fixed length records with variable length fields. (c) Counting fields: six fields per record.**

six, outputting record boundary information to the screen every time the count starts over.

4.4.2 METHOD 2: BEGINNING EACH RECORD WITH A LENGTH INDICATOR

We know how many bytes are in fixed length records because the record length is some predetermined constant throughout the file. We can also communicate the length of records, making them recognizable, by beginning each record with a field containing an integer that indicates how many bytes there are in the rest of the record (Fig. 4.6a). This is a commonly used method for handling variable length records. We look at it more closely in the next section.

4.4.3 METHOD 3: USING A SECOND FILE TO KEEP TRACK OF ADDRESSES

We can use a second, *index* file to keep a byte offset for each record in the original file. The byte offsets allow us to find the beginning of each successive record and also let us compute the length of each record. We

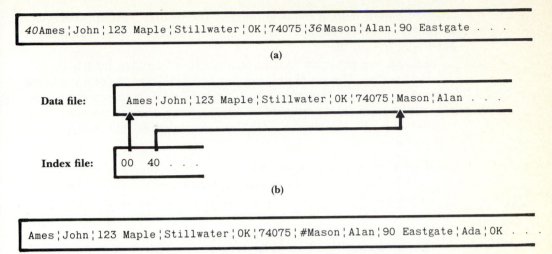

```
40Ames┊John┊123 Maple┊Stillwater┊OK┊74075┊36Mason┊Alan┊90 Eastgate . . .
```
(a)

Data file:
```
Ames┊John┊123 Maple┊Stillwater┊OK┊74075┊Mason┊Alan . . .
```

Index file:
```
00   40 . . .
```
(b)

```
Ames┊John┊123 Maple┊Stillwater┊OK┊74075┊#Mason┊Alan┊90 Eastgate┊Ada┊OK . . .
```
(c)

FIGURE 4.6 ▪ Record structures for variable length records. (a) Beginning each record with a length indicator. (b) Using an index file to keep track of record addresses. (c) Placing the delimiter '#' at the end of each record.

look up the position of a record in the index and then seek to the record in the data file. Figure 4.6(b) illustrates this two-file mechanism.

4.4.4 METHOD 4: PLACING A DELIMITER AT THE END OF EACH RECORD

This is the option that, at a record level, is exactly analogous to the solution we used to keep the *fields* distinct in the sample program we developed. An end-of-line mark is often used as a record delimiter (carriage return/linefeed pair or, on UNIX systems, just a linefeed ('\n') character). In Fig. 4.6(c) we use a '#' character as the record delimiter.

4.5 A RECORD STRUCTURE THAT USES A LENGTH INDICATOR

No one of these different approaches to preserving the idea of a *record* in a file is appropriate for all situations. Selection of a method for record organization depends on the nature of the data and on what you need to do with it. We begin by looking at a record structure that uses a record length field at the beginning of the record. This approach lets us preserve the *variability* in the length of records that is inherent in our initial stream file.

We call the program that builds this new, variable length record structure *writrec*. The set of programs at the end of the chapter contains versions of this program in C and Turbo Pascal. Implementing this program is partially a matter of building on the *writstrm* program that we created earlier in this chapter, but also involves addressing some new problems:

☐   If we want to put a length indicator at the *beginning* of every record (before any other fields) we must know the sum of the lengths of the fields in each record before we can begin writing the record to the file. We need to accumulate the entire contents of a record in a *buffer* before writing it out.

☐   In what form should we write the record length field to the file? As a binary integer? As a series of ASCII characters?

The concept of buffering is one we run into again and again as we work with files. In the case of *writrec* the buffer can simply be a character array into which we place the fields and field delimiters as we collect them. Resetting the buffer length to zero and adding information to the buffer can be handled using the loop logic provided in Fig. 4.7.

The question of how to represent the record length is a little more difficult. One option would be to write the length in the form of a

```
get LAST name as input
while ( LAST name has a length > 0 )
    set length of string in BUFFER to zero
    concatenate: BUFFER + LAST name + DELIMITER

    while ( input fields exist for record )
        get the FIELD
        concatenate: BUFFER + FIELD + DELIMITER
    endwhile

    write length of string in BUFFER to the file
    write the string in BUFFER to the file

    get LAST name as input
endwhile
```

FIGURE 4.7 ▪ **Main program logic for *writrec*.**

binary integer before each record. This is a natural solution in C, since it does not require us to go to the trouble of converting the record length into character form. It is also conceptually interesting, since it illustrates the use of a fixed length, binary field in combination with variable length character fields.

Although we could use this same solution for a Pascal implementation, we might choose, instead, to account for some important differences between C and Pascal:

☐   Unlike C, Pascal automatically converts binary integers into character representations of those integers if we are writing to a text file. Consequently, it is no trouble at all to convert the record length into a character form: it happens automatically.

☐   In Pascal, a file is defined as a sequence of elements of a single type. Since we have a file of variable length strings of characters, the natural type for the file is that of a character. We *can* store two-byte integers in the file if we go to the trouble of breaking them up into their constituent byte values and converting them with the CHR() function. However, it is much simpler just to let Pascal perform the automatic conversion of length into character form.

In short, the easiest thing to do in C is to store the integers in the file as fixed length, two-byte fields containing integers. In Pascal it is easier to make use of the automatic conversion of integers into characters for text files. File structure design is always an exercise in flexibility. Neither of these approaches is correct; good design consists of choosing the approach that is most *appropriate* for a given language and computing environment. In the programs included at the end of the chapter, we have implemented our record structure both ways, using integer length fields in C and character representations in Pascal. The output from the Pascal implementation is shown in Fig. 4.8. (The output wraps around to the next line after 64 characters.) Each record now has a record length field preceding the data fields. This field is delimited by a blank. For example, the first record (for John Ames) contains 40 characters, counting from the first 'A' in "Ames" to the final delimiter after "74075," so the characters '4' and '0' are placed before the record, followed by a blank.

```
40 Ames¦John¦123 Maple¦Stillwater¦OK¦74075¦36 Mason¦Alan¦90
Eastgate¦Ada¦OK¦74820:
```

FIGURE 4.8 ▪ Records preceded by record length fields in character form.

Before we can look at the output from the C version of *writrec*, in which we use binary integers for the record lengths, we need to take a brief look at the use of hex dumps so that we can interpret the non-character portion of this output.

4.6
MIXING NUMBERS AND CHARACTERS—USE OF A HEX DUMP

Hex dumps give us the ability to look inside a file at the actual bytes that are stored there. Consider, for instance, the record length information in Pascal program output that we were examining a moment ago. The length of the Ames record, which is the first one in the file, is 40 characters, including delimiters. In the Pascal version of *writrec*, where we store the ASCII character representation of this decimal number, the actual bytes stored *in the file* look like the representation in Fig. 4.9.

As you can see, the *number* 40 is not the same as the set of characters '4' and '0'. The hex value of the *binary integer* 40 is 0x28; the hexadecimal values of the *characters* '4' and '0' are 0x34 and 0x30. (We are using the C language convention of identifying hexadecimal numbers through the use of the prefix 0x.) So, when we are storing a number in ASCII form, it is the hex values of the *ASCII characters* that go into the file, not the hex value of the number itself.

In the C implementation we choose to represent the length field for each record as a short integer rather than as ASCII characters. There are two advantages to this:

1. We can represent much bigger numbers with a two-byte integer than we can with two ASCII bytes (32,767 versus 99).
2. We do not need to translate the record length from ASCII to integer when we want to *use* it as an integer.

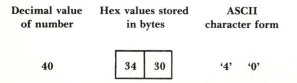

Decimal value of number	Hex values stored in bytes	ASCII character form
40	34 | 30	'4' '0'

FIGURE 4.9 ▪ The number 40, stored as ASCII characters.

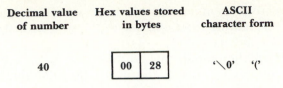

Decimal value of number	Hex values stored in bytes	ASCII character form
40	00 | 28	'\0' '('

FIGURE 4.10 ▪ **The number 40, stored as a short integer.**

Figure 4.10 shows the byte representation of the number 40 stored as an integer (this is called storing the number in *binary* form, even though we usually view the output as a hexadecimal number). Now the hexadecimal value stored in the file is that of the number itself. The ASCII characters that happen to be associated with the number's actual hexadecimal value have no obvious relationship to the number.

Given this background in the difference between storing numbers in ASCII character form and storing them as binary quantities, and given that our two records had lengths of 40 (hex value 0x28) and 36 (hex value 0x24), here is what the version of the file that uses binary integers for record lengths looks like if we simply print it on a terminal screen.

```
(  Ames¦John¦123 Maple¦Stillwater¦OK¦74075¦$ Mason¦Alan¦90 Eastgate...
```
──────Blank, since '\0' is unprintable   ──Blank, same reason
──────0x28 is ASCII code for '('   ──0x24 is ASCII code for '$'

The ASCII representations of characters and numbers in the actual record come out nicely enough, but the binary representations of the length fields are displayed cryptically. Also, note that the order of the bytes for the binary digits is reversed. We see "(" rather than " (" for the number 40. Before discussing this anomaly, let's take a different look at the file, this time using a hex dump.

Range		Hex values				ASCII values
0 −	F	2800416D	65737C4A	6F686E7C	31323320	(.Ames¦John¦123
10 −	1F	4D61706C	657C5374	696C6C77	61746572	Maple¦Stillwater
20 −	2F	7C4F4B7C	37343037	347C2400	4D61736F	¦OK¦74075¦$.Maso
30 −	3F	6E7C416C	616E7C39	30204561	73746761	n¦Alan¦90 Eastga
40 −	4F	74657C41	64617C4F	4B7C3734	3832307C	te¦Ada¦OK¦74820¦

As you can see, the display created by this particular hex dump program is divided into three different kinds of data. The area of the display labeled *Range* is the range of byte offsets that is being displayed.

The byte offsets are given in hexadecimal form; since each line contains 16 (decimal) bytes, moving from one line to the next adds 0x10 to the range.

The part of the hex dump that we label *Hex values* contains the hexadecimal value of each byte found in the file. The third byte has the value 0x41, which is the ASCII code for the character 'A'. Each of the spaces we inserted in the file result in a byte with the value 0x20, which is the ASCII code for a blank space.

Let's look at the hex values of the bytes that represent numbers. In some cases, such as 123, the representations are ASCII codes (0x31, 0x32, 0x33); in other cases, such as the record length 40 which begins the file, they are actual two-byte hexadecimal values (0x28). But the hexadecimal number corresponding to 40 seems to be 0x2800 instead of 0x0028. Why are the bytes reversed?

The answer is that this hex dump is the kind of output produced by a computer that stores the values for numbers in backwards byte order. For two-byte integers the low-order byte is always stored at a lower address than the high-order byte. So the byte with 0x28 is placed into a memory address preceding the one used to hold 0x00. This reverse order is also applied to long, four-byte integers on these machines. For example, the hexadecimal value of the number 500,000,000 is 0x1DCD6500. If you write this value out to a file on a VAX, IBM PC, or some other reverse-order machine, a hex dump of the file created looks like this:

```
0 - F  0065CD1D 00000000  00000000 00000000  .e............
```

Not all computers reverse the order of bytes this way. For example, large IBM machines do not. It is an aspect of files that you need to be aware of if you expect to make sense out of hex dumps. It is also something to keep in mind if you intend to transfer files containing binary data between two machines that order bytes differently. Note that the problem does not arise if you are using ASCII files in which all numbers are represented as sequences of characters.

Let's return to the hex dump of the name and address file and look at the rightmost column. This is the list of ASCII values represented by the bytes in the file. As you would expect, the data placed in the file in ASCII form appears in this column in a readable way. But there are hexadecimal values for which there is no printable ASCII representation. The only such value appearing in this file is 0x00. But there could be many others. If you look at the dump containing the number 500,000,000, you see that the only printable byte is the one with the value 0x65 ('e'). This particular hex dump program handles all of the others by placing a period ('.') in the ASCII representation to hold the place for the byte value.

The hex dump of this output from the C version of *writrec* shows how this file structure represents an interesting mix of a number of the organizational tools we have encountered. In a single record we have both binary and ASCII data. Each record consists of a fixed length field (the byte count) and several delimited, variable length fields. This kind of mixing of different data types and organizational methods is common in real-world file structures.

4.7 READING THE VARIABLE LENGTH RECORDS FROM THE FILE

Given our file structure of variable length records preceded by record length fields, it is easy to write a program that reads through the file, record by record, displaying the fields from each of the records on the screen. The program logic is shown in Fig. 4.11. The main program calls the function *get_rec()* that reads records into a buffer; this call continues until *get_rec()* returns a value of 0. Once *get_rec()* places a record's contents into a buffer, the buffer is passed to a function called *get_fld()*. The call to *get_fld()* includes a scanning position (SCAN_POS) in the argument list. Starting at the SCAN_POS, *get_fld()* reads characters from the buffer into a field until either a delimiter or the end of the record is reached. Function *get_fld()* returns the SCAN_POS for use on the next call. Implementations of *readrec* in both C and Pascal are included along with the other programs at the end of the chapter.

4.8 RETRIEVING RECORDS BY KEY: CANONICAL FORMS FOR KEYS

Since our new file structure so clearly focuses on the notion of a record as the quantity of information that is being read or written, it makes sense to think in terms of retrieving just one specific record rather than having to read all the way through the file, displaying everything. When looking for an individual record, it is convenient to identify the record with a *key* based on the record's contents. For example, in our name and address file we might want to access the "Ames record" or the "Mason record" rather than thinking in terms of the "first record" or "second record." (Can you remember which record comes first?)

```
PROGRAM: readrec

    open input file as INP_FILE
    initialize SCAN_POS to 0
    RECORD_LENGTH := get_rec(INP_FILE, BUFFER)
    while (RECORD_LENGTH > 0)
        SCAN_POS := get_fld(FIELD,BUFFER,SCAN_POS,RECORD_LENGTH)
        while (SCAN_POS > 0)
            print FIELD on the SCREEN
            SCAN_POS := get_fld(FIELD,BUFFER,SCAN_POS,RECORD_LENGTH)
        endwhile

        RECORD_LENGTH := get_rec(INP_FILE, BUFFER)
    endwhile
end PROGRAM


FUNCTION: get_rec(INP_FILE, BUFFER)

    if EOF (INP_FILE) then return 0

    read the RECORD_LENGTH
    read the record contents into the BUFFER
    return the RECORD_LENGTH

end FUNCTION


FUNCTION: get_fld(FIELD,BUFFER,SCAN_POS,RECORD_LENGTH)

    if SCAN_POS == RECORD_LENGTH then return 0

    get a character CH at the SCAN_POS in the BUFFER
    while (SCAN_POS < RECORD_LENGTH and CH is not a DELIMITER)
        place CH into the FIELD
        increment the SCAN_POS
        get a character CH at the SCAN_POS in the BUFFER
    endwhile

    return the SCAN_POS

end FUNCTION
```

FIGURE 4.11 ▪ **Main program logic for** *readrec,* **along with functions** *get_rec()* **and** *get_fld().*

This notion of a content-based *key* is another fundamental conceptual tool. We need to develop a more exact idea of what a key is.

When we are looking for a record containing the last name Ames, we want to recognize it even if the user enters the key in the form "AMES", "ames", or "Ames ". To do this, we must define a standard form for keys, along with associated rules and procedures for converting keys into this standard form. A standard form of this kind is often called a *canonical form* for the key. One meaning of the word canon is rule, and the word canonical means conforming to the rule. A canonical form for a search key is the *single* representation for that key that conforms to the rule.

As a simple example, we could state that the canonical form for a key requires that the key consist solely of uppercase letters and have no extra blanks at the end. So, if a user enters "Ames ", we would convert the key to the canonical form "AMES" before searching for it.

A key does not have to correspond to a single field in a record; it is possible to construct keys that combine information from more than one field in a file. For example, we might want to use both a person's first name and last name when trying to find a record. To do this we need to develop a rule that combines the last name and first name fields into a single key in canonical form. A very simple rule might be:

Trim each field, concatenate a blank to the end of the last name field, then concatenate the first name field. Convert the whole string to uppercase.

This rule converts the name John Ames to the canonical form "AMES JOHN". This key, when compared to a last-name-only key, is much more likely to identify a record *uniquely*.

It is often very desirable to have *distinct keys*, or keys that uniquely identify a single record. If there is not a one-to-one relationship between the key and a single record, then the program has to provide additional mechanisms to allow the user to resolve the confusion that can result when more than one record fits a particular key. Suppose, for example, that we are looking for John Ames' address. If there are several records in the file for several different people named John Ames, how should the program respond? Certainly it should not just give the address of the first John Ames that it finds. Should it give all the addresses at once? Should it provide a way of scrolling through the records?

The simplest solution is to *prevent* such confusion. The prevention takes place as new records are added to the file. When the user enters a new record, we form a canonical key for that record and then search the file for that key. If it already exists in the file, we tell the user to modify the key fields in some way so that the key is unique.

This concern about uniqueness applies only to *primary keys*. A primary key is, by definition, the key that is used to identify a record uniquely. It is also possible, as we see later, to search on *secondary keys*. An example of a secondary key might be the city field in our name and address file. If we wanted to find all the records in the file for people who live in towns named Stillwater, we would use some canonical form of "Stillwater" as a secondary key. Typically, secondary keys do not uniquely identify a record.

4.9
A SEQUENTIAL SEARCH

Now that we have access to the concept of a canonical key, we are ready to write a program called *find* that reads through the file, record by record, looking for a record with a particular key. Such sequential

```
PROGRAM: find

    open input file as INP_FILE
    get LAST and FIRST names for which we will search
    form canonical SEARCH_KEY from LAST and FIRST

    set MATCHED to FALSE
    RECORD_LENGTH := get_rec(INP_FILE, BUFFER)
    while (not MATCHED and RECORD_LENGTH > 0)
        initialize SCAN_POS to 0
        SCAN_POS := get_fld(LAST,BUFFER,SCAN_POS,RECORD_LENGTH)
        SCAN_POS := get_fld(FIRST,BUFFER,SCAN_POS,RECORD_LENGTH)
        form canonical RECORD_KEY from LAST and FIRST

        if (RECORD_KEY == SEARCH_KEY)
            set MATCHED to TRUE
        else
            RECORD_LENGTH := get_rec(INP_FILE, BUFFER)
    endwhile

if (MATCHED)
    call get_fld() to get and display the fields in the record
```

FIGURE 4.12 ▪ **Main loop logic for *find*.**

searching is just a simple extension of our *readrec* program, adding a comparison operation to the main loop to see if the key for the record matches the key we are seeking. The logic for the main portion of *find* is illustrated in pseudocode in Fig. 4.12. The *get_rec()* and *get_fld()* functions are the same as those used in *readrec*. Implementation details are provided in versions of the *find* program, written in both C and Pascal, at the end of the chapter.

4.10 EVALUATING PERFORMANCE OF SEQUENTIAL SEARCH

In the chapters that follow we find ways to search for records that are faster than the sequential search mechanism. We can use sequential searching as a kind of baseline against which to measure the improvements that we make. It is important, therefore, to find some way of expressing the amount of time and work expended in a sequential search.

Developing a performance measure requires that we decide on a unit of work that usefully represents the constraints on the performance of the whole process. When we describe the performance of searches that take place in electronic RAM, where comparison operations are more expensive than fetch operations to bring data in from memory, we usually use the *number of comparisons* required for the search as the measure of work. But, given that the cost of a comparison in RAM is so small compared to the cost of a disk access, comparisons do not fairly represent the performance constraints for a search through a file on secondary storage. Instead, we count low-level READ() calls. We assume that each READ() call requires a seek and that any one READ() call is as costly as any other. We know from the discussions of matters such as system buffering in Chapter 3 that these assumptions are not strictly accurate. But, in a multiuser environment where many processes are using the disk at once, they are close enough to correct to be useful.

Suppose we have a file with 1000 records and we want to use a sequential search to find Al Smith's record. How many READ() calls are required? If Al Smith's record is the first one in the file, the program has to read in only a single record. If it is the last record in the file, the program makes 1000 READ() calls before concluding the search. For an average search, 500 calls are needed.

If we double the number of records in a file, we also double both the average and the maximum number of READ() calls required. Using a sequential search to find Al Smith's record in a file of 2000 records, requires, on the average, 1000 calls. In other words, the amount of work required for a sequential search is directly proportional to the number of records in the file.

In general, the work required to search sequentially for a record in a file with n records is proportional to n; it takes at most n comparisons; on average it takes approximately $n/2$ comparisons. A sequential search is said to be of the order $O(n)$ because the time it takes is proportional to n.†

Much of the remainder of this text is devoted to identifying better ways to access individual records; sequential searching is just too expensive for most retrieval situations. There are, however, some applications in which a sequential search *might be* reasonable, such as searching files with very few records (e.g., 10 records), searching files that hardly ever need to be searched (e.g., tape files usually used for other kinds of processing), and searching files for all records with a certain secondary key value, where a large number of matches is expected.

4.11
IMPROVING SEQUENTIAL SEARCH PERFORMANCE: RECORD BLOCKING

It is interesting and useful to apply some of the information from Chapter 3 about disk performance to the problem of improving sequential search performance. We see in Chapter 3 that the major cost associated with a disk access is the time required to perform a seek to the right location on the disk. Once data transfer begins, it is relatively fast, although still much slower than a data transfer within RAM. Consequently, the cost of seeking and reading a record and then seeking and reading another record is greater than the cost of seeking just once and then reading two successive records. (Once again, we are assuming a multiuser environment in which a seek is required for each separate READ() call.) It follows that we should be able to improve the performance of sequential searching by reading in a *block* of several records all at once and then processing that block of records in RAM.

We started out this chapter with a stream of bytes. We then grouped the bytes into fields, and just recently grouped the fields into records. Now we are considering a yet higher level of organization, grouping records into blocks. This new level of grouping, however, dif-

---

†If you are not familiar with this "big-oh" notation, you should look it up. Knuth [1973a] is a good source.

fers from the others. Whereas fields and records are ways of maintaining the logical organization within the file, blocking is done strictly as a performance measure. As such, the block size is usually related more to the physical properties of the disk drive than to the content of the data. For instance, on sector-oriented disks the block size is almost always some multiple of the sector size.

Suppose we have a file of 1000 records and that the average length of a record is 64 bytes. An unblocked sequential search requires, on the average, 500 READ() calls before it can retrieve a particular record. By blocking the records in groups of 32 per block, so that each READ() call brings in 2 kilobytes worth of records, the number of READs required for an average search comes down to 15. Each READ() requires slightly more time, since more data is transferred from the disk, but this is a cost that is usually well worth paying for such a large reduction in the number of reads.

Note that although the blocking of records can result in substantial performance improvements, it does not change the order of the sequential search operation. The cost of searching is still $O(n)$, increasing in direct proportion to increases in the size of the file. Also note that this new tool is one that clearly reflects the differences between RAM access speed and the cost of accessing secondary storage. Blocking records does not change the number of comparisons that must be done in RAM, and it very probably increases the amount of data transferred between disk and RAM. (We always read a whole block, even if the record we are seeking is the first one in the block.) Blocking saves time because it decreases the amount of seeking. We find, again and again, that this differential between the cost of seeking and the cost of other operations, such as data transfer or RAM access, is the force that drives file structure design.

4.12 DIRECT ACCESS

The most radical alternative to searching sequentially through a file for a record is a retrieval mechanism known as *direct access*. We have direct access to a record when we can seek directly to the beginning of the record and read it in. Whereas sequential searching is an $O(n)$ operation, direct access is $O(1)$; no matter how large the file is, we can still get to the record we want with a single seek.

Direct access is predicated on knowing where the beginning of the required record is. Sometimes this information about record location is carried in a separate index file. But, for the moment, we assume that we do not have an index. We assume, instead, that we know the *relative record number* (RRN) of the record that we want. The idea of an RRN is an important concept that emerges from viewing a file as a collection of records rather than a collection of bytes. If a file is a sequence of records, then the RRN of a record gives its position relative to the beginning of the file. The first record in a file has RRN 0, the next has RRN 1, and so forth.[†]

In our name and address file we might tie a record to its RRN by assigning membership numbers that are related to the order in which we enter the records in the file. The person with the first record might have a membership number of 1001, the second a number of 1002, and so on. Given a membership number, we can subtract 1001 to get the RRN of the record.

What can we do with this RRN? Not much, given the file structures we have been using so far, which consist of variable length records. The RRN tells us the relative position of the record we want in the sequence of records, but we still have to read sequentially through the file, counting records as we go, to get to the record we want. Exercise 20 at the end of this chapter explores a method of moving through the file called *skip sequential* processing, which can improve performance somewhat, but looking for a particular RRN is still an $O(n)$ process.

To support direct access by RRN we need to work with records of fixed, known length. If the records are all the same length, then we can use a record's RRN to calculate the *byte offset* of the start of the record relative to the start of the file. For instance, if we are interested in the record with an RRN of 546 and our file has a fixed length record size of 128 bytes per record, we can calculate the byte offset as follows:

$$\text{Byte offset} = 546 \times 128 = 69{,}888.$$

In general, given a fixed length record file where the record size is r, the byte offset of a record with an RRN of n is

$$\text{Byte offset} = n \times r.$$

Programming languages and operating systems differ with regard to where this byte offset calculation is done and even with regard to whether byte offsets are used for addressing within files. In C (and the UNIX and MS-DOS operating systems), where a file is treated as just a sequence of bytes, the application program does the calculation and uses the *lseek()* command to jump to the byte that begins the record. All movement within a file is in terms of bytes. This is a very low-level view

---

[†]In keeping with the conventions of C and Turbo Pascal, we assume that the RRN is a *zero-based* count. In some file systems, the count starts at 1, rather than 0.

of files; the responsibility for translating an RRN into a byte offset belongs wholly to the application program.

The PL/I language and the operating environments in which PL/I is often used (OS/MVS, VMS) are examples of a much different, higher-level view of files. The notion of a sequence of bytes is simply not present when you are working with record-oriented files in this environment. Instead, files are viewed as collections of records that are accessed by keys. The operating system takes care of the translation between a key and a record's location. In the simplest case, the key is, in fact, just the record's RRN, but the determination of actual location within the file is still not the programmer's concern.

If we limit ourselves to the use of standard Pascal, the question of seeking by bytes or seeking by records is not an issue: there is no seeking at all in standard Pascal. But, as we said earlier, many implementations of Pascal extend the standard definition of the language to allow direct access to different locations in a file. The nature of these extensions varies according to the differences in the host operating systems around which the extensions were developed. All the same, one feature that is consistent across implementations is that a file in Pascal always consists of elements of a single type. A file is a sequence of integers, or characters, or arrays, or records, and so on. Addressing is always in terms of this fundamental element size. For example, we might have a *file of datarec*, where *datarec* is defined as:

> TYPE datarec = packed array [0..64] of char;

Seeking within this file is in terms of multiples of the elementary unit *datarec*, which is to say in multiples of a 65-byte entity. If I ask to jump to *datarec* number 3 (zero-based count), I am jumping 195 bytes $(3 \times 65 = 195)$ into the file.

4.13 CHOOSING A RECORD STRUCTURE AND RECORD LENGTH

Once we decide to fix the length of our records so that we can use the RRN to give us direct access to a record, we have to decide on a record length. Clearly this decision is related to the size of the fields we want to store in the record. Sometimes the decision is easy. Suppose we are building a file of sales transactions that contain the following information about each transaction:

- ☐ A 6-digit account number of the purchaser;
- ☐ Six digits for the date field;

☐   A 5-character stock number for item purchased;
☐   A 3-digit field for quantity; and
☐   A 10-position field for total cost.

These are all fixed length fields; the sum of the field lengths is 30 bytes. If we intend to store the records on a typical sectored disk (see Chapter 3) with a sector size of 512 bytes or some other power of 2, we might decide to pad the record out to 32 bytes so that we can place an integral number of records in a sector.

The choice of a record length is more complicated when the lengths of the fields can vary, as in our name and address file. If we choose a record length that is the sum of our estimates of the largest possible values for all the fields, we can be reasonably sure that we have enough space for everything, but we also waste a lot of space. If, on the other hand, we are conservative in our use of space and fix the lengths of fields at smaller values, we may have to leave information out of a field. Fortunately, we can avoid this problem to some degree through appropriate design of the field structure *within* a record.

In our discussion of record structures back in Section 4.4, we see that there are two general approaches we can take toward organizing fields within a fixed length record. The first, illustrated in Fig. 4.13(a), uses fixed length fields inside the fixed length record. This is the approach we took for the sales transaction file previously described. The second approach, illustrated in Fig. 4.13(b), uses the fixed length record as a kind of standard-size container for holding something that looks like a variable length record. The first approach has the virtue of

Ames	John	123 Maple	Stillwater	OK74075
Mason	Alan	90 Eastgate	Ada	OK74820

(a)

Ames ¦ John ¦ 123 Maple ¦ Stillwater ¦ OK ¦ 74075 ¦ ◄———— Unused space ————►
Mason ¦ Alan ¦ 90 Eastgate ¦ Ada ¦ OK ¦ 74820 ¦ ◄———— Unused space ————►

(b)

FIGURE 4.13 ▪ Two fundamental approaches to field structure within a fixed length record. (a) Fixed length records with fixed length fields. (b) Fixed length records with variable length fields.

simplicity: it is very easy to "break out" the fixed length fields from within a fixed length record. The second approach lets us take advantage of an averaging out effect that usually occurs: the longest names are not likely to appear in the same record as the longest address field. By letting the field boundaries vary, we can make more efficient use of a fixed amount of space. Also, note that the two approaches are not mutually exclusive. Given a record that contains a number of truly fixed length fields and some fields that have variable length information, we might design a record structure that combines these two approaches.

The programs *update.c* and *update.pas*, which are included in the set of programs at the end of the chapter, use direct access to allow a user to retrieve a record, change it, and then write it back. These programs create a file structure that uses variable length fields within fixed length records. Given the variability in the length of the fields in our name and address file, this is an appropriate choice.

One of the interesting questions that must be resolved in the design of this kind of structure is that of distinguishing the real data portion of the record from the unused space portion. The range of possible solutions parallels that of the solutions for recognizing variable length records in any other context: we can place a record length count at the beginning of the record, we can use a special delimiter at the end of the record, we can count fields, and so on. Because both *update.c* and *update.pas* use a character string buffer to collect the fields, and because we are handling character strings differently in C than in Pascal (strings are null-terminated in C; we keep a byte count of the string length at the beginning of the Pascal strings), it is convenient to use a slightly different file structure for the two implementations. In the C version we fill out the unused portion of the record with null characters. In the Pascal version we actually place a fixed length field (an integer) at the start of the record to tell how many of the bytes in the record are valid. As usual, there is no single right way to implement this file structure; instead we seek the solution that is most appropriate for our needs and situation.

Figure 4.14 shows the hex dump output from each of these programs. The output introduces a number of other ideas, such as the use of *header records*, which we discuss in the next section. For now, however, just look at the structure of the data records. We have italicized the length fields at the start of the records in the output from the Pascal program. Although we filled out the records created by the Pascal program with blanks to make the output more readable, this blank fill is unnecessary. The length field at the start of the record guarantees that we do not read past the end of the data in the record.

```
 0  -  F    02000000 00000000   00000000 00000000    . . . . . . . . . . . . . . .   Header record
10  - 1F    00000000 00000000   00000000 00000000    . . . . . . . . . . . . . . .   Record count in
                                                                                     first 2 bytes


20  - 2F    416D6573 7C4A6F68   6E7C3132 33204D61    Ames¦John¦123 Ma   First record
30  - 3F    706C657C 5374696C   6C776174 65727C4F    ple¦Stillwater¦O
40  - 4F    4B7C3734 3037357C   00000000 00000000    K¦74075¦. . . . . . . .
50  - 5F    00000000 00000000   00000000 00000000    . . . . . . . . . . . . . . .


60  - 6F    4D61736F 6E7C416C   616E7C39 30204561    Mason¦Alan¦90 Ea   Second record
70  - 7F    73746761 74657C41   64617C4F 4B7C3734    stgate¦Ada¦OK¦74
80  - 8F    3832307C 00000000   00000000 00000000    820¦. . . . . . . . . . .
90  - 9F    00000000 00000000   00000000 00000000    . . . . . . . . . . . . . . .
```

                                (a)


```
 0  -  F    02000000 00000000   00000000 00000000    . . . . . . . . . . . . . . .   Header record
10  - 1F    00000000 00000000   00000000 00000000    . . . . . . . . . . . . . . .   Record count in
20  - 2F    00000000 00000000   00000000 00000000    . . . . . . . . . . . . . . .   first 2 bytes
30  - 3F    00000000 00000000   00000000 00000000    . . . . . . . . . . . . . . .
40  - 41    0000                                     . .


42  - 4F         2800 416D6573   7C4A6F68 6E7C3132    ( .Ames¦John¦12    First record
50  - 5F    33204D61 706C657C   5374696C 6C776174    3 Maple¦Stillwat   Integer in first
60  - 6F    65727C4F 4B7C3734   3037357C 20202020    er¦OK¦74075¦       2 bytes contains
70  - 7F    20202020 20202020   20202020 20202020                       the number of
80  - 83    20202020                                                    bytes of data in
                                                                        the record


84  - 8F         24004D61   736F6E7C 416C616E    $.Mason¦Alan      Second record
90  - 9F    7C393020 45617374   67617465 7C416461    ¦90 Eastgate¦Ada
A0  - AF    7C4F4B7C 37343832   307C2020 20202020    ¦OK¦74820¦
B0  - BF    20202020 20202020   20202020 20202020
C0  - C5    20202020 2020                            
```

                                (b)

FIGURE 4.14 ▪ Two different record structures that carry variable length
fields in a fixed length record. (a) Record structure created by *update.c*:
fixed length records containing variable length fields that are terminated by
a null character. (b) Record structure created by *update.pas*: fixed length
records beginning with a fixed length (integer) field that indicates the
number of usable bytes in the record's variable length fields.

4.14 HEADER RECORDS

It is often necessary or useful to keep track of some general information about a file to assist in future use of the file. For example, in some versions of Pascal there is no easy way to jump to the end of a file, even though the implementation supports direct access. One simple solution to this problem is to keep a count of the number of records in the file and to store that count somewhere. A *header record* is often placed at the beginning of the file to hold this kind of information.

The header record usually has a different structure than the data records in the file. The output from *update.c*, for instance, uses a 32-byte header record, whereas the data records each contain 64 bytes. Furthermore, the data records created by *update.c* contain only character data, whereas the header record contains an integer that tells how many data records are in the file. The difference between the header records and the data records becomes even more pronounced if we find it useful to include information such as the record length of the data records, the date and time of the file's most recent update, and so on.

A programmer implementing header records in Pascal often accommodates the differences between data records and the header record through the use of a *variant* record. An even simpler solution is available in *update.pas*: we just use the initial integer field in the record for a different purpose in the header record. In the data records this field holds a count of the bytes of valid data within the record; in the header record it holds a count of the data records in the file.

Header records are a widely used, important file design tool. For example, when we reach the point where we are discussing the construction of indexes for files, we see that header records are often placed at the beginning of the index to keep track of matters such as the RRN of the record that is the root of the index.

4.15 FILE ACCESS AND FILE ORGANIZATION

In the course of our discussions in this chapter we look at:

☐ Variable length records;
☐ Fixed length records;
☐ Sequential access; and
☐ Direct access.

The first two of these terms relate to aspects of *file organization*. The second pair of terms has to do with *file access*. The distinction between file organization and file access is a useful one; we need to look at it more closely before concluding the chapter.

Most of what we have considered so far falls into the category of file organization. Can the file be divided into fields? Is there a higher level of organization to the file that combines the fields into records? Do all the records have the same number of bytes or fields? How do we distinguish one record from another? How do we organize the internal structure of a fixed length record so that we can distinguish between data and extra space? We have seen that there are many possible answers to these questions, and that the choice of a particular file organization depends on many things, including the file-handling facilities of the the language you are using and the *use you want to make of the file*.

Using a file implies access. We looked first at sequential access, ultimately developing a *sequential search* in the programs *find.c* and *find.pas*. So long as we did not know where individual records began, sequential access was the only option open to us. When we wrote our *update* program, we wanted *direct access*, so we fixed the length of our records, and this allowed us to calculate precisely where each record began and to seek directly to it.

In other words, our desire for direct *access* caused us to choose a fixed length record file *organization*. Does this mean that we can equate fixed length records with direct access? Definitely not. There is nothing about our having fixed the length of the records in a file that precludes sequential access; we certainly could write a program that reads sequentially through a fixed length record file.

Not only can we elect to read through the fixed length records sequentially, but we can also provide direct access to *variable length* records simply by keeping a list of the byte offsets from the start of the file for the placement of each record. We chose the record structure that we did in *update.c* and *update.pas* because it is simple and adequate for the data that we want to store. Although the lengths of our names and addresses vary, the variation is not so great that we cannot accommodate it in a fixed length record. Consider, however, the effects of using a fixed length record organization to provide direct access to records that are documents that can range in length from a few hundred bytes to over a hundred kilobytes. Fixed length records would be disastrously wasteful of space, so some form of variable length record structure would have to be found. Developing file structures to handle such situations requires that you clearly distinguish between the matter of *access* and your options regarding *organization*.

The restrictions imposed by the language and file system used to develop your applications do, surely, impose limits on your ability to take advantage of this distinction between access method and organization. For example, the C language provides the programmer with the ability to implement direct access to variable length records, since it allows access to any byte in the file. On the other hand, Pascal, even when seeking is supported, imposes limitations related to Pascal's definition of a file as a collection of elements that are all of the same *type* and, consequently, size. Seeking is usually only to the beginning of an element. Since the elements must all be of the same size, direct access to variable length records is difficult, at best, in Pascal.

Each of the two basic access modes, sequential and direct, has important uses. Direct access is clearly preferable when you need just a few specific records. But direct access is not always the most appropriate retrieval method. For example, if you are preparing paychecks from a file of employee records, there is usually no reason to bother with calculating record positions. Since all of the records in the file need to be processed, it is faster and simpler just to start at the beginning and work through the file, record by record, until reaching the end.

SUMMARY

The lowest level of organization that we normally impose on a file is that of a *stream of bytes*. Unfortunately, by storing data in a file merely as a stream of bytes, we lose the ability to distinguish among the fundamental informational units of our data. We call these fundamental pieces of information *fields*. Fields are grouped together to form *records*. Recognizing fields and recognizing records requires us to impose structure on the data in the file.

There are many ways to separate one field from the next and one record from the next:

1. Fix the length of each field or record.
2. Begin each field or record with a count of the number of bytes that it contains.
3. Use delimiters to mark the divisions between entities.

In the case of records, another useful technique is to use a second, index file that tells where each record begins.

One higher level of organization, in which records are grouped into *blocks*, is also often imposed on files. This level is imposed to improve I/O performance rather than our logical view of the file.

In this chapter we use the record structure that uses a length indicator at the beginning of each record to develop programs for writing and reading a simple file of variable length records containing names and addresses of individuals. We use buffering to accumulate the data in an individual record before we know its length to write it to the file. Buffers are also useful in allowing us to read in a complete record at one time. We represent the length field of each record as a binary number or as a sequence of ASCII digits. In the former case, it is useful to use a *hex dump* to examine the contents of our file.

Sometimes we identify individual records by their *relative record numbers* (RRNs) in a file. It is also common, however, to need to identify a record by a *key* whose value is based on some of the record's content. Key values must occur in, or be converted to, some predetermined *canonical form* if they are to be recognized accurately and unambiguously by programs. If every record's key value is distinct from all others, the key can be used to identify and locate the unique record in the file. Keys that are used in this way are called *primary keys*.

In this chapter we look at a program called *find*, which searches sequentially through a file looking for a record with a particular key. Sequential search can perform poorly for long files, but there are times when sequential searching is reasonable. Record blocking can be used to improve the I/O time for a sequential search substantially.

In the earlier discussion of ways to separate records, it is clear that some of the methods provide a mechanism for looking up or calculating the *byte offset* of the beginning of a record. This, in turn, opens up the possibility of accessing the record *directly*, by RRN, rather than sequentially.

The simplest record formats for permitting direct access by RRN involve the use of fixed length records. When the data itself actually comes in fixed-size quantities (e.g., zip codes), fixed length records can provide good performance and good space utilization. If there is a lot of variation in the amount and size of data in records, however, the use of fixed length records can result in expensive waste of space. In such cases the designer should look carefully at the possibility of using variable length records.

Sometimes it is helpful to be able to keep track of general information about files, such as the number of records they contain. A *header record*, stored at the beginning of the file it pertains to, is a useful tool for storing this kind of information.

It is important to be aware of the difference between *file access* and *file organization*. We try to organize files in such a way that they give us the types of access we need for a particular application. For example, one of the advantages of a fixed length record *organization* is that it allows *access* that is either sequential or direct.

KEY TERMS

Block. A collection of records stored as a physically contiguous unit on secondary storage. In this chapter, we use record blocking to improve I/O performance during sequential searching.

Byte count field. A field at the beginning of a variable length record that gives the number of bytes used to store the record. The use of a byte count field allows a program to transmit (or skip over) a variable length record without having to deal with the record's internal structure.

Canonical form. A standard form for a key that can be derived, by the application of well-defined rules, from the particular, nonstandard form of the data found in a record's key field(s) or provided in a search request supplied by a user.

Delimiter. One or more characters used to separate fields and records in a file.

Direct access. A file accessing mode that involves jumping to the exact location of a record. Direct access to a fixed length record is usually accomplished by using its *relative record number* (RRN), then computing its byte offset, then seeking to the first byte of the record.

Field. The smallest logically meaningful unit of information in a file. A record in a file is usually made up of several fields.

File access method. The approach used to locate information in a file. In general, the two alternatives are *sequential access* and *direct access*.

File organization method. The combination of conceptual and physical structures used to distinguish one record from another and one field from another. An example of a kind of file organization is: fixed length records containing variable numbers of variable length delimited fields.

Fixed length record. A file organization in which all records have the same length. Records are padded with blanks, nulls, or other characters so that they extend to the fixed length. Since all the records have the same length, it is possible to calculate the beginning position of any record, making *direct access* possible.

Header record. A record placed at the beginning of a file that is used to store information about the file contents and the file organization.

Key. An expression derived from one or more of the fields within a record that can be used to locate that record. The fields used to build the key are sometimes called the *key fields*. Keyed access provides a way of performing content-based retrieval of records, rather than retrieval based merely on a record's position.

Primary key. A key that uniquely identifies each record and which is used as the primary method of accessing the records.

Record. A record is a collection of related fields. For example, the name, address, etc., of an individual in a mailing list file would probably make up one record.

Relative record number (RRN). An index giving the position of a record relative to the beginning of its file. If a file has fixed length records, the RRN can be used to calculate the *byte offset* of a record so that the record can be accessed directly.

Sequential access. Sequential access to a file means reading the file from the beginning and continuing until you have read in everything that you need. The alternative is direct access.

Sequential search. A method of searching a file by reading the file from the beginning and continuing until the desired record has been found.

Stream of bytes. Term describing the lowest-level view of a file. If we begin with the basic *stream-of-bytes* view of a file, we can then impose our own higher levels of order on the file, including field, record, and block structures.

Variable length record. A file organization in which the records have no predetermined length. They are just as long as they need to be, hence making better use of space than fixed length records do. Unfortunately, we cannot calculate the byte offset of a variable length record by knowing only its relative record number.

EXERCISES

1. Find situations for which each of the three field structures described in the text might be appropriate. Do the same for each of the record structures described.

2. Discuss the appropriateness of using the following characters to delimit fields or records: carriage-return, linefeed, space, comma, period, colon, escape. Can you think of situations in which you might want to use different delimiters for different fields?

3. Suppose you want to change our programs to include a phone number field in each record. What changes need to be made?

4. Suppose you need to keep a file in which every record has both fixed and variable length fields. For example, suppose you want to create a file of employee records, using fixed length fields for each employee's ID (primary key), sex, birthdate, and department, and using variable length fields for each name and address. What advantages might there be to using such a structure? Should we put the variable length portion first or last? Either approach is possible; how can each be implemented?

5. One record structure not described in this chapter is called *labeled*. In a labeled record structure each field that is represented is preceded by a label describing its contents. For example, if the labels LN, FN, AD, CT, ST, and ZP are used to describe the six fixed length fields for a name and address record, it might appear as follows:

`LNAmesbbbbbbFNJohnbbbbbbAD123 MaplebbbbbbCTStillwaterSTOKZP74075bbbb`

Under what conditions might this be a reasonable, even desirable, record structure?

6. Give meanings to the terms *stream of bytes*, *stream of fields*, and *stream of records*.

7. Find out what basic file structures are available to you in the progamming language that you are currently using. For example, does your language recognize a sequence-of-bytes type structure? Does it recognize lines of text? Record blocking? For those types of structures that your language does not recognize, describe how you might implement them using structures that your language does recognize.

8. Report on the basic field and record structures available in PL/I or COBOL.

9. Compare the use of ASCII characters to represent *everything* in a file with the use of binary and ASCII data mixed together.

10. If you list the contents of a file containing both binary and ASCII characters on your terminal screen, what results can you expect? What happens when you list a completely binary file on your screen? (Warning! If you actually try this, do so with a very small file. You could lock up or reconfigure your terminal, or even log yourself off!)

11. If a key in a record is already in canonical form and the key is the first field of the record, it is possible to search for a record by key without ever separating out the key field from the rest of the fields. Explain.

12. It has been suggested (Sweet, 1985) that primary keys should be "dataless, unchanging, unambiguous, and unique." Discuss the importance of each of these, and show by example how their absence can cause problems. Does the primary key used in our example file violate any of the criteria?

13. How many comparisons would be required on average to find a record using sequential search in a 10,000-record disk file? If the record is not in the file, how many comparisons are required? If the file is blocked so that 20 records are stored per block, how many disk accesses are required on average? What if only one record is stored per block?

14. In our evaluation of performance for sequential search, we assume that every read results in a seek. How do the assumptions change on a single user machine with access to a magnetic disk? How do these changed assumptions affect the analysis of sequential searching?

15. Give a formula for finding the byte offset of a fixed length record where the RRN of the first record is 1 rather than 0.

16. Why is a variable length record structure unworkable for the *update* program? Does it help if we have an index that points to the beginning of each variable length record?

17. The *update* program lets the user change records, but not delete records. How do the file structure and the access procedures have to be modified to allow for deletion if we do not care about reusing the space from deleted records? How do the file structures and procedures change if we do want to reuse the space?

18. In our discussion of the uses of relative record numbers (RRNs), we suggest that you can create a file in which there is a direct correspondence between a primary key such as membership number and RRN, so that we can find a person's record by knowing just the name or membership number. What kinds of difficulties can you envision with this simple correspondence between membership number and RRN? What happens if we want to delete a name? What happens if we change the information in a record in a variable length record file and the new record is longer?

19. The following hex dump describes the first few bytes from a file of the type produced by the C version of *writerec*, but the right-hand column is not filled in. How long is the first record? What are its contents?

```
 0 -     F   26004475 6D707C46  7265647C 38323120   . . . . . . . . . . . . . .
10 -    1F   4B6C7567 657C4861  636B6572 7C50417C   . . . . . . . . . . . . . .
20 -    2F   36353533 357C2E2E  48657861 64656369   . . . . . . . . . . . . . .
```

20. Assume we have a variable length record file with long records (greater than 1000 bytes each, on the average). Assume that we are looking for a record with a particular RRN. Describe the benefits of using the contents of a byte count field to skip sequentially from record to record to find the one we want. This is called *skip sequential* processing. Use your knowledge of system buffering to describe why this is useful only for long records. If the records are sorted in order by key and blocked, what information do you have to place at the start of each block to permit even faster skip sequential processing?

21. Suppose you have a fixed length record with fixed length fields, and the sum of the field lengths is 30 bytes. A record with a length of 30 bytes would hold them all. If we intend to store the records on a sectored disk with 512-byte sectors (see Chapter 3) we might decide to pad the record out to 32 bytes so that we can place an integral number of records in a sector. Why would we want to do this?

22. Why is it important to distinguish between file access and file organization?

PROGRAMMING EXERCISES

23. Rewrite *writstrm* so that it uses delimiters as field separators. The output of the new version of *writstrm* should be readable by *readstrm.c* or *readstrm.pas*.

24. Create versions of *writrec* and *readrec* that use the following fixed field lengths rather than delimiters.

Last name: 15 characters
First name: 15 characters
Address: 30 characters
City: 20 characters
State: 2 characters
Zip: 5 characters

25. Write the program described in the preceding problem so that it uses blocks. Make it store five records per block.

26. Implement the program *find*.

27. Rewrite program *find* so that it can find a record on the basis of its position in the file. For example, if requested to find the 547th record in a file, it would read through the first 546 records, then print the contents of the 547th record. Use skip sequential search (see Exercise 20) to avoid reading the contents of unwanted records.

28. Write a program similar to *find*, but with the following differences. Instead of getting record keys from the keyboard, it reads them from a separate transaction file that contains only the keys of the records to be extracted. Instead of printing the records on the screen, it writes them out to a separate output file. First, assume that the records are in no particular order. Then assume that both the main file and the transaction file are sorted by key. In the latter case, how can you make your program more efficient than find?

29. Make any or all of the following alterations *update.pas* or *update.c*.

- Let the user identify the record to be changed by name, rather than RRN;
- Let the user change individual fields without having to change an entire record; and
- Let the user choose to view the entire file.

30. Modify *update.c* or *update.pas* to signal the user when a record exceeds the fixed record length. The modification should allow the user to bring the record down to an acceptable size and input it again. What are some other modifications that would make the program more robust?

31. Change *update.c* or *update.pas* to a batch program that reads a transaction file in which each transaction record contains an RRN of a record that is to be updated, followed by the new contents of the record, then makes the changes in a batch run. Although not necessary, it might be desirable to sort the transaction file by RRN. Why?

32. Write a program that reads a file and outputs the file contents as a hex dump. The hex dump should have a format similar to the one used in the examples in this chapter. The program should accept the name of the input file on the command line. Output should be to standard output (terminal screen).

33. Develop a set of rules for translating the dates August 7, 1949, Aug. 7, 1949, 8-7-49, 08-07-49, 8/7/49, and other, similar variations into a common canonical form. Write a function that accepts a string containing a date in one of these forms and returns the canonical form, according to your rules. Be sure to document the limitations of your rules and function.

FURTHER READINGS

Many textbooks cover basic material on field and record structure design, but only a few go into the options and design considerations in much detail. Teorey and Fry [1982] and Wiederhold [1983] are two possible sources. Hanson's [1982] chapter, "Choice of File Organization," is excellent, but is more meaningful after you read the material in the later chapters of this text. One can learn a lot about alternative types of file organization and access by studying descriptions of options available in certain languages and file management systems. PL/I offers a particularly rich set of alternatives, and Pollack and Sterling [1980] describe them thoroughly and well.

Sweet [1985] is a short but stimulating article on key field design. A number of interesting algorithms for improving performance in sequential searches are described in Gonnet [1984] and, of course, Knuth [1973b].

C PROGRAMS

The C programs listed in the following pages correspond to the programs discussed in the text. The programs are contained in the following files.

writstrm.c	Writes out name and address information as a stream of consecutive bytes.
readstrm.c	Reads a stream file as input and prints it to the screen.
writrec.c	Writes a variable length record file that uses a byte count at the beginning of each record to give its length.
readrec.c	Reads through a file, record by record, displaying the fields from each of the records on the screen.
getrf.c	Contains support functions for reading individual records or fields. These functions are needed by programs in *readrec.c* and *find.c*
find.c	Searches sequentially through a file for a record with a particular key.
makekey.c	Combines first and last names and converts them to a key in canonical form. Calls *strtrim()* and *ucase()*, found in *strfuncs.c*.
strfuncs.c	Contains two string support functions: *strtrim()* trims the blanks from the ends of strings; *ucase()* converts alphabetic characters to uppercase.
update.c	Allows new records to be added to a file, or old records to be changed.

FILEIO.H

All of the programs include a header file called *fileio.h* which contains some useful definitions. Some of the these are system dependent. If the programs were to be run on a UNIX system *fileio.h* might look like this:

```
/*
    fileio.h --- header file containing file I/O definitions
*/

#define PMODE      0755
#define READONLY   0
#define WRITEONLY  1
```

```
#define READWRITE 2
#define DELIM_STR     "|"
#define DELIM_CHR     '|'

#define MAX_REC_SIZE 512
```

▬▬▬ WRITSTRM.C

```
/* writstrm.c

    creates name and address file that is strictly a stream
    of bytes (no delimiters, counts, or other information to help
    distinguish fields and records).

    A simple modification to the out_str macro:

        #define out_str(fd,s)     write((fd),(s),strlen(s));  \
                                  write((fd),DELIM_STR,1);

    changes the program so that it creates delimited fields.
*/

#include "fileio.h"
#define  out_str(fd,s)           write((fd),(s),strlen(s))

main () {

        char first[30], last[30], address[30], city[20];
        char state[15], zip[9];
        char filename[15];
        int fd;

        printf("Enter the name of the file you wish to create: ");
        gets(filename);

        if ((fd = creat(filename,PMODE)) < 0) {
            printf("file opening error --- program stopped\n");
            exit(1);
        }
        printf("\n\nType in a last name (surname), or <CR> to exit\n>>>");
        gets(last);
        while (strlen(last) > 0)
        {
            printf("\nFirst Name:");
            gets(first);
            printf("   Address:");
            gets(address);
```

(continued)

```
        printf("      City:");
        gets(city);
        printf("      State:");
        gets(state);
        printf("        Zip:");
        gets(zip);

        /* output the strings to the buffer and then to the file */

        out_str(fd,last);
        out_str(fd,first);
        out_str(fd,address);
        out_str(fd,city);
        out_str(fd,state);
        out_str(fd,zip);

        /* prepare for next entry */

        printf("\n\nType in a last name (surname), or <CR> to exit\n>>>");
        gets(last);
    }

    /* close the file before leaving */
    close(fd);
}
```

▬▬▬ READSTRM.C

```
/* readstrm.c

    reads a stream of delimited fields
*/
#include "fileio.h"

main() {

        int fd,n;
        char s[30];
        char filename[15];
        int fld_count;

        printf("Enter name of file to read: ");
        gets(filename);
        if ((fd = open(filename,READONLY)) < 0) {
            printf("file opening error --- program stopped\n");
            exit(1);
        }
```

```
        /* main program loop -- calls readfield() until all fields are read */
        fld_count = 0;
        while ((n = readfield(fd,s)) > 0)
            printf("\tField # %3d:  %s\n",++fld_count,s);

        close(fd);
}

readfield(fd,s)
        int fd;
        char s[];
{

        int i;
        char c;

        i = 0;
        while ( read(fd,&c,1) > 0  && c != DELIM_CHR)
            s[i++] = c;

        s[i] = '\0';    /* append null to end string */
        return (i);
}
```

▆▆▆▆ WRITREC.C

```
/* writrec.c

    creates name and address file using fixed length (2-byte) record
    length field ahead of each record
*/
#include "fileio.h"
#define  fld_to_recbuff(rb,s)  strcat(rb,s); strcat(rb,DELIM_STR);

char recbuff[MAX_REC_SIZE + 1];
char *prompt[] = {
        "Enter Last Name -- or <CR> to exit: ",
        "                         First name: ",
        "                            Address: ",
        "                               City: ",
        "                              State: ",
        "                                Zip: ",
        ""                  /* null string to terminate the prompt loop */
};

main () {

        char response[50];
        char filename[15];
```

(continued)

```
        int fd,i;
        int rec_lgth;

        printf("Enter the name of the file you wish to create: ");
        gets(filename);

        if ((fd = creat(filename,PMODE)) < 0) {
            printf("file opening error --- program stopped\n");
            exit(1);
        }
        printf("\n\n%s",prompt[0]);
        gets(response);
        while (strlen(response) > 0)
        {
            recbuff[0] = '\0';
            fld_to_recbuff(recbuff,response);
            for (i=1; *prompt[i] != '\0' ; i++)
            {
                printf("%s",prompt[i]);
                gets(response);
                fld_to_recbuff(recbuff,response);
            }

            /* write out the record length and buffer contents */
            rec_lgth = strlen(recbuff);
            write(fd,&rec_lgth,2);
            write(fd,recbuff,rec_lgth);

            /* prepare for next entry */

            printf("\n\n%s",prompt[0]);
            gets(response);
        }

        /* close the file before leaving */
        close(fd);
}

/* Questions:

    How does the termination condition work in the for loop:
            for (i=1; *prompt[i] != '\0' ; i++)?

    What does the "i" refer to?  Why do we need the "*"?
*/
```

≡ READREC.C

```
/* readrec.c

        reads through a file, record by record, displaying the
        fields from each of the records on the screen.
*/
#include "fileio.h"

main() {

        int fd, rec_count, fld_count;
        int scan_pos, rec_lgth;
        char filename[15];
        char recbuff[MAX_REC_SIZE + 1];
        char field[MAX_REC_SIZE + 1];

        printf("Enter name of file to read: ");
        gets(filename);
        if ((fd = open(filename,READONLY)) < 0) {
            printf("file opening error --- program stopped\n");
            exit(1);
        }

        rec_count = 0;
        scan_pos = 0;
        while  ((rec_lgth = get_rec(fd,recbuff)) > 0)
        {
            printf ("Record %d\n", ++rec_count);
            fld_count > 0;
            while ((scan_pos = get_fld(field,recbuff,scan_pos,rec_lgth)) > 0)
                printf ("\tField %d: %s\n",++fld_count,field);
        }
        close(fd);
}

/* Question: Why can we assign 0 to scan_pos just once, outside of the
   while loop for records?  */
```

≡ GETRF.C

```
/*  getrf.c ...
```

Two functions are used by programs in readrec.c and find.c:

get_rec() reads a variable length record from file fd into
          the character array recbuff.

(continued)

```
              get_fld() moves a field from recbuff into the character array
                    field, inserting a '\0' to make it a string.
*/
#include "fileio.h"

get_rec(fd, recbuff)
        int fd;
        char recbuff[];
{
        int rec_lgth;

        if (read(fd, &rec_lgth, 2) == 0)        /* get record length */
            return(0);                          /* return 0 if EOF    */
        rec_lgth = read(fd, recbuff, rec_lgth); /* read record        */
        return(rec_lgth);
}

get_fld(field,recbuff,scan_pos,rec_lgth)
        char field[],recbuff[];
        short scan_pos, rec_lgth;
{
        short fpos = 0;                     /*  position in "field" array */

        if (scan_pos == rec_lgth)           /* if no more fields to read, */
            return(0);                      /*    return scan_pos of 0.    */

        /* scanning loop */
        while ( scan_pos < rec_lgth &&
                (field[fpos++] = recbuff[scan_pos++]) != DELIM_CHR)
            ;

        if (field[fpos - 1] == DELIM_CHR) /* if last character is a field  */
            field[--fpos] = '\0';         /* delimiter, replace with null  */
        else
            field[fpos] = '\0';           /* otherwise, just ensure that
                                             the field is null-terminated  */
        return(scan_pos);    /* return position of start of next field     */
}
```

≡ FIND.C

```
/* find.c

        searches sequentially through a file for a record with a
        particular key.
*/
#include "fileio.h"
#define   TRUE    1
#define   FALSE   0
```

```
main()  {

        int fd, rec_lgth, scan_pos;
        int matched;
        char search_key[30], key_found[30], last[30], first[30];
        char filename[15];
        char recbuff[MAX_REC_SIZE + 1];
        char field[MAX_REC_SIZE + 1];

        printf("Enter name of file to search: ");
        gets(filename);
        if ((fd = open(filename,READONLY)) < 0) {
            printf("file opening error --- program stopped\n");
            exit(1);
        }

        printf("\n\nEnter last name: ");              /* get search key */
        gets(last);
        printf("\nEnter first name: ");
        gets(first);
        makekey(last, first, search_key);

        matched = FALSE;
        while  (!matched && (rec_lgth = get_rec(fd,recbuff)) > 0 )
        {
            scan_pos = 0;
            scan_pos = get_fld(last, recbuff, scan_pos, rec_lgth);
            scan_pos = get_fld(first, recbuff, scan_pos, rec_lgth);
            makekey(last, first, key_found);
            if (strcmp (key_found, search_key) == 0)
                matched = TRUE;
        }

        /* if record found, print the fields */
        if (matched)
        {
            printf("\n\nRecord found:\n\n");
            scan_pos = 0;

            /* break out the fields */
            while ((scan_pos = get_fld(field,recbuff,scan_pos,rec_lgth)) > 0)
                printf("\t%s\n",field);
        } else
            printf("\n\nRecord not found.\n");
}

/* Questions:

    Why does scan_pos get set to zero inside the while loop here?

    What would happen if we wrote the loop that reads records like this:
        while  ((rec_lgth = get_rec(fd,recbuff)) > 0 && !matched )?

*/
```

▤ MAKEKEY.C

```
/* makekey(last,first,s) ...

        function to make a key from the first and last names passed
        through the function's arguments.  Returns the key in canonical
        form through the address passed through the argument s.  Calling
        routine is responsible for ensuring that s is large enough to hold
        the return string.

        Value returned through the function name is the length of the
        string returned through s.
*/

makekey(last,first,s)

        char last[], first[], s[];
{
        int lenl,lenf;

        lenl = strtrim(last);    /* trim the last name              */
        strcpy(s,last);          /* place it in the return string   */
        s[lenl++] = ' ';         /* append a blank at the end       */
        s[lenl] = '\0';
        lenf = strtrim(first);   /* trim the first name             */
        strcat(s,first);         /* append it to the string         */
        ucase(s,s);              /* convert everything to uppercase */
        return(lenl + lenf);
}
```

▤ STRFUNCS.C

```
/* strfuncs.c ...

   module containing the following functions:

   strtrim(s) trims blanks from end of the (null-terminated) string
       referenced by the string address s.  The function works from
       right to left, removing blanks until it comes to a nonblank
       character. When the function is complete, the parameter s
       points to the trimmed string.  The function returns the length
       of the trimmed string through its name.

   ucase(si,so) converts all lowercase alphabetic characters in the
       string at address si into uppercase characters, returning the
       converted string through the address so.

*/
```

```
strtrim(s)
        char s[];
{
        int i;

        for (i = strlen(s) - 1; i >= 0 && s[i] == ' '; i-- )
                ;

        /* now that the blanks are trimmed, reaffix null on the end
           to form a string  */

        s[++i] = '\0';
        return(i);
}


ucase(si,so)
        char si[],so[];
{
        while (*so++ = (*si >= 'a' && *si <= 'z') ? *si & 0x5F : *si )
            si++;
}
```

═══ UPDATE.C

```
/* update.c ...
        program to open or create a fixed length record file for
        updating.  Records may be added or changed. Records to be
        changed must be accessed by relative record number
*/
#include "fileio.h"
#define REC_LGTH  64
#define  fld_to_recbuff(rb,s)  strcat(rb,s); strcat(rb,DELIM_STR);

static char *prompt[]= {"      Last Name: ",
                        "     First name: ",
                        "        Address: ",
                        "           City: ",
                        "          State: ",
                        "            Zip: ",
                        ""                        };

static int fd;
static struct {
        short  rec_count;
        char   fill[30];
}  head;
```

(continued)

```
main() {

        int i,menu_choice,rrn;
        int byte_pos;
        char filename[15];
        long lseek();
        char recbuff[MAX_REC_SIZE + 1];  /* buffer to hold a record */

        printf("Enter the name of the file: ");
        gets(filename);
        if (( fd = open(filename, READWRITE)) < 0)  /* if OPEN fails    */
        {
            fd = creat(filename, PMODE);              /* then CREAT        */
            head.rec_count = 0;                       /* initialize header */
            write(fd,&head,sizeof(head));             /* write header rec  */
        }
        else                          /* existing file opened -- read in header */
            read(fd,&head,sizeof(head));

        /* main program loop -- call menu and then jump to options */
        while((menu_choice = menu()) < 3)
        {
            switch(menu_choice)
            {
                case 1:            /* add a new record */
                    printf("Input the information for the new record --\n\n");
                    ask_info(recbuff);
                    byte_pos = head.rec_count * REC_LGTH + sizeof(head);
                    lseek(fd,(long) byte_pos,0);
                    write(fd,recbuff,REC_LGTH);
                    head.rec_count++;
                    break;

                case 2:            /* update existing record */
                    rrn = ask_rrn();

                    /* if rrn is too big, print error message ... */
                    if (rrn >= head.rec_count) {
                        printf("Record Number is too large");
                        printf("... returning to menu ...");
                        break;
                    }

                    /* otherwise, seek to the record ... */
                    byte_pos = rrn * REC_LGTH + sizeof(head);
                    lseek(fd,(long) byte_pos,0);

                    /* display it and ask for changes ... */
                    read_and_show();
                    if (change())
                    {
                        printf("\n\nInput the revised Values:\n\n");
                        ask_info(recbuff);
```

```
                                lseek(fd,(long) byte_pos,0);
                                write(fd,recbuff,REC_LGTH);
                        }
                        break;
                }
        }
        /* rewrite correct record count to header before leaving */
        lseek(fd,0L,0);
        write(fd,&head,sizeof(head));
        close(fd);
}


/* menu() ...
        local function to ask user for next operation.
        Returns numeric value of user response
*/
static menu() {
        int choice;
        char response[10];

        printf("\n\n\n\n                          FILE UPDATING PROGRAM\n");
        printf("\n\nYou May Choose to:\n\n");
        printf("\t1.  Add a record to the end of the file\n");
        printf("\t2.  Retrieve a record for Updating\n");
        printf("\t3.  Leave the Program\n\n");
        printf("Enter the number of your choice: ");
        gets(response);
        choice = atoi(response);
        return(choice);
}


/* ask_info() ...
        local function to accept input of name and address fields, writing
        them to the buffer passed as a parameter
*/
static ask_info(recbuff)
        char recbuff[];
{
        int field_count,i;
        char response[50];

        /* clear the record buffer */
        for (i = 0; i < REC_LGTH; recbuff[i++] = '\0')
                ;
        /* get the fields */
        for (i=0; *prompt[i] != '\0' ; i++)
        {
                printf("%s",prompt[i]);
                gets(response);
                fld_to_recbuff(recbuff,response);
        }
}
```

(continued)

```
/* ask_rrn() ...
        local function to ask for the relative record number of the record
        that is to be updated.
*/
static ask_rrn() {

        int rrn;
        char response[10];

        printf("\n\nInput the relative record number of the record that\n");
        printf("\tyou want to update:  ");
        gets(response);
        rrn = atoi(response);
        return(rrn);
}


/* read_and_show() ...
        local function to read and display a record.  Note that this function
        does not include a seek -- reading starts at the current position
        in the file
*/
static read_and_show()  {

        char recbuff[MAX_REC_SIZE + 1], field[MAX_REC_SIZE + 1];
        int scan_pos, data_lgth;

        scan_pos = 0;
        read(fd, recbuff, REC_LGTH);

        printf("\n\n\n\nExisting Record Contents\n");

        recbuff[REC_LGTH] = '\0';   /* ensure that record ends with null */
        data_lgth = strlen(recbuff);
        while ((scan_pos = get_fld(field, recbuff, scan_pos, data_lgth)) > 0)
            printf ("\t%s\n", field);
}


/* change() ...
        local function to ask user whether or not he wants to change the
        record.  Returns 1 if the answer is yes, 0 otherwise
*/
static change()  {
        char response[10];

        printf("\n\nDo you want to change this record?\n");
        printf("     Answer Y or N, followd by <CR> ==>");
        gets(response);
        ucase(response, response);
        return((response[0] == 'Y') ? 1 : 0);
}
```

PASCAL PROGRAMS

The Pascal programs listed in the following pages correspond to the programs discussed in the text. Each program is organized into one or more files, as follows.

writstrm.pas	Writes out name and address information as a stream of consecutive bytes.
readstrm.pas	Reads a stream file as input and prints it to the screen.
writrec.pas	Writes a variable length record file that uses a byte count at the beginning of each record to give its length.
readrec.pas	Reads through a file, record by record, displaying the fields from each of the records on the screen.
get.prc	Supports functions for reading individual records or fields. These functions are needed by the program in *readrec.pas*.
find.pas	Searches sequentially through a file for a record with a particular key.
update.pas	Allows new records to be added to a file, or old records to be changed.
stod.prc	Support function for *update.pas*, which converts a variable of type *strng* to a variable of type *datarec*.

In addition to these files, there is a file called *tools.prc*, which contains the tools for operating on variables of type *strng*. A listing of *tools.prc* is contained in Appendix B at the end of the textbook.

We have added line numbers to some of these Pascal listings to assist the reader in finding specific program statements.

The files that contain Pascal functions or procedures but do not contain main programs are given the extension *.prc*, as in *get.prc* and *stod.prc*.

WRITSTRM.PAS

Some things to note about *writstrm.pas*:

☐ The comment {$B-} on line 6 is a directive to the Turbo Pascal compiler, instructing it to handle keyboard input as a standard Pascal file. Without this directive we would not be able to handle the *len_str()* function properly in the WHILE loop on line 36.

□ The comment {$I tools.prc} on line 24 is also a directive to the Turbo Pascal compiler, instructing it to include the file *tools.prc* in the compilation. The procedures *read_str, len_str,* and *fwrite_str* are in the file *tools.prc.*

□ Although Tubo Pascal supports a special string type, we choose not to use that type here to come closer to conforming to standard Pascal. Instead, we create our own *strng* type, which is a packed array [0..MAX_REC_SIZE] of char. The length of the *strng* is stored in the zeroth byte of the array as a character value. If *X* is the character value in the zeroth byte of the array, then ORD(*X*) is the length of the string.

□ The assign statement on line 31 is one that is nonstandard. It is a Turbo Pascal procedure, which, in this case, assigns *filename* to *outfile,* so all further operation on *outfile* will operate on the disk file.

```
 1: PROGRAM writstrm (INPUT,OUTPUT);
 2:
 3: {     writes out name and address information as a stream of
 4:       consecutive bytes }
 5:
 6: {$B-}    { Directive to the Turbo Pascal compiler, instructing it to
 7:            handle keyboard input as a standard Pascal file }
 8:
 9: CONST
10:      DELIM_CHR    = '|';
11:      MAX_REC_SIZE = 255;
12:
13: TYPE
14:      strng       = packed array[0..MAX_REC_SIZE] of char;
15:      inp_list    = (last,first,address,city,state,zip);
16:      filetype    = packed array[1..40] of char;
17:
18: VAR
19:      response    : array [inp_list] of strng;
20:      resp_type   : inp_list;
21:      filename    : filetype;
22:      outfile     : text;
23:
24: {$I tools.prc}
25: { Another directive, instructing the compiler to include the file
26:      tools.prc }
27:
28: BEGIN {main}
29:      write('Enter the name of the file: ');
30:      readln(filename);
31:      assign(outfile,filename);
32:      rewrite(outfile);
33:
34:      write('Type in a last name, or press <CR> to exit: ');
```

```
35:      read_str(response[last]);
36:      while (len_str(response[last]) > 0 ) DO
37:      BEGIN
38:          { get all the input for one person }
39:          write(' First Name: ');
40:          read_str(response[first]);
41:          write('    Address: ');
42:          read_str(response[address]);
43:          write('       City: ');
44:          read_str(response[city]);
45:          write('      State: ');
46:          read_str(response[state]);
47:          write('        Zip: ');
48:          read_str(response[zip]);
49:
50:          { write the responses to the file }
51:          for resp_type := last TO zip DO
52:              fwrite_str(outfile,response[resp_type]);
53:
54:          { start the next round of input }
55:          write('Type in a last name, or press <CR> to exit: ');
56:          read_str(response[last])
57:      END;
58:      close(outfile)
59: END.
```

▅▅▅▅ **READSTRM.PAS**

```
PROGRAM readstrm (INPUT,OUTPUT);

   { A program that reads a stream file (fields separated by
     delimiters) as input and prints it to the screen }

CONST
   DELIM_CHR = '|';
   MAX_REC_SIZE = 255;

TYPE
   strng    = packed array [0..MAX_REC_SIZE] of char;
   filetype = packed array [1..40] of char;

VAR
   filename  : filetype;
   infile    : text;
   fld_count : integer;
   fld_len   : integer;
   str       : strng;

{$I tools.prc}
```

(continued)

```
FUNCTION readfield (VAR infile : text; VAR str : strng): integer;

{ Function readfield reads characters from file infile until it
  reaches end of file of a "|".  Readfield puts the characters in
  str and returns the length of str }

VAR
    i  : integer;
    ch : char;
BEGIN
  i := 0;
  ch := ' ';
  while (not EOF(infile)) and (ch <> DELIM_CHR) DO
    BEGIN
      read (infile,ch);
      i := i + 1;
      str[i] := ch
    END;
i := i - 1;
str[0] := CHR(i);
readfield := i
END;

BEGIN {main}
    write ('Enter the name of the file that you wish to open: ');
    readln (filename);
    assign(infile,filename);
    reset (infile);

    fld_count := 0;

    fld_len := readfield(infile,str);
    while (fld_len > 0) DO
      BEGIN
      fld_count := fld_count + 1;
      write(' field #':10,fld_count:1,':':2);
      write_str(str);                     { write_str() is in tools.prc }
      fld_len := readfield(infile,str)
      END;
    close (infile)
END.
```

▬▬▬ WRITREC.PAS

Note about *writrec.pas*: After writing the *rec_lgth* to outfile on line 69, we write a space to the file. This is because in Pascal values to be read into integer variables must be separated by spaces, tabs, or end-of-line markers.

```
1: PROGRAM writrec (INPUT,OUTPUT);
2:
3: {$B-}
```

```
 4:
 5: CONST
 6:     DELIM_CHR = '¦';
 7:     MAX_REC_SIZE = 255;
 8:
 9: TYPE
10:     strng = packed array [0..MAX_REC_SIZE] of char;
11:     filetype = packed array [1..40] of char;
12:
13: VAR
14:     filename : filetype;
15:     outfile  : text;
16:     response : strng;
17:     buffer   : strng;
18:     rec_lgth : integer;
19:
20: {$I tools.prc}
21:
22:
23: PROCEDURE fld_to_buffer(VAR buff: strng; s: strng);
24:
25: { This procedure concatenates s and a delimiter to end of
26:   buff }
27:
28: VAR
29:     d_str    : strng;
30: BEGIN
31:     cat_str(buff,s);
32:     d_str[0] := CHR(1);
33:     d_str[1] := DELIM_CHR;
34:     cat_str(buff,d_str)
35: END;
36:
37:
38: BEGIN {main}
39:     write('Enter the name of the file you wish to create: ');
40:     readln(filename);
41:     assign(outfile,filename);
42:     rewrite(outfile);
43:
44:     write('Enter Last Name -- or <CR> to exit: ');
45:     read_str(response);
46:     while (len_str(response) > 0) DO
47:         BEGIN
48:         buffer[0] := CHR(0);                    {Set length of string
49:                                                   in buffer to 0}
50:         fld_to_buffer(buffer,response);
51:         write('                        First name: ');
52:         read_str(response);
53:         fld_to_buffer(buffer,response);
54:         write('                           Address: ');
55:         read_str(response);
56:         fld_to_buffer(buffer,response);                        (continued)
```

```
57:              write('                              City: ');
58:              read_str(response);
59:              fld_to_buffer(buffer,response);
60:              write('                             State: ');
61:              read_str(response);
62:              fld_to_buffer(buffer,response);
63:              write('                               Zip: ');
64:              read_str(response);
65:              fld_to_buffer(buffer,response);
66:
67:              { write out the record length and buffer contents }
68:              rec_lgth := len_str(buffer);
69:              write(outfile,rec_lgth);
70:              write(outfile,' ');
71:              fwrite_str(outfile,buffer);
72:
73:              { prepare for next entry }
74:              write('Enter Last Name -- or <CR> to exit: ');
75:              read_str(response)
76:           END;
77:        close(outfile)
78:  END.
```

▬▬▬ READREC.PAS

```
PROGRAM readrec (INPUT,OUTPUT);

{ This program reads through a file, record by record, displaying the
  fields from each of the records on the screen. }

{$B-}

CONST
    input_size = 255;
    DELIM_CHR = '¦';
    MAX_REC_SIZE = 255;

TYPE
    strng = packed array [0..input_size] of char;
    filetype = packed array [1..40] of char;

VAR
    filename  : filetype;
    outfile   : text;
    rec_count : integer;
    scan_pos  : integer;
    rec_lgth  : integer;
    fld_count : integer;
    buffer    : strng;
    field     : strng;
```

```
{$I tools.prc}
{$I get.prc}


BEGIN {main}
    write('Enter name of file to read: ');
    readln (filename);
    assign(outfile,filename);
    reset(outfile);

    rec_count := 1;
    scan_pos := 0;
    rec_lgth := get_rec(outfile,buffer);
    while rec_lgth > 0 DO
        BEGIN
        writeln('Record ',rec_count);
        rec_count := rec_count + 1;
        fld_count := 1;
        scan_pos := get_fld(field,buffer,scan_pos,rec_lgth);
        while scan_pos > 0 DO
            BEGIN
            write('     Field ',fld_count,': ');
            write_str(field);
            fld_count := fld_count + 1;
            scan_pos := get_fld(field,buffer,scan_pos,rec_lgth)
            END;
        rec_lgth := get_rec(outfile,buffer)
        END;

    close(outfile)

END.
```

▬▬▬ GET.PRC

```
FUNCTION get_rec(VAR fd: text; VAR buffer: strng): integer;

{ A function that reads a record and its length from file fd.  The
  function returns the length of the record.  If EOF is encountered
  get_rec() returns 0  }

VAR
    rec_lgth    : integer;
    space       : char;
BEGIN
    if EOF(fd) then
        get_rec := 0
    else
        BEGIN
        read(fd,rec_lgth);
```

(continued)

```
        read(fd,space);
        fread_str(fd,buffer,rec_lgth);
        get_rec := rec_lgth
        END
END;


FUNCTION get_fld(VAR field:strng;buffer:strng;VAR scanpos: integer;
                 rec_lgth: integer): integer;

{ A function that starts reading at scanpos and reads characters from
  the buffer until it reaches a delimiter or the end of the record.  It
  returns scanpos for use on the next call. }

VAR
    fpos   : integer;
BEGIN
    if scanpos = rec_lgth then
        get_fld := 0
    else
        BEGIN
        fpos := 1;
        scanpos := scanpos + 1;
        field[fpos] := buffer[scanpos];
        while (field[fpos] <> DELIM_CHR) and (scanpos < rec_lgth) DO
            BEGIN
            fpos := fpos + 1;
            scanpos := scanpos +1;
            field[fpos] := buffer[scanpos]
            END;
        if field[fpos] = DELIM_CHR then
            field[0] := CHR(fpos - 1)
        else
            field[0] := CHR(fpos);
        get_fld := scanpos
        END
END;
```

FIND.PAS

```
PROGRAM find (INPUT,OUTPUT);

{ This program reads through a file, record by record, looking for
  a record with a particular key.  If a match occurs, then all the
  fields in the record are displayed.  Otherwise a message is
  displayed indicating that the record was not found. }

{$B-}
```

```
CONST
    MAX_REC_SIZE = 255;
    DELIM_CHR = '¦';

TYPE
    strng = packed array [0..MAX_REC_SIZE] of char;
    filetype = packed array [1..40] of char;

VAR
    filename  : filetype;
    outfile   : text;
    last      : strng;
    first     : strng;
    search_key: strng;
    length    : integer;
    matched   : boolean;
    rec_lgth  : integer;
    buffer    : strng;
    scan_pos  : integer;
    key_found : strng;
    field     : strng;

{$I tools.prc}
{$I get.prc}
BEGIN {main}
    write('Enter name of file to search: ');
    readln(filename);
    assign(outfile,filename);
    reset(outfile);

    write('Enter last name: ');
    read_str(last);
    write('Enter first name: ');
    read_str(first);
    makekey(last,first,search_key);

    matched := FALSE;
    rec_lgth := get_rec(outfile,buffer);
    while ((not matched) and  (rec_lgth  > 0)) DO
        BEGIN
        scan_pos := 0;
        scan_pos := get_fld(last,buffer,scan_pos,rec_lgth);
        scan_pos := get_fld(first,buffer,scan_pos,rec_lgth);
        makekey(last,first,key_found);
        if cmp_str(key_found,search_key) = 0 then
            matched := TRUE
        else
            rec_lgth := get_rec(outfile,buffer);
        END;
    close(outfile);
```

(continued)

```
        { if record found, print the fields }
    if matched then
        BEGIN
        writeln('Record found:');
        writeln;
        scan_pos := 0;

        { break out the fields }
        scan_pos := get_fld(field,buffer,scan_pos,rec_lgth);
        while scan_pos > 0 DO
            BEGIN
            write_str(field);
            scan_pos := get_fld(field,buffer,scan_pos,rec_lgth)
            END;
        END
    else
        writeln(' Record not found.');
END.
```

UPDATE.PAS

Some things to note about *update.pas*:

☐ In the procedure *ask_info()*, the name and address fields are read in as *strngs*, and procedure *fld_to_buffer()* writes the fields to *strbuff* (also of type *strng*). Writing *strbuff* to *outfile* would result in a type mismatch, since *outfile* is a file of type *datarec*. However, the procedure *stod()*, located in *stod.prc*, converts a variable of type *strng* to a variable of type *datarec* to write the buffer to the file. The calls to *stod()* are located on lines 210 and 237.

☐ The seek() statements on lines 212, 229, 239, and 250 are not standard; they are features of Turbo Pascal.

```
 1: PROGRAM update (INPUT,OUTPUT);
 2:
 3: {$B-}
 4:
 5: { A program to open or create a fixed length record file for
 6:   updating.  Records may be added or changed.  Records to be
 7:   changed must be accessed by relative record number }
 8:
 9: CONST
10:     MAX_REC_SIZE = 255;
11:     REC_LGTH     = 64;
12:     DELIM_CHR    = '|';
13:
```

```
14: TYPE
15:     strng     = packed array [0..MAX_REC_SIZE] of char;
16:     filetype  = packed array [1..40] of char;
17:     datarec   = RECORD
18:                     len   : integer;
19:                     data  : packed array [1..REC_LGTH] of char
20:                 END;
21:
22: VAR
23:     filename     : filetype;
24:     outfile      : file of datarec;
25:     response     : char;
26:     menu_choice  : integer;
27:     strbuff      : strng;
28:     byte_pos     : integer;
29:     head         : datarec;
30:     rrn          : integer;
31:     drecbuff     : datarec;
32:     i            : integer;
33:     rec_count    : integer;
34: {$I tools.prc}
35: {$I stod.prc }
36: {$I get.prc  }
37:
38:
39: PROCEDURE fld_to_buffer(VAR buff: strng; s: strng);
40:
41: { fld_to_buffer concatenates strng s and a delimiter to the
42:   end of buff }
43:
44: VAR
45:     d_str  : strng;
46: BEGIN
47:     cat_str(buff,s);
48:     d_str[0] := CHR(1);
49:     d_str[1] := DELIM_CHR;
50:     cat_str(buff,d_str)
51: END;
52:
53:
54: FUNCTION menu:integer;
55:
56: {local function to ask user for next operation. Returns numeric
57:  value of user response }
58:
59: VAR
60:     choice : integer;
61: BEGIN
62:     writeln;
63:     writeln('                   FILE UPDATING PROGRAM');
64:     writeln;
65:     writeln('You May Choose to: ');
```

(continued)

```
 66:     writeln;
 67:     writeln('    1.   Add a record to the end of the file');
 68:     writeln('    2.   Retrieve a record for updating');
 69:     writeln('    3.   Leave the program');
 70:     writeln;
 71:     write('Enter the number of your choice: ');
 72:     readln(choice);
 73:     writeln;
 74:     menu := choice
 75: END;
 76: PROCEDURE ask_info(VAR strbuff: strng);
 77:
 78: {local procedure to accept input of name and address fields,
 79:   writing them to the buffer passed as a parameter }
 80:
 81: VAR
 82:     response  : strng;
 83: BEGIN
 84:     { clear the record buffer }
 85:     clear_str(strbuff);
 86:
 87:     { get the fields }
 88:     write('    Last Name: ');
 89:     read_str(response);
 90:     fld_to_buffer(strbuff,response);
 91:     write('    First Name: ');
 92:     read_str(response);
 93:     fld_to_buffer(strbuff,response);
 94:     write('        Address: ');
 95:     read_str(response);
 96:     fld_to_buffer(strbuff,response);
 97:     write('           City: ');
 98:     read_str(response);
 99:     fld_to_buffer(strbuff,response);
100:     write('          State: ');
101:     read_str(response);
102:     fld_to_buffer(strbuff,response);
103:     write('            Zip: ');
104:     read_str(response);
105:     fld_to_buffer(strbuff,response);
106:     writeln
107: END;
108:
109:
110: FUNCTION ask_rrn: integer;
111:
112: { function to ask for the relative record number of the record
113:   that is to be updated.  }
114:
115: VAR
116:     rrn       : integer;
```

```
117: BEGIN
118:     writeln('Input the relative record number of the record that');
119:     write('   you want to update: ');
120:     readln(rrn);
121:     writeln;
122:     ask_rrn := rrn
123: END;
124: PROCEDURE read_and_show;
125:
126: {procedure to read and display a record.  This procedure does not
127:  include a seek -- reading starts at the current file position }
128:
129: VAR
130:     scan_pos    : integer;
131:     drecbuff    : datarec;
132:     i           : integer;
133:     data_lgth   : integer;
134:     field       : strng;
135:     strbuff     : strng;
136: BEGIN
137:     scan_pos := 0;
138:     read(outfile,drecbuff);
139:
140:     { convert drecbuff to type strng }
141:     strbuff[0] := CHR(drecbuff.len);
142:     for i := 1 to drecbuff.len DO
143:         strbuff[i] := drecbuff.data[i];
144:
145:     writeln('Existing Record Contents');
146:     writeln;
147:
148:     data_lgth := len_str(strbuff);
149:     scan_pos := get_fld(field,strbuff,scan_pos,data_lgth);
150:     while scan_pos > 0 DO
151:         BEGIN
152:         write_str(field);
153:         scan_pos := get_fld(field,strbuff,scan_pos,data_lgth)
154:         END
155: END;
156:
157:
158: FUNCTION change: integer;
159:
160: { function to ask the user whether or not to change the
161:   record.  Returns 1 if the answer is yes, 0 otherwise.        }
162:
163: VAR
164:     response  : char;
165: BEGIN
166:     writeln('Do you want to change this record?');
167:     write('    Answer Y or N, followed by <CR> ==>');
```

(continued)

```
168:        readln(response);
169:        writeln;
170:        if (response = 'Y') or (response = 'y') then
171:            change := 1
172:        else
173:            change := 0
174: END;
175: BEGIN {main}
176:        write('Enter the name of the file: ');
177:        readln(filename);
178:        assign(outfile,filename);
179:
180:        write('Does this file already exist? (respond Y or N): ');
181:        readln(response);
182:        writeln;
183:        if (response = 'Y') OR (response = 'y') then
184:            BEGIN
185:            reset(outfile);                  { open outfile          }
186:            read(outfile,head);              { get header            }
187:            rec_count := head.len            { read in record count }
188:            END
189:        else
190:            BEGIN
191:            rewrite(outfile);                { create outfile          }
192:            rec_count := 0;                  { initialize record count }
193:            head.len := rec_count;           { place in header record  }
194:            for i := 1 to REC_LGTH DO
195:                head.data[i] := CHR(0);      { set header data to nulls}
196:            write(outfile,head)              { write header rec        }
197:            END;
198:
199:        { main program loop -- call menu and then jump to options }
200:        menu_choice := menu;
201:        while menu_choice < 3 DO
202:            BEGIN
203:            CASE menu_choice OF
204:                1 :                     { add a new record }
205:                    BEGIN
206:                    writeln('Input the information for the new record --');
207:                    writeln;
208:                    writeln;
209:                    ask_info(strbuff);
210:                    stod(drecbuff,strbuff); {convert strbuff to type datarec}
211:                    rrn := rec_count + 1;
212:                    seek(outfile,rrn);
213:                    write(outfile,drecbuff);
214:                    rec_count := rec_count + 1
215:                    END;
216:                2 :                     { update existing record }
217:                    BEGIN
218:                    rrn := ask_rrn;
```

```
219:
220:                    { if rrn is too big, print error message ... }
221:                    if (rrn > rec_count) or (rrn < 1) then
222:                        BEGIN
223:                        write('Record Number is out of range');
224:                        writeln('...returning to menu ...')
225:                        END
226:
227:                    else                    { otherwise, seek to the record ... }
228:                        BEGIN
229:                        seek(outfile,rrn);
230:
231:                        { display it and ask for changes ... }
232:                        read_and_show;
233:                        if change = 1 then
234:                            BEGIN
235:                            writeln('Input the revised Values: ');
236:                            ask_info(strbuff);
237:                            stod(drecbuff,strbuff);   { convert strbuff to type
238:                                                        datarec }
239:                            seek(outfile,rrn);
240:                            write(outfile,drecbuff)
241:                            END
242:                        END
243:                    END
244:          END; { CASE }
245:          menu_choice := menu
246:          END; { while }
247:
248:          { rewrite correct record count to header before leaving }
249:          head.len := rec_count;
250:          seek(outfile,0);
251:          write(outfile,head);
252:          close(outfile)
253: END.
```

══════ **STOD.PRC**

```
PROCEDURE stod (VAR drecbuff: datarec; strbuff: strng);

{ A procedure that converts a variable of type strng to a variable of
  type datarec }

VAR
    i : integer;
```

(continued)

```
BEGIN
    drecbuff.len := min(REC_LGTH,len_str(strbuff));
    for i := 1 to drecbuff.len DO
        drecbuff.data[i] := strbuff[i];

    { Clear the rest of the buffer }
    while i < REC_LGTH DO
        BEGIN
        i := i + 1;
        drecbuff.data[i] := ' '
        END
END;
```

OBJECTIVES

Look at *storage compaction* as a simple way of reusing space in a file.

Develop a procedure for deleting fixed length records that allows the vacated file space to be reused dynamically.

Illustrate the use of *linked lists* and *stacks* to manage an *avail list*.

Consider several approaches to the problem of deleting variable length records.

Introduce the concepts associated with the terms *internal fragmentation* and *external fragmentation*.

Outline some *placement strategies* associated with the reuse of space in a variable length record file.

5

FILE MAINTENANCE AND RECORD DELETION

CHAPTER OUTLINE

5.1
FILE MAINTENANCE

We have already seen how important it is for the file systems designer to consider the way a file is to be accessed when deciding on how to organize a file. In this chapter we see that the designer must also consider the kinds of *changes* that are likely to take place over the life of a file. If a file is very *volatile* (undergoing frequent additions or deletions) and is used in a real-time environment, the organization of the file should facilitate rapid changes to individual records in real time, without interfering with user access to the file. A reservations file in an online reservation system is an example of a volatile file used in real time.

At the other extreme is an offline file that undergoes relatively few changes and does not need to be kept absolutely up to date; it can be updated in a batch mode and need not include extra structures to facilitate rapid changes. A mailing list file might be an example of this kind of file.

File maintenance is important because performance deteriorates as changes are made to a file. For example, suppose a record in a variable length record file is modified in such a way that the new record is longer than the original record. What do you do with the extra data? You could append it to the end of the file and put a pointer from the original record space to the extension of the record. You could rewrite the whole record at the end of the file (unless the file needs to be sorted), leaving a hole at the original location of the record. Each solution has a drawback: in the former case, the job of processing the record is more awkward than it was originally; in the latter case, the file contains wasted space.

In this chapter we take a close look at the way file organization deteriorates as a file is modified. In general, modifications can take any one of three forms:

□ Record addition;
□ Record updating; and
□ Record deletion.

If the only kind of change to a file is record addition, there is no deterioration of the kind we cover in this chapter. (Previous chapters describe how to handle the simple addition of new records.) It is only when variable length records are updated, or when either fixed or variable length records are deleted, that maintenance issues become complicated and interesting. Since record updating can always be treated as a record deletion followed by a record addition, our focus will be in the effects of record deletion. When a record has been deleted, we want to reuse the space. We begin by looking at *storage compaction*, which is the simplest and most widely used of the storage reclamation methods we discuss.

5.2 STORAGE COMPACTION

Any record deletion strategy must provide some way for us to recognize records as deleted. A simple and usually workable approach is to place a special mark in each deleted record. For example, in the name and address file developed in the preceding chapters, we might simply place an asterisk as the first field in a deleted record. Figures 5.1(a) and (b) show a name and address file similar to the one in Chapter 4 before and after the second record is marked as deleted. (The dots at the ends of records 0 and 2 represent padding between the last field and the end of each record.)

Once we are able to recognize a record as deleted, the next question is how to reuse the space from the record. Approaches to this problem that rely on storage compaction do nothing at all to reuse the space for a while. The records are simply marked as deleted and left in the file for a period of time. Programs using the file must include logic that causes them to ignore records that are marked as deleted. One nice side effect of this approach is that it is usually possible to allow the user to

```
Ames¦John¦123 Maple¦Stillwater¦OK¦74075¦........................
Morrison¦Sebastian¦9035 South Hillcrest¦Forest Village¦OK¦74820¦
Brown¦Martha¦625 Kimbark¦Des Moines¦IA¦50311¦...................
```
(a)

```
Ames¦John¦123 Maple¦Stillwater¦OK¦74075¦........................
*¦rrison¦Sebastian¦9035 South Hillcrest¦Forest Village¦OK¦74820¦
Brown¦Martha¦625 Kimbark¦Des Moines¦IA¦50311¦..................
```
(b)

```
Ames¦John¦123 Maple¦Stillwater¦OK¦74075¦........................
Brown¦Martha¦625 Kimbark¦Des Moines¦IA¦50311¦..................
```
(c)

FIGURE 5.1 ▪ **Storage requirements of sample file using 64-byte fixed length records. (a) Before deleting the second record. (b) After deleting the second record. (c) After compaction—the second record is gone.**

"undelete" a record with very little effort. This is particularly easy if you keep the deleted mark in a special field, rather than destroy some of the original data, as in our example.

The reclamation of the space from the deleted records happens all at once. After deleted records have accumulated for some interval, a special storage compaction program is used to reconstruct the file with all the deleted records squeezed out (Fig. 5.1c). If there is enough space, the simplest way to do this compaction is through a file copy program that skips over the deleted records. It is also possible, though more complicated and time consuming, to do the compaction in place. Either of these approaches can be used with both fixed and variable length records.

The decision about how often to run the storage compaction program can be based on either the number of deleted records or on the calendar. In accounting programs, for example, it often makes sense to run a compaction procedure on certain files at the end of the fiscal year or some other point associated with closing the books.

Storage compaction is an acceptable way to reclaim space for many applications. There are other applications, however, that are too volatile and interactive for storage compaction to be useful. In these situations we want to reuse the space from deleted records as soon as possible. We begin our discussion of such dynamic storage reclamation with a look at fixed length record files, since fixed length records make the reclamation problem much simpler.

5.3 OVERVIEW OF FIXED LENGTH RECORD DELETION

In general, to provide a mechanism for record deletion with subsequent reutilization of the freed space, we need to be able to guarantee two things:

□ That deleted records be marked in some special way; and
□ That we can find the space that deleted records once occupied so that we can reuse that space when we add records.

We have already identified a method of meeting the first requirement: we mark records as deleted by putting a field containing an '*' at the beginning of deleted records.

If you are working with fixed length records and are willing to search sequentially through a file before adding a record, you can always provide the second guarantee if you have provided the first. If the program can recognize a deleted record, then space reutilization can take the form of looking through the file, record by record, until a deleted record is found. If the program reaches the end of the file without finding a deleted record, then the new record can be appended there at the end.

Unfortunately, this approach makes adding records an intolerably slow process if the program is an interactive one and the user has to sit at the terminal and wait as the record addition takes place. What we need to make record reuse happen more quickly are:

□ A way to know immediately if there are empty slots in the file; and
□ A way to jump directly to one of those slots if they exist.

LINKED LISTS. The use of a *linked list* for stringing together all of the available records can meet both of these needs. A linked list is a data structure in which each element or *node* contains some kind of reference to its successor in the list.

If you have a head reference to the first node in the list, you can move through the list by looking at each node, then at the node's pointer field, so that you know where the next node is located. When you finally encounter a pointer field with some special, predetermined end-of-list value, you stop the traversal of the list. In Fig. 5.2 we use a − 1 in the pointer field to mark the end of the list.

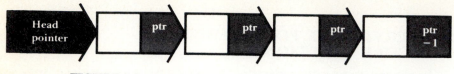

FIGURE 5.2 ▪ A linked list.

When a list is made up of deleted records that have become *available space* within the file, the list is usually called an *avail list*. When inserting a new record into a fixed length record file, any one available record is just as good as any other. There is no reason to prefer one open slot over another since all the slots are the same size. It follows that there is no reason for ordering the avail list in any particular way. (As we see later, this situation changes for variable length records.)

STACKS.   The simplest way to handle a list is as a stack. A stack is a list in which all insertions and removals of nodes take place at one end of the list. So, if we have an avail list managed as a stack that contains relative record numbers (RRN) 5 and 2, and then add RRN 3, it looks like this before and after the addition of the new node:

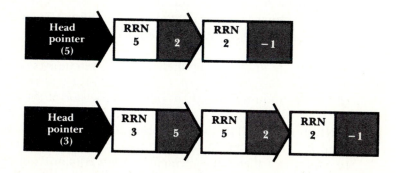

When a new node is added to the top or front of a stack, we say that it is *pushed* onto the stack. If the next thing that happens is a request for some available space, the request is filled by taking relative record number 3 from the avail list. This is called *popping* the stack. The list returns to a state in which it contains only records 5 and 2.

LINKING AND STACKING DELETED RECORDS.   Now we can meet the two criteria for rapid access to reusable space from deleted records. We need:

☐   A way to know immediately if there are empty slots in the file; and
☐   A way to jump directly to one of those slots if they exist.

Placing the deleted records on a stack meets both criteria. If the pointer to the top of the stack contains the end-of-list value, then we know that there are not any empty slots and that we have to add new records by appending them to the end of the file. If the pointer to the stack top contains a valid node reference, then we know not only that a reusable slot is available, but also exactly where to find it.

Where do we keep the stack? Is it a separate list, perhaps maintained in a separate file, or is it somehow embedded within the data file? Once again, we need to be careful to distinguish between *physical* and *conceptual* structures. The deleted, available records are not actually moved anywhere when they are pushed onto the stack. They stay right where we need them, located in the file. The stacking and linking is done by arranging and rearranging the links used to make one available record slot point to the next. Since we are working with fixed length records in a disk file, rather than with memory addresses, the pointing is not done with *pointer* variables in the formal sense, but through relative record numbers (RRNs).

Suppose we are working with a fixed length record file that once contained seven records (RRNs 0–6). Furthermore, suppose that records 3 and 5 have been deleted, *in that order*, and that deleted records are marked by replacing the first field with an asterisk. We can then use the second field of a deleted record to hold the link to the next record on the avail list. Leaving out the details of the valid, in-use records, Fig. 5.3(a) shows how the file might look.

Record number 5 is the first record on the avail list (top of the stack) since it is the record that is most recently deleted. Following the linked list, we see that record 5 points to record 3. Since the *link field* for record 3 contains -1, which is our end-of-list marker, we know that record 3 is the last slot available for reuse.

Figure 5.3(b) shows the same file after record number 1 is also deleted. Note that the contents of all the other records on the avail list remain unchanged. Treating the list as a stack results in a minimal amount of list reorganization when we push and pop records to and from the list.

List head (first available record) → 5

0	1	2	3	4	5	6
Edwards . . .	Bates . . .	Wills . . .	*−1	Masters . . .	*3	Chavez . . .

(a)

List head (first available record) → 1

0	1	2	3	4	5	6
Edwards . . .	*5	Wills . . .	*−1	Masters . . .	*3	Chavez . . .

(b)

List head (first available record) → −1

0	1	2	3	4	5	6
Edwards . . .	1st new rec	Wills . . .	3rd new rec	Masters . . .	2nd new rec	Chavez . . .

(c)

FIGURE 5.3 ▪ Sample file showing linked lists of deleted records. (a) After deletion of records 3 and 5, in that order. (b) After deletion of records 3, 5, and 1, in that order. (c) After insertion of three new records.

If we now add a new name to the file, it is placed in record number 1, since RRN 1 is the first available record. The avail list would return to the configuration shown in Fig. 5.3(a). Since there are still two record slots on the avail list, we could add yet two more names to the file without increasing the size of the file. After that, however, the avail list would be empty (Fig. 5.3c). If yet another name is added to the file, the program knows that the avail list is empty and that the name requires the addition of a new record at the end of the file.

5.4 ▬ IMPLEMENTING FIXED LENGTH RECORD DELETION

Implementing mechanisms that place deleted records on a linked avail list and that treat the avail list as a stack is relatively straightforward. Some important details that we must consider are as follows.

☐ We need a suitable place to keep the pointer to the first available record on the avail list.

☐ When we delete a record we must be able to mark the record in some special way, and then place it on the avail list.

☐ When we add records we must be able to reuse space from the avail list if it is not empty.

☐ We must be able to verify if a record has been deleted before we try to use it.

A POINTER TO THE TOP OF THE AVAIL LIST.   We begin with the first item: finding a place to keep the RRN of the first record on the avail list. Since this is information that is specific to the data file, it is information that can be carried in a header record at the start of the file. Let us assume that this has been done—that there is a field in the header record called HEAD.FIRST_AVAIL† that holds the relative record number of the first available record. If this element contains a − 1, we take this to mean that the avail list is empty.

PLACING THE RECORD ON THE AVAIL LIST.   The next item on the list of important details concerns placing the deleted record on the avail list. The record must be marked as deleted and must, as an avail list member, be given a link field in place of the usual name and address fields. Placing an '*' (or some other special mark) in the record as a deletion mark is easy: We simply write the character '*' at the beginning of the record.

Handling the link field is a little more complicated than handling the '*' because we have a choice: should we store the link in ASCII or binary format? This is analogous to the choice we faced in Chapter 4 when we had to decide how to express the record length for variable length records. Once again, in C we would opt for binary format because it does not require translations and saves a little space, whereas in Pascal we would be better off writing it in the form of a character string.

Figure 5.4 contains a pseudocode description of a function that deletes records from our fixed length record file.

ADDING RECORDS—REUSING SPACE.   Until now, adding records to a file always meant placing them at the end of the file. Now that we have a list of available records within a file, we can reuse the space previously

---

†We are assuming that the header would be read into a structure in C and a record in Pascal.

```
FUNCTION:  del_rec(RRN)

    move file pointer to RRN position in file
    write delete flag field ('*') in current position in file
    write HEAD.FIRST_AVAIL in new current position in file
    set HEAD.FIRST_AVAIL to RRN

end FUNCTION
```

FIGURE 5.4 ▪ **Function** *del_rec(RRN)* **deletes record number** *RRN*. **The space opened by the deletion is pushed onto the avail list.**

occupied by deleted records. What we need is a single function that returns

☐ The RRN of a reusable record slot; or
☐ The RRN of the next record to be appended if no reusable slots are available.

The function *pop_avail()* (Fig. 5.5) does this. The logic underlying this function should be clear from a reading of the code and comments.

RECOGNIZING DELETED RECORDS. The last implementation detail we need to address involves ensuring that we be able to check to see if a record has been deleted before trying to use it. Since the very first character in a deleted record is an asterisk, it is possible to check for

```
FUNCTION: pop_avail()

    if HEAD.FIRST_AVAIL == -1 then  /* avail list empty */
        return RRN of next record to be appended

    else  /* pop avail list    */
        set RET_VAL to HEAD.FIRST_AVAIL
        move file pointer to HEAD.FIRST_AVAIL position in file
        skip over '*' field
        read link field from file into RRN
        set HEAD.FIRST_AVAIL to RRN
        return RET_VAL

end FUNCTION
```

FIGURE 5.5 ▪ **Function** *pop_avail()* **returns the RRN of the first available slot in the file. If the avail list of deleted records is empty, the function returns the RRN of the next record to be appended at the end of the file.**

deletion using a simple test, such as

```
If the first position in BUFFER is '*' then
                notify the caller that the record is deleted
```

5.5 VARIABLE LENGTH RECORD DELETION

Now that we have a mechanism for handling an avail list of available space once records are deleted, let's try to apply this mechanism to the more complex problem of reusing space from deleted variable length records. We have seen that, to support record reuse through an avail list, we need:

☐ A way to link the deleted records together into a list (i.e., a place to put a link field);
☐ An algorithm for adding newly deleted records to the avail list; and
☐ An algorithm for finding and removing records from the avail list when we are ready to use them.

AN AVAIL LIST OF VARIABLE LENGTH RECORDS.   What kind of file structure do we need to support an avail list of variable length records? Since we will want to delete whole records and then place records on an avail list, we need a structure in which the record is a clearly defined entity. The file structure in which we define the length of each record by placing a byte count of the record contents at the beginning of each record will serve us well in this regard.

Since this record structure is insensitive to the number of fields in a record, we can handle the contents of a deleted variable length record just as we did with fixed length records. That is, we can place a single asterisk in the first field, followed by a binary link field pointing to the next deleted record on the avail list. The avail list itself can be organized just as it was with fixed length records, but with one small but important difference. Without fixed length records, we cannot use relative record numbers (RRNs) for *links*. Since we cannot compute the byte offset of variable length records from their RRNs, the links must contain the byte offsets themselves.

To illustrate, suppose we begin with a variable length record file containing the three records for Ames, Morrison, and Brown introduced earlier. Figure 5.6(a) shows what the file looks like (minus the header) before any deletions, and Fig. 5.6(b) shows what it looks like after the deletion of the second record. The periods in the deleted record signify discarded characters.

```
HEAD.FIRST_AVAIL: -1

40 Ames¦John¦123 Maple¦Stillwater¦OK¦74075¦64 Morrison¦Sebastian
¦9035 South Hillcrest¦Forest Village¦OK¦74820¦45 Brown¦Martha¦62
5 Kimbark¦Des Moines¦IA¦50311¦
```
(a)

```
HEAD.FIRST_AVAIL: 43

40 Ames¦John¦123 Maple¦Stillwater¦OK¦74075¦64 *¦ -1.............
.........................................................45 Brown¦Martha¦62
5 Kimbark¦Des Moines¦IA 50311¦
```
(b)

FIGURE 5.6 ▪ **A sample file for illustrating variable length record deletion. (a) Original sample file stored in variable length format with byte count (header record not included). (b) Sample file after deletion of the second record (periods show discarded characters).**

ADDING AND REMOVING RECORDS. Let's address the questions of adding and removing records to and from the list together, since they are clearly related. With fixed length records we could access the avail list as a stack because one member of the avail list is just as usable as any other. That is not true when the record slots on the avail list differ in size, as they do in a variable length record file. We now have two conditions that must be met before we can reuse a record:

1. The record must be deleted. This is the only condition required for fixed length record reuse.
2. The record must be the right size. For the moment we define "right size" as "big enough." Later we find that it is sometimes useful to be more particular about the meaning of "right size."

All records on the avail list are known to meet the first condition, but not all members of the avail list necessarily meet the second condition for a given instance of reuse. It is possible, even likely, that we need to *search through* the avail list for a record slot that is the right size. Because we need to search, we cannot organize the avail list as a stack.

The inability to use stack popping as an access scheme does not mean that we cannot still *organize* the avail list as a linked list, but it does mean that we *access* it differently. Since it is organized as a linked list, finding a proper slot simply means traversing the list until a record slot is found that is big enough to hold the new record that is to be inserted.

For example, suppose the avail list contains the deleted record slots shown in Fig. 5.7(a), and a record that requires 55 bytes is to be added.

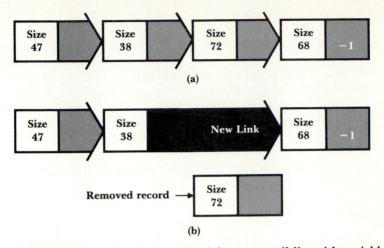

FIGURE 5.7 ▪ Removal of a record from an avail list with variable length records: (a) before removal; and (b) after removal.

Since the avail list is not empty, we traverse the records whose sizes are 47 (too small), 38 (too small), and 72 (big enough). Having found a slot big enough to hold our record, we remove it from the avail list by creating a new link that jumps over the record (Fig. 5.7b). If we had reached the end of the avail list before finding a record that was large enough, we would have appended the new record at the end of the file.

Figure 5.8 contains a description of an algorithm for finding a record slot on the avail list.

```
FUNCTION: get_avail()

    find the first record on the avail list

    while (the record is not big enough AND not end of list)
        jump to the next available record

    if the record is big enough
        rearrange the linked list to remove the record
        return the byte offset of the record slot

    else    /* end of list reached before a big enough slot found */
        return byte offset of the end of the file

end FUNCTION
```

FIGURE 5.8 ▪ A function for getting a slot from the avail list for variable length record insertion.

```
FUNCTION: delete_record(RRN)

    read sequentially through the file until record RRN is found

    set BYTE_POS to the byte offset of the record to be deleted
    place a deleted record marker ("*") in the first field
    place the value of HEAD.FIRST_AVAIL in the next field as a link
    set HEAD.FIRST_AVAIL to BYTE_POS

end FUNCTION
```

FIGURE 5.9 ▪ **A procedure for placing deleted records on the avail list.**

Since this procedure for finding a reusable record looks through the entire avail list if necessary, we do not need a sophisticated method for putting newly deleted records onto the list. If a record of the right size is somewhere on this list, our get-available-record procedure eventually finds it. It follows that we can continue to push new members onto the front of the list, just as we do with fixed length records. Figure 5.9 contains an outline of a procedure that deletes a record, given its relative record number (RRN), and that then pushes the record onto the avail list.

5.6
STORAGE FRAGMENTATION

Let's look again at the fixed length record version of our three-record file (Fig. 5.10). The dots at the ends of the records represent characters we use as padding between the last field and the end of the records. The padding is wasted space; it is part of the cost of using fixed length records. Wasted space *within* a record is called *internal fragmentation*.

Clearly we want to minimize internal fragmentation. If we are working with fixed length records, we attempt such minimization by choosing a record length that is as close as possible to what we need for each record. But unless the actual data is fixed in length, we have to

```
Ames¦John¦123 Maple¦Stillwater¦OK¦74075¦.......................
Morrison¦Sebastian¦9035 South Hillcrest¦Forest Village¦OK¦74820¦
Brown¦Martha¦625 Kimbark¦Des Moines¦IA¦50311¦..................
```

FIGURE 5.10 ▪ **Storage requirements of sample file using 64-byte fixed length records.**

```
40 Ames¦John¦123 Maple¦Stillwater¦OK¦74075¦64 Morrison¦Sebastian
¦9035 South Hillcrest¦Forest Village¦OK¦74820¦45 Brown¦Martha¦62
5 Kimbark¦Des Moines¦IA¦50311¦
```

FIGURE 5.11 ▪ **Storage requirements of sample file using variable length records with a count field.**

put up with a certain amount of internal fragmentation in a fixed length record file.

One of the attractions of variable length records is that they minimize wasted space by doing away with internal fragmentation when the file is first written out. The space set aside for each record is exactly as long as it needs to be. Compare the fixed length example with the one in Fig. 5.11, which uses the variable length record structure—a byte count followed by delimited data fields. The only space (other than the delimiters) that is not used for holding data in each record is the count field. If we assume that this field uses two bytes, this amounts to only six bytes for the three-record file. The fixed length record file wastes 24 bytes in the very first record.

But before we start congratulating ourselves for solving the problem of wasted space due to internal fragmentation, we should consider what happens in a variable length record file after a record is deleted and replaced with a shorter record. If the shorter record takes less space than the original record, internal fragmentation results. Figure 5.12 shows how the problem could occur with our sample file when the

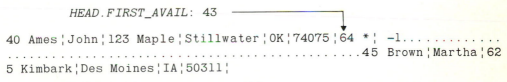

```
HEAD.FIRST_AVAIL: 43
40 Ames¦John¦123 Maple¦Stillwater¦OK¦74075¦64 *¦ -1............
.......................................................45 Brown¦Martha¦62
5 Kimbark¦Des Moines¦IA¦50311¦
```

(a)

```
HEAD.FIRST_AVAIL: -1

40 Ames¦John¦123 Maple¦Stillwater¦OK¦74075¦64 Ham¦Al¦28 Elm¦Ada¦
OK¦70332¦.............................................45 Brown¦Martha¦62
5 Kimbark¦Des Moines¦IA¦50311¦
```

(b)

FIGURE 5.12 ▪ **Illustration of fragmentation with variable length records. (a) After deletion of the second record (unused characters in the deleted record are replaced by periods). (b) After the subsequent addition of the record for Al Ham.**

second record in the file is deleted and the following record is added:

Ham¦Al¦28 Elm¦Ada¦OK¦70332¦

It appears that escaping internal fragmentation does not turn out to be so easy. The slot vacated by the deleted record is 37 bytes larger than is needed for the new record. Since we treat the extra 37 bytes as part of the new record, they are not on the avail list and are therefore unusable. But instead of keeping the 64-byte record slot intact, suppose we break it into two parts: one part to hold the new Ham record, and the other to be placed back on the avail list? Since we would take only as much space as necessary for the Ham record, there would be no internal fragmentation.

Figure 5.13 shows what our file looks like if we use this approach to insert the record for Al Ham. We steal the space for the Ham record *from the end* of the 64-byte slot, and leave the first 35 bytes of the slot on the avail list. (The available space is 35 rather than 37 bytes because we need two bytes to form a new size field for the Ham record.)

The 35 bytes still on the avail list can be used to hold yet another record. Figure 5.14 shows the effect of inserting the following 25-byte record:

Lee¦Ed¦Rt 2¦Ada¦OK¦74820¦

As we would expect, the new record is carved out of the 35-byte record that is on the avail list. The data portion of the new record requires 25 bytes, and then we need two more bytes for another size field. This leaves eight bytes in the record still on the avail list.

What are the chances of finding a record that can make use of these eight bytes? Our guess would be that the probability is very close to zero. These eight bytes are not usable, even though they are not trapped inside any other record. This is an example of *external fragmentation*. The space is actually on the avail list rather than being locked inside some other record, but is too fragmented to be reused.

```
HEAD.FIRST_AVAIL: 43  ─────────────────────┐
                                            ↓
40 Ames¦John¦123 Maple¦Stillwater¦OK¦74075¦35 *¦ −1.............
.................26 Ham¦Al¦28 Elm¦Ada¦OK¦70332¦45 Brown¦Martha¦6
25 Kimbark¦Des Moines¦IA¦50311¦
```

FIGURE 5.13 ▪ **Combatting internal fragmentation by putting the unused part of the deleted slot back on the avail list.**

HEAD, FIRST_AVAIL: 43

```
40 ¦ Ames ¦ John ¦ 123 Maple ¦ Stillwater ¦ OK ¦ 74075 ¦ 8 * ¦ −1...25 Lee ¦ Ed ¦
Rt 2 ¦ Ada ¦ OK ¦ 74820 ¦ 26 Ham ¦ Al ¦ 28 Elm ¦ Ada ¦ OK ¦ 70332 ¦ 45 Brown ¦ Martha ¦ 6
25 Kimbark ¦ Des Moines ¦ IA ¦ 50311 ¦
```

FIGURE 5.14 ▪ Addition of the second record into the slot originally occupied by a single deleted record.

There are some interesting ways to combat external fragmentation. One way, which we discuss at the beginning of this chapter, is *storage compaction*. We could simply regenerate the file when external fragmentation becomes intolerable. Two other approaches are:

☐ When possible, combine small fragments to make larger, more useful fragments. If the program notices that two record slots on the avail list are adjacent, it can combine them to make a single, larger record slot. This is called *coalescing the holes* in the storage space.

☐ Try to minimize fragmentation before it happens by adopting a placement strategy that the program can use as it selects a record slot from the avail list.

Coalescing holes presents some interesting problems. The avail list is not kept in *physical* record order; if there are two deleted records that are physically adjacent, there is no reason to presume that they are linked adjacent to each other on the avail list. Exercise 15 at the end of the chapter provides a discussion of this problem along with a framework for developing a solution.

The development of better *placement strategies*, however, is a different matter. It is a topic that warrants a separate discussion, since the choice among alternative strategies is not as obvious as it might seem at first glance.

5.7
PLACEMENT STRATEGIES

Earlier we presented two functions for dealing with variable length record deletion, *delete_rec()* and *get_avail()*. Function *delete_rec()* treats the avail list as a stack, putting newly deleted records at the front. Since the records are placed on the avail list in a most-recently-deleted-is-first order, they are not ordered by size. When a record slot is needed to hold a new record, *get_avail()* looks through the list, starting from the beginning, until it either finds a record slot that is big enough to hold the new record or reaches the end of the list.

This is called a *first-fit* placement strategy. The least possible amount of work is expended when we place newly available space on the list, and we are not very particular about the closeness of fit as we look for a record slot to hold a new record. We accept the first available record slot that will do the job, regardless of whether the slot is 10 times bigger than what is needed or whether it is a perfect fit.

We could, of course, develop a more orderly approach for placing records on the avail list, keeping them in either ascending or descending sequence by size. Rather than always putting the newly deleted records at the front of the list, these approaches involve moving through the list, looking for the place to insert the record to maintain the desired sequence.

If we order the avail list in *ascending* order by size, what is the effect on the closeness of fit of the records that *get_avail()* would retrieve from the list? Since *get_avail()* searches sequentially through the avail list until it encounters a record that is big enough to hold the new record, the first record encountered by *get_avail()* is the *smallest* record that would do the job. The fit between the available slot and the new record's needs would be as close as we can make it. This is called a *best-fit* placement strategy.

A best-fit strategy is intuitively appealing. There is, of course, a price to be paid for obtaining this fit. We end up having to search through at least a part of the list not only when we get records from the list, but also when we put newly deleted records on the list. In a real-time environment the extra processing time could be significant.

A less obvious disadvantage of the best-fit strategy is related to the very idea of finding the best possible fit: The free area left over after inserting a new record into a slot is as small as possible. Often this remaining space is too small to be useful, resulting in external fragmentation. Furthermore, the slots that are least likely to be useful are the ones that will be placed toward the beginning of the list, making first-fit searches increasingly long as time goes on.

These problems suggest an alternative strategy: What if we arrange the avail list so that it is in *descending* order by size? Then the largest record slot on the avail list would always be at the head of the list. Since *get_avail()* starts its search at the beginning of the avail list, it always returns the largest available record slot if it returns any slot at all. This is known as a *worst-fit* placement strategy. The amount of space in the record slot beyond what is actually needed is as large as possible.

A *worst-fit* strategy does not, at least initially, sound very appealing. But consider:

□ The *get_avail()* procedure can be simplified so that it looks only at the first element of the avail list. If the first record slot is not large enough to do the job, none of the others will be.

□ By extracting the space we need from the *largest* available slot, we are assured that the unused portion of the slot is as large as possible. This is important because external fragmentation begins to develop when the unused space in the file consists of pieces that are too small to be useful.

What can you conclude from all of this? It should be clear that no one placement strategy is superior for all circumstances. The best you can do is formulate a series of general observations and then, given a particular design situation, try to select the strategy that seems most appropriate. Here are some general observations. The judgment will have to be yours.

□ Placement strategies make sense only with regard to variable length record files. With fixed length records placement is simply not an issue.

□ If space usage due to record deletion and reuse is not an important factor, either because there is lots of space or because there is very little deletion, first fit is probably the strategy of choice because it takes the least time.

□ If space is lost due to *internal fragmentation*, then the choice is between first fit and best fit. A worst-fit strategy truly makes internal fragmentation worse.

□ If the space is lost due to *external fragmentation*, and if something other than first fit is called for, then one should give careful consideration to a worst-fit strategy, which takes less time than best fit and might tend to decrease the degree of external fragmentation.

SUMMARY

The original organization of a file influences the ways in which it can be altered, and also the ways in which it can respond to deterioration. A volatile file, one that undergoes many changes, can deteriorate very rapidly unless measures are taken to adjust the file organization to the changes. One result of making changes to files is storage fragmentation.

Internal fragmentation occurs when there is wasted space within a record. In a fixed length record file, internal fragmentation can result when variable length records are stored in fixed slots. It can also occur in a variable length record file when one record is replaced by another record of a smaller size. *External fragmentation* occurs when holes of unused space between records are created, normally because of record deletions.

There are a number of ways to combat fragmentation. The simplest is *storage compaction*, which squeezes out unused space caused by external fragmentation by sliding all of the undeleted records together. Compaction is generally done in a batch mode.

Fragmentation can be dealt with *dynamically* by reclaiming deleted space when records are added. The need to keep track of the space to be reused makes this approach more complex than compaction. Moreover, if a file has variable length records, just keeping a list of available record slots or positions in the file is not sufficient. One also needs to develop a *placement strategy* for choosing a slot that is the right size for the new record. Most of the chapter is devoted to developing techniques and strategies for dynamically reclaiming space lost due to record deletion.

We begin with the problem of deleting fixed length records. Since finding the first field of a fixed length record is very easy, deleting a record can be accomplished by placing a special mark in the first field. We use an asterisk ("*") to mark a record as deleted.

Since all records in a fixed length record file are the same size, the reuse of deleted records need not be complicated. The solution we adopt consists of collecting all the available record slots into an *avail list*. The avail list is created by stringing together all the deleted records to form a *linked list*. The list is formed by arranging *link fields* in deleted record spaces (right after the "*" field) so that each record on the list contains a field that gives the relative record number of the next record on the list.

In a fixed length record file any one record slot is just as usable as any other slot; they are interchangeable. Consequently, the simplest way to maintain the linked avail list is to treat it as a *stack*. Newly available records are added to the avail list by *pushing* them on to the front of the list; record slots are removed from the avail list by *popping* them from the front of the list.

After a discussion of some of the implementation details associated with providing record deletion and reuse for the file structures developed in Chapter 4, we consider the more difficult matter of deleting *variable* length records. We find that we can place "*" fields and link fields in variable length records in the same way we put them in fixed length records, but there is an important difference. With variable length records, we need to be sure that a record slot is the right size to hold the new record. Our initial definition of right size is simply in terms of being big enough. Consequently, we develop a *get_avail()* function that can search through the avail list until it finds a record slot that is big enough to hold the new record. Given such a function, and a complementary function that simply places newly deleted records on the front of the avail list, we can implement a system that deletes and reuses variable length records.

We then consider the amount and nature of fragmentation that develops inside a file due to record deletion and reuse. The fragmentation can happen *internally* if the space is lost because it is locked up inside of a record. We develop a procedure that breaks a single large variable length record slot into two or more smaller ones, using exactly as much space as is needed for a new record, leaving the remainder on the avail list. We see that, although this could decrease the amount of wasted space, eventually the remaining fragments are too small to be useful. When this happens, the space is lost to *external fragmentation*.

There are a number of things that one can do to minimize external fragmentation. They include:

- *Compacting* the file in a batch mode when the level of fragmentation becomes excessive;
- *Coalescing* adjacent record slots (holes) on the avail list to make larger, more generally useful slots; and
- Adopting a *placement strategy* to select slots for reuse in a way that minimizes fragmentation.

Development of algorithms for coalescing holes is left to the reader as part of the exercises found at the end of the chapter. Placement strategies, on the other hand, need more careful discussion.

The placement strategy used up to this point by the variable length record deletion and reuse procedures is a *first-fit* strategy. This strategy is simply, "if the record slot is big enough, use it." By keeping the avail list in sorted order, it is easy to implement either of two other placement strategies:

- *Best fit*, in which a new record is placed in the smallest slot that is still big enough to hold it. This is an attractive strategy for variable length record files in which the fragmentation is *internal*. It involves more overhead than other placement strategies.

■ *Worst fit*, in which a new record is placed in the largest record slot available. The idea is to have the left-over portion of the slot be as large as possible.

There is no firm rule for selecting a placement strategy; the best one can do is use informed judgment based on a number of guidelines.

KEY TERMS

Avail list. A list of the space, freed through record deletion, that is available for holding new records. In the examples considered in this chapter this list of space took the form of a linked list of deleted records.

Best fit. A placement strategy for selecting the space on the avail list used to hold a new record. Best-fit placement finds the available record slot that is closest in size to what is needed to hold the new record.

Coalescence. If two deleted, available records are physically adjacent, they can be combined to form a single, larger available record space. This process of combining smaller available spaces into a larger one is known as *coalescing holes*. Coalescence is a way to counteract the problem of external fragmentation.

Compaction. A way of getting rid of all *external fragmentation* by sliding all the records together so that there is no space lost between them.

External fragmentation. A form of fragmentation that occurs in a file when here is unused space outside of or between individual records.

First fit. A kind of placement strategy for selecting a space from the avail list. First-fit placement selects the first available record slot large enough to hold the new record.

Fragmentation. The unused space within a file. The space can be locked within individual records (*internal fragmentation*) or outside of or between individual records (*external fragmentation*).

Internal fragmentation. A form of fragmentation that occurs when space is wasted in a file because it is locked up, unused, inside of records. Fixed length record structures often result in internal fragmentation.

Linked list. A collection of nodes that have been organized into a specific sequence by means of references placed in each node that point to a single successor node. The *logical* order of a linked list is often different than the actual physical order of the nodes in the computer's memory.

Placement strategy. As used in this chapter, a placement strategy is a mechanism for selecting the space on the avail list that is to be used to hold a new record added to the file.

Stack. A kind of list in which all additions and deletions take place at the same end.

Worst fit. A kind of placement strategy for selecting a space from the avail list. Worst-fit placement selects the largest record slot, regardless of how small the new record is. Insofar as this leaves the largest possible record slot for reuse, worst fit can sometimes help minimize *external fragmentation*.

EXERCISES

1. What is the difference between internal and external fragmentation? How can compaction affect the amount of internal fragmentation in a file? What about external fragmentation?

2. In-place compaction purges deleted records from a file without creating a separate new file. What are the advantages and disadvantages of in-place compaction compared to compaction in which a separate compacted file is created.

3. Why is a worst-fit placement strategy a bad choice if there is significant loss of space due to internal fragmentation?

4. Conceive of an inexpensive way to keep a continuous record of the amount of fragmentation in a file. This fragmentation measure could be used to trigger the batch processes used to reduce fragmentation.

5. Suppose a file must remain sorted. How does this affect the range of placement strategies available?

6. Develop a pseudocode description of a procedure for performing in-place compaction in a variable length record file that contains size fields at the start of each record.

7. Consider the process of updating rather than deleting a variable length record. Outline a procedure for handling such updating, accounting for the fact that the update might result in either a longer or a shorter record.

8. In Section 5.4, we raise the question of where to keep the stack containing the list of available records. Should it be a separate list, perhaps maintained in a separate file, or should it be embedded within the data file? We choose the latter organization for our implementation. What advantages and disadvantages are there to the second approach? What other kinds of file structures can you think of to facilitate various kinds of record deletion?

9. In some files, each record has a delete bit that is set to 1 to indicate that the record is deleted. This bit can also be used to indicate that a record is inactive rather than deleted. What is required to reactivate an inactive record? Could reactivation be done with the deletion procedures we have used?

10. In this chapter we outline three general approaches to the problem of minimizing storage fragmentation:

- Implementation of a placement strategy;
- Coalescing of holes; and
- Compaction.

Assuming an interactive programming environment, which of these strategies would be used "on the fly," as records are added and deleted? Which strategies would be used as batch processes that could be run periodically?

11. Why do placement strategies make sense only with variable length record files?

PROGRAMMING EXERCISES

12. Rewrite the program *update.c* or *update.pas* so that it can delete and add records to a fixed length record file using one of the replacement procedures discussed in this chapter.

13. Write a program similar to the one described in the preceding exercise, but that works with variable length record files.

14. In Section 5.6 we show that the function *get_avail()* for reusing deleted variable length record space can result in a large amount of internal fragmentation, and suggest an alternative approach that allows record slots to be split up to form new records. Modify *get_avail()* to implement this splitting when the original record slot is large enough to accommodate it.

15. Develop a pseudocode description of a variable length record deletion procedure that checks to see if the newly deleted record is contiguous with any other deleted records. If there is contiguity, coalesce the records to make a single, larger available record slot. Some things to consider as you address this problem:

- The avail list does not keep records arranged in physical order; the next record on the avail list is not necessarily the next deleted record in the physical file. Is it possible to merge these two views of the avail list, the physical order and the logical order, into a single list? If you do this, what placement strategy will you use?
- Physical adjacency can include records that precede as well as follow the newly deleted record. How will you look for a deleted record that precedes the newly deleted record?
- Maintaining two views of the list of deleted records implies that as you discover physically adjacent records you have to rearrange links to update the nonphysical avail list. What additional complications would we encounter if we were combining the coalescing of holes with a best-fit or worst-fit strategy?

FURTHER READINGS

Somewhat surprisingly, the literature concerning storage fragmentation and reuse does not often consider these issues from the standpoint of secondary storage. Typically, storage fragmentation, placement strategies, coalescing of holes, and garbage collection are considered in the context of reusing space within electronic random access memory (RAM). As one reads this literature with the idea of applying the concepts to secondary storage, it is necessary to evaluate each strategy in light of the cost of accessing secondary storage. Some strategies that are attractive when used in electronic RAM are too expensive on secondary storage.

Discussions about space management in RAM are usually found under the heading "Dynamic Storage Allocation." Knuth [1973a] provides a good, though technical, overview of the fundamental concerns associated with dynamic storage allocation, including placement strategies. Much of Knuth's discussion is reworked and made more approachable by Tremblay and Sorenson [1984]. Standish [1980] provides a more complete overview of the entire subject, reviewing much of the important literature on the subject.

CHAPTER

OBJECTIVES

Provide an introduction to the idea underlying a binary search.

Develop a sort procedure based on a Shell's sort in internal memory.

Introduce, by example, the concept of *indirection* and demonstrate the power of this conceptual tool.

Undertake an examination of the limitations of binary searching.

Develop a *keysort* procedure for sorting larger files; investigate the costs associated with keysort.

Introduce the concept of a *pinned* record.

6

FINDING THINGS QUICKLY IN A FILE: AN INTRODUCTION TO SORTING AND BINARY SEARCHING

CHAPTER OUTLINE

This book begins with a discussion of the cost of accessing secondary storage. You may remember that the magnitude of the difference between accessing RAM and seeking information on a fixed disk is such that, if we magnify the time for a RAM access to 20 seconds, a similarly magnified disk access would take 116 days.

So far we have not had to pay much attention to this cost. This chapter, then, marks a kind of turning point. Once we move from fundamental organizational issues to the matter of searching a file for a particular piece of information, the cost of a seek becomes a major factor in determining our approach. And what is true for searching is all the more true for sorting. If you have studied sorting algorithms you know that even a good sort involves making many comparisons. If each of these comparisons involves a seek, the sort is agonizingly slow.

Our discussion of sorting and searching, then, goes beyond simply getting the job done. We develop approaches that minimize the number of disk accesses and that therefore minimize the amount of time expended. This concern with minimizing the number of seeks continues to be a major focus throughout the rest of the book. This chapter is just the beginning of a quest for ways to order and find things quickly.

6.1

FINDING THINGS IN THE FILES ALREADY DEVELOPED

We have implemented some file structures that let the user do some rather sophisticated things. But all of the programs we have written up to this point in the book, despite any other strengths they offer, share a major failing: the only way to retrieve or find a record with any degree of rapidity is to look for it by relative record number (RRN). If the file has fixed length records, knowing the RRN lets us jump to the record using *direct access*.

But what if we do not know the RRN of the record we want? The examples in the preceding chapters are often associated with a simple name and address file. How likely is it that a question about this file would take the form, "What is the address stored in RRN 23?" Not very likely, of course. We are much more likely to know the identity of a record by its key.

Given the methods of organization developed so far, access by key implies a sequential search, looking at record after record until we find one that contains the key. What if there is no record containing the requested key? Then we would have to look through the entire file. What if we suspect that there might be more than one record that contains the key, and we want to find them all? Once again, we would be doomed to looking at every record in the file. Clearly, we need to find a better way to handle keyed access. Fortunately, there are many better ways.

We begin our investigation of alternate organizations by considering ways to find things by guessing.

6.2

SEARCH BY GUESSING— BINARY SEARCH

Suppose we are looking for a record for Bill Kelly in a file of 1000 fixed length records, and suppose the file is sorted so that the records appear in ascending order by key. The relative record numbers in the file range from 0 to 999. We start by comparing KELLY BILL (the canonical form of the search key) with the middle key in the file, which is the key whose RRN is 500. The result of the comparison tells us which half of the file contains Bill Kelly's record. If we find, for example, that record 500 is for Sam Miller, we know that the remainder of the search can concentrate on the first half of the file, records 0 through 499. Next we compare KELLY BILL with the middle key among records 0 through 499 to find out which *quarter* of the file Bill Kelly's record is in. This process is repeated until either Bill Kelly's record is found or we have narrowed the number of potential records to zero.

This kind of searching, in which half of the remaining items are eliminated with each comparison, is called *binary searching*. An algorithm for binary searching is shown in Fig. 6.1. Binary searching takes

```
/* function to perform a binary search in the file associated with the
   logical name INPUT.  Assumes that INPUT contains RECORD_COUNT records.
   Searches for the key KEY_SOUGHT.  Returns RRN of record containing
   key if the key is found; otherwise returns -1
*/

FUNCTION: bin_search(INPUT, KEY_SOUGHT, RECORD_COUNT)

    LOW := 0                    /* initialize lower bound for searching   */
    HIGH := RECORD_COUNT - 1    /* initialize high bound -- we subtract 1
                                   from the count since RRNs start from 0 */

    while (LOW <= HIGH)
        GUESS := (LOW + HIGH) / 2      /* find midpoint                   */

        read record with RRN of GUESS
        place canonical form of key from record GUESS into KEY_FOUND

    if (KEY_SOUGHT < KEY_FOUND)               /* GUESS is too high        */
        HIGH := GUESS - 1                     /* so reduce upper bound    */
    else if (KEY_SOUGHT > KEY_FOUND)          /* GUESS is too low         */
        LOW := GUESS + 1                      /* increase lower bound     */
    else
        return(GUESS)                 /* match -- return the RRN          */
    endwhile

    return (-1)       /* if loop completes, then key was not found        */
```

FIGURE 6.1 ▪ The *bin_search()* function in pseudocode.

at most ten comparisons to find Bill Kelly's record, if it is in the file, or to determine that it is not in the file. Compare this with a sequential search for the record. If there are 1000 records, then it takes *at most* 1000 comparisons to find a given record (or establish that it is not present); on the average, 500 comparisons are needed.

In general, a binary search of a file with *n* records takes at most

$$\lfloor \log n \rfloor + 1 \text{ comparisons}†$$

and on average approximately

$$\lfloor \log n \rfloor + 1/2 \text{ comparisons.}$$

A binary search is therefore said to be $O(\log n)$. In contrast, you may recall that a sequential search of the same file requires at most *n* comparisons, and on average $1/2 \, n$ which is to say that a sequential search is $O(n)$.

The difference between a binary search and a sequential search becomes even more dramatic as we increase the size of the file to be searched. If we double the number of records in the file, we double the number of comparisons required for sequential search; when binary search is used, doubling the file size adds only one more guess to our worst case. This makes sense, since we know that each guess eliminates half of the possible choices. So, if we tried to find Bill Kelly's record in a file of 2000 records, it would take *at most*

$$1 + \lfloor \log 2000 \rfloor = 11 \text{ comparisons,}$$

whereas a sequential search would *average*

$$1/2 \, n = 1000 \text{ comparisons,}$$

and could take up to 2000 comparisons.

Binary searching is clearly a more attractive way to find things than is sequential searching. But, as you might expect, there is a price to be paid before we can use binary searching: Binary searching works only when the list of records is ordered in terms of the key we are using in the search. So, to make use of binary searching, we have to be able to *sort* a list on the basis of a key.

Since sorting is such an excellent illustration of the problems encountered in file structure design, we will take the time to look carefully at a number of approaches to sorting, starting in this chapter with sorts that take place in RAM.

---

†In this text, *log x* refers to the logarithm function to the base 2. When any other base is intended, it is so indicated.

6.3

SORTING A DISK FILE IN RAM

Consider the operation of any internal sorting algorithm with which you are familiar. The algorithm requires multiple passes over the list that is to be sorted, comparing and reorganizing the elements. Some of the items in the list are moved a long distance from their original positions in the list. If such an algorithm were applied directly to data stored on a disk, it is clear that there would be a lot of jumping around, seeking, and rereading of data. This would be a very slow operation. Unthinkably slow.

If the entire contents of the file can be held in RAM, a very attractive alternative is to read the entire file from the disk into memory, and then do the sorting there. We still have to access the data on the disk, but this way we can access it sequentially, sector after sector, without having to incur the cost of a lot of seeking and the cost of multiple passes over the disk.

This is one instance of a general class of solutions to the problem of minimizing disk usage: force your disk access into a sequential mode, performing the more complex, nonsequential accesses in RAM. Unfortunately it is often not possible to use this very simple kind of solution, but when you can, you should take advantage of it.

The first step in this particular approach to sorting is to read all the data records from the file into memory. To keep things simple, we assume that we are dealing with a fixed length record file of the kind created by the *update.c* and *update.pas* programs developed in Chapter 4. The files created by these programs contain header records that tell us how many records there are in the file. Once we have read the right number of data records into RAM, we have an array of identically sized character vectors, with each row of the array containing a record's contents (Fig. 6.2). Let's call this array RECORDS[].

Once we have read all the records into memory, we need to sort them. Unfortunately, we cannot simply treat the collection of records as a set of character strings, literally sorting the elements of our array. The problem is that the sort must be on the canonical form of the keys. For example, if we sort the records in Fig. 6.2 without converting the keys to canonical form, the record for Harrison would precede that of Harris. We need to *extract* a second array consisting of only the keys in canonical form and then do our sorting on those keys.

There must, of course, be some way of relating the keys back to the records from which they have been extracted. Consequently, each node of the new array has a second field that contains the RRN of the record associated with the key. We call this array KEYNODES[]. This arrange-

RECORDS

Harrison ¦ Susan ¦ 387 Eastern . . .
Kellogg ¦ Bill ¦ 17 Maple . . .
Harris ¦ Margaret ¦ 4343 West . . .
. . .
.
.
.
Bell ¦ Robert ¦ 8912 Hill . . .

FIGURE 6.2 ▪ **Data records after loading the file into the RECORDS array in RAM (minus header).**

ment is illustrated schematically in Fig. 6.3(a). We start with an RRN of 1, reserving the RRN of 0 for the header record. This mechanism of building a chain of references, in this case a reference from a key back to the copy of the original record, is known as *indirection*.

Conceptually, after sorting, the arrangement is as in Fig. 6.3(b). We stress the word *conceptually* because we really would not want to reorganize the array of canonical keys physically. Each element of KEYNODES[] contains a character string. If we sort the array of keys by physically moving the keynode elements, we have to do a lot of *copying* of strings. Sorts can require a large number of moves. If each of these moves required copying a string with 30 or more characters from one place to another, performance would be unnecessarily slow.

We say unnecessarily slow because we really do not need to move the keys. Each key is an element in the array KEYNODES and therefore can be referenced through an integer *subscript*. For example, if we want to reference the key for Susan Harrison in Fig. 6.3(a), all we need to keep track of is the integer 1, so we have the necessary subscript in the expression KEYNODES[1]. Consequently, we can reorder the keys without moving them if we form a third array, this one consisting simply of the subscripts in the KEYNODES array. We call this third array INDEX[] since, after we rearrange it, it forms an index to the correctly ordered sequence of the KEYNODES array. This sounds more complicated than it is. You should be able to get the idea by looking at Fig. 6.4, which illustrates the before and after arrangements of the three arrays we have discussed so far.

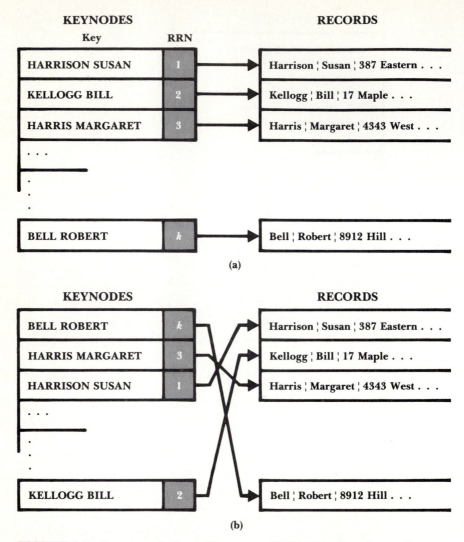

FIGURE 6.3 ▪ Conceptual view of key array (KEYNODES) and record array (a) before sorting, and (b) *conceptually*, after sorting. (The array on the left is not actually rearranged. See text.)

The attraction of using the INDEX array is that we can reorder the KEYNODES array by simply moving around the integer values within INDEX[], which is much faster and less expensive than moving around the KEYNODES elements themselves. Although this performance improvement is the really important consequence of introducing yet another level of indirection in the form of the INDEX array, there is an

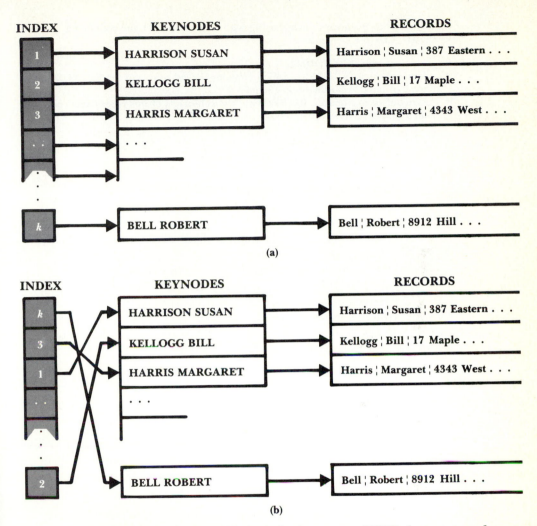

FIGURE 6.4 ▪ Conceptual view of pointer array (PTRS), key array, and record array (a) before sorting, and (b) after sorting. Note that the canonical key array has not been rearranged, but the pointer array has.

interesting secondary result: since we no longer intend to move the elements of the KEYNODES array, there is no need for an RRN reference within KEYNODES[]. As you can see from examining Fig. 6.4(b), there is now a fixed relationship between the subscript number in the KEYNODES array and the RRNs of the data records stored in the RECORDS array. Elements within KEYNODES[] can now be just

Given the following arrays, each starting with a subscript of 1 and containing RECORD_COUNT elements:

- Array of keys, KEYNODES[]
- Array of integers, INDEX[], which contains the subscripts of the KEYNODES[] array ordered according to key sequence
- Array of record images, RECORDS[]. The subscripts of this record array are such that KEYNODES[i] corresponds to RECORD[i]

for i := 1 to RECORD_COUNT
    write RECORD [INDEX[i]] to the output file
next i

FIGURE 6.5 ▪ Writing out the records in order by key.

character vectors; we no longer need a chain of references from KEY-NODES[] to RECORDS[].

Once the elements of INDEX[] are resequenced according to key values in KEYNODES[], we are ready to write out all of the REC-ORDS[] sorted in order by key. That process is described in Fig. 6.5. In other words, the subscript of the next RECORD to be written out in sorted order is contained in the INDEX element INDEX[i]. You can see that this record output logic works by applying it to Fig. 6.4(b).

6.4 ALGORITHM FOR THE RAM SORT

It is a relatively simple matter to turn the foregoing diagrams and discussion into pseudocode that can subsequently be implemented in C, Pascal, or some other language. Looking at the procedure from a high level, the basic steps are as follows:

1. Read the records from the input file into the RECORDS array;
2. Extract the keys, building the KEYNODES array;
3. Build an INDEX array of subscripts for KEYNODES[] and RECORDS[];
4. Order the INDEX[] based on the values in KEYNODES[]; and
5. Use the newly ordered INDEX[] to write out RECORDS[] to a new file in sorted order.

The pseudocode in Fig. 6.6 fills out this skeletal outline. The array names RECORDS[], KEYNODES[], and INDEX[] refer to the structures described in the preceding section. The actual sorting process is done by a function called *shell_sort()*, which we describe in the section that follows. Implementations of *ramsort* in both C and Pascal are provided at the end of this chapter.

```
PROGRAM: ramsort

    open input file as IN_FILE
    create output file as OUT_FILE

    read header record from IN_FILE
    write copy of header record to OUT_FILE
    REC_COUNT := record count from header record

    /* read in records, fill arrays */
    for i := 1 to REC_COUNT
        read record from IN_FILE to RECORDS[i]
        extract canonical key, place it in KEYNODES[i]
        INDEX[i] := i
    next i

    /* order INDEX[] according to KEYNODES[] values */
    shell_sort (INDEX, KEYNODES, REC_COUNT)

    /* write out records in sorted order */
    for i := 1 to REC_COUNT
        write RECORD [ INDEX[i] ] to OUT_FILE
    next i

    close IN_FILE and OUT_FILE
end PROGRAM
```

FIGURE 6.6 ▪ Pseudocode for *ramsort*.

6.5 THE SORT FUNCTION: *shell_sort()*

Once the main program in *ramsort* has extracted the canonical keys and formed an index of subscripts to this array of keys, it passes control to a sorting routine that is responsible for rearranging the index. There are many different sorting algorithms that could be used for this task; we use Shell's sort, which is named after D.L. Shell, who first suggested the method. Sometimes this approach is referred to as simply *shellsort*. It is a moderately fast algorithm that is easy to implement. Baase [1978] provides an excellent description of the algorithm; the approach taken in the pseudocode in Fig. 6.7 closely parallels Baase's description insofar as it is based on an insertion sort. Knuth [1973b] undertakes a detailed analysis of the algorithm's performance.

Fundamental to the design of any version of Shell's sort is the choice of a sequence of intervals used to divide and then subdivide the original list. For our pseudocode program (Fig. 6.7), we employ the

```
FUNCTION: shell_sort(INDEX, KEYNODES, REC_COUNT)

   variables:
     GAP:        current interval between elements being compared.
                 Starts at REC_COUNT/2 and reduces to 1.
     INS_KEY:    key to be inserted in a given cycle of the sort.
                 (The key is not actually inserted—instead the
                 subscript to the key is moved within INDEX[].)
     INS_SUBSCR: subscript (within KEYNODES[]) of the INS_KEY.  This
                 subscript will be the element that is actually moved
                 in the INDEX[] array.

     GAP := REC_COUNT / 2

     while (GAP > 0)
         /* Begin the insertion sort for this value of GAP */
         for j := (GAP + 1) to REC_COUNT
             INS_KEY := KEYNODES [INDEX[j]]
             INS_SUBSCR := INDEX[j]

             /* work backwards looking for the insertion location */
             i := j — GAP
             while ((i > 0) and (KEYNODES [INDEX[i]] > INS_KEY))
                 INDEX[i + GAP] := INDEX[i] /* slide for insertion  */
                 i := i — GAP                  /* move down 1 interval */
             endwhile

             INDEX[i + gap] := INS_SUBSCR   /* do the insertion     */
         next j

         GAP := GAP / 2        /* reduce the GAP, start next cycle  */
     endwhile
end FUNCTION
```

FIGURE 6.7 ▪ Pseudocode for *shell_sort().*

simple method of using an initial interval that is one-half the list length and then dividing the interval by two on successive passes over the list.

The array names used in Fig. 6.7 (KEYNODES, INDEX) have the same meaning as in previous sections. Note that the sort routine must receive both the INDEX and KEYNODES arrays since it is sorting on values within KEYNODES but actually doing the rearrangement in the INDEX array. This indirection is reflected in the use of the expression

```
KEYNODES [INDEX[i]]
```

to access elements of the KEYNODES array. Implementations of the *shell_sort()* function in both C and Pascal are included at the end of the chapter.

THE LIMITATIONS OF BINARY SEARCHING AND IN-RAM SORTING

Given the ability to sort files, we can now look for a particular record on the basis of a key without having to do a sequential search. We have made a first cut at a solution to the problem with which we began this chapter, the problem of finding things quickly through the use of a key. But our solution is only a first step. Let's look at some of the problems associated with our "sort, then binary search" approach to finding things.

PROBLEM 1: BINARY SEARCHING REQUIRES MORE THAN ONE OR TWO ACCESSES.   Earlier in the chapter we assert that, in the average case, a binary search requires approximately $\lfloor \log n \rfloor + 1/2$ comparisons. If each comparison requires a disk access, a series of binary searches on a list of 1000 items requires, on the average, 9.5 accesses per request. If the list is expanded to 100,000 items, the average search length extends to 16.5 accesses.

Although this is a *tremendous* improvement over the cost of a sequential search for the key, it is also true that 16 accesses, or even nine or ten accesses, is not a negligible cost. The cost of this seeking is particularly noticeable, and objectionable, if we are doing a large enough number of repeated accesses by key.

When we access records by relative record number (RRN) rather than by key, we are able to retrieve a record with a single access. That is an order of magnitude of improvement over the ten or more accesses that binary searching requires with even a moderately large file. Ideally, we would like to approach RRN retrieval performance, while still maintaining the advantages of access by key. In the next chapter, which is on the use of index structures, we begin to look at ways to move toward this ideal.

PROBLEM 2: KEEPING A FILE SORTED IS VERY EXPENSIVE.   Our ability to use a binary search has a price attached to it: We must keep the file in sorted order by key. Suppose we are working with a file to which we add records as often as we search for existing records. If we leave the file in unsorted order, doing sequential searches for records, then on the average each search requires reading through half the file. Each record addition, however, is very fast, since it involves nothing more than jumping to the end of the file and writing a record.

If, as an alternative, we keep the file in sorted order, we can cut down substantially on the cost of searching, reducing it to a handful of accesses. But we encounter difficulty when we add a record, since we want to keep all the records in sorted order. Inserting a new record into the file requires, on the average, that we not only read through half the records, but that we also *shift* the records to open up the space required for the insertion. We are actually doing *more* work than if we simply do sequential searches on an unsorted file.

Clearly the costs of maintaining a file that can be accessed through binary searching are not always as large as in this example involving frequent record addition. For example, it is often the case that searching is required much more frequently than is record addition. In such a circumstance, the benefits of faster retrieval can more than offset the costs of keeping the file sorted. As another example, there are many applications in which record additions can be accumulated in a transaction file and made in a batch mode. By sorting the list of new records before adding them to the main file, it is possible to *merge* them with the existing records. As we see in Chapter 8, such merging is a sequential process, passing only once over each record in the file. This can be an efficient, attractive approach to maintaining the file.

So, despite its problems, there are situations in which binary searching appears to be a useful strategy. However, knowing the costs of binary searching also lets us see what the requirements will be for better solutions to the problem of finding things by key. Better solutions will have to meet at least one of the following two conditions.

☐   They will not involve reordering of the records in the file when a new record is added; and

☐   They will be associated with data structures that allow for substantially more rapid, efficient reordering of the file.

In the chapters that follow we develop approaches that fall into each of these categories. Solutions of the first type can involve the use of simple indexes. They can also involve *hashing*. Solutions of the second type can involve the use of *tree structures*, such as a B-tree, to keep the file in order.

PROBLEM 3: AN IN-RAM SORT WORKS ONLY ON SMALL FILES. Our ability to use binary searching is limited by our ability to sort the file. The *ramsort* program works only if we can read the entire contents of a file into the computer's electronic memory. If the file is so large that we cannot do that, then we need a different kind of sort.

In what remains of this chapter we develop a variation on *ramsort* called a *keysort*. Like *ramsort*, *keysort* is limited in terms of how large a file it can sort, but its limit is larger. More important, our work on *keysort* will begin to illuminate a new approach to the problem of finding things that will allow us to avoid altogether the sorting of the records in a file.

6.7 KEYSORTING

6.7.1 DESCRIPTION OF THE METHOD

Keysorting, sometimes referred to as *tag sorting*, is simply a modification of our RAM sort. The difference is that we do not read the actual records into memory; we read in only the canonical keys.

Figure 6.8 shows a diagram that is much like the earlier ones that illustrate the relationship between the copies of the file's records, the array of keys, and the index array of subscripts. The difference is that

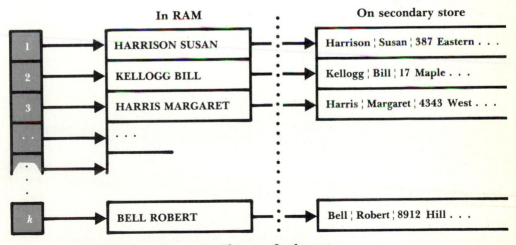

FIGURE 6.8 ▪ **Placement of arrays for *keysort*.**

the diagram in Fig. 6.8 is divided down the middle by a dotted line. The area on the left side of the line is titled *In RAM*, the area on the right is titled *On secondary store*.

Keysort, then, maintains the same fundamental components as *ramsort*. The actual sorting process rearranges the array of subscripts for the canonical keys, exactly as in *ramsort*. But, since *keysort* never reads the complete set of records into memory, it does not need to use nearly as much RAM as *ramsort* uses. This means that *keysort* can sort larger files, given the same amount of RAM.

Given the similarity between the two approaches, only minor modifications need to be made to the code for *ramsort* to turn it into a new program called *keysort*. Figure 6.9 outlines the *keysort* procedure in pseu-

```
PROGRAM: keysort

    open input file as IN_FILE
    create output file as OUT_FILE

    read header record from IN_FILE
    write copy of header record to OUT_FILE
    REC_COUNT := record count from header record

    /* read in records, fill arrays */
    for i := 1 to REC_COUNT
        read record from IN_FILE into temporary BUFFER
        extract canonical key, place in KEYNODES[i]
        INDEX[i] := i
    next i

    /* order INDEX[] according to KEYNODES[] values */
    shell_sort (INDEX, KEYNODES, REC_COUNT)

    /* write out records in sorted order */
    for i := 1 to REC_COUNT
        seek in IN_FILE to the record with RRN of INDEX[i]
        read the record into BUFFER from IN_FILE
        write BUFFER contents to OUT_FILE
    next i

    close IN_FILE and OUT_FILE
end PROGRAM
```

FIGURE 6.9 ▪ **Pseudocode for *keysort* (lines that differ from *ramsort* are shaded).**

docode. The few lines that differ from *ramsort* have been italicized. The differences are:

- ☐ Rather than read in all of the records into a RAM array, we simply read each record into a temporary BUFFER and then discard it; and
- ☐ When we are writing the records out in sorted order, we have to read them in a second time, since they are not all stored in RAM.

6.7.2 LIMITATIONS OF THE KEYSORT METHOD

At first glance, keysorting appears to be an obvious improvement over *ramsort*; it might even appear to be a case of getting something for nothing. We know that sorting is an expensive operation and that we want to do it in RAM. Keysorting allows us to achieve this objective without having to hold the entire file in RAM at once. After all, we *are* sorting on the basis of a *key*, so why should we bother to carry around all the rest of the record in memory? With keysorting it appears we are able to perform the expensive part of a sort operation in RAM while leaving the bulky part out on secondary storage. How elegant.

But, while reading about the operation of writing the records out in sorted order, even a casual reader probably senses a cloud on this apparently bright horizon. In *keysort* we need to read in the records a second time before we can write out the new sorted file. Doing something twice is never very desirable. But the problem is worse than that.

Look carefully at the *for* loop that reads in the records before writing them out to the new file. You can see that we are *not* reading through the input file sequentially. Instead, we are working in sorted order, moving from the sorted INDEX[] to the RRNs of the records. (The index is sorted as a set of subscripts into the KEYNODE array, but the relationship between KEYNODES[] and the file is such that KEYNODES[i] corresponds to the record with RRN = i.) Since we have to seek to each record and read it in before writing it back out, creating the sorted file requires as many *random seeks* into the input file as there are records. As we have noted a number of times, there is an enormous difference between the time required to read all the records in a file sequentially and the time required to read those same records if we must seek to each record separately. What is worse, we are performing all of these accesses in alternation with write statements to the

output file. So, even the writing of the output file, which would otherwise appear to be sequential, in most cases involves seeking. The disk
drive must move the head back and forth between the two files as it
reads and writes.

The getting-something-for-nothing aspect of keysort has suddenly
evaporated. Even though keysort does the hard work of sorting in
RAM, it turns out that creating a sorted version of the file from the
map supplied by the INDEX array is not at all a trivial matter when the
only copies of the records are kept on secondary store. Exercise 5 at
the end of the chapter involves using buffers to minimize the disadvantages of keysorting while still maintaining the fundamental advantage
of requiring less memory than *ramsort*.

6.7.3 ANOTHER SOLUTION: WHY BOTHER TO WRITE THE FILE BACK?

The fundamental idea behind *keysort* is an attractive one; why work with
an entire record when the only parts of interest, as far as sorting and
searching are concerned, are the fields used to form the key? There is
a compelling kind of parsimony behind this idea, and it makes keysorting look promising. The promise fades only when we run into the
problem of rearranging all the records in the file so that they reflect
the new, sorted order.

It is interesting to ask whether we can avoid this problem by simply
not bothering with the task that is giving us trouble: What if we just
skip the time-consuming business of writing out a sorted version of the
file? What if, instead, we simply write out a copy of the vector of canonical key nodes? Suppose, for example, that KEYNODES is an array
of C structures or Pascal records in which each individual KEYNODE
is defined as follows so that it can hold an RRN for the original data
record in addition to the canonical key.†

In C:	In Pascal:
| ```
typedef struct{
    char  key[30];
    short rrn;
} KEYNODE;
``` | ```
KEYNODE = record
    key : packed array [0..29] of char;
    rrn : integer
END;
``` |

†We use an array starting with 0 in Pascal so that we can place the length of the key
string in the zeroth position of the array. In C, the string is null terminated, as one would
expect.

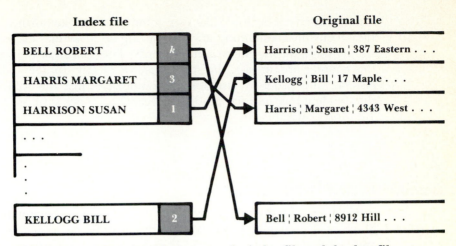

FIGURE 6.10 ▪ Relationship between the index file and the data file.

If we do without writing the records back in sorted order, writing out the contents of our KEYNODES[] array instead, we will have written a program that outputs an *index* to the original file. The relationship between the two files is illustrated in Fig. 6.10.

This is an instance of one of our favorite categories of solutions to computer science problems: If some part of a process begins to look like a bottleneck, consider skipping it altogether. Can you do without it? Instead of creating a new, sorted copy of the file to use for searching, we have created a second kind of file, an index file, that is to be used in conjunction with the original file. If we are looking for a particular record, we do our binary search on the index file, then use the RRN stored in the index file record to find the corresponding record in the original file.

There is much to say about the use of index files, enough to fill up several chapters. The next chapter is about the various ways we can use simple indexes, which is the kind of index we illustrate here. In later chapters we talk about different ways of organizing the index to provide more flexible access and easier maintenance.

All of these index structures can be seen as a kind of logical extension of the ideas we discuss in this chapter. Like our sorting programs, the various index structures involve extracting keys from the records in a file. These index structures also usually involve *indirection*, accessing the records through a chain of one or more pointers or relative record number references. And, like our solution to the keysorting problem, they focus on maintaining and organizing an *index* file, rather than on simply reorganizing the original records. The concerns we introduce in this chapter are, in fact, the root concerns of any storage and retrieval system. The problem remains the same, it is just the solutions that change, building on each other and becoming more sophisticated, flexible, and powerful.

6.8 PINNED RECORDS

In Chapter 5 we discuss the problem of updating and maintaining files. Much of that chapter revolves around the problems of deleting records and keeping track of the space vacated by deleted records so that it can be reused. In Chapter 5 an avail list of deleted record slots is created by linking all of the available slots together. In the case of fixed length record deletion the linking is done by writing a field into each deleted record that points to the relative record number (RRN) of the next deleted record. With variable length records, the link field consists of the actual *byte offset* of the next record on the avail list. In both cases the link fields give very specific information about the exact *physical location* of the next available record.

When a file contains such references to the physical locations of records, we say that these records are *pinned*. You can gain an appreciation for this particular choice of terminology if you consider the effects of sorting one of these files containing an avail list of deleted records. A *pinned record*, then, is one that cannot be moved. Other records in the same file or in some other file (such as an index file) contain references to the physical location of the record. If the record is moved, these references no longer lead to the record; they become what are called *dangling pointers*, pointers leading to incorrect, meaningless locations in the file.

Clearly the use of pinned records in a file can make sorting more difficult and sometimes impossible. But what if we want to support rapid access by key, while still reusing the space made available by record deletion? One solution is to use an index file to keep the sorted order of the records, while keeping the actual data file in its original order. Once again, the problem of finding things leads to the suggestion that we need to take a close look at the use of indexes, which, in turn, leads us to the next chapter.

SUMMARY

The primary problem addressed in this chapter is finding things quickly in a file through the use of a key. In preceding chapters it was not possible to access a record rapidly without knowing its physical location or relative record number. The present chapter explores some of the problems and opportunities associated with keyed direct access.

   This chapter actually develops only one method of finding records by key—*binary searching*. Binary searching requires $O(\log n)$ comparisons to find a record in a file with n records, and hence is far superior to sequential searching. The main work of this chapter is associated with functions and operations required to support binary searching of a file.

   Since binary searching works only on a sorted file, a sorting procedure is an absolute necessity. The problem of sorting is complicated by three factors:

- We want to sort the file on the basis of the canonically formed keys corresponding to each record, rather than on the actual contents of the records themselves.
- We want the sort to run quickly, which implies that we do *not* want to perform a lot of physical movement of data. More specifically, we do not want to be moving and copying entire key fields.
- We are sorting files on secondary storage rather than vectors in RAM. We need to develop a sorting procedure that does not require seeking back and forth over the file.

   Our RAM sort program responds to all three of these requirements. It does so by using *indirection*. We read in the records from the file sequentially into an array, forming at the same time a vector of keys that are related by their position to the record images. We also form a vector of subscripts related to positions within the vector of keys. Although the sorting is by key, the vector that is rearranged is the vector of subscripts. We use Shell's sort to do the actual sorting work.

   At this point in the chapter we have solved the initial problem of organizing and searching a file so that we can find a record with a specific primary key without having to do a sequential search. The next step is to evaluate what we have done. Three disadvantages are associated with sorting and binary searching as developed up to this point in the chapter:

- Although binary searching is an enormous improvement over sequential searching, the fact remains that, even with files containing just a few thousand records, we would be accessing the disk a dozen or more times. We would much rather have a method that requires only one, or at most, three or four disk accesses per record. This need for fewer disk accesses per record becomes especially acute in applications where a large number of records are to be accessed by key.
- The requirement that the file be kept in sorted order is an expensive one. For active files to which records are added as frequently as they are accessed, the cost of keeping the file in sorted order can outweigh the benefits of binary searching.
- The RAM sort can be used only on relatively small files, since the entire file must be held in memory. This limits the size of the files that we could organize for binary searching, given our sorting tools.

The third problem can be solved partially by developing more powerful sorting procedures, such as the method known as a *keysort*. This approach to sorting resembles our RAM sort in most respects, but does not use RAM to hold the entire file. Instead, it reads in only the *keys* from the records, and then sorts the keys. The keysort then uses the sorted list of keys to rearrange the records on secondary storage so that they are in sorted order.

The disadvantage to a keysort is that rearranging a file of *n* records requires *n* random seeks out to the original file. Such seeking can take much more time than does a sequential reading of the same number of records. The inquiry into keysorting is not a wasted effort, however. Keysorting *is* a simple, easy-to-implement way to sort many files that are too large to fit into memory. Perhaps more importantly, it naturally leads to the suggestion that we merely write the sorted list of keys off on to secondary storage, setting aside the expensive matter of rearranging the file. This list of keys, coupled with RRN tags pointing back to the original records, is an example of an index. Indexing is a topic we look at much more closely in Chapter 7.

Chapter 6 closes with a discussion of another, potentially hidden, cost of sorting and searching. Pinned records are records that are referenced elsewhere (in the same file or in some other file) according to their physical position in the file. Sorting and binary searching cannot be applied to a file containing pinned records, since the sorting, by definition, is likely to change the physical position of the record. Such a change causes other references to this record to become inaccurate, creating the problem of dangling pointers.

KEY TERMS

Binary search. A binary search algorithm locates a key in a sorted list by repeatedly selecting the middle element of the list, dividing the list in half, and forming a new, smaller list from the half that contains the key. This process is continued until the selected element is the key that is sought.

Indirection. A term that describes the process of referencing things indirectly through the use of a series of pointers or other kinds of locators. The method used in *ramsort* in this chapter provides a small study in indirection, since the actual rearrangement is done on a vector of subscripts into an array containing canonical keys. The elements of this key array, in turn, are related through position to the records that, ultimately, are the objects of the sort. The power of indirection as a general tool for making problems more tractable becomes even more evident as we talk about indexing in later chapters.

Keysort. A method of sorting a file that does not require holding the entire file in memory. Only the keys are held in memory, along with pointers that tie these keys to the records in the file from which they are extracted. The keys are sorted, and the sorted list of keys is used to construct a new version of the file that has the records in sorted order. The primary advantage of a keysort is that it requires less RAM than does a RAM sort. The disadvantage is that the process of constructing a new file requires a lot of seeking for records.

Pinned record. A record is pinned when there are other records or file structures that refer to it by its physical location. It is *pinned* in the sense that we are not free to alter the physical location of the record; doing so destroys the validity of the physical references to the record. These references become useless dangling pointers.

Shell's sort. Shell's sort is a relatively fast internal sorting algorithm that sorts a list by first ordering widely separated elements, followed by successive passes over the list that order elements that are separated by smaller and smaller intervals. We used it to perform the in-RAM portions of the sorts developed in this chapter.

EXERCISES

1. Compare the average case performance of binary search with sequential search for records, assuming:
  a) That the records being sought are guaranteed to be in the file;
  b) That half of the time the records being sought are not in the file; and
  c) That half of the time the records being sought are not in the file and that missing records must be inserted.
Make a table showing your performance comparisons for files of 1,000, 2,000, 4,000, 8,000, and 16,000 records.

2. If the records in Problem 1 are blocked with 20 records per block, how does this affect the performance of the binary and sequential searches?

3. The sort used in *ramsort* does not sort the data file. Instead, it sorts an array of keys in canonical form. Suppose the keys in the data records are already in canonical form and are stored in the first field of the RECORDS[] array. Why would this eliminate the need for the array of keynodes? How would *ramsort* have to be changed to bypass the use of the array of keynodes? What savings would be incurred if this approach could be used?

4. The *ramsort* program works only with files small enough to fit in RAM. Some computing systems provide users with an almost unlimited amount of RAM with a memory management technique called *virtual storage*. Discuss the use of *ramsort* to sort large files on systems that use virtual storage.

5. Our discussion of keysorting covers the considerable expense associated with the process of actually creating the sorted output file, given the sorted vector of pointers to the canonical key nodes. The expense revolves around two primary areas of difficulty:

- Having to jump around in the input file, performing many seeks to retrieve the records in their new, sorted order; and
- Writing the output file at the same time we are reading the input file; jumping back and forth between the files can involve seeking.

Design an approach to this problem that uses buffers to hold a number of records, therefore mitigating these difficulties. If your solution is to be viable, obviously the buffers must use less RAM than would a sort taking place entirely within electronic memory.

PROGRAMMING EXERCISES

6. Implement the *bin_search()* function in either C or Pascal. Write a driver program named *search* to test the function *bin_search()*. Assume the files are created with the *update* program developed in Chapter 4, and then sorted with the *ramsort* program provided at the end of this chapter. Include enough debug information in the *search* driver and *bin_search()* function to watch the binary searching logic as it makes successive guesses about where to place the new record.

7. Modify the *bin_search()* function so that, if the key is not in the file, it returns the relative record number that the key *would* occupy, were it in the file. The function should also continue to indicate whether the key was found or not.

8. Rewrite the *search* driver from Problem 6 so that it uses the new *bin_search()* function developed in Problem 7. If the sought-after key is in the file, the program should display the record contents. If the key is not found, the program should display a list of the keys that surround the position that the key would have occupied. You should be able to move backward or forward through this list at will. Given this modification, you do not have to remember an *entire* key to retrieve it. If, for example, you know that you are looking for someone named Smith, but cannot remember the person's first name, this new program lets you jump to the area where all the Smith records are stored. You can then scroll back and forth through the keys until you recognize the right first name.

9. Write a version of *ramsort* that can sort a *variable length record* file of the kind produced by the *writrec* programs in Chapter 4. Since *writrec* does not create a header record, the *ramsort* program must count the records as it reads them in. One side effect of this is that the C version of *ramsort* can no longer allocate all of the space for the arrays dynamically with a series of *calloc()* statements. Change the C version so that, as in the Pascal version, it fixes the size of the arrays at some maximum number of records.

FURTHER READINGS

This chapter only touches the surface of issues relating to searching and sorting files. A large part of the remainder of this book is devoted to exploring the issues in more detail, so one source for further reading is the present text. But there is much more that has been written about even the relatively simple issues raised in this chapter.

The classic reference on sorting and searching is Knuth [1973b]. Knuth provides an excellent discussion of the limitations of keysort methods. He also develops a very complete discussion of binary searching, clearly bringing out the analogy between binary searching and the use of binary trees.

Baase [1978] provides a clear, understandable analysis of binary search performance. She also explains the workings of Shell's sort. The version of Shell's sort we use closely mirrors the one developed by Baase.

C.A.R. Hoare presented a spoken address upon receiving the Turing award from the Association for Computing Machinery (ACM). In this address he recounts the development of Quicksort, which began as he was implementing Shell's sort. His remarks are very readable and interesting from perspectives that go far beyond sorting and searching. They are printed in the February 1981 *Communications of the ACM*.

C PROGRAMS

In this chapter we describe the structure of the *ramsort* program in detail. What follows is an implementation of *ramsort* in C. Some notes about this implementation:

☐ Functions *get_infile()*, *get_outfile()*, and *extract_key()* are static, local functions that should be included in the same file as the main routine for *ramsort*. The *shell_sort()* function is written in a way that allows it to be placed in a separate file for separate compilation.

☐ The *makekey()* and *get_fld()* functions are listed at the end of Chapter 4. The *get_fld()* function is part of a module called *getrf.c*. As before, *makekey()* must be linked with the functions *strtrim()* and *ucase()* that are included in the file *strfuncs.c*.

☐ Because the C language allows the programmer to be very flexible in choosing to work with either pointers or subscripts, it is relatively easy to allocate the RECORDS[], KEYNODES[], and INDEX[] arrays *dynamically*. All we need to do is use the *calloc()* function to request the right amount of space, and then *cast* the resulting address to the correct pointer type. The use of a *cast* operator is absolutely necessary so that the transition between, for example, RECORDS[0] and RECORDS[1] is a jump of one entire record rather than a jump of a single byte.

☐ The *shell_sort()* function makes use of a macro titled KEY_FLD() to simplify the referencing of the KEYNODES[] array through the subscripts contained in INDEX[].

```
/* ramsort.c ...
        Prompts for an input file in the fixed record format created
        by update.c and prompts for the name of an output file.
        Sorts the records in the input file and writes them to the
        output file.  Preserves the header records at the beginning of
        the file.

        This sort takes place in RAM. In this C version, RAM space
        is allocated dynamically.  The size of the file that can be
        sorted is limited by the amount of RAM available.
*/
#include "fileio.h"
#define   REC_LGTH      64
```

(continued)

```
typedef char KEYNODE [30];
typedef char DATAREC [REC_LGTH + 1];
static struct {
        short   rec_count;
        char    fill[30];
} head;

main ()
{
        int in_fd,out_fd,i,rec_count;
        char *calloc();
        DATAREC *records;       /* address of array of records    */
        KEYNODE *keynodes;      /* address of keynodes array      */
        short   *index;         /* address of index array         */

        in_fd = get_infile();   /* open input file    */
        out_fd = get_outfile(); /* create output file */

        if (in_fd<0 || out_fd<0)  /* quit if open or create failed */
        {
            printf("program stopped\n");
            exit(1);
        }
        rec_count = head.rec_count;  /* convert record count to
                                        int for use in calloc()    */

        /* allocate memory for the entire file, for the array of key
           nodes, and for the index array of key node subscripts   */
        records  = (DATAREC *)  calloc(rec_count,sizeof(DATAREC));
        keynodes = (KEYNODE *)  calloc(rec_count,sizeof(KEYNODE));
        index    = (short *)    calloc(rec_count,sizeof(short));

        /* check to see that all the allocations succeeded          */
        if (records == 0L || keynodes == 0L || index == 0L) {
            printf ("Could not allocate the requested space\n");
            printf ("File may be too large to sort in memory\n");
            exit(1);
        }

        /* read in the records sequentially, placing them in the
           records[] array.  Extract keys and assign index[] values
           as we go                                                 */
        for (i = 0; i < rec_count; i++) {
            read(in_fd, records[i], REC_LGTH);
            extract_key(keynodes[i], records[i]);
            index[i] = i;
        }

        shell_sort(index, keynodes, rec_count);
```

```
        /* write out the records in the order of the subscripts in
            the now sorted index[] array                            */
        for (i = 0; i < rec_count; i++)
            write(out_fd, records[index[i]], REC_LGTH);

        close(in_fd);
        close(out_fd);
}


/* get_infile()...
        gets the name of the input file, tries to open it,
        and, if successful, reads the header record into head
*/
static get_infile() {
        char    filename[30];
        int     fd;

        printf("Enter the name of the file to be sorted: ");
        gets(filename);
        if (( fd = open(filename, READWRITE)) < 0)   /* OPEN fails? */
            printf ("The file %s cannot be opened\n",filename);
        else
            read(fd,&head,sizeof(head));

        return(fd);
}


/* get_outfile()...
        gets the name of the output file, creates it, and writes
        out the header record that was read in during get_infile.
*/
static get_outfile() {
        char    filename[30];
        int     fd;

        printf("Enter the name of the output file: ");
        gets(filename);

        if ((fd = creat(filename, PMODE)) < 0)    /* CREAT fails?    */
            printf ("The file %s cannot be created\n",filename);
        else
            write(fd,&head,sizeof(head));

        return(fd);
}
```

(continued)

```
/* extract_key(key, record) ...
        extract last and first names from first two fields in
        "record" and store in "key" in canonical form.
*/
static extract_key(key, record)
        DATAREC record;
        char key[];
{
        int scan_pos;
        char first[30], last[30];

        scan_pos = 0;
        scan_pos = get_fld(last, record, scan_pos, REC_LGTH);
        scan_pos = get_fld(first, record, scan_pos, REC_LGTH);
        makekey(last, first, key);
}


/* shell_sort(index, keynodes, n) ...
        index[] is an array of subscripts into the keynodes[] array,
        which contains keys in canonical form.  Both arrays contain
        n valid elements.  This function uses Shell's sort to order
        the subscripts in the index[] array so that they reference
        the keys in keynodes[] in sorted order by key
*/

#define KEY_FLD(i)   keynodes[index[(i)]]
typedef char KEYNODE [30];

shell_sort(index,keynodes,n)
        short index[];
        KEYNODE keynodes[];
        int n;
{
        int gap,i,j;
        char *ins_key;
        short ins_subscr;

        for (gap = n >> 1; gap > 0; gap >>= 1)
        {
            /* begin insertion sort for this gap */
            for (j = gap; j < n; j++)
            {
                ins_key = KEY_FLD(j);
                ins_subscr = index[j];

                /* work backwards looking for the insertion location */
                for (i = j - gap; i >= 0; i -= gap)
                {
                    if (strcmp(KEY_FLD(i),ins_key) <=0)
                        break;
                    index[i + gap] = index[i];
                }
                index[i + gap] = ins_subscr;
            }
        }
}
```

202

PASCAL PROGRAMS

In this chapter we describe the structure of the *ramsort* program in detail. What follows is an implementation of *ramsort* in Pascal. Some notes about this implementation:

□   As before, this is a Turbo Pascal implementation. We use the {$B −} compiler option and our own *strng* type to come closer to conforming to standard Pascal. See the comments associated with earlier Pascal programs at the ends of Chapters 2 and 4 for more details about the variations between these programs, standard Pascal, and typical Turbo Pascal usage.

□   We use the {$I tools.prc }, {$I get.prc }, and {$I stod.prc } compiler directives to include a number of procedures that are defined elsewhere. File *tools.prc* contains the functions required to perform basic operations on variables of type *strng* (see Appendix B); *get.prc* contains the *get_fld()* function (see programs at the end of Chapter 4); *stod.prc* contains the *stod()* function which transfers characters from a *strng* variable to a DATAREC record (see the programs at the end of Chapter 4).

□   In the C implementation it is easy to allocate the required arrays dynamically, requesting exactly as much RAM as is necessary, given the number of records to be sorted. Although Pascal supports dynamic allocation, Pascal does its dynamic allocation one record at a time. Thus we cannot work in terms of a contiguous, dynamically allocated array of records. Consequently, we allocate arrays of fixed size in this implementation.

```
PROGRAM ramsort (INPUT,OUTPUT);

{ Prompts for an input file in the fixed record format created by
  update.pas and prompts for the name of an output file.  Sorts the
  records in the input file and writes them to the output file.
  Preserves the header records at the beginning of the file.

  This sort takes place in RAM.  In this Pascal version, a fixed,
  predetermined amount of RAM is allocated for the arrays.  The
  number of records that can be sorted is indicated by the constant
  MAX_REC_CNT.
```

(continued)

```
}
{$B-}
CONST
    REC_LGTH = 64;
    MAX_REC_CNT = 100;
    MAX_REC_SIZE = 255;
    DELIM_CHR = '¦';

TYPE
    DATAREC   = RECORD
                    len : integer;
                    data : packed array [1..REC_LGTH] of char
                    END;
    fixed_rec_file = file of DATAREC;
    fname  = packed array [1..40] of char;
    strng  = packed array [0..REC_LGTH] of char;
    KEYREC = strng;
    INDEX_ARRAY    = packed array [1..MAX_REC_CNT] of integer;
    KEYNODE_ARRAY  = packed array [1..MAX_REC_CNT] of KEYREC;
    RECORD_ARRAY   = packed array [1..MAX_REC_CNT] of DATAREC;


VAR
    in_fd     : fixed_rec_file;
    out_fd    : fixed_rec_file;
    head      : DATAREC;
    rec_count : integer;
    i         : integer;
    index     : INDEX_ARRAY;
    keynodes  : KEYNODE_ARRAY;
    records   : RECORD_ARRAY;
    strbuff   : strng;
    drecbuff  : DATAREC;
    key       : strng;

{$I tools.prc }
{$I get.prc   }
{$I stod.prc  }


PROCEDURE get_infile(VAR in_file: fixed_rec_file);

{ get_infile gets the name of the input file,
  resets the file and reads the header record into head  }

VAR
    filename : fname;
BEGIN
    write('Enter the name of the file to be sorted: ');
    readln(filename);
```

```
      assign(in_file,filename);
      reset(in_file);
      read(in_file,head)
END;  { get_infile }


PROCEDURE  get_outfile(VAR out_file: fixed_rec_file);

{ get_outfile gets the name of the output file, sets
  the file into rewrite mode, and writes out the header
  record that was read in during get_infile.}

VAR
      filename : fname;
      i        : integer;
BEGIN
      write('Enter the name of output file: ');
      readln(filename);
      assign(out_file,filename);
      rewrite(out_file);
      write(out_file,head)
END; { get_outfile }


PROCEDURE read_rec (VAR fd : fixed_rec_file; VAR strbuff : strng);

{ read_rec reads a record from file fd into the record buffer
  and converts the buffer contents to a variable of type strng }

VAR
      drecbuff  : datarec;
      i         : integer;
BEGIN
      read(fd,drecbuff);

      strbuff[0] := CHR(drecbuff.len);
      for i := 1 to drecbuff.len DO
          strbuff[i] := drecbuff.data[i]
END; { read_rec }


PROCEDURE extract_key (VAR key: strng; strbuff : strng);

{ extract last and first names from first two fields in string buffer
  and store in key in canonical form. }

VAR
      scan_pos  : integer;
      last      : strng;
      first     : strng;
```

(continued)

```
BEGIN
    scan_pos := 0;
    scan_pos := get_fld(last,strbuff,scan_pos,REC_LGTH);
    scan_pos := get_fld(first,strbuff,scan_pos,REC_LGTH);
    makekey(last,first,key)
END; { extract_key }


PROCEDURE shell_sort(VAR index: INDEX_ARRAY; keynodes: KEYNODE_ARRAY;
                     n: integer);
{ index[] is an array of subscripts into the keynodes[] array, which
  contains keys in canonical form.  Both arrays contain n valid
  elements.  This function uses Shell's sort to order the subscripts
  in the index[] array so that they reference the keys in the
  keynodes[] in sorted order by key. }

VAR
    gap         : integer;
    i,j         : integer;
    ins_subscr  : integer;
    ins_key     : strng;
BEGIN
    gap := n div 2;
    while gap > 0 DO
        BEGIN                        { begin insertion sort for this gap }
        for j := (gap + 1) to n DO
            BEGIN
            ins_key := keynodes[index[j]];
            ins_subscr := index[j];

            { work backwards looking for the insertion location }
            i := j - gap;
            while (i>0) and (cmp_str(keynodes[index[i]],ins_key)>0) DO
                BEGIN
                index[i + gap] := index[i];
                i := i - gap
                END;
            index[i + gap] := ins_subscr
            END;
        gap := gap div 2
        END
END;  { shell_sort }


BEGIN { main }
    get_infile(in_fd);              { open input file              }
    get_outfile(out_fd);            { create output file           }
    rec_count := head.len;          { read record count from header }
```

```
{ read in the records sequentially, placing them in the records[]
  array.  Extract keys and assign index[] values as we go }
for i := 1 to rec_count DO
    BEGIN
    read_rec(in_fd,strbuff);
    stod(records[i],strbuff);
    extract_key(keynodes[i], strbuff);
    index[i] := i
    END;

shell_sort(index, keynodes, rec_count);

{ write out the records in the order of the subscripts in the
  now sorted index[] array }
for i := 1 to rec_count DO
    write(out_fd,records[index[i]]);

close(in_fd);
close(out_fd)
END.
```

7

INDEXING

CHAPTER OUTLINE

7.1
WHAT IS AN INDEX?

The last few pages of many books contain an index. Such an index is a table containing a list of topics (keys) and numbers of pages where the topics can be found (reference fields).

All indexes are based on the same basic concept—keys and reference fields. The types of indexes we examine in this chapter are called *simple indexes* because they are represented using *simple arrays* of structures that contain the keys and reference fields. In later chapters we look at indexing schemes that use more complex data structures, especially trees. In this chapter, however, we want to emphasize that indexes can be very simple and still provide powerful tools for file processing.

The index to a book provides a way to find a topic quickly. If you have ever had to use a book without a good index, you already know that an index is a desirable alternative to scanning through the book sequentially to find a topic. In general, indexing is another way to handle the problem that we explored in Chapter 6: An index is a way to find things.

Consider what would happen if we tried to apply the previous chapter's methods, sorting and binary searching, to the problem of finding things in a book. Rearranging all the words in the book so that they were in alphabetical order certainly would make finding any particular term easier, but would obviously have disastrous effects on the meaning of the book. In a sense, the terms in the book are pinned records. This is an absurd example, but clearly underscores the power and importance of the index as a conceptual tool. Since it works by indirection, *an index lets you impose order on a file without actually rearranging the file.* This not only keeps us from disturbing pinned records, but also makes matters such as record addition much less expensive than they are with a sorted file.

Take, as another example, the problem of finding books in a library. We want to be able to locate books by a specific author, by their title, or by subject area. One way of achieving this is to have three copies of each book and three separate library buildings. All of the books in one building would be sorted by author's name, another building would contain books arranged by title, and the third would have them ordered by subject. Again, this is an absurd example, but one that underscores another important advantage of indexing. Instead of using multiple arrangements, a library uses a card catalog. The card catalog is actually a set of three indexes, each using a different *key field*; and all of them using the same catalog number as a *reference field*. Another use of indexing, then, is to provide *multiple access paths* to a file.

We also find that indexing gives us *keyed access to variable length record files.* Let's begin our discussion of indexing by exploring this problem of access to variable length records and the simple solution that indexing provides.

7.2 A SIMPLE INDEX WITH AN ENTRY SEQUENCED FILE

Suppose we own an extensive collection of musical recordings and we want to keep track of the collection through the use of computer files. For each recording we keep the information shown in Fig. 7.1. The data file records are variable length. Figure 7.2 illustrates such a collection of data records. We refer to this data record file as *Datafile.*

Identification number

Title

Composer or composers

Artist or artists

Label (publisher)

FIGURE 7.1 ▪ Contents of a data record.

Rec. addr.	Label	ID number	Title	Composer(s)	Artist(s)
32†	LON	2312	Romeo and Juliet	Prokofiev	Maazel
77	RCA	2626	Quartet in C Sharp Minor	Beethoven	Julliard
132	WAR	23699	Touchstone	Corea	Corea
167	ANG	3795	Symphony No. 9	Beethoven	Giulini
211	COL	38358	Nebraska	Springsteen	Springsteen
256	DG	18807	Symphony No. 9	Beethoven	Karajan
300	MER	75016	Coq d'or Suite	Rimsky-Korsakov	Leinsdorf
353	COL	31809	Symphony No. 9	Dvorak	Bernstein
396	DG	139201	Violin Concerto	Beethoven	Ferras
442	FF	245	Good News	Sweet Honey in the Rock	Sweet Honey in the Rock

†Assume there is a header record that uses the first 32 bytes.

FIGURE 7.2 ▪ **Sample contents of *Datafile*.**

There are a number of approaches that could be used to create a variable length record file to hold these records; the record addresses used in Fig. 7.2 suggest that each record be preceded by a size field that permits skip sequential access and easier file maintenance. This is the structure we use.

Suppose we formed a *primary key* for these records consisting of the initials for the record company label combined with the record company's ID number. This will make a good primary key since it should provide a *unique* key for each entry in the file. We call this key the *Label ID*. The canonical form for the Label ID consists of the uppercase form of the Label field followed immediately by the ASCII representation of the ID number. For example,

LON2312

How could we organize the file to provide rapid keyed access to individual records? Could we sort the file, then use binary searching? Unfortunately, binary searching depends on being able to jump to the middle record in the file. This is not possible in a variable length record file because direct access by relative record number is not possible— there is no way to know where the middle record is in any group of records.

An alternative to sorting is to construct an index for the file. Figure 7.3 illustrates such an index. On the right is the data file containing information about our collection of recordings, with one variable length data record per recording. Only four fields are shown (Label, ID number, Title, and Composer), but it is easy to imagine the other information filling out each record.

On the left is the index file, each record of which contains a twelve-character *key* (left justified, blank filled) corresponding to a certain Label ID in the data file. Each key is associated with a *reference field* giving the address of the first byte of the corresponding data record. ANG3795, for example, corresponds to the reference field containing the number 167, meaning that the record containing full information on the recording with Label ID ANG3795 can be found starting at byte number 167 in the record file.

The structure of the index file is very simple. It is a fixed length record file in which each record has two fixed length fields: a key field and a byte-offset field. There is one record in the index file for every record in the data file.

Note also that the index is sorted, whereas the data file is not. Consequently, although Label ID ANG3795 is the first entry in the index, it is not necessarily the first entry in the data file. In fact, the data file is *entry sequenced,* which means that the records occur in the order that

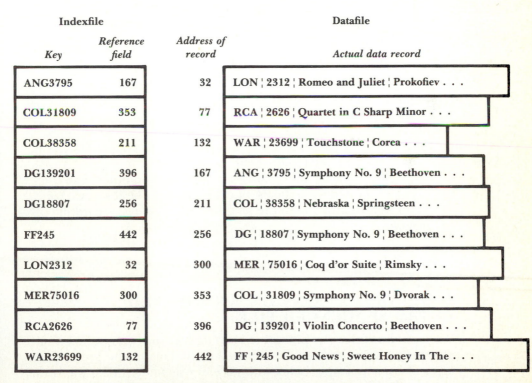

| Indexfile | | Datafile | |
Key	Reference field	Address of record	Actual data record
ANG3795	167	32	LON ¦ 2312 ¦ Romeo and Juliet ¦ Prokofiev . . .
COL31809	353	77	RCA ¦ 2626 ¦ Quartet in C Sharp Minor . . .
COL38358	211	132	WAR ¦ 23699 ¦ Touchstone ¦ Corea . . .
DG139201	396	167	ANG ¦ 3795 ¦ Symphony No. 9 ¦ Beethoven . . .
DG18807	256	211	COL ¦ 38358 ¦ Nebraska ¦ Springsteen . . .
FF245	442	256	DG ¦ 18807 ¦ Symphony No. 9 ¦ Beethoven . . .
LON2312	32	300	MER ¦ 75016 ¦ Coq d'or Suite ¦ Rimsky . . .
MER75016	300	353	COL ¦ 31809 ¦ Symphony No. 9 ¦ Dvorak . . .
RCA2626	77	396	DG ¦ 139201 ¦ Violin Concerto ¦ Beethoven . . .
WAR23699	132	442	FF ¦ 245 ¦ Good News ¦ Sweet Honey In The . . .

FIGURE 7.3 ▪ **Sample index with corresponding data file.**

```
PROCEDURE retrieve_record(KEY)

    find position of KEY in Indexfile  /* Probably using binary search */
    look up the BYTE_OFFSET of the corresponding record in Datafile
    use SEEK() and the byte_offset to move to the data record
    read the record from Datafile

end PROCEDURE
```

FIGURE 7.4 ▪ *Retrieve_record()*: **a procedure to retrieve a single record from** *Datafile* **through** *Indexfile*.

they are entered into the file. As we see soon, the use of an entry se-quenced file can make record addition and file maintenance much sim-pler than is the case with a data file that is kept sorted by some key.

Using the index to provide access to the data file by Label ID is a simple matter. The steps needed to retrieve a single record with key KEY from *Datafile* are shown in the procedure *retrieve_record()* in Fig. 7.4. Although this retrieval strategy is relatively straightforward, it contains some features that deserve comment:

☐ We are now dealing with two files—the index file and the data file. The index file is considerably easier to work with than the data file because it uses fixed length records (which is why we can search it with a binary search), and because it is likely to be much smaller than the data file.

☐ By requiring that the index file have fixed length records, we impose a limit on the sizes of our keys. In this example we assume that the primary key field is long enough to retain every key's unique identity. The use of a small, fixed key field in the index could cause problems if a key's uniqueness is truncated away as it is placed in the fixed index field.

☐ In the example, the index carries no information other than the keys and the reference fields, but this need not be the case. We could, for example, keep the length of each *Datafile* record in *Indexfile*.

7.3
BASIC OPERATIONS ON AN INDEXED, ENTRY SEQUENCED FILE

We have noted that the process of keeping files sorted to permit binary searching for records can be very expensive. One of the great advan-tages of using a simple index with an entry-sequenced data file is that record addition can take place much more quickly than with a sorted data file as long as the index is small enough to be held entirely in memory. If the index record length is short, this is not a difficult condition to meet for small files consisting of no more than a few thousand records. For the moment our discussions assume that the condition is met and that the index is read from secondary storage into an array of structures called INDEX[]. Later we consider what should be done when the index is too large to fit into memory.

Keeping the index in memory as the program runs also lets us find records by key more quickly with an indexed file than with a sorted one since the binary searching can be performed entirely in memory. Once the byte offset for the data record is found, then a single seek is all that is required to retrieve the record. The use of a sorted data file, on the other hand, requires a seek for each step of the binary search.

The support and maintenance of an entry sequenced file coupled with a simple index requires the development of procedures to handle a number of different tasks. Besides the *retrieve_record()* algorithm described previously, other procedures used to find things by means of the index include the following:

☐   Create the original empty index and data files;
☐   Load the index file into memory before using it;
☐   Rewrite the index file from memory after using it;
☐   Add records to the data file and index;
☐   Delete records from the data file; and
☐   Update records in the data file.

CREATING THE FILES.   Both the index file and the data file are created as empty files, with header records and nothing else. This can be accomplished quite easily by creating the files and writing headers to both files.

LOADING THE INDEX INTO MEMORY.   We assume that the index file is small enough to fit into primary memory, so we define an array *INDEX[]* to hold the index records. Each array element has the structure of an index record. Loading the index file into memory, then, is simply a matter of reading in and saving the index header record, and then reading the records from the index file into the INDEX[] array. Since this will be a sequential read, and since the records are short, the procedure should be written so that it reads a large number of index records at once, rather than one record at a time. Do you understand why?

REWRITING THE INDEX FILE FROM MEMORY.   When processing of an indexed file is completed, it is necessary to rewrite INDEX[] back into the index file if the array has been changed in any way. In Fig. 7.5, the procedure *rewrite_index()* describes the steps for doing this:

```
PROCEDURE rewrite_index()

    check a status flag that tells whether the INDEX[] array
        has been changed in any way.

    if there were changes, then
        open the index file as a new empty file
        update the header record and rewrite the header
        write the index out to the newly created file

    close the index file

end PROCEDURE
```

FIGURE 7.5 ▪ The *rewrite_index()* procedure.

It is important to consider what happens if this rewriting of the index does not take place, or takes place incompletely. The fact is that programs do not always run to completion. A program designer needs to guard against power failures, against the operator turning the machine off at the wrong time, and other such disasters. One of the serious dangers associated with reading an index into memory and then writing it out when the program is over is that the copy of the index on disk will be out of date and incorrect if the program is interrupted. It is imperative that a program contain at least the following two safeguards to protect against this kind of error:

☐ There should be a mechanism that permits the program to know when the index is out of date. One possibility involves setting a status flag as soon as the copy of the index in memory is changed. This status flag could be written into the header record of the index file on disk as soon as the index is read into memory, and then subsequently cleared when the index is rewritten. All programs could check the status flag before using an index. If the flag is found to be set, then the program would know that the index is out of date.

☐ If a program detects that an index is out of date, the program must have access to a procedure that reconstructs the index from the data file. This should happen automatically, taking place before any attempt is made to use the index.

RECORD ADDITION. Adding a new record to the data file requires that we also add a record to the index file. Adding to the data file itself is easy. The exact procedure depends, of course, on the kind of variable length file organization being used. In any case, when we add a data record we should know the starting *byte_offset* of the file location at which we wrote the record. This information, along with the canonical form of the record's key, must be placed in the INDEX[] array.

Since the INDEX[] array is kept in sorted order by key, insertion of the new index record probably requires some rearrangement of the index. In a way, the situation is similar to the one we face as we add records to a sorted data file. We have to shift or slide all the records that have keys that come in order after the key of the record we are inserting. The shifting opens up a space for the new record. The big difference between the work we have to do on the index records and the work required for a sorted data file is that the INDEX[] array is contained *wholly in memory*. All of the index rearrangement can be done without any file access.

One troubling aspect of this otherwise straightforward procedure is the time it takes to shift the index records. In Chapter 6 we confront this same problem when we rearrange the vector of keys and pointers in the *ramsort* program. You will remember that we avoid actually moving the structures containing the keys by forming a vector of pointers to the structures containing the keys. We then rearrange the vector of pointers rather than the structures themselves. A similar mechanism can be implemented for the maintenance of our index file vector.

RECORD DELETION. In Chapter 5 we describe a number of approaches to deleting records in variable length record files that allow for the reuse of the space occupied by these records. These approaches are completely viable for our data file since, unlike a sorted data file, the records in this file need not be moved around to maintain an ordering on the file. This is one of the great advantages of an indexed file organization: We have rapid access to individual records by key without disturbing pinned records. In fact, the indexing itself pins all the records.

Of course, when we delete a record from the data file we must also delete the corresponding entry from our index file. Since the index is contained in an array during program execution, deleting the index record and shifting the other records to close up the space may not be an overly expensive operation. Once again, opportunities exist to make this file rearrangement go even more quickly by employing some additional indirection through the use of a vector of pointers to structures. Alternatively, we could simply mark the index record as deleted, just as we might mark the corresponding data record.

RECORD UPDATING. Record updating falls into two categories:

☐ *The update changes the value of the key field.* This kind of update can bring about a reordering of the index file as well as the data file.

Conceptually, the easiest way to think of this kind of change is as a deletion followed by an addition. This delete/add approach can be implemented while still providing the program user with the view that he or she is merely changing a record.

□ *The update does not affect the key field.* This second kind of update does not require rearrangement of the index file, but may well involve rearrangement of the data file. If the record size is unchanged or decreased by the update, the record can be written directly into its old space, but if the record size is increased by the update, a new slot for the record will have to be found. In the latter case the starting address of the rewritten record must replace the old address in the *byte_offset* field of the corresponding index record.

7.4 INDEXES THAT ARE TOO LARGE TO HOLD IN MEMORY

The methods we have been discussing, and, unfortunately, many of the advantages associated with them, are tied to the assumption that the index file is small enough to be loaded into memory in its entirety. If the index is too large for this approach to be practical, then index access and maintenance must be done on secondary storage. With simple indexes of the kind we have been discussing, accessing the index on a disk has the following disadvantages:

□ Binary searching of the index requires several seeks rather than taking place at electronic memory speeds. Binary searching of an index on secondary storage is not substantially faster than the binary searching of a sorted file.

□ Index rearrangement due to record addition or deletion requires shifting or sorting records on secondary storage. This is literally millions of times more expensive than the cost of these same operations when performed in electronic memory.

Although these problems are no worse than those associated with the use of any file that is sorted by key, they are severe enough to warrant the consideration of alternatives. Any time a simple index is too large to hold in memory, you should consider using:

□ A *hashed* organization if access speed is a top priority; or

□ A *tree-structured* index, such as a *B-tree*, if you need the flexibility of both keyed access and ordered, sequential access.

These alternative file organizations are discussed at length in the chapters that follow. But, before writing off the use of simple indexes on secondary storage altogether, we should note that they provide some important advantages over the use of a data file sorted by key even if the index cannot be held in memory:

☐ A simple index makes it possible to use a binary search to obtain keyed access to a record in a variable length record file. The index provides the service of associating a fixed length and therefore binary-searchable record with each variable length data record.

☐ If the index records are substantially smaller than the data file records, sorting and maintaining the index can be less expensive than would be sorting and maintaining the data file. This is simply a result of the fact that there is less information to move around in the index file.

☐ If there are pinned records in the data file, the use of an index lets us rearrange the keys without moving the data records.

There is another advantage associated with the use of simple indexes, one that we have not yet discussed. It, in itself, can be reason enough to use simple indexes even if they do not fit into memory. Remember the analogy between an index and a library card catalog? The card catalog provides multiple views or arrangements of the library's collection, even though there is only one set of books arranged in a single order. Similarly, we can use multiple indexes to provide multiple views of a data file.

7.5 INDEXING TO PROVIDE ACCESS BY MULTIPLE KEYS

One question that might very reasonably arise at this point is, "All this indexing business is pretty interesting, but who would ever want to find a record using a key such as COL38358? What I want is the *Nebraska* record by Bruce Springsteen."

Let's return to our analogy between our index and a library card catalog. Suppose we think of our primary key, the Label ID, as a kind of catalog number. Like the catalog number assigned to a book, we have taken care to make our Label ID unique. Now, in a library it is very unusual to begin by looking for a book with a particular catalog number (e.g., "I am looking for a book with catalog number QA331T5 1959."). Instead, one generally begins by looking for a book on a particular subject, with a particular title, or by a particular author (e.g., "I am looking for a book on functions," or "I am looking for *The Theory of Functions* by Titchmarsh."). Given the subject, author, or title, one looks in the card catalog to find the *primary key,* the catalog number.

Similarly, we could build a catalog for our record collection consisting of entries for album title, composer, and artist. These fields are *secondary key fields.* Just as the library catalog relates an author entry (secondary key) to a card catalog number (primary key), so can we build an index file that relates Composer to Label ID, as illustrated in Fig. 7.6.

Along with the similarities, there is an important difference between this kind of secondary key index and the card catalog in a library. In a library, once you have the catalog number you can usually go directly to the stacks to find the book since the books are arranged in order by catalog number. In other words, the books are sorted by primary key. The actual data records in our file, on the other hand, are *entry sequenced.* Consequently, after consulting the composer index to find the Label ID, you must consult one additional index, our primary

Composer index

Secondary key	Primary key
BEETHOVEN	ANG3795
BEETHOVEN	DG139201
BEETHOVEN	DG18807
BEETHOVEN	RCA2626
COREA	WAR23699
DVORAK	COL31809
PROKOFIEV	LON2312
RIMSKY-KORSAKOV	MER75016
SPRINGSTEEN	COL38358
SWEET HONEY IN THE R	FF245

FIGURE 7.6 ▪ Secondary key index organized by composer.

```
PROCEDURE search_on_secondary(KEY)

    search for KEY in the secondary index

    once the correct secondary index record is found, set LABEL_ID
        to the primary key value in the record's reference field

    call retrieve_record(LABEL_ID) to get the data record

end PROCEDURE
```

FIGURE 7.7 ▪ *Search_on_secondary*: **an algorithm to retrieve a single record from** *Datafile* **through a secondary key index.**

key index, to find the actual byte offset of the record that has this particular Label ID. The procedure is summarized in Fig. 7.7.

Clearly it is possible to relate secondary key references (e.g., Springsteen) directly to a byte offset (211) rather than to a primary key (COL38358). However, there are excellent reasons for postponing this binding of a secondary key to a specific address for as long as possible. These reasons become clear as we discuss the way that fundamental file operations such as record deletion and updating are affected by the use of secondary indexes.

RECORD ADDITION. When a secondary index is present, adding a record to the file means adding a record to the secondary index. The cost of doing this is very similar to the cost of adding a record to the primary index: Either records must be shifted or a vector of pointers to structures needs to be rearranged. As with primary indexes, the cost of doing this decreases greatly if the secondary index can be read into electronic memory and changed there.

Note that the key field in the secondary index file is stored in canonical form (all of the composers' names are capitalized), since this is the form that we want to use when we are consulting the secondary index. If we want to print out the name in normal, mixed upper- and lowercase form, we can pick up that form from the original data file. Also note that the secondary keys are held to a fixed length, which means that sometimes they are truncated. The definition of the canonical form should take this length restriction into account if searching the index is to work properly.

One important difference between a secondary index and a primary index is that a secondary index can contain duplicate keys. In the sample index illustrated in Fig. 7.6, there are four records with the key BEETHOVEN. Duplicate keys are, of course, grouped together.

Within this group, they should be ordered according to the values of the reference fields. In this example, that means placing them in order by Label ID. The reasons for this second level of ordering become clear a little later, as we discuss retrieval based on combinations of two or more secondary keys.

RECORD DELETION. Deleting a record usually implies removing all references to that record in the file system. So, removing a record from the data file would mean removing not only the corresponding record in the primary index, but also all of the records in the secondary indexes that refer to this primary index record. The problem with this is that secondary indexes, like the primary index, are maintained in sorted order by key. Consequently, deleting a record would involve rearranging the remaining records to close up the space left open by deletion.

This delete-all-references approach would indeed be advisable if the secondary index referenced the data file directly. If we did not delete the secondary key references, and if the secondary keys were associated with actual byte offsets in the data file, it could be difficult to tell when these references were no longer valid. This is another instance of the pinned-record problem. The reference fields associated with the secondary keys would be pointing to byte offsets that could, after deletion and subsequent space reuse in the data file, be associated with different data records.

But we have carefully avoided referencing actual addresses in the secondary key index. After we search to find the secondary key, we do another search, this time on primary key. Since the primary index *does* reflect changes due to record deletion, a search for the primary key of a record that has been deleted will fail, returning a record-not-found condition. In a sense, the updated primary key index acts as a kind of final check, protecting us from trying to retrieve records that no longer exist.

Consequently, one option that is open to us when we delete a record from the data file is to modify and rearrange only the primary key index. We could safely leave intact the references to the deleted record that exist in the secondary key indexes. Searches starting from a secondary key index that lead to a deleted record are caught when we consult the primary key index.

If there are a number of secondary key indexes, the savings that result from not having to rearrange all of these indexes when a record is deleted can be substantial. This is especially important when the secondary key indexes are kept on secondary storage. It is also important in an interactive system, where the user is waiting at a terminal for the deletion operation to complete.

There is, of course, a cost associated with this short cut: Deleted records take up space in the secondary index files. With a file system that undergoes few deletions, this is not usually a problem. With a somewhat more volatile file structure, it is possible to address the problem by periodically removing from the secondary index files all records that contain references that are no longer in the primary index. If a file system is so volatile that even periodic purging is not adequate, it is probably time to consider another index structure, such as a B-tree, which allows for deletion without having to rearrange a lot of records.

RECORD UPDATING.   In our discussion of record deletion we find that the primary key index serves as a kind of protective buffer, insulating the secondary indexes from changes in the data file. This insulation extends to record updating as well. If our secondary indexes contain references directly to byte offsets in the data file, then updates to the data file that result in changing a record's physical location in the file also require updating the secondary indexes. But, since we are confining such detailed information to the primary index, data file updates affect the secondary index only when they change either the primary or the secondary key. There are three possible situations:

☐ *Update Changes the Secondary Key*: If the secondary key is changed, then we may have to rearrange the secondary key index so that it stays in sorted order. This can be a relatively expensive operation.

☐ *Update Changes the Primary Key*: This kind of change has a large impact on the primary key index, but often requires only that we update the affected reference field (*Label_id* in our example) in all the secondary indexes. This involves searching the secondary indexes (on the unchanged secondary keys) and rewriting the affected fixed length field. It does not require reordering of the secondary indexes unless the corresponding secondary key occurs more than once in the index. If a secondary key does occur more than once, there may be some local reordering, since records having the same secondary key are ordered by the reference field (primary key).

☐ *Update Confined to Other Fields*: All updates that do not affect either the primary or secondary key fields do not affect the secondary key index, even if the update is substantial. Note that if there are several secondary key indexes associated with a file, updates to records often affect only a subset of the secondary indexes.

7.6

RETRIEVAL USING COMBINATIONS OF SECONDARY KEYS

One of the most important applications of secondary keys involves using two or more of them in combination to retrieve special subsets of records from the data file. To provide an example of how this can be done, we will extract another secondary key index from our file of recordings. This one uses the recording's *title* as the key, as illustrated in Fig. 7.8. Now we can respond to requests such as:

☐ Find the record with Label ID COL38358 (primary key access);

☐ Find all the recordings of Beethoven's work (secondary key—composer); and

☐ Find all the recordings titled "Violin Concerto" (secondary key—title).

What is more interesting, however, is that we can also respond to a request that *combines* retrieval on the composer index with retrieval on

Title index

Secondary key	Primary key
COQ D'OR SUITE	MER75016
GOOD NEWS	FF245
NEBRASKA	COL38358
QUARTET IN C SHARP M	RCA2626
ROMEO AND JULIET	LON2312
SYMPHONY NO. 9	ANG3795
SYMPHONY NO. 9	COL31809
SYMPHONY NO. 9	DG18807
TOUCHSTONE	WAR23699
VIOLIN CONCERTO	DG139201

FIGURE 7.8 ▪ Secondary key index organized by recording title.

the title index, such as: Find all recordings of Beethoven's Symphony No. 9. Without the use of secondary indexes, this kind of request requires a sequential search through the entire file. Given a file containing thousands, or even just hundreds of records, this is a very expensive process. But, with the aid of secondary indexes, responding to this request is simple and quick.

We begin by recognizing that this request can be rephrased as a *Boolean AND* operation, specifying the intersection of two subsets of the data file:

> *Find all data records with*:
> composer = "BEETHOVEN" AND title = "SYMPHONY NO. 9"

We begin our response to this request by searching the composer index for the list of Label IDs that identify records with Beethoven as the composer. (An exercise at the end of this chapter describes a binary search procedure that can be used for this kind of retrieval.) This yields the following list of Label IDs:

```
ANG3795
DG139201
DG18807
RCA2626
```

Next we search the title index for the Label IDs associated with records that have SYMPHONY NO. 9 as the title key:

```
ANG3795
COL31809
DG18807
```

Now we perform the Boolean AND, which is a match operation, combining the lists so that only the members that appear in *both* lists are placed in the output list.

Composers	Titles	Matched list
ANG3795	ANG3795	ANG3795
DG139201	COL31809	DG18807
DG18807	DG18807	RCA2626
RCA2626		

We give careful attention to algorithms for performing this kind of match operation in Chapter 8. Note that this kind of matching is much easier if the lists that are being combined are in sorted order. That is the reason why, when we have more than one entry for a given secondary key, the records are ordered by the primary key reference fields.

Finally, once we have the list of primary keys occurring in both lists, we can proceed to the primary key index to look up the addresses of the data file records. Then we can retrieve the records:

```
ANG ¦ 3795 ¦ Symphony No. 9 ¦ Beethoven ¦ Giulini
DG ¦ 18807 ¦ Symphony No. 9 ¦ Beethoven ¦ Karajan
```

This is the kind of operation that makes computer indexed file systems useful in a way that far exceeds the capabilities of manual systems. We have only one copy of each data file record, and yet, working through the secondary indexes, we have multiple views of these records: We can look at them in order by title, by composer, or by any other field that interests us. Using the computer's ability to combine sorted lists rapidly, we can even combine different views, retrieving *intersections* (Beethoven AND Symphony No. 9) or *unions* (Beethoven OR Prokofiev OR Symphony No. 9) of these views. And since our data file is entry sequenced, we can do all of this without having to sort data file records, confining our sorting to the smaller index records which can often be held in electronic memory.

Now that we have a general idea of the design and uses of secondary indexes, we can look at ways to improve these indexes so that they take less space and require less sorting.

7.7 IMPROVING THE SECONDARY INDEX STRUCTURE— INVERTED LISTS

The secondary index structures that we have developed so far result in two distinct difficulties:

☐ We have to rearrange the index file *every time* a new record is added to the file, even if the new record is for an existing secondary key. For example, if we add another recording of Beethoven's Symphony No. 9 to our collection, both the composer and title indexes would have to be rearranged, even though both indexes already contain entries for secondary keys (but not the Label IDs) that are being added.

☐ If there are duplicate secondary keys, the secondary key field is repeated for each entry. This wastes space, making the files larger than necessary. Larger index files are less likely to be able to fit in electronic memory.

7.7.1 A FIRST ATTEMPT AT A SOLUTION

One simple response to these difficulties is to change the secondary index structure so that it associates an *array* of references with each secondary key. For example, we might use a record structure that allows us to associate up to four Label ID reference fields with a single secondary key, as in:

BEETHOVEN	ANG3795	DG139201	DG18807	RCA2626

Figure 7.9 provides a schematic example of how such an index would look if used with our sample data file.

The major contribution of this revised index structure is toward the solution of our first difficulty: the need to rearrange the secondary index file every time a new record is added to the data file. Looking at Fig. 7.9, we can see that the addition of another recording of a work by Prokofiev does not require the addition of another record to the index. For example, if we add the recording

```
ANG   36193  Piano Concertos 3 and 5   Prokofiev   Francois
```

we need to modify only the corresponding secondary index record by inserting a second Label ID:

PROKOFIEV	ANG36193	LON2312

Revised composer index

Secondary key	*Set of primary key references*			
BEETHOVEN	ANG3795	DG139201	DG18807	RCA2626
COREA	WAR23699			
DVORAK	COL31809			
PROKOFIEV	LON2312			
RIMSKY-KORSAKOV	MER75016			
SPRINGSTEEN	COL38358			
SWEET HONEY IN THE R	FF245			

FIGURE 7.9 ▪ Secondary key index containing space for multiple references for each secondary key.

Since we are not adding another record to the secondary index, there is no need to rearrange any records. All that is required is a rearrangement of the fields in the existing record for Prokofiev.

Although this new structure helps avoid the need to rearrange the secondary index file so often, it does have some problems. For one thing, it provides space for only four Label IDs to be associated with a given key. In the very likely case that more than four Label IDs will go with some key, we need a mechanism for keeping track of the extra Label IDs.

A second problem has to do with space usage. Although the structure does help avoid the waste of space due to the repetition of identical keys, this space savings comes at a potentially high cost. By extending the fixed length of each of the secondary index records to hold more reference fields, we might easily lose more space to internal fragmentation than we gained by not repeating identical keys.

Since we don't want to waste any more space than we have to, we need to ask whether we can improve on this record structure. Ideally, what we would like to do is develop a new design, a revision of our revision, that

☐   Retains the attractive feature of not requiring reorganization of the secondary indexes for every new entry to the data file;
☐   Allows more than four Label IDs to be associated with each secondary key; and
☐   Does away with the waste of space due to internal fragmentation.

7.7.2 A BETTER SOLUTION: LINKING THE LIST OF REFERENCES

Files such as our secondary indexes, in which a secondary key leads to a set of one or more primary keys, are called *inverted lists*. The sense in which the list is inverted should be clear if you consider that we are working our way backward from a secondary key to the primary key to the record itself.

The second word in the term inverted list also tells us something important: that we are, in fact, dealing with a *list* of primary key references. Our revised secondary index, which collects together a number of Label IDs for each secondary key, reflects this list aspect of the data more directly than did our initial secondary index. Another way of conceiving of this list aspect of our inverted list is illustrated in Fig. 7.10.

As Fig. 7.10 shows, an ideal situation would be to have each secondary key point to a different list of primary key references. Each of these lists could grow to be just as long as it needs to be. If we add the

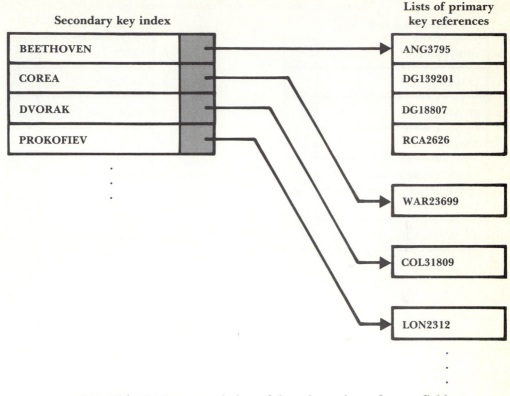

FIGURE 7.10 ▪ **Conceptual view of the primary key reference fields as a series of lists.**

new Prokofiev record the list of Prokofiev references becomes

Similarly, adding two new Beethoven recordings adds just two additional elements to the list of references associated with the Beethoven key. Unlike our record structure that allocates enough space for four Label IDs for each secondary key, the lists could contain hundreds of references, if needed, while still requiring only one instance of a secondary key. On the other hand, if a list requires only one element, then no space is lost to internal fragmentation. Most important of all, we need to rearrange only the file of secondary keys if a new composer is added to the file.

Improved revision of the composer index

Secondary Index file

0	BEETHOVEN	3
1	COREA	2
2	DVORAK	7
3	PROKOFIEV	10
4	RIMSKY-KORSAKOV	6
5	SPRINGSTEEN	4
6	SWEET HONEY IN THE R	9

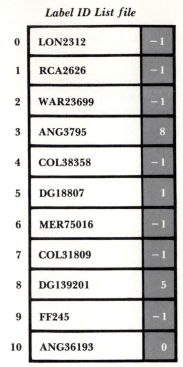

Label ID List file

0	LON2312	−1
1	RCA2626	−1
2	WAR23699	−1
3	ANG3795	8
4	COL38358	−1
5	DG18807	1
6	MER75016	−1
7	COL31809	−1
8	DG139201	5
9	FF245	−1
10	ANG36193	0

FIGURE 7.11 ▪ **Secondary key index referencing linked lists of primary key references**

How can we set up an unbounded number of different lists, each of varying length, without creating a large number of small files? The simplest way is through the use of linked lists. We could redefine our secondary index so that it consists of records with two fields—a secondary key field, and a field containing the relative record number of the first corresponding primary key reference (Label ID) in the inverted list. The actual primary key references associated with each secondary key would be stored in a separate, entry sequenced file.

Given the sample data we have been working with, this new design would result in a secondary key file for composers and an associated Label ID file that are organized as illustrated in Fig. 7.11. Following the links for the list of references associated with Beethoven helps us see how the Label ID List file is organized. We begin, of course, by searching the secondary key index of composers for Beethoven. The record that we find points us to relative record number (RRN) 3 in the Label ID List file. Since this is a fixed length file, it is easy to jump to RRN 3 and read in its Label ID (ANG3795). Associated with this Label ID is a link to a record with RRN 8. We read in the Label ID for that record, adding it to our list (ANG379 DG139201). We continue following links and collecting Label IDs until the list looks like this:

```
ANG3795      DG139201      DG18807      RCA2626
```

The link field in the last record read from the Label ID List file contains a value of −1. As in our earlier programs, this indicates end of list, so we know that we now have all the Label ID references for Beethoven records.

To illustrate how record addition affects the Secondary Index and Label ID List files, we add the Prokoviev recording mentioned earlier:

```
ANG    36193  Piano Concertos 3 and 5   Prokofiev   Francois
```

You can see (Fig. 7.11) that the Label ID for this new recording is the last one in the Label ID List file, since this file is entry sequenced. Before this record is added, there is only one Prokofiev recording. It has a Label ID of LON2312. Since we want to keep the Label ID Lists in order by ASCII character values, the new recording is inserted in the list for Prokofiev so that it logically precedes the LON2312 recording.

Associating the Secondary Index file with a new file containing linked lists of references provides some advantages over any of the structures considered up to this point:

- □ The only time we need to rearrange the Secondary Index file is when a new composer's name is added or an existing composer's name is changed (e.g., it was misspelled on input). Deleting or adding recordings for a composer who is already in the index involves changing only the Label ID List file. Deleting *all* the recordings for a composer could be handled by modifying the Label ID List file, while leaving the entry in the Secondary Index file in place, using a value of −1 in its reference field to indicate that the list of entries for this composer is empty.
- □ In the event that we do need to rearrange the Secondary Index file, the task is quicker now since there are fewer records and each record is smaller.
- □ Since there is less need for sorting, it follows that there is less of a penalty associated with keeping the Secondary Index files off on secondary storage, leaving more room in RAM for other data structures.
- □ The Label ID List file is entry sequenced. That means that it *never* needs to be sorted.
- □ Since the Label ID List file is a fixed length record file, it would be very easy to implement a mechanism for reusing the space from deleted records, as described in Chapter 5.

There is also at least one potentially significant disadvantage to this kind of file organization: the Label IDs associated with a given composer are no longer guaranteed to be physically grouped together. The technical term for such "togetherness" is *locality*; with a linked, entry sequenced structure such as this, it is less likely that there will be locality associated with the logical groupings of reference fields for a given secondary key. Note, for example, that our list of Label IDs for Prokofiev consists of the very last and the very first records in the file. This lack of locality means that picking up the references for a composer that has a long list of references could involve a large amount of *seeking* back and forth on the disk. Note that this kind of seeking would not be required for our original Secondary Index file structure.

One obvious antidote to this seeking problem is to keep the Label ID List file in memory. This could be expensive and impractical, given many secondary indexes, except for the interesting possibility of using the same Label ID List file to hold the lists for a number of Secondary Index files. Even if the file of reference lists were too large to hold in memory, it might be possible to obtain a performance improvement by holding only a part of the file in memory at a time, paging sections of the file in and out of memory as they are needed.

Several exercises at the end of the chapter explore these possibilities more thoroughly. These are very important problems, since the notion of dividing the index into pages is fundamental to the design of B-trees and other methods for handling large indexes on secondary storage.

7.8 ━━━ SELECTIVE INDEXES

Another interesting feature of secondary indexes is that they can be used to divide a file into parts, providing a selective view. For example, it is possible to build a *selective index* that contains only the titles of classical recordings in the record collection. If we have additional information about the recordings in the data file, such as the date the recording was released, we could build selective indexes such as "recordings released prior to 1970" and "recordings since 1970." Such selective index information could be combined into Boolean AND operations to respond to requests such as, "List all the recordings of Beethoven's Ninth Symphony released since 1970." Selective indexes are sometimes useful when the contents of a file fall naturally and logically into several broad categories.

7.9
BINDING

A recurrent and very important question that emerges in the design of file systems that utilize indexes is: *At what point in time is the key bound to the physical address of its associated record?*

In the file system we are designing in the course of this chapter, the *binding* of our primary keys to an address takes place *at the time the files are constructed*. The secondary keys, on the other hand, are bound to an address *at the time that they are actually used*.

Binding at the time of the file construction results in faster access. Once you have found the right index record, you have in hand the byte offset of the data record you are seeking. If we elected to bind our secondary keys to their associated records at the time of file construction, so that when we find the DVORAK record in the composer index we would know immediately that the data record begins at byte 353 in the data file, secondary key retrieval would be simpler and faster. The improvement in performance is particularly noticeable if both the primary and secondary index files are used on secondary storage rather than in memory. Given the arrangement we designed, we would have to perform a binary search of the composer index and then a binary search of the primary key index before being able to jump to the data record. Binding early, at file construction time, does away entirely with the need to search on the primary key.

The disadvantage of binding directly in the file, of *binding tightly,* is that reorganizations of the data file must result in modifications to all bound index files. This reorganization cost can be very expensive, particularly with simple index files in which modification would often mean shifting records. By postponing binding until execution time, when the records are actually being used, we are able to develop a secondary key system that involves a minimal amount of reorganization when records are added or deleted.

Another important advantage of postponing binding until a record is actually retrieved is that this approach is safer. As we see in the system that we set up, associating the secondary keys with reference fields consisting of primary keys allows the primary key index to act as a kind of final check of whether a record is really in the file. The secondary indexes can afford to be wrong. This situation is very different if the secondary index keys are tightly bound, containing addresses. We would then be jumping directly from the secondary key into the data file; the address would need to be right.

This brings up a related safety aspect: It is always more desirable to have to make important changes in one place, rather than having to make them in many places. With a bind-at-retrieval-time scheme such as we developed, we need to remember to make a change in only one place, the primary key index, if we move a data record. With a more tightly bound system, we have to make many changes successfully to keep the system internally consistent, braving power failures, user interruptions, and so on.

When designing a new file system, it is better to deal with this question of binding *intentionally* and *early* in the design process, rather than letting the binding just happen. In general, tight, in-the-data binding is most attractive when:

☐ The data file is static or nearly so, requiring little or no adding, deleting, and updating of records; and
☐ Rapid performance during actual retrieval is a high priority.

For example, tight binding is desirable for file organization on a mass-produced, read-only optical disc. The addresses will never change since no new records can ever be added; consequently, there is no reason not to obtain the extra performance associated with tight binding.

For file applications in which record addition, deletion, and updating do occur, however, binding at retrieval time is usually the more desirable option. Postponing binding for as long as possible usually makes these operations simpler and safer. If the file structures are carefully designed, and, in particular, if the indexes use more sophisticated organizations such as B-trees, retrieval performance is usually quite acceptable, even given the additional work required by a bind-at-retrieval system.

SUMMARY

We began this chapter with the assertion that indexing is an alternative to sorting as a way of structuring a file so that records can be found *by key*. Unlike sorting, indexing permits us to perform *binary searches* for keys in variable length record files. If the index can be held in memory, record addition, deletion, and retrieval can be done much more quickly with an indexed, entry sequenced file than with a sorted file.

Indexes can do much more than merely improve on access time: they can provide us with new capabilities that are inconceivable with access methods based on sorted data records. The most exciting new capability involves the use of multiple secondary indexes. Just as a library card catalog allows us to regard a collection of books in author order, title order, or subject order, so index files allow us to maintain different views of the records in a data file. We find that we can not only use secondary indexes to obtain different views of the file, but that we can also combine the associated lists of primary key references and thereby combine particular views.

In this chapter we address the problem of how to rid our secondary indexes of two liabilities:

- The need to repeat duplicate secondary keys and;
- The need to rearrange the secondary indexes every time a record is added to the data file.

A first solution to these problems involves associating a fixed-size *vector* of reference fields with each secondary key. This solution results in an overly large amount of internal fragmentation, but serves to illustrate the attractiveness of handling the reference fields associated with a particular secondary key as a group, or *list*.

Our next iteration of solutions to our secondary index problems is more successful and much more interesting. We can treat the primary key references themselves as an entry sequenced file, forming the necessary lists through the use of *link fields* associated with each primary record entry. This allows us to create a secondary index file that, in the case of the composer index, needs rearrangement only when we add new composers to the data file. The entry sequenced file of linked reference lists never requires sorting. We call this kind of secondary index structure an *inverted list*.

There are also, of course, disadvantages associated with our new solution. The most serious disadvantage is that our file demonstrates less locality: Lists of associated records are less likely to be physically adjacent. A good antidote to this problem is to hold the file of linked lists in memory. We note that this is made more plausible because a single file of primary references can link the lists for a number of secondary indexes.

As indicated by the length and breadth of our consideration of secondary indexing, multiple keys, and inverted lists, these topics are among the most interesting aspects of indexed access to files. The concepts of secondary indexes and inverted lists become even more powerful later, as we develop index structures that are themselves more powerful than the simple indexes that we consider here. But, even so, we already see that for small files consisting of no more than a few thousand records, approaches to inverted lists that rely merely on simple indexes can provide a user with a great deal of capability and flexibility.

KEY TERMS

Binding. Binding takes place when a key is associated with a particular physical record in the data file. In general, binding can take place either during the preparation of the data file and indexes or during program execution. In the former case, which is called *tight binding,* the indexes contain explicit references to the associated physical data record. In the latter case the connection between a key and a particular physical record is postponed until the record is actually retrieved in the course of program execution.

Entry sequenced file. A file in which the records occur in the order that they are entered into the file.

Index. An index is a tool for finding records in a file. It consists of a *key field* on which the index is searched and a *reference field* that tells where to find the data file record associated with a particular key.

Inverted list. The term *inverted list* refers to indexes in which a key may be associated with a *list* of reference fields pointing to documents that contain the key. The secondary indexes developed toward the end of this chapter are examples of inverted lists.

Key field. The key field is the portion of an index record that contains the canonical form of the key that is being sought.

Locality. Locality exists in a file when records that will be accessed in a given temporal sequence are found in physical proximity to each other on the disk. Increased locality usually results in better performance, since records that are in the same physical area can often be brought into memory with a single *read* request to the disk.

Reference field. The reference field is the portion of an index record that contains information about where to find the data record containing the information listed in the associated key field of the index.

Selective index. A selective index contains keys for only a portion of the records in the data file. Such an index provides the user with a view of a specific subset of the file's records.

Simple index. All the index structures discussed in this chapter are simple indexes insofar as they are all built around the idea of an ordered, linear sequence of index records. All these simple indexes share a common weakness: Adding records to the index is expensive. As we see later, tree-structured indexes provide an alternate, more efficient solution to this problem.

EXERCISES

1. Until now, it was not possible to perform a binary search on a variable length record file. Why does indexing make binary search possible? With a fixed length record file it *is* possible to perform a binary search. Does this mean that indexing need not be used with fixed length record files?

2. Why is *title* not used as a primary key in the data file described in this chapter? If it were used as a secondary key, what problems would have to be considered in deciding on a canonical form for titles?

3. What is the purpose of keeping an out-of-date-status flag in the header record of an index? In a multiprogramming environment, this flag might be found to be set by one program because another program is in the process of reorganizing the index. How should the first program respond to this situation?

4. Explain how the use of an index pins the data records in a file.

5. When a record in a data file is updated, corresponding primary and secondary key indexes may or may not have to be altered, depending on whether the file has fixed or variable length records, and depending on the type of change made to the data record. Make a list of the different updating situations that can occur, and explain how each affects the indexes.

6. Discuss the problem that occurs when you add the following recording to the recordings file, assuming that the composer index shown in Fig. 7.9 is used. How might you solve the problem without substantially changing the secondary key index structure?

```
LON       1259       Fidelio       Beethoven       Maazel
```

7. What is an inverted list, and when is it useful?

8. How are the structures in Fig. 7.11 changed by the addition of the recording

```
LON       1259       Fidelio       Beethoven       Maazel
```

9. Suppose you have the data file described in this chapter, greatly expanded, with a primary key index and secondary key indexes organized by composer, artist, and title. Suppose that an inverted list structure is used to organize the secondary key indexes. Give step-by-step descriptions of how a program might answer the following queries:
  a) List all recordings of Bach or Beethoven; and
  b) List all recordings by Perleman of pieces by Mozart or Joplin.

10. One possible antidote to the problem of diminished locality when using inverted lists is to use the same Label ID List file to hold the lists for several of the secondary index files. This increases the likelihood that the secondary indexes can be kept in primary memory. Draw a diagram of a single Label ID List file that can be used to hold references for both the secondary index of composers and the secondary index of titles. How would you handle the difficulties that this arrangement presents with regard to maintaining the Label ID List file?

11. Discuss the following structures as antidotes to the possible loss of locality in a secondary key index.

- Leave space for multiple references for each secondary key (Fig. 7.9).
- Allocate variable length records for each secondary key value, where each record contains the secondary key value, followed by the Label IDs, followed by free space for later addition of new Label IDs. The amount of free space left could be fixed, or it could be a function of the size of the original list of Label IDs.

12. The method and timing of binding affect two important attributes of a file system—speed and flexibility. Discuss the relevance of these attributes, and the effect of binding time on them, for a hospital patient information system designed to provide information about current patients by patient name, patient ID, location, medication, doctor or doctors, and illness.

PROGRAMMING AND DESIGN EXERCISES

13. Implement the *retrieve_record()* procedure outlined in Fig. 7.4.

14. In solving the preceding problem you have to create a mechanism for deciding how many bytes to read from the *Datafile* for each record. At least four options are open to you:
a) Jump to the *byte_offset*, read the size field, then use this information to read the record.
b) Build an index file that contains a record size field that reflects the *true* size of the data record, including the size field carried in the *Datafile*. Use the size field carried in the index file to decide how many bytes to read.
c) Follow much the same strategy as in option (b), except use a *Datafile* that does not contain internal size fields.
d) Jump to the *byte_offset* and read a fixed, overly large number of bytes (e.g., 512 bytes). Once these bytes are read into a memory buffer, use the size field at the start of the buffer to decide how many bytes to break out of the buffer.

Evaluate each of these options, listing the advantages and disadvantages of each.

15. Implement procedures to read in and to write back the *INDEX[]* array to the index file.

16. When searching secondary indexes that contain multiple records for some of the keys, we do not want to find just *any* record for a given secondary key; we want to find the *first* record containing that key. Finding the first record allows us to read ahead, sequentially, extracting all of the records for the given key. Write a variation of a binary search function that returns the relative record number of the *first* record containing the given key. The function should return a negative value if the key cannot be found.

17. If a Label ID List file such as the one shown in Fig. 7.11 is too large to be held in memory in its entirety, it might still be possible to improve performance by retaining a number of blocks of the file in memory. These blocks are called *pages*. Since the records in the Label ID List file are each 16 bytes long, a page might consist of 32 records (512 bytes). Write a function that would hold the most-recently used eight pages in memory. Calls for a specific record from the Label ID List file would be routed through this function. It would check to see if the record exists in one of the pages that is already in memory. If so, the function would return the values of the record fields immediately. If not, the function would read in the page containing the desired record, either writing out or dumping the page that was used least recently. Clearly, if a page has been changed, it needs to be written out rather than dumped. When the program is over, all pages still in memory must be checked to see if they should be written out.

18. Assuming the use of a paged index as described in the preceding problem, and given that the Label ID List file is entry sequenced, is there any particular order of data entry (initial file loading) that tends to give better performance than other methods? How does the use of an organization method such as that described in Problem 10, which combines the linked lists from several secondary indexes into a single file, affect your answer about performance?

19. The Label ID List file is entry sequenced. Development of paging schemes is simpler for entry sequenced files than for files that are kept in sorted order. List the additional difficulties involved in the design of a paging system for a sorted index, such as the primary key index. Accepting the possibility that there will be a number of pages that are only partially full, design such a paging system. How will you handle the insertion of a new key when the page in which it belongs is full?

FURTHER READINGS

We have much more to say about indexing in later chapters, where we take up the subjects of tree-structured indexes and of indexed sequential file organizations. The topics developed in the current chapter, particularly those relating to secondary indexes and inverted files, are also covered by many other file and data structure texts. The few texts that we list here are of interest because they either develop certain topics in more detail or present the material from a different viewpoint.

Wiederhold [1983] provides a survey of many of the index structures we discuss, along with a number of others. His treatment is more mathematical than that provided in our text. Users interested in looking at indexed files in the context of PL/I and of large IBM mainframes will want to see Bradley [1981]. A brief, readable overview of a number of different file organizations is provided in J.D. Ullman [1980].

Tremblay and Sorenson [1984] provide a comparison of inverted list structures with an alternative organization called *multilist* files. M.E.S. Loomis [1983] provides a similar discussion, along with some examples oriented toward COBOL users. Salton and McGill [1983] discuss inverted lists in the context of their application in information retrieval systems.

CHAPTER

OBJECTIVES

Describe a class of frequently used processing activities known as *cosequential processes*.

Provide a general model for implementing all varieties of cosequential processes.

Illustrate the use of the model to solve a number of different kinds of cosequential processing problems, including problems other than simple merges and matches.

Show how cosequential merging provides the basis for sorting very large files.

Examine the costs of *K*-way merges on disk and find ways to reduce that cost.

Introduce the notion of *replacement selection*.

Examine some of the fundamental concerns associated with sorting large files using tapes rather than disks.

8

COSEQUENTIAL PROCESSING AND THE SORTING OF LARGE FILES

CHAPTER OUTLINE

Cosequential operations involve *the coordinated processing of two or more sequential lists to produce a single output list*. Sometimes the processing results in a *merging*, or *union* of the input lists, sometimes the goal is a *matching* or *intersection* of the lists, and other times the operation is a combination of matching and merging. These kinds of operations on sequential lists are the basis of a great deal of file processing.

In the first half of the chapter we develop a general model for doing cosequential operations, illustrate its use for simple matching and merging operations, then apply it to the development of a more complex general ledger program. Next we apply the model to multiway merging, which is an essential component of external sort-merge operations. We conclude the chapter with a discussion of sort-merge procedures, strategies, and trade-offs, paying special attention to performance considerations.

8.1
A MODEL FOR IMPLEMENTING COSEQUENTIAL PROCESSES

Cosequential operations usually appear to be simple to construct; given the information that we provide in this chapter, this appearance of simplicity can be turned into reality. However, it is also true that approaches to cosequential processing are often confused, poorly organized, and incorrect. These examples of bad practice are by no means limited to student programs; the problems also arise in commercial programs and in textbooks. The difficulty with these incorrect programs is usually that they are not organized around a single, clear model for cosequential processing. Instead, they seem to deal with the various exception conditions and problems in a cosequential process in an *ad hoc* rather than systematic way.

This section addresses such lack of organization head on. We present a single, simple model that can be the basis for the construction of any kind of cosequential process. By understanding and adhering to the design principles inherent in the model, you will be able to write cosequential procedures that are simple, short, and robust.

8.1.1 MATCHING NAMES IN TWO LISTS

Suppose we want to output the names common to the two lists shown in Fig. 8.1. This operation is usually called a *match operation,* or an *intersection.* We assume, for the moment, that we will not allow duplicate keys within a list, and that the lists are sorted in ascending order.

We begin by reading in the initial name from each list, and we find that they match. We output this first name as a member of the *match set,* or *intersection set.* We then read in the next name from each list. This time the name in List 2 is less than the name in List 1. When we are processing these lists visually, as we are now, we remember that we are trying to match the name CARTER from List 1, and scan down List 2 until we either find it or jump beyond it. In this case, we eventually find a match for CARTER, so we output it, read in the next name from each list, and continue the process. Eventually we come to the end of one of the lists. Since we are looking for names common to both lists, we know we can stop at this point.

Although the match procedure appears to be quite simple, there are a number of matters that have to be dealt with to make it work reasonably well.

List 1	List 2
ADAMS	ADAMS
CARTER	ANDERSON
CHIN	ANDREWS
DAVIS	BECH
FOSTER	BURNS
GARWICK	CARTER
JAMES	DAVIS
JOHNSON	DEMPSEY
KARNS	GRAY
LAMBERT	JAMES
MILLER	JOHNSON
PETERS	KATZ
RESTON	PETERS
ROSEWALD	ROSEWALD
TURNER	SCHMIDT
	THAYER
	WALKER
	WILLIS

FIGURE 8.1 ▪ **Sample input lists for cosequential operations.**

☐ *Initializing*: We need to arrange things in such a way that the procedure gets going properly.

☐ *Synchronizing*: We have to make sure that the current name from one list is never so far ahead of the current name on the other list that a match will be missed. Sometimes this means reading the next name from List 1, sometimes from List 2, sometimes from both lists.

☐ *Handling end-of-file conditions*: When we get to the end of either file 1 or file 2, we need to halt the program.

☐ *Recognizing errors*: When an error occurs in the data (e.g., duplicate names or names out of sequence) we want to detect it and take some action.

Finally, we would like our algorithm to be reasonably efficient, simple, and easy to alter to accommodate different kinds of data. The key to accomplishing these objectives in the model we are about to present lies in the way we deal with the second item in our list—synchronization.

At each step in the processing of the two lists we can assume that we have two names to compare: a *current name* from List 1 and a current name from List 2. Let's call these two current names NAME_1 and NAME_2. We can compare the two names to determine whether

NAME_1 is less than, equal to, or greater than NAME_2:

☐   If NAME_1 is *less than* NAME_2, we read the next name from
      List 1;
☐   If NAME_1 is *greater than* NAME_2, we read the next name from
      List 2; and
☐   If the names are the same, we output the name and read the next
      names from the two lists.

It turns out that this can be handled very cleanly with a single loop
containing one three-way conditional statement, as illustrated in the algorithm in Fig. 8.2. The key feature of this algorithm is that *control
always returns to the head of the main loop after every step of the operation.*
This means that no extra logic is required within the loop to handle the
case when List 1 gets ahead of List 2, or List 2 gets ahead of List 1, or
the end-of-file condition is reached on one list before it is on the other.

```
PROGRAM: match

        call initialize() procedure to:
            - open input files LIST_1 and LIST_2
            - create output file OUT_FILE
            - set MORE_NAMES_EXIST to TRUE
            - initialize sequence checking variables

        call input() to get NAME_1 from LIST_1
        call input() to get NAME_2 from LIST_2

        while (MORE_NAMES_EXIST)

            if (NAME_1 < NAME_2)
                call input() to get NAME_1 from LIST_1

            else if (NAME_1 > NAME_2)
                call input() to get NAME_2 from LIST_2

            else    /* match -- names are the same */
                write NAME_1 to OUT_FILE
                call input() to get NAME_1 from LIST_1
                call input() to get NAME_2 from LIST_2
            endif
        endwhile
        finish_up()

end PROGRAM
```

FIGURE 8.2 ▪ **Cosequential match procedure based on a single loop.**

Since each pass through the main loop looks at the next pair of names, the fact that one list may be longer than the other does not require any special logic. Nor does the end-of-file condition—the while statement simply checks the MORE_NAMES_EXIST flag on every cycle.

The logic inside the loop is equally simple. Only three possible conditions can exist after reading a name; the *if...else* logic handles all of them. Since we are implementing a match process here, output occurs only when the names are the same.

Note that the main program does not concern itself with such matters as sequence checking and end-of-file detection. Since their presence in the main loop would only obscure the main synchronization logic, they have been relegated to subprocedures.

Since the end-of-file condition is detected during input, the setting of the MORE_NAMES_EXIST flag is done in the *input()* procedure. The *input()* procedure can also be used to check the condition that the lists be in strictly ascending order (no duplicate entries within a list).

```
PROCEDURE: input()      /* input routine for MATCH procedure */

    input arguments:
        INP_FILE            : file descriptor for input file to be used
                              (could be LIST_1 OR LIST_2)
        PREVIOUS_NAME       : last name read from this list

    arguments used to return values:
        NAME                : name to be returned from input procedure
        MORE_NAMES_EXIST    : flag used by main loop to halt processing

        read next NAME from INP_FILE

        /* check for end of file, duplicate names, names out of order    */
        if (EOF)
            MORE_NAMES_EXIST := FALSE       /* set flag to end processing */

        else if (NAME <= PREVIOUS_NAME)
            issue sequence check error
            abort processing
        endif

        PREVIOUS_NAME := NAME

end PROCEDURE
```

FIGURE 8.3 ▪ Input routine for match procedure.

```
PROCEDURE: initialize()

    arguments used to return values:
      PREV_1, PREV_2    : previous name variables for the 2 lists
      LIST_1, LIST_2    : file descriptors for input files to be used
      MORE_NAMES_EXIST  : flag used by main loop to halt processing


        /* set both the previous_name variables (one for each list) to
           a value that is guaranteed to be less than any input value */
        PREV_1 := LOW_VALUE
        PREV_2 := LOW_VALUE

        open file for List 1 as LIST_1
        open file for List 2 as LIST_2

        if (both open statements succeed)
            MORE_NAMES_EXIST := TRUE

end PROCEDURE
```

FIGURE 8.4 ▪ **Initialization procedure for cosequential processing.**

The algorithm in Fig. 8.3 illustrates one method of handling these tasks. This "filling out" of the *input()* procedure also indicates the arguments that the procedure would use.

All we need now to complete the logic is a description of the *initialize()* procedure that begins the main cosequential match procedure. The *initialize()* procedure, shown in Fig. 8.4, performs three tasks:

1. It opens the input and output files.
2. It sets the MORE_NAMES_EXIST flag to TRUE.
3. It sets the *previous_name* variables (one for each list) to a value that is guaranteed to be less than any input value. The effect of setting PREV_1 and PREV_2 to LOW_VALUE is that the procedure *input()* does not need to treat the reading of the first two records in any special way.

Given these program fragments, you should be able to work through the two lists provided in Fig. 8.1, following the pseudocode, and demonstrate to yourself that these simple procedures can handle the various resynchronization problems that these sample lists present.

8.1.2 MERGING TWO LISTS

The three-way test, single-loop model for cosequential processing can easily be modified to handle *merging* of lists as well as matching, as illustrated in Fig. 8.5. Note that we now produce output for every case of the *if...else* construction since a merge is a *union* of the list contents.

An important difference between matching and merging is that with merging we must read *completely* through each of the lists. This necessitates a change in our *input()* procedure, since the version used for matching sets the MORE_NAMES_EXIST flag to FALSE as soon we detect end of file for one of the lists. We need to keep this flag set to TRUE as long as there are records in *either* list. At the same time, we must recognize that one of the lists has been read completely, and we should avoid trying to read from it again. Both of these goals can be

```
PROGRAM: merge

        call initialize() procedure to:
           — open input files LIST_1 and LIST_2
           — create output file OUT_FILE
           — set MORE_NAMES_EXIST to TRUE
           — initialize sequence checking variables

        call input() to get NAME_1 from LIST_1
        call input() to get NAME_2 from LIST_2

        while (MORE_NAMES_EXIST)

           if (NAME_1 < NAME_2)
               write NAME_1 to OUT_FILE
               call input() to get NAME_1 from LIST_1

            else if (NAME_1 > NAME_2)
               write NAME_2 to OUT_FILE
               call input() to get NAME_2 from LIST_2

           else    /* match -- names are the same */
               write NAME_1 to OUT_FILE
               call input() to get NAME_1 from LIST_1
               call input() to get NAME_2 from LIST_2
           endif
        endwhile
        finish_up()

end PROGRAM
```

FIGURE 8.5 ▪ Cosequential merge procedure based on a single loop.

```
PROCEDURE: input()    /* input routine for MERGE procedure */

    input arguments
      INP_FILE            : file descriptor for input file to be used
                            (could be LIST_1 OR LIST_2)
      PREVIOUS_NAME       : last name read from this list
      OTHER_LIST_NAME     : most recent name read from the other list

    arguments used to return values:
      NAME                : name to be returned from input procedure
      MORE_NAMES_EXIST    : flag used by main loop to halt processing

        read next NAME from INP_FILE

        if (EOF) and (OTHER_LIST_NAME == HIGH_VALUE)
            MORE_NAMES_EXIST := FALSE      /* end of both lists    */

        else if (EOF)
            NAME := HIGH_VALUE            /* just this list ended */

        else if (NAME <= PREVIOUS_NAME)   /* sequence check       */
            issue sequence check error
            abort processing
        endif

        PREVIOUS_NAME := NAME

end PROCEDURE
```

FIGURE 8.6 ▪ Input routine for merge procedure.

achieved if we simply set the NAME variable for the completed list to some value that:

☐ Cannot possibly occur as a legal input value; and
☐ Has a *higher* collating sequence value than any possible legal input value. In other words, this special value would come *after* all legal input values in the file's ordered sequence.

We refer to this special value as HIGH_VALUE. The pseudocode in Fig. 8.6 shows how HIGH_VALUE can be used to ensure that both input files are read to completion. Note that we have to add the argument OTHER_LIST_NAME to the argument list so that the function knows whether the other input list has reached its end.

Once again, you should use this logic to work, step by step, through the lists provided in Fig. 8.1 to see how the resynchronization is handled and how the use of the HIGH_VALUE forces the procedure to finish both lists before terminating. Note that the version of *input()* incorporating the HIGH_VALUE logic can also be used for *matching* procedures, producing correct results. The only disadvantage to doing so is that the matching procedure would no longer terminate as soon as one list is completely processed, but would go through the extra work of reading all the way through the unmatched entries at the end of the other list.

With these two examples, we have covered all of the pieces of our model. Now let us summarize the model before adapting it to a more complex problem.

8.1.3 SUMMARY OF THE COSEQUENTIAL PROCESSING MODEL

Generally speaking, the model can be applied to problems that involve the performance of set operations (union, intersection, and more complex processes) on two or more sorted input files to produce one or more output files. In this summary of the cosequential processing model, we assume that there are only two input files and one output file. It is important to understand that the model makes certain general assumptions about the nature of the data and type of problem to be solved. Here is a list of the assumptions, together with clarifying comments.

Assumptions	Comments
Two or more input files are to be processed in a parallel fashion to produce one or more output files.	In some cases an output file may be the same file as one of the input files.
Each file is sorted on one or more key fields, and all files are ordered in the same ways on the same fields.	It is not necessary that all files have the same record structures.
In some cases, there must exist a high key value that is greater than any legitimate record key, and a low key value that is less than any legitimate record key.	The use of a high key value and a low key value is not absolutely necessary, but can help avoid the need to deal with beginning-of-file and end-of-file conditions as special cases, hence decreasing complexity.
Records are to be processed in logical sorted order.	The *physical* ordering of records is irrelevant to the model, but in practice it may be very important to the way the model is implemented. Physical ordering can have a large impact on processing efficiency.

Assumptions	Comments
For each file there is only one current record. This is the record whose key is accessible within the main synchronization loop.	The model does not prohibit looking ahead or looking back at records, but such operations should be restricted to subprocedures and should not be allowed to affect the structure of the main synchronization loop.
Records can be manipulated only in internal memory.	A program cannot alter a record in place on secondary storage.

Given these assumptions, here are the essential components of the model.

1. Initialization. Current records for all files are read from the first logical records in the respective files. *Previous_key* values for all files are set to the low value.
2. One main synchronization loop is used, and the loop continues as long as relevant records remain.
3. Within the body of the main synchronization loop is a selection based on comparison of the record keys from respective input file records. If there are two input files, the selection takes a form such as

```
if (current_file1_key > current_file2_key) then
    .
    .
else if (current_file1_key < current_file2_key) then
    .
    .
else    /* current keys equal */
    .
    .
endif
```

4. Input files and output files are sequence checked by comparing the *previous_key* value with the *current_key* value when a record is read in. After a successful sequence check, *previous_key* is set to *current_key* to prepare for the next input operation on the corresponding file.
5. High values are substituted for actual key values when end-of-file occurs. The main processing loop terminates when high values have occurred for all relevant input files. The use of high values eliminates the need to add special code to deal with each end-of-file condition. (This step is not needed in a pure match procedure since a match procedure halts when the first end-of-file condition is encountered.)

6. All possible I/O and error detection activities are to be relegated to subprocesses, so the details of these activities do not obscure the principal processing logic.

This three-way test, single-loop model for creating cosequential processes is both simple and robust. You will find very few applications requiring the coordinated sequential processing of two files that cannot be handled neatly and efficiently with the model. We now look at a problem that is much more complex than a simple match or merge, but that nevertheless lends itself nicely to solution by means of the model.

8.2 APPLICATION OF THE MODEL TO A GENERAL LEDGER PROGRAM

8.2.1 THE PROBLEM

Suppose we are given the problem of designing a general ledger program as part of an accounting system. The system includes a journal file and a ledger file. The ledger contains the month-by-month summaries of the values associated with each of the bookkeeping accounts. A sample portion of the ledger, containing only checking and expense accounts, is illustrated in Fig. 8.7.

Acct. no.	Account title	Jan	Feb	Mar	Apr
101	Checking account #1	1032.57	2114.56	5219.23	
102	Checking account #2	543.78	3094.17	1321.20	
505	Advertising expense	25.00	25.00	25.00	
510	Auto expenses	195.40	307.92	501.12	
515	Bank charges	0.00	5.00	5.00	
520	Books and publications	27.95	27.95	87.40	
525	Interest expense	103.50	255.20	380.27	
530	Legal expense				
535	Miscellaneous expense	12.45	17.87	23.87	
540	Office expense	57.50	105.25	138.37	
545	Postage and shipping	21.00	27.63	57.45	
550	Rent	500.00	1000.00	1500.00	
555	Supplies	112.00	167.50	241.80	
560	Travel and entertainment	62.76	198.12	307.74	
565	Utilities	84.89	190.60	278.48	

FIGURE 8.7 ▪ Sample ledger fragment containing checking and expense accounts.

Acct. no.	Check no.	Date	Description	Debit/ Credit
101	1271	04/02/86	Auto expense	− 78.70
510	1271	04/02/86	Tune up and minor repair	78.70
101	1272	04/02/86	Rent	− 500.00
550	1272	04/02/86	Rent for April	500.00
101	1273	04/04/86	Advertising	− 87.50
505	1273	04/04/86	Newspaper ad re: new product	87.50
102	670	04/07/86	Office expense	− 32.78
540	670	04/07/86	Printer ribbons (6)	32.78
101	1274	04/09/86	Auto expense	− 12.50
510	1274	04/09/86	Oil change	12.50

FIGURE 8.8 ▪ Sample journal entries.

The journal file contains the monthly transactions that are ultimately to be posted to the ledger file. Figure 8.8 shows what these journal transactions look like. Note that the entries in the journal file are paired. This is because every check involves both subtracting an amount from the checking account balance and adding an amount to at least one expense account. The accounting program package needs procedures for creating this journal file interactively, probably outputting records to the file as checks are keyed in and then printed.

Once the journal file is complete for a given month, which means that it contains all of the transactions for that month, the journal must be posted to the ledger. *Posting* involves associating each transaction with its account in the ledger. For example, the printed output produced for accounts 101, 102, 505, and 510 during the posting operation, given the journal entries in Fig. 8.8, might look like the output illustrated in Fig. 8.9.

How is the posting process implemented? Clearly, it uses the account number as a *key* to relate the journal transactions to the ledger records. One possible solution involves building an index for the ledger, so that we can work through the journal transactions, using the account number in each journal entry to look up the correct ledger record. But this solution involves seeking back and forth across the ledger file as we work through the journal. Moreover, this solution does not really address the issue of creating the output list, in which all the journal entries relating to an account are collected together. Before we could print out the ledger balances and collect journal entries for even the first account, 101, we would have to proceed all the way through

```
101  Checking Account #1
     1271  04/02/86  Auto expense                      -  78.70
     1272  04/02/86  Rent                              - 500.00
     1273  04/04/86  Advertising                       -  87.50
     1274  04/09/86  Auto expense                      -  12.50
                          Prev. bal: 5219.23    New bal: 4540.53

102  Checking account #2
      670  04/07/86  Office expense                    -  32.78
                          Prev. bal: 1321.20    New bal: 1288.42

505  Advertising expense
     1273  04/04/86  Newspaper ad re: new product         87.50
                          Prev. bal:   25.00    New bal:  112.50

510  Auto expenses
     1271  04/02/86  Tune up and minor repair             78.70
     1274  04/09/86  Oil change                           12.50
                          Prev. bal:  501.12    New bal:  592.32
```

FIGURE 8.9 ▪ Sample ledger printout showing the effect of posting from the journal.

the journal list. Where would we save the transactions for account 101 as we collect them during this complete pass through the journal?

A much better solution is to begin by collecting all the journal transactions that relate to a given account. This involves sorting the journal transactions by account number, producing a list ordered as in Fig. 8.10.

Acct no.	Check no.	Date	Description	Debit/ Credit
101	1271	04/02/86	Auto expense	- 78.70
101	1272	04/02/86	Rent	- 500.00
101	1273	04/04/86	Advertising	- 87.50
101	1274	04/09/86	Auto expense	- 12.50
102	670	04/07/86	Office expense	- 32.78
505	1273	04/04/86	Newspaper ad re: new product	87.50
510	1271	04/02/86	Tune up and minor repair	78.70
510	1274	04/09/86	Oil change	12.50
540	670	04/07/86	Printer ribbons (6)	32.78
550	1272	04/02/86	Rent for April	500.00

FIGURE 8.10 ▪ List of journal transactions sorted by account number

Ledger list		Journal list		
101	Checking account #1	101	1271	Auto expense
		101	1272	Rent
		101	1273	Advertising
		101	1274	Auto expense
102	Checking account #2	102	670	Office expense
505	Advertising expense	505	1273	Newspaper ad re: new product
510	Auto expenses	510	1271	Tune up and minor repair
		510	1274	Oil change

FIGURE 8.11 ▪ **Conceptual view of cosequential matching of the ledger and journal files.**

Now we can create our output list by working through both the ledger and the sorted journal *cosequentially,* meaning that we process the two lists sequentially and in parallel. This concept is illustrated in Fig. 8.11. As we start working through the two lists, we note that we have an initial match on account number. We know that multiple entries are possible in the journal file, but not in the ledger, so we move ahead to the next entry in the journal. The account numbers still match. We continue doing this until the account numbers no longer match. We then *resynchronize* the cosequential action by moving ahead in the ledger list.

This matching process seems simple, as it in fact is, as long as every account in one file also appears in another. But there will be ledger accounts for which there is no journal entry, and there can be typographical errors that create journal account numbers that do not actually exist in the ledger. Such situations can make resynchronization more complicated and can result in erroneous output or infinite loops if the programming is done in an *ad hoc* way. By using the cosequential processing model, we can guard against these problems. Let us now apply the model to our ledger problem.

8.2.2 APPLICATION OF THE MODEL TO THE LEDGER PROGRAM

The ledger program must perform two tasks:

☐ It needs to update the ledger file with the correct balance for each account for the current month.

☐ It must produce a printed version of the ledger that not only shows the beginning and current balance for each account, but also lists all the journal transactions for the month.

```
101   Checking account #1
        1271  04/02/86  Auto expense              -  78.70
        1272  04/02/86  Rent                      - 500.00
        1273  04/04/86  Advertising               -  87.50
        1274  04/09/86  Auto expense              -  12.50
                        Prev. bal: 5219.23     New bal: 4540.53

102   Checking account #2
         670  04/07/86  Office expense            -  32.78
                        Prev. bal: 1321.20     New bal: 1288.42

505   Advertising expense
        1273  04/04/86  Newspaper ad re: new product   87.50
                        Prev. bal:   25.00     New bal:  112.50

510   Auto expenses
        1271  04/02/86  Tune up and minor repair       78.70
        1274  04/09/86  Oil change                     12.50
                        Prev. bal:  501.12     New bal:  592.32

515   Bank charges
                        Prev. bal:    5.00     New Bal:    5.00

520   Books and publications
                        Prev. bal:   87.40     New bal:   87.40
```

FIGURE 8.12 ▪ Sample ledger printout for the first six accounts.

We focus on the second task since it is the most difficult. Let's look again at the form of the printed output, this time extending the output to include a few more accounts as shown in Fig. 8.12. As you can see, the printed output from the ledger program shows the balances of all ledger accounts, whether or not there were transactions for the account. From the point of view of the ledger accounts, the process is a *merge,* since even unmatched ledger accounts appear in the output.

What about unmatched journal accounts? The ledger accounts and journal accounts are not equal in authority. The ledger file *defines* the set of legal accounts; the journal file contains entries that are to be *posted* to the accounts listed in the ledger. The existence of a journal account that does not match a ledger account indicates an error. From the point of view of the journal accounts, the posting process is strictly one of *matching.* Our procedure needs to implement a kind of combined merging/matching algorithm while simultaneously handling the chores of printing account title lines, individual transactions, and summary balances.

Another difference between the ledger posting operation and the straightforward matching and merging algorithms is that the ledger procedure must accept duplicate entries for account numbers in the journal while still treating a duplicate entry in the ledger as an error. Recall that our earlier matching and merging routines accept keys only in strict ascending order, rejecting all duplicates.

The inherent simplicity of the three-way test, single-loop model works in our favor as we make these modifications. First, let's look at the input functions that we use for the ledger and journal files, identifying the variables that we need for use in the main loop. Figure 8.13 presents pseudocode for the procedure that accepts input from the ledger. We have treated individual variables within the ledger record as

```
PROCEDURE: ledger_input()

    input arguments:
      L_FILE                : file descriptor for ledger file
      J_ACCT                : current value of journal account number

    arguments used to return values:
      L_ACCT                : account number of new ledger record
      L_BAL                 : balance for this ledger record
      MORE_RECORDS_EXIST    : flag used by main loop to halt processing

    static, local variable that retains its value between calls
      PREV_L_ACCT           : last acct number read from ledger file

        read next record from L_FILE, assigning values to L_ACCT and L_BAL

        if (EOF) and (J_ACCT == HIGH_VALUE)
            MORE_RECORDS_EXIST := FALSE         /* end of both files     */

        else if (EOF)
            L_ACCT := HIGH_VALUE                /* just ledger is done   */

        else if (L_ACCT <= PREV_L_ACCT)         /* sequence check        */
            issue sequence check error          /* (permit no duplicates) */
            abort processing
        endif

        PREV_L_ACCT := L_ACCT

end PROCEDURE
```

FIGURE 8.13 ▪ Input routine for ledger file.

return values to draw attention to these variables; in practice the procedure would probably return the entire ledger record to the calling routine so that other procedures could have access to things such as the account title as they print the ledger. We are overlooking such matters here, focusing instead on the variables that are involved in the cosequential logic. Note that, since this function is strictly for use with ledger entries, we can keep track of the previous ledger account number locally within the procedure rather than pass this value in as an argument.

Figure 8.14 outlines the logic for the procedure used to accept input from the journal file. It is similar to the *ledger_input()* procedure in most respects, including the fact that it returns values for individual variables, even though a working implementation would probably re-

```
PROCEDURE: journal_input()

    input arguments:
        J_FILE                  : file descriptor for journal file
        L_ACCT                  : current value of ledger account number

    arguments used to return values:
        J_ACCT                  : account number of new journal record
        TRANS_AMT               : amount of this journal transaction
        MORE_RECORDS_EXIST      : flag used by main loop to halt processing

    static, local variable that retains its value between calls
        PREV_J_ACCT             : last acct number read from journal file

        read next record from J_FILE, assigning values to J_ACCT
            and TRANS_AMT

        if (EOF) and (L_ACCT == HIGH_VALUE)
            MORE_RECORDS_EXIST := FALSE          /* end of both files      */

        else if (EOF)
            J_ACCT := HIGH_VALUE                 /* just ledger is done    */

        else if (J_ACCT < PREV_J_ACCT)           /* sequence check         */
            issue sequence check error           /* (permit duplicates)    */
            abort processing
        endif

        PREV_J_ACCT := J_ACCT

end PROCEDURE
```

FIGURE 8.14 ▪ **Input routine for journal file.**

```
PROGRAM: ledger

    call initialize() procedure to:
        - open input files L_FILE and J_FILE
        - set MORE_RECORDS_EXIST to TRUE

    call ledger_input()
    PREV_L_BAL := L_BAL              /* set starting ledger balance
                                        for this first ledger account */
    call journal_input()

    while (MORE_RECORDS_EXIST)

        if (L_ACCT < J_ACCT)        /* we have read all the journal
                                       entries for this account       */
            print PREV_L_BAL and L_BAL
            call ledger_input()
            if (L_ACCT < HIGH_VALUE)
                print account number and title for new ledger account
                PREV_L_BAL := L_BAL
            endif

        else if (L.ACCT > J.ACCT)   /* bad journal account number     */
            print error message
            call journal_input()

        else            /* match -- add journal transaction amount    */
                        /* to ledger balance for this account         */
            L_BAL := L_BAL + TRANS_AMT
                output the transaction to the printed ledger
            call journal_input()
        endif
    endwhile

end PROGRAM
```

FIGURE 8.15 ▪ Cosequential procedure to process ledger and journal files to produce printed ledger output.

turn the entire journal record. Note, however, that the sequence-checking logic is different in *journal_input()*. In this procedure we need to accept records that have the same account number as previous records. Given these input procedures, we can handle our cosequential processing and output as illustrated in Fig. 8.15.

The reasoning behind the three-way test is as follows:

1. If the ledger account is less than the journal account, then there are no more transactions to add to this ledger account (perhaps

there were none at all), so we print out the ledger account balances and read in the next ledger account. If the account exists (value < HIGH_VALUE), we print the title line for the new account and update the PREV_BAL variable.

2. If the journal account is less than the ledger account, then it is an unmatched journal account, perhaps due to an input error. We print an error message and continue.

3. If the account numbers match, then we have a journal transaction that is to be posted to the current ledger account. We add the transaction amount to the account balance, print the description of the transaction, and then read in the next journal entry. Note that unlike the match case in either the matching or merging algorithms, we do not read in a new entry from both accounts. This is a reflection of our acceptance of more than one journal entry for a single ledger account.

The development of this ledger-posting procedure from our basic cosequential processing model illustrates how the simplicity of the model contributes to its adaptability. We can also generalize the model in an entirely different direction, extending it to enable cosequential processing of more than two input files at once. To illustrate this, we now extend the model to include multiway merging.

8.3
EXTENSION OF THE MODEL TO INCLUDE MULTIWAY MERGING

The most common application of cosequential processes requiring more than two input files is a *K-way merge*, in which we want to merge *K* input lists to create a single, sequentially ordered output list.

Recall the synchronizing loop we use to handle a two-way merge of two lists of names (Fig. 8.5). This merging operation can be viewed as a process of deciding which of two input names has the *minimum* value, outputting that name, and then moving ahead in the list from which that name is taken. In the event of duplicate input entries, we move ahead in each list.

Given a *min()* function that returns the name with the lowest collating sequence value, there is no reason to restrict the number of input names to two. The procedure could be extended to handle three (or more) input lists as shown in Fig. 8.16.

```
while (MORE_NAMES_EXIST)

    OUT_NAME = min(NAME_1, NAME_2, NAME_3, ... NAME_K)
    write OUT_NAME to OUT_FILE

    if (NAME_1 == OUT_NAME)
        call input() to get NAME_1 from LIST_1

    if (NAME_2 == OUT_NAME)
        call input() to get NAME_2 from LIST_2

    if (NAME_3 == OUT_NAME)
        call input() to get NAME_3 from LIST_3
    .

    .

    .
    if (NAME_K == OUT_NAME)
        call input() to get NAME_K from LIST_K

endwhile
```

FIGURE 8.16 ▪ *K*-way merge loop, accounting for duplicate names.

Clearly the expensive part of this procedure is the series of tests to see in which lists the name occurs and which files therefore need to be read. Note that since the name can occur in several lists, every one of these *if* tests must be executed on every cycle through the loop. However, it is often possible to guarantee that a single name, or key, occurs in only one list. In this case, the procedure becomes much simpler and more efficient. Suppose we reference our lists through a vector of list names:

```
list[1], list[2], list[3], ... list[K]
```

and suppose that we reference the names (or keys) that are being used from these lists at any given point in the cosequential process through another vector:

```
name[1], name[2], name[3], ... name[K]
```

Then the procedure shown in Fig. 8.17 can be used, assuming once again that the *input()* procedure attends to the MORE_NAMES_EXIST flag.

```
/* initialize the process by reading in a name from each list    */
for i := 1 to K
    call input() to get name[i] from list[i]
next i

/* now start the K-way merge */
while (MORE_NAMES_EXIST)

    /* find subscript of name that has the lowest collating
       sequence value among the names available on the K lists    */
    LOWEST := 1
    for i := 2 to K
        if (name[i] < name[LOWEST])
            LOWEST := i
    next i

    write name[LOWEST] to OUT_FILE

    /* now replace the name that was written out                   */
    call input() to get name[LOWEST] from list[LOWEST]
endwhile
```

FIGURE 8.17 ▪ *K*-way merge loop, assuming no duplicate names.

This procedure clearly differs in many ways from our initial three-way test, single-loop procedure that merges two lists. But, even so, the single-loop parentage is still evident: There is no looping within a list. We determine which list has the key with the lowest value, output that key, move ahead one key in that list, and loop again. The procedure is as simple as it is powerful.

The *K*-way merge described in Fig. 8.17 works nicely if *K* is no larger than 8 or so. When we begin merging a larger number of lists, the set of sequential comparisons to find the key with the minimum value begins to become noticeably expensive. We see later that for practical reasons it is rare to want to merge more than eight files at one time, so the use of sequential comparisons is normally a good strategy. If there is a need to merge considerably more than eight lists, we could replace the loop of comparisons with a *selection tree*.

Use of a selection tree is an example of the classic time versus space trade-off that we so often encounter in computer science. We reduce the time required to find the key with the lowest value by using a data structure to save information about the relative key values across cycles of the procedure's main loop. The concept underlying a selection tree can be readily communicated through a diagram such as that in Fig.

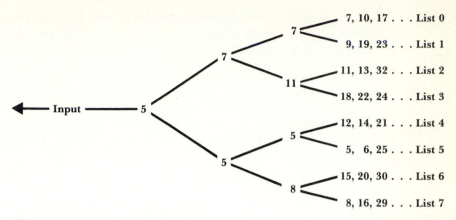

FIGURE 8.18 ▪ **Use of a selection tree to assist in the selection of a key with minimum value in a *K*-way merge.**

8.18. Here we have used lists in which the keys are numbers rather than names.

The selection tree is a kind of *tournament* tree in which each higher-level node represents the "winner" (in this case the *minimum* key value) of the comparison between the two descendent keys. The minimum value is always at the root node of the tree. If each key has an associated reference to the list from which it came, it is a simple matter to take the key at the root, read the next element from the associated list, and then run the tournament again. Since the tournament tree is a binary tree, its depth is

$$\lceil \log_2 K \rceil$$

for a merge of *K* lists. The number of comparisons required to establish a new tournament winner is, of course, related to this depth, rather than being a linear function of *K*.

8.4
MERGING AS A WAY OF SORTING LARGE FILES ON DISK

In Chapter 6 we ran into problems when we needed to sort files that were too large to be wholly contained in electronic random access memory (RAM). The chapter offered a partial, but ultimately unsatisfactory, solution to this problem in the form of a *keysort,* in which we needed to hold only the keys in RAM, along with pointers to each key's corresponding record. Keysort had two shortcomings:

☐   Once the keys were sorted, we then had to bear the substantial cost of seeking to each record in sorted order, reading each record in and then writing it out into the new, sorted file.

☐   With keysorting, the size of the file that can be sorted is limited by the number of key/pointer pairs that can be contained in RAM. Consequently, we still cannot sort really large files.

As an example of the kind of file we cannot sort with either a RAM sort or a keysort, suppose we have a file with 400,000 records, each of which is 100 bytes long and contains a key field that is ten bytes long. The total length of this file is about 40 megabytes. Let us further suppose that we have one megabyte of RAM available as a work area, not counting RAM used to hold the program, operating system, and so forth. Clearly we cannot sort the whole file in RAM. We cannot even sort all the keys in RAM.

The multiway merge algorithm in Section 8.3 provides the beginning of an attractive solution to the problem of sorting large files such as this one. Since RAM sorting algorithms such as Quicksort can work in place, using only a small amount of overhead for maintaining a stack and some temporary variables, we can create a sorted subset of our full file by reading records into RAM until the RAM work area is almost full, sorting the records in this work area, and then writing the sorted records back to disk as a sorted subfile. We call such a sorted subfile a *run.* Given the memory constraints and record size in our example, a run could contain approximately

$$\frac{1,000,000 \text{ bytes of RAM}}{100 \text{ bytes per record}} = 10,000 \text{ records.}$$

Once we create the first run, we then read in a new set of records, once again filling RAM, and create another run of 10,000 records. In our example, we repeat this process until we have created 40 runs, with each run containing 10,000 sorted records.

Once we have the 40 runs in 40 separate files on disk, we can perform a 40-way merge of these runs, using the multiway merge logic outlined in Section 8.3, to create a completely sorted file containing all the original records. A schematic view of this run creation and merging process is provided in Fig. 8.19.

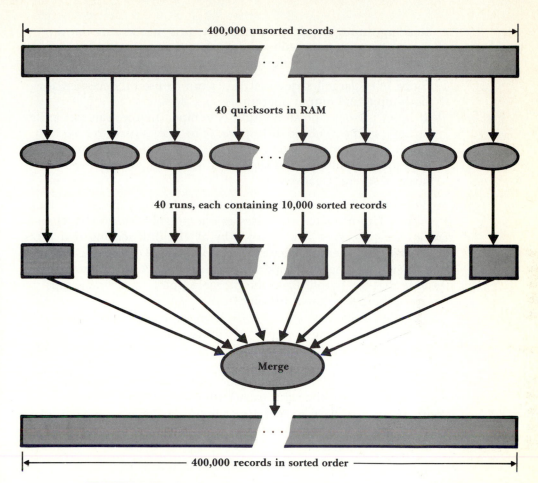

FIGURE 8.19 ▪ **Sorting through the creation of runs (sorted subfiles) and subsequent merging of runs.**

This solution to our sorting problem has the following features:

☐ It can, in fact, sort large files, and can be extended to files of any size.

☐ Reading of the input file during the run creation step is completely sequential, hence is much faster than input that requires seeking (as in a keysort).

□ Reading through each run during merging and writing out the sorted records is also sequential. Seeking is required only as we switch from run to run during the merge operation.

□ Since I/O is largely sequential, tapes can be used if necessary for both input and output operations.

□ If input is from tape and output is to tape, then we can sort a file as large as the available disk space. (The disk is used to hold only the runs.) For many system installations this means we can sort files up to hundreds of megabytes in size, and perhaps even as large as several gigabytes.

This general approach to the problem of sorting large files looks promising. Unfortunately, it possesses one notably undesirable characteristic: the process is slowed down by all the disk seeking that takes place during the merging phase of the operation. To illustrate this, let's consider the seeking associated only with the *input* to the merge step. (Assume that the output from the merge is going to magnetic tape, so that no seeking is required for output.)

For the sample data we are considering, the seeking is between the 40 runs that are being merged. Of course, we buffer the input from each run so that we do not have to seek for every single item. How big can each buffer be? Since each of the 40 runs is as large as the work area available in RAM, it follows that when we divide that same work area into buffers for the runs, each buffer will only hold 1/40 of a run. Consequently, we have to seek to each run 40 times to read all of it. Since there are 40 runs, to complete the merge operation (Fig. 8.20) we end up making

$$40 \text{ runs} \times 40 \text{ seeks/run} = 1600 \text{ seeks.}†$$

We know by now that seeking is expensive, and that any operation that requires 1600 seeks for completion is an operation that ought to be scrutinized to see if there is some way to reduce the amount of seeking that is required.

---

†In general, for a K-way merge of K runs where each run is as large as the RAM work area available, the buffer size for each of the runs is

$$(1/K) \times \text{size of RAM space} = (1/K) \times \text{size of each run,}$$

so K seeks are required to read in all of the records in each individual run. Since there are K runs altogether, the merge operation therefore requires K^2 seeks. Hence, measured in terms of seeks, our sort-merge is an $O(K^2)$ operation. Since K is directly proportional to N (if we double the number of records from 400,000 to 800,000, K doubles from 40 to 80) it also follows that our sort-merge is an $O(N^2)$ operation, measured in terms of seeks. In other words, performance can deteriorate rapidly as N increases.

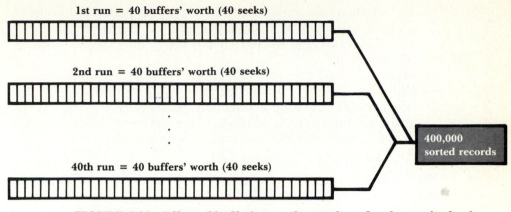

1st run = 40 buffers' worth (40 seeks)

2nd run = 40 buffers' worth (40 seeks)

40th run = 40 buffers' worth (40 seeks)

400,000
sorted records

FIGURE 8.20 ▪ **Effect of buffering on the number of seeks required, where each run is as large as the available work area in RAM.**

There are two ways we can reduce the number of seeks required for the merge step of our sort:

☐   Perform the merge in more than one step, reducing the order of each merge and increasing the buffer size; and

☐   Increase the size of the initial sorted runs.

We look at each of these improvements separately. They are not, however, mutually exclusive—a good sorting program may well make use of both of them.

8.4.1 MULTIPLE-STEP MERGE PATTERNS

One of the hallmarks of a solution to a file structure problem, as opposed to the solution of a mere data structure problem, is the attention given to the enormous difference in cost between seeking on disk and accessing information in RAM. If our merging problem involved only RAM operations, the relevant measure of work, or expense, would be the number of *comparisons* required to complete the merge. The *merge pattern* that would minimize the number of comparisons for our sample problem, in which we want to merge 40 runs, would be the 40-way merge considered in the preceding section. Considered from a point of view that ignores the cost of seeking, this K-way merge has the following desirable characteristics:

☐   Each record is read only once.

☐ If a selection tree is used for the comparisons performed in the merging operation, as described in Section 8.3, then the number of comparisons required for a K-way merge of N records (total) is a function of

$$N \times \log K.$$

☐ Since K is directly proportional to N, this is an $O(N \times \log N)$ operation (measured in numbers of comparisons), which is to say that it is reasonably efficient even as N grows large.

This would all be very good news, were we working exclusively in RAM, but the very purpose of this *merge-sort* procedure is to be able to sort files that are too large to fit into RAM. Given the task at hand, the costs associated with disk seeks are orders of magnitude greater than the costs of operations in RAM. Consequently, if we can sacrifice the advantages of a 40-way merge, trading them for savings in seek time, we may be able to obtain a net gain in performance.

Rather than merging all 40 runs at once, we could merge them as five sets of eight runs each, followed by a five-way merge of the *intermediate* runs. Using the same notation as Knuth [1973b], we refer to this as an 8:8:8:8:8 merge (five sets of eight-way merges). This scheme is illustrated in Fig. 8.21.

When compared to our original 40-way merge, this approach has the disadvantage of requiring that we read every record twice: once to form the intermediate runs and then again to form the final sorted file. But, since each step of the merge is reading from, at most, eight input files at a time, we are able to use larger buffers and avoid a large amount of disk seeking. When we analyzed the seeking required for

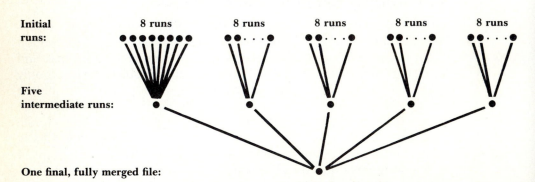

FIGURE 8.21 ▪ 8:8:8:8:8 merge (two steps) of 40 runs.

the 40-way merge, disregarding seeking for the output file, we calculated that the 40-way merge involved 1600 seeks between the input files. Let's perform similar calculations for our 8:8:8:8:8 merge.

1. *For each of the eight-way merges of the initial runs:*
   - Each of the eight input buffers can hold 1/8 run;
   - Therefore: 8 seeks/run × 8 runs = 64 seeks for each of these merges;
   - Total for all five of these eight-way merges: 5 × 64 = *320 seeks.*
2. *Five-way merge of the intermediate runs:*
   - Each intermediate run is eight times as long as an initial run;
   - Each of five input buffers can hold 1/40 of an intermediate run;
   - Therefore: 40 seeks/run × 5 runs = *200 seeks.*
3. *Total seeks for the entire 8:8:8:8:8 merge:*
   - 320 seeks + 200 seeks = *520 seeks.*

So, by accepting the cost of processing each record twice, we reduce the number of seeks by two-thirds. It is interesting to look at what happens if we double the number of records to be sorted from 400,000 to 800,000, and therefore the number of initial runs from 40 to 80. Once again ignoring buffering for output, an 80-way merge requires *6400 seeks*! Replacing the 80-way merge with a two-step, 10:10:10:10:10:10:10:10 merge (eight separate ten-way merges, followed by a final eight-way merge), we can reduce the number of seeks to 1440, which is certainly a much more workable number of seeks than is 6400.

A careful analysis of the trade-offs between seek time and transmission time (which is related to the number of times we read each record), accounting for output buffers as well as input buffers, is more complicated than these calculations indicate. In fact, it is necessary to account for the specific characteristics of the hardware involved. Given certain hardware configurations, for example, it might make sense to do a merge in three steps rather than two.

For example, what would be the effect of merging the original 40 runs, containing 400,000 records, by performing two two-step, 5:5:5:5 merges of 200,000 records apiece, followed by a third step in which the two 200,000-record intermediate runs are combined through a two-way merge? How does this change if the merging can be done on four disk packs with separate seek arms? References cited at the end of this chapter, especially Knuth [1973b], contain detailed analyses of these kinds of issues.

We should be careful, in the face of these complexities and options, not to lose sight of the main point: when sorting large files on disk through the merging of a large number of runs, it is almost always advantageous to pay the price of reading the records more than once to reduce the amount of disk seeking involved.

8.4.2 INCREASING RUN LENGTHS BY USING REPLACEMENT SELECTION

What would happen if we could somehow increase the size of the initial runs? Consider, for example, our earlier sort of 400,000 records in which each record was 100 bytes. Our initial runs were limited to approximately 10,000 records because the RAM work area was limited to one megabyte. Suppose we are somehow able to create runs of twice this length, containing 20,000 records each. Then, rather than needing to perform a 40-way merge, we need to do only a 20-way merge. The available RAM is divided into 20 buffers, each of which can hold 1/40th of a run. (Why?) Hence, the number of seeks required per run is 40, and the total number of seeks is

$$40 \text{ seeks/run} \times 20 \text{ runs} = 800 \text{ seeks,}$$

half the number required for the 40-way merge of 10,000-byte runs.

In general, if we can somehow increase the size of the initial runs, we decrease the amount of work required during the merge step of the sorting process. A longer initial run means fewer total runs, which means a lower order merge, which means bigger buffers, which means fewer seeks. But how, short of buying twice as much memory for the computer, can we create initial runs that are twice as large as the number of records that we can hold in RAM? The answer, once again, involves trading off some efficiency within our in-RAM operations in return for decreasing the amount of work to be done on disk. In particular, the answer involves the use of an algorithm known as *replacement selection*.

Replacement selection is based on the very simple idea of always *selecting* the key from memory that has the lowest value, outputting that key, and then *replacing* it with a new key from the input list. Key selection can be implemented through use of a selection tree of the kind we described earlier. Some of the time the new key brought in as a replacement has a value higher than that of the key that has been output. When this happens, it is possible to include the new key in the run along with the other keys that are being selected for output. This makes

Input:
21, 67, 12, 5, 47, 16

⌐—Front of input string

Remaining input	Memory ($P = 3$)			Output run					
21, 67, 12	5	47	16						−
21, 67	12	47	16						5
21	67	47	16					12,	5
−	67	47	21				16,	12,	5
−	67	47	−			21,	16,	12,	5
−	67	−	−		47,	21,	16,	12,	5
−	−	−	−	67,	47,	21,	16,	12,	5

FIGURE 8.22 ▪ **Example of the principle underlying replacement selection.**

it possible to form runs that are actually larger than the number of keys that can be held in memory at any one time.

To see how this works, let's begin with a simple example, using an input list of only six keys and a memory work area that can hold only three keys. As Fig. 8.22 illustrates, we begin by reading into RAM the three keys that fit there. We select the key in RAM with the minimum value, which happens to be 5 in this example, and output that key. We now have room in memory for another key, so we read one from the input list. The new key, which has a value of 12, now becomes a member of the set of keys to be sorted into the output run. In fact, since it is smaller than the other keys in RAM, 12 is the next key that is output. A new key is read into its place, and the process continues. When the process is complete, it produces a sorted list of six keys while using only three memory locations.

A study of this example naturally raises such questions as, "What if the fourth key in the input list is 2 rather than 12?" It is obvious that this key would arrive in memory too late to be output into its proper position relative to the other keys: The 5 has already been written to the output list. The solution is simply to hold the 2 until we complete outputting the first run, incorporating it in the next run. In general, when a key that has been input has a value that is less than that of the key that has been most recently output, that key is marked as a member of the next run.

Figure 8.23 illustrates how this process works. During the first run, when keys that are too small to be included in that run are brought into memory, we mark them with parentheses, indicating that they have to be held for the second run.

Input:

33, 18, 24, 58, 14, 17, 7, 21, 67, 12, 5, 47, 16

└── Front of input string

Remaining input	Memory (P = 3)	Output run
33, 18, 24, 58, 14, 17, 7, 21, 67, 12	5 47 16	–
33, 18, 24, 58, 14, 17, 7, 21, 67	12 47 16	5
33, 18, 24, 58, 14, 17, 7, 21	67 47 16	12, 5
33, 18, 24, 58, 14, 17, 7	67 47 21	16, 12, 5
33, 18, 24, 58, 14, 17	67 47 (7)	21, 16, 12, 5
33, 18, 24, 58, 14	67 (17) (7)	47, 21, 16, 12, 5
33, 18, 24, 58	(14) (17) (7)	67, 47, 21, 16, 12, 5

First run complete; start building the second

33, 18, 24, 58	14 17 7	–
33, 18, 24	14 17 58	7
33, 18	24 17 58	14, 7
33	24 18 58	17, 14, 7
–	24 33 58	18, 17, 14, 7
–	– 33 58	24, 18, 17, 14, 7
–	– – 58	33, 24, 18, 17, 14, 7
–	–	58, 33, 24, 18, 17, 14, 7

FIGURE 8.23 ▪ **Step-by-step operation of replacement selection working to form two sorted runs.**

It is interesting to use this example to compare the action of replacement selection to the procedure we have been using up to this point, namely that of reading keys into RAM, sorting them, and outputting a run that is the size of the RAM space. In this example our input list contains 13 keys. A series of successive RAM sorts, given only three memory locations, results in five runs. The replacement selection procedure results in only two runs. Since the disk seeking during a multiway merge can be a major expense, replacement selection's ability to create longer, and therefore fewer, runs can be an important advantage.

Two questions emerge at this point:

1. Given P locations in memory, how long a run can we expect replacement selection to produce, on the average?
2. By this time we have learned that there is only very rarely a free lunch to be had while working with file structures. What are the costs of using replacement selection?

8.4.3 AVERAGE RUN LENGTH FOR REPLACEMENT SELECTION

The answer to the first question is that, on the average, we can expect a run length of $2P$, given P memory locations. Knuth [1973b]† provides an excellent description of an intuitive argument for why this is so:

> A clever way to show that $2P$ is indeed the expected run length was discovered by E. F. Moore, who compared the situation to a snowplow on a circular track [*U.S. Patent. 2983904* (1961), Cols. 3–4]. Consider the situation shown [below]; flakes of snow are falling uniformly on a circular road, and a lone snowplow is continually clearing the snow. Once the snow has been plowed off the road, it disappears from the system. Points on the road may be designated by real numbers x, $0 \leqslant x < 1$; a flake of snow falling at position x represents an input record whose key is x, and the snowplow represents the output of replacement selection. The ground speed of the snowplow is inversely proportional to the height of the snow that it encounters, and the situation is perfectly balanced so that the total amount of snow on the road at all times is exactly P. A new run is formed in the output whenever the plow passes point 0.

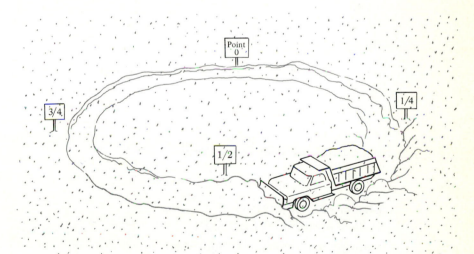

After this system has been in operation for awhile, it is intuitively clear that it will approach a stable situation in which the snowplow runs at constant speed (because of the circular symmetry of the

†From Donald Knuth, *The Art of Computer Programming,* ©1973, Addison-Wesley, Reading, Mass. Pages 254–255 and Figs. 64 and 65. Reprinted with permission.

track). This means that the snow is at constant height when it meets the plow, and the height drops off linearly in front of the plow as shown [below]. It follows that the volume of snow removed in one revolution (namely the run length) is twice the amount present at any one time (namely P).

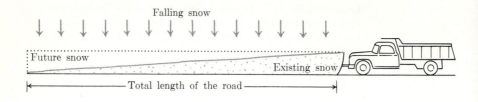

So, given a random ordering of keys, we can expect replacement selection to form runs that contain about twice as many records as we can hold in memory at one time. It follows that replacement selection creates half as many runs as does a series of RAM sorts of memory contents, assuming that the replacement selection and the RAM sort have access to the same amount of memory. (As we see in a moment, the replacement selection does, in fact, have to make do with less memory than does the RAM sort.)

It is actually often possible to create runs that are substantially longer than $2P$. In many applications, the order of the records is *not* wholly random; the keys are often already partially in ascending order. In these cases replacement selection can produce runs that, on the average, exceed $2P$. (Consider what would happen if the input list is already sorted.) Replacement selection becomes an especially valuable tool for such partially ordered input files.

8.4.4 COST OF USING REPLACEMENT SELECTION

Unfortunately, the no-free-lunch rule applies to replacement selection, as it does to so many other areas of file structure design. In the worked-by-hand examples we have looked at up to this point, we have been inputting records into memory one at a time. We know, in fact, that the cost of seeking out to disk for every single input record is prohibitive. Instead, we want to buffer the input, which means, in turn, that we are not able to use *all* of the memory for the operation of replacement selection. Some of it has to be used for input and output buffering. (Because replacement selection always needs exactly one record for input immediately after outputting one record, a single buffer can be used for both input and output.)

To see the effects of this need for buffering during the replacement selection step, let's return to our example in which we sort 400,000 records, given a memory area that can hold only 10,000 records. In our earlier examination of this example, we counted only the seeks required during the merge step, after we had already formed runs. Now we will also account for the seeking required to read records from disk into memory for the initial formation of the runs.

For the RAM sorting methods, which simply read records into memory until it is full, we can perform sequential reads of 10,000 records at a time. This means that reading in the whole file requires only 40 seeks. (We assume we are on a multiuser system, and that when we finish reading, someone else's request causes the disk to seek away to some other location.)

For replacement selection we might use an input/output buffer that can hold, for example, 2,500 records, leaving enough space to hold 7,500 records for the actual replacement selection process. As a consequence, we need 160 seeks to read the entire 400,000 record file. If the records occur in a random key sequence, the average run length will be 15,000 records.

Table 8.1 compares the number of seeks required to sort the 400,000 records using both a RAM sort, such as Quicksort, and replacement selection. The table includes our initial 40-way merge, our improved multistep merge, and two replacement selection examples. The second replacement selection example, which produces runs of 40,000 records while using only 7,500 record storage locations in memory, assumes that there is already a good deal of sequential ordering within the input records.

It is clear that even given randomly distributed input data, replacement selection can substantially reduce the number of runs formed; in this case the reduction is from 40 down to 27. But the consequent reduction in the amount of seeking effort required to merge the runs is more than offset by the amount of seeking that is required to form the runs. The 160 seeks required for run formation bring the total number of seeks for the entire replacement selection sort to 583; the process based on successive RAM sorts requires a total of only 560 seeks. Only when the original data is assumed to possess enough order to make the runs four times as long as those produced by RAM sorting does replacement selection require substantially less seeking.

Table 8.1 also lets us consider what happens if the original, unsorted input file comes from tape rather than disk. If the input is from

TABLE 8.1

Comparison of run formation through successive RAM sorts and through replacement selection (Considers only the seeks required for input.)

Approach	Number of records read in at once to form runs	Size of runs formed	Number of runs formed	Total number of seeks required to form runs	Merge pattern used	Total number of seeks required for merging	Total seeks (run formation plus merging)
40 RAM sorts followed by a 40-way merge	10,000	10,000	40	40	40	1600	1640
40 RAM sorts followed by a multistep merge	10,000	10,000	40	40	8:8:8:8:8	520	560
Replacement selection followed by a multistep merge (records in random order)	2,500	15,000	27	160	5:5:5:6:6	423	583
Replacement selection followed by a multistep merge (records partially sorted)	2,500	40,000	10	160	3:3:4	256	416

tape, then there is *no* seeking required to form the initial runs; input is truly sequential from the tape into the buffer. The fifth column of the table, Total number of seeks required to form runs, is zero in each case. It is clear that, given tape input, replacement selection outperforms the RAM sorting method. This positive association between replacement selection and tape operations is something we explore in Section 8.5, when we look at sorts that do not use the disk at all.

8.4.5 DISK CONFIGURATIONS

Since seek time seems to be the source of our greatest delay, we ought to ask whether there are situations in which seek time does not play a role. We have seen that one way to decrease the number of seeks is to decrease the number of runs. The reason this works is that merging fewer runs requires the read/write head to move from file to file less frequently. This suggests that another approach to decreasing the number of seeks is to increase the number of independent read/write heads.

If we could have one read/write head for every file and no other users contending for use of the same read/write heads, there would be no delay due to seek time after the original runs are generated. The primary source of delay would now be rotational delays, which would occur every time a new block had to be read in. As with seeks, the number of rotational delays can be lessened by decreasing the merge order (increasing the internal buffer size), so it is still generally advantageous to keep the order of the merge low.

8.4.6 SUMMARY CONCERNING DISK SORTING

A few summarizing remarks about disk sorting are in order before we turn our attention to the problem of sorting on tape.

- ☐ If the disk sort involves a merge of more than five runs, it is probably advantageous to perform the merge in two or more steps. For example, a six-way merge is probably best handled as a 3:3 merge: a pair of three-way merges followed by a final two-way merge of the resulting intermediate runs.
- ☐ When the input data comes from a disk, the use of replacement selection to form the initial runs, as opposed to a series of RAM sorts, is probably not worth the trouble unless there is already a significant amount of order in the input data.
- ☐ If the data can be distributed across several disks, each disk having a separate access arm, performance can be improved substantially.

This is especially true if there are not other users on the system. (In many installations, it is possible to arrange for a quiet system when it is necessary to perform very large sorts.)
□ If the input file comes from tape, it is possible to use replacement selection advantageously.

8.5 SORTING FILES ON TAPE

Most small- to medium-sized computer installations can do more sorting on disk than on tape for the very simple reason that the majority of installations of this size have only one or two tape drives. However, if a facility has a number of tape drives, it is often possible to sort large files more rapidly on tape than on disk. This is particularly true when six or more tape drives are available. The reasons for the improvement are, of course, related to the seeking cost that is incurred when working on disk.

There are a large number of approaches to sorting files on tape. After approximately 100 pages of closely reasoned discussion of different alternatives for tape sorting, Knuth [1973b] summarizes his analysis in the following way:

Theorem A. It is difficult to decide which merge pattern is best in a given situation.

Because of the complexity and number of alternative approaches and because of the way that these alternatives depend so closely on the specific characteristics of the hardware at a particular computer installation, our objective here is merely to communicate some of the fundamental issues associated with tape sorting and merging. For a more comprehensive (and more mathematical) discussion of specific alternatives we recommend Knuth's [1973b] work as a starting point.

Viewed from a most general perspective, the steps involved in sorting on tape resemble those that we discussed with regard to sorting on disk:

1. Distribute the unsorted file into sorted *runs;* and
2. Merge the runs into a single sorted file.

Replacement selection is almost always a good choice as a method for creating the initial runs during a tape sort. You will remember that the problem with replacement selection when we are working on disk is that the amount of seeking required during run creation more than offsets the advantage of creating longer runs. As we point out earlier, this seeking problem disappears when the input is from tape. So, for a tape-to-tape sort, it is almost always advisable to take advantage of the longer runs created by replacement selection.

8.5.1 THE BALANCED MERGE

Given that the question of how to create the initial runs has such a straightforward answer, it is clear that it is in the merging process that we encounter all of the choices and complexities implied by Knuth's tongue-in-cheek theorem. These choices begin with the question of how to *distribute* the initial runs on tape and extend into questions about the process of merging from this initial distribution. Let's turn again to our example of a file containing 400,000 records to show what we mean.

In Table 8.1, where we summarize some analyses for disk sorting, the last example listed is one in which replacement selection is used on a set of records that is already partially ordered. Because of the ordering, replacement selection is able to fit the 400,000 records into ten 40,000-record runs. We look at a number of different methods for merging these runs on tape, assuming that our computer system has four tape drives. Because the replacement selection process is, itself, using one of the drives, we have the choice of initially distributing the ten runs on two or three of the other drives. We begin with a method called *balanced merging*, which requires that the initial distribution be on two drives. Balanced merging is the simplest tape merging algorithm that we look at; it is also, as you will see, the slowest.

The balanced merge proceeds according to the pattern illustrated in Fig. 8.24.

Step 1. The initial runs are distributed evenly on tape drives 1 and 2 so that there are five runs on each tape.

Step 2. Working cosequentially, we merge each of the five pairs of runs as we work through the tapes, writing the resulting longer runs alternately on tapes 3 and 4.

Step 3. We merge the runs on tapes 3 and 4, writing the results back to tapes 1 and 2. Note that there is one more run on tape 3 than there is on tape 4. When this occurs, the extra run (R9–R10) is merged with an empty run, effectively copying it to the target tape.

Step 4. We merge the runs on tapes 1 and 2, writing the results to tapes 3 and 4. Again, the extra run (R9–R10) is merged with an empty run, so we end up with one long run on tape 3 and a short run on tape 4.

Step 5. We do one final merge to produce a single run consisting of the whole file.

This balanced merge process is expressed in an alternate, more compact form in Fig. 8.25. The numbers inside the table are the run lengths measured in terms of the number of initial runs included in each merged run. For example, in Step 1 all the runs consist of a single initial run. By Step 2 the runs each consist of a pair of initial runs. At the start of Step 3, tape drive T1 contains one run consisting of four initial runs, followed by a run consisting of two initial runs. This method of illustration more clearly shows the way some of the inter-

Tape	Contains runs				
T1	R1	R3	R5	R7	R9
Step 1 T2	R2	R4	R6	R8	R10
T3	—				
T4	—				
T1	—				
Step 2 T2	—				
T3	R1–R2	R5–R6	R9–R10		
T4	R3–R4	R7–R8			
T1	R1–R4	R9–R10			
Step 3 T2	R5–R8				
T3	—				
T4	—				
T1	—				
Step 4 T2	—				
T3	R1–R8				
T4	R9–R10				
T1	R1–R10				
Step 5 T2	—				
T3	—				
T4	—				

FIGURE 8.24 ▪ Balanced four-tape merge of ten runs.

	T1	T2	T3	T4	
Step 1	1 1 1 1 1	1 1 1 1 1	—	—	
					Merge ten runs
Step 2	—	—	2 2 2	2 2	
					Merge ten runs
Step 3	4 2	4	—	—	
					Merge ten runs
Step 4	—	—	8	2	
					Merge ten runs
Step 5	10	—	—	—	

FIGURE 8.25 ▪ Balanced four-tape merge of ten runs expressed in more compact table notation.

mediate runs combine and grow into runs of lengths 2, 4, and 8, whereas the one run that is copied again and again stays at length 2 until the end. The form used in this illustration is the form we use as we discuss alternative approaches to merging.

8.5.2 MULTIPHASE MERGES

The balanced merging algorithm has the advantage of being very simple; it is easy to write a program to perform this algorithm. Unfortunately, one reason it is simple is that it is "dumb" and cannot take advantage of opportunities to save work. As you can see, the balanced merge must read and write 40 runs of the initial, 40,000-record run size. Let's see how we can improve on it.

We can begin by noting that when we merge the extra run (R9–R10) with empty runs in Steps 3 and 4, we don't really accomplish anything. Figure 8.26 shows how we can dramatically reduce the amount of work that has to be done by simply not copying the extra run between Steps 2 and 3. Instead of merging this run with a dummy run, we simply stop tape 3 where it is. Tapes 1 and 2 now each contain a single, long (160,000 record) run made up of four of the initial runs. We rewind all the tapes but T3, and then perform a three-way merge of the runs on tapes T1, T2, and T3, writing the final result on T4. Adding this intelligence to the merging procedure reduces the number of initial runs that must be read and written from 40 down to 28.

The example in Fig. 8.26 clearly indicates that there are ways to improve on the performance of balanced merging. It is important to be

	T1	T2	T3	T4	
Step 1	1 1 1 1 1	1 1 1 1 1	—	—	
					Merge ten runs
Step 2	—	—	2 2 2	2 2	
					Merge eight runs
Step 3	4	4	. . 2	—	
					Merge ten runs
Step 4	—	—	—	10	

FIGURE 8.26 ▪ **Modification of balanced four-tape merge that does not rewind tape 3 between Steps 2 and 3 to avoid copying runs.**

able to state, in general terms, what it is about this second merging pattern that saves work:

☐ We use a higher-order merge. In place of two two-way merges, we use one three-way merge.
☐ We extend the merging of runs from one tape over several steps. Specifically, we merge some of the runs from T3 in Step 3 and some in Step 4. We could say that we merge the runs from T3 in two *phases*.

Note that these two aspects are related: Without the ability to do a three-way merge, it would not make sense to save the last part of T3 for use in a second phase. Conversely, if we do not leave part of T3 unmerged, there is no opportunity to do a three-way merge.

These ideas, the use of higher-order merge patterns and the merging of runs from a tape in *phases,* are the basis for two well-known approaches to merging called *polyphase merging* and *cascade merging.* In general, these merges share the following characteristics:

☐ The initial distribution of runs is such that at least the initial merge is a $J-1$ way merge, where J is the number of available tape drives.
☐ The distribution of the runs across the tapes is such that the tapes often contain different numbers of runs.

Figure 8.27 illustrates how a polyphase merge can be used to merge our ten runs distributed on four tape drives. This merge pattern reduces the number of initial runs that must be read and written to 25. It is easy to see that this reduction is a consequence of the use of several thee-way merges in place of the two-way merges in earlier examples. It should also be clear that the ability to do these operations as three-way

	T1	T2	T3	T4
Step 1	1 1 1 1 1	1 1 1	1 1	—
Step 2	. . 1 1 1	. . 1	—	3 3
Step 3	. . . 1 1	—	5	. 3
Step 4	 1	4	5	—
Step 5	—	—	—	10

Merge six runs

Merge five runs

Merge four runs

Merge ten runs

FIGURE 8.27 ▪ **Polyphase four-tape merge of ten runs.**

merges is related to the uneven nature of the initial distribution. Consider, for example, what happens if the initial distribution of runs is 4-3-3 rather than 5-3-2. We can perform three three-way merges to open up space on T3, but this also clears all the runs off of T2 and leaves only a single run on T1. Obviously, we are not able to perform another three-way merge as a second step.

Several questions arise at this point:

1. How does one choose an initial distribution that leads readily to an efficient merge pattern?
2. Are there algorithmic descriptions of the merge patterns, given an initial distribution?
3. Given N runs and J tape drives, is there some way to compute the *optimal* merging performance so that we have a yardstick against which to compare the performance of any specific algorithm?

Precise answers to these questions are beyond the scope of this text; in particular, the answer to Question 3 requires a more mathematical approach to the problem than the one we have taken here. Readers wanting more than an intuitive understanding of how to set up initial distributions should consult Knuth [1973b].

8.6 SORT/MERGE PACKAGES

Many very good utility programs are available for users who need to sort large files. Often the progams have enough intelligence to choose from one of several strategies, depending on the nature of the data to be sorted and the available system configuration. They also often allow users to exert some control (if they want it) over the organization of data and strategies used. Consequently, even if you are using a commercial sort package rather than designing your own sorting procedure, it is useful to be familiar with the variety of different ways to design merge-sorts. It is especially important to have a good general understanding of the most important factors and trade-offs influencing performance.

SUMMARY

In the first half of the chapter, we develop a cosequential processing model and apply it to two common problems—updating a general ledger and merge sorting. In the second half of the chapter we identify the most important factors influencing performance in merge-sorting operations and suggest some strategies for achieving good performance.

The cosequential processing model can be applied to problems that involve operations such as matching and merging (and combinations of these) on two or more sorted input files. We begin the chapter by illustrating the use of the model to perform a simple match of the elements common to two lists, and a merge of two lists. The procedures we develop to perform these two operations embody all the basic elements of the model.

In its most complete form, the model depends on certain assumptions about the data in the input files. We enumerate these assumptions in our formal description of the model. Given these assumptions, we can describe the processing components of the model.

The real value of the cosequential model is that it can be adapted to more substantial problems than simple matches or merges without too much alteration. We illustrate this by using the model to design a general ledger accounting program.

All of our early sample applications of the model involve only two input files. We next adapt the model to a multiway merge to show how the model might be extended to deal with more than two input lists. The problem of finding the minimum key value during each pass through the main loop becomes more complex as the number of input files increases. Its solution involves replacing the three-way selection statement with either a multiway selection or a procedure that keeps current keys in a list structure that can be processed more conveniently.

We see that the application of the model to K-way merging performs well for small values of K, but that for values of K greater than eight or so, it is more efficient to find the minimum key value by means of a selection tree.

After discussing multiway merging, we shift our attention to a problem that we encountered in a previous chapter—how to sort large files. The generally accepted solution when a file is too large for in-RAM sorts is some form of *merge sort*. A merge sort involves two steps:

1. Break the file into two or more sorted subfiles, or runs, using internal sorting methods; and
2. Merge the runs.

Ideally, we would like to keep every run in a separate file so we can perform the merge step with one pass through the runs. Unfortunately, practical considerations make it difficult to do this effectively. These considerations can differ depending on whether we are using tapes or disks (or a combination) to hold our files. We begin by looking at the factors influencing disk performance.

The critical element when merging many files on disk is seek time. The number of seeks depends largely on two interrelated factors: the number of different runs being merged, and the amount of internal buffer space available to hold parts of the runs. We can reduce the number of seeks in two ways:

- By performing the merge in more than one step; and/or
- By increasing the sizes of the initial sorted runs.

In both cases, the order of each merge step can be reduced, increasing the sizes of the internal buffers, and allowing more data to be processed per seek.

Looking at the first alternative first, we see how performing the merge in several steps can decrease the number of seeks dramatically, though it also means that we need to read through the data more than once (increasing total data transmission time).

The second alternative is realized through use of an algorithm called *replacement selection*. Replacement selection, which can be implemented by using the selection tree mentioned earlier, involves selecting the key from memory that has the lowest value, outputting that key, and replacing it with a new key from the input list.

With randomly organized files, replacement selection can be expected to produce runs twice as long as the number of internal storage locations available for performing the algorithms. Although this represents a major step toward decreasing the number of runs needing to be merged, it carries with it an additional cost. The need for a large buffer for performing the replacement selection operation leaves relatively little space for the I/O buffer, which means that many more seeks are involved in forming the runs than are needed when the sort step uses an in-RAM sort. If we compare the total number of seeks required by the two different approaches, we find that replacement selection can actually require more seeks; it performs substantially better only when there is a great deal of order in the initial file.

Next we turn our attention to file sorting on tapes. Since file I/O with tapes does not involve seeking, the problems and solutions associated with tape sorting can differ from those associated with disk sorting, although the fundamental goal of working with fewer, longer runs remains. With tape sorting, the primary measure of performance is the number of times each record must be transmitted. (Other factors, such as tape rewind time, can also be important, but we do not consider them here.)

Since tapes do not require seeking, replacement selection is almost always a good choice for creating initial runs. Since the number of drives available to hold run files is limited, the next question is how to distribute the files on the tapes. In most cases, it is necessary to put several runs on each of several tapes, reserving one or more other tapes for the results. This generally leads to merges of several steps, with the total number of runs being decreased after each merge step. Two approaches to doing this are *balanced merges* and *multiphase merges*. In a K-way balanced merge, all input tapes contain approximately the same number of runs, there are the same number of output tapes as there are input tapes, and the input tapes are read through entirely during each step. The number of runs is decreased by a factor of K after each step.

A multiphase merge (such as a *polyphase merge* or a *cascade merge*) requires that the runs initially be distributed unevenly among all but one of the available tapes. This increases the order of the merge, and as a result can decrease the number of times each record has to be read. It turns out that the initial distribution of runs among the first set of input tapes has a major effect on the number of times each record has to be read.

We conclude the chapter with a brief mention of sort/merge utilities, which are available on most large systems and can be very flexible and effective.

KEY TERMS

Balanced merge. A multistep merging technique that uses the same number of input devices as output devices. A two-way balanced merge uses two input tapes, each with approximately the same number of runs on it, and produces two output tapes, each with approximately half as many runs as the input tapes. A balanced merge is suitable for merge sorting with tapes, though it is not generally the best method (see multiphase merging).

Cosequential operations. Operations applied to problems that involve the performance of union, intersection, and more complex set operations on two or more sorted input files to produce one or more output files built from some combination of the elements of the input files. Cosequential operations commonly occur in matching, merging, and file-updating problems.

HIGH_VALUE. A value used in the cosequential model that is greater than any possible key value. By assigning HIGH_VALUE as the current key value for files for which an end-of-file condition has been encountered, extra logic for dealing with end-of-file conditions can be simplified.

K-way merge. A merge in which K input files are merged to produce one output file.

LOW_VALUE. A value used in the cosequential model that is less than any possible key value. By assigning LOW_VALUE as the previous key value during initialization, the need for certain other special start-up code is eliminated.

Match. The process of forming a sorted output file consisting of all the elements common to two or more sorted input files.

Merge. The process of forming a sorted output file that consists of the union of the elements from two or more sorted input files.

Multiphase merge. A multistep tape merge in which the initial distribution of runs is such that at least the initial merge is a J-1-way merge (J is the number of available tape drives), and where the distribution of runs across the tapes is such that the merge performs efficiently at every step. (See polyphase merge.)

Multistep merge. A merge in which not all runs are merged in one step. Rather, several sets of runs are merged separately, each set producing one long run consisting of the records from all of its runs. These new, longer sets are then merged, either all together or in several sets. After each step, the number of runs is decreased and the length of the runs is increased. The output of the final step is a single run consisting of the entire file. (Be careful not to confuse our use of the term *multistep merge* with *multiphase merge*.)

Although a multistep merge is theoretically more time consuming than is a single-step merge, it can involve much less seeking when performed on a disk, and it may be the only reasonable way to perform a merge on tape if the number of tape drives is limited.

Polyphase merge. A multiphase merge in which, ideally, the merge order is maximized at every step.

Replacement selection. A method of creating initial runs based on the idea of always *selecting* the record from memory whose key has the lowest value, outputting that record, and then *replacing* it in memory with a new record from the input list. When new records are brought in whose keys are greater than those of the most recently output records, they eventually become part of the run being created. When new records have keys that are less than those of the most recently output records, they are held over for the next run.

Replacement selection generally produces runs that are substantially longer than runs that can be created by in-RAM sorts, and hence can help improve performance in merge sorting. When using replacement selection with merge sorts on disk, however, one must be careful that the extra seeking required for replacement selection does not outweigh the benefits of having longer runs to merge.

Run. A sorted subset of a file resulting from the sort step of a sort merge or one of the steps of a multistep merge.

Selection tree. A binary tree in which each higher-level node represents the winner of the comparison between the two descendent keys. The minimum (or maximum) value in a selection tree is always at the root node, making the selection tree a good data structure for merging several lists. It is also a key structure in replacement selection algorithms, which can be used for producing long runs for merge sorts. (*Tournament sort,* an internal sort, is also based on the use of a selection tree.)

Sequence checking. Checking that records in a file are in the expected order. It is recommended that all files used in a cosequential operation be sequence checked.

Synchronization loop. The main loop in the cosequential processing model. A primary feature of the model is to do all synchronization within a single loop, rather than in multiple nested loops. A second objective is to keep the main synchronization loop as simple as possible. This is done by restricting the operations that occur within the loop to those that involve current keys, and by relegating as much special logic as possible (such as error checking and end-of-file checking) to subprocedures.

EXERCISES

1. Write an output procedure to go with the procedures described in Section 8.1 for doing cosequential matching. As a defensive measure, it is a good idea to have the output procedure do sequence checking in the same manner as the input procedure does.

2. Consider the cosequential initialization routine in Fig. 8.4. If PREV_1 and PREV_2 were not set to LOW_VALUE in this routine, how would *input()* have to be changed? How would this affect the adaptability of *input()* for use in other cosequential processing algorithms?

3. Consider the cosequential merge procedures described in Section 8.1. Comment on how they handle the following situations. If they do not correctly handle a situation, indicate how they might be altered to do so.
a) List 1 empty and List 2 not empty.
b) List 1 not empty and List 2 empty.
c) List 1 empty and List 2 empty.

4. In the ledger procedure example in Section 8.2, modify the procedure so that it also updates the ledger file with the new account balances for the month.

5. Use the K-way merge example as the basis for a procedure that is a K-way match.

6. Figure 8.17 shows a loop for doing a K-way merge, assuming that there are no duplicate names. If duplicate names are allowed, one could add to the procedure a facility for keeping a *list* of subscripts of duplicate lowest names. Alter the procedure to do this.

7. In Section 8.3, two methods are presented for choosing the lowest of K keys at each step in a K-way merge: a linear search and use of a selection tree. Compare the performances of the two approaches in terms of numbers of comparisons for $K = 2, 4, 8, 16, 32$, and 100. Why do you think the linear approach is recommended for values of K less than 8?

8. How much seek time is required to perform a one-step K-way merge such as the one described in Section 8.4 if the time for an average seek is 50 msec and the amount of available internal buffer space is 500K? 100K?

9. Performance in sorting is often measured in terms of the number of comparisons. Explain why the number of comparisons is not adequate for measuring performance in sorting large files.

10. Derive two formulas for the number of seeks required to perform the merge step of a one-step K-way sort-merge of a file with r records divided into k runs, where the amount of available RAM is equivalent to M records. If an internal sort such as Quicksort is used for the sort phase, you can assume that the length of each run is M, but if replacement selection is used, you can assume that the length of each run is about $2M$. Why?

11. Assume a quiet system with four separately addressable disk drives, each of which is able to hold several hundred megabytes. Assume that the 40 megabyte file of 400,000 records described in Section 8.4 is already on one of the drives. Design a sorting procedure for this sample file that uses the separate drives to minimize the amount of seeking required. Assume that the final sorted file is written off to tape and that buffering for this tape output is handled invisibly by the operating system. Is there any advantage to be gained by using replacement selection?

12. Use replacement selection to produce runs from the following files, assuming $P = 4$.

a) 23   29   5   17   9   55   41   3   51   33   18   24   11   47

b) 3   5   9   11   17   18   23   24   29   33   41   47   51   55

c) 55   51   47   41   33   29   24   23   18   17   11   9   5   3

13. Suppose you have a disk drive that has ten read/write heads per surface, so that ten cylinders may be accessed at any one time without having to move the actuator arm. If you could control the *physical* organization of runs stored on disk, how might you be able to exploit this arrangement in performing a sort-merge?

14. Assume we need to merge 14 runs on four tape drives. Develop merge patterns starting from each of these initial distributions:

8-4-2

7-4-3

6-5-3

5-5-4

15. A four-tape polyphase merge is to be performed to sort the list 24 36 13 25 16 45 29 38 23 50 22 19 43 30 11 27. The original list is on tape 4. Initial runs are of length 1. After initial sorting, tapes 1, 2, and 3 contain the following runs (a slash separates runs).

Tape 1: 24 / 36 / 13 / 25
Tape 2: 16 / 45 / 29 / 38 / 23 / 50
Tape 3: 22 / 19 / 43 / 30 / 11 / 27 / 47

a) Show the contents of tape 4 after one merge phase.
b) Show the contents of all four tapes after the sixth and fourth phases.
c) Comment on the appropriateness of the original 4-6-7 distribution for performing a polyphase merge.

16. Obtain a copy of the manual for one or more commercially available sort-merge packages. Identify the different kinds of choices available to users of the packages. Relate the options to the performance issues discussed in this chapter.

PROGRAMMING EXERCISES

17. Implement the cosequential match procedures described in Section 8.1 in C or Pascal.

18. Implement the cosequential merge procedures described in Section 8.1 in C or Pascal.

19. Implement a complete program corresponding to the solution to the general ledger problem presented in Section 8.2.

20. Design and implement a program to do the following:
a) Examine the contents of two sorted files M1 and M2.
b) Produce a third file COMMON containing a copy of records from the original two files that are identical.
c) Produce a fourth file DIFF that contains all records from the two files that are not identical.

FURTHER READINGS

The subject matter treated in this chapter can be divided into two separate topics: the presentation of a model for cosequential processing, and discussion of external merging procedures on tape and disk. Although most file processing texts discuss cosequential processing, they usually do it in the context of specific applications, rather than presenting a general model that can be adapted to a variety of applications. We found this useful and flexible model through Dr. James VanDoren, who developed this form of the model himself for presentation in the file structures course that he teaches. We are not aware of any discussion of the cosequential model elsewhere in the literature.

Quite a bit of work has been done towards developing simple and effective algorithms to do sequential file updating, which is an important instance of cosequential processing. The results deal with some of the same problems the cosequential model deals with, and some of the solutions are similar. See Levy [1982] and Dwyer [1981] for more.

Unlike cosequential processing, external sorting is a topic that is covered widely in the literature. The most complete discussion of the subject, by far, is in Knuth [1973b]. Students interested in the topic of external sorting must, at some point, familiarize themselves with Knuth's definitive summary of the subject. Knuth also describes replacement selection, as evidenced by our quoting from his book in this chapter.

Lorin [1975] spends several chapters on sort-merge techniques. Bradley [1981] provides a good treatment of replacement selection and multiphase merging, including some interesting comparisons of processing time on different devices. Tremblay and Sorenson [1984], Loomis [1983], and Claybrook [1983] also have chapters on external sorting.

Since the sorting of large files accounts for a large percentage of data processing time, most systems have sorting utilities available. IBM's DFSORT (described in IBM, 1985) is a flexible package for handling sorting and merging applications. A VAX sort utility is described in Digital [1984].

OBJECTIVES

Place the development of B-trees in the historical context of the problems they were designed to solve.

Look briefly at other tree structures that might be used on secondary storage, such as paged AVL trees.

Provide an understanding of the important properties possessed by B-trees, and show how these properties are especially well suited to secondary storage applications.

Describe fundamental operations on B-trees.

Introduce the notion of page buffering and virtual B-trees.

Describe variations of the fundamental B-tree algorithms, such as those used to build B* trees and B-trees with variable length records.

9 B-TREES AND OTHER TREE-STRUCTURED FILE ORGANIZATIONS

CHAPTER OUTLINE

9.1

INTRODUCTION—THE INVENTION OF THE B-TREE

Computer science is a young discipline. As evidence of this youth, consider that at the start of 1970, after astronauts had twice travelled to the moon, B-trees did not yet exist. Today, only fifteen years later, it is hard to think of a major general-purpose file system that is not built around a B-tree design.

Douglas Comer, in his excellent survey article, "The Ubiquitous B-Tree" [1979], recounts the competition among computer manufacturers and independent research groups that developed in the late 1960s. The goal was the discovery of a general method for storing and retrieving data in large file systems that would provide rapid access to the data with minimal overhead cost. Among the competitors were R. Bayer and E. McCreight, who were working for Boeing Corporation at that time. In 1972 they published an article, "Organization and Maintenance of Large Ordered Indexes," which announced B-trees to the world. By 1979, when Comer published his survey article, B-trees had already become so widely used that Comer was able to state that "the B-tree is, *de facto,* the standard organization for indexes in a database system."

We have reprinted the first few paragraphs of the 1972 Bayer and McCreight article† because it so concisely describes the facets of the problem that B-trees were designed to solve: how to access and maintain efficiently an index that is too large to hold in memory. You will remember that this is the same problem that is left unresolved in Chapter 7, on simple index structures. It will be clear as you read Bayer and McCreight's introduction that their work goes straight to the heart of the issues we raise back in the indexing chapter.

> In this paper we consider the problem of organizing and maintaining an index for a dynamically changing random access file. By an *index* we mean a collection of index elements which are pairs (x, a) of fixed size physically adjacent data items, namely a key x and some associated information a. The key x identifies a unique element in the index, the associated information is typically a pointer to a record or a collection of records in a random access file. For this paper the associated information is of no further interest.
>
> We assume that the index itself is so voluminous that only rather small parts of it can be kept in main store at one time. Thus the bulk of the index must be kept on some backup store. The class of backup stores considered are *pseudo random access devices* which have rather long access or wait time—as opposed to a true random access device like core store—and a rather high data rate once the transmission of physically sequential data has been initiated. Typical pseudo random access devices are: fixed and moving head disks, drums, and data cells.
>
> Since the data file itself changes, it must be possible not only to search the index and to retrieve elements, but also to delete and to insert keys—more accurately index elements—economically. The index organization described in this paper allows retrieval, insertion, and deletion of keys in time proportional to $\log_k I$ or better, where I is the

†From *Acta-Informica,* 1:173–189, © 1972, Springer Verlag, New York. Reprinted with permission.

size of the index, and k is a device dependent natural number which describes the page size such that the performance of the maintenance and retrieval scheme becomes near optimal.

Exercises 17, 18, and 19 at the end of Chapter 7 introduce the notion of a paged index. Bayer and McCreight's statement that they have developed a scheme with retrieval time proportional to $\log_k I$, where k is related to the page size, is very significant. As we will see, the use of a B-tree with a page size of 64 to index a file with a million records results in being able to find the key for any record in no more than four seeks to the disk. A binary search on the same file can require as many as 20 seeks. Moreover, we are talking about getting this kind of performance from a system that requires only minimal overhead as keys are inserted and deleted.

Before looking in detail at Bayer and McCreight's solution, let's first return to a more careful look at the problem, picking up where we left off in Chapter 7. We will also look at some of the data and file structures that were routinely used to attack the problem before the invention of B-trees. Given this background, it will be easier to appreciate the contribution made by Bayer and McCreight's work.

One last matter before we begin: Why the name *B-tree*? Comer [1979] provides this footnote:

> The origin of "B-tree" has never been explained by [Bayer and McCreight]. As we shall see, "balanced," "broad," or "bushy" might apply. Others suggest that the "B" stands for Boeing. Because of his contributions, however, it seems appropriate to think of B-trees as "Bayer"-trees.

9.2
STATEMENT OF THE PROBLEM

The fundamental problem with keeping an index on secondary storage is, of course, that accessing secondary storage is slow. This fundamental problem can be broken down into two more specific problems:

☐ *Binary searching requires too many seeks.* Searching for a key on a disk often involves seeking to different disk tracks. Since seeks are expensive, a search that has to look in more than three or four locations before finding the key often requires more time than is desirable. If we are using a binary search, four seeks is only enough to differentiate between 15 items. An average of about 9.5 seeks is required to find a key in an index of 1,000 items using a binary search. We need to find a way to home in on a key using fewer seeks.

◻ *It can be very expensive to keep the index in sorted order so we can perform a binary search.* As we see in Chapter 7, if inserting a key involves moving a large number of the other keys in the index, index maintenance is very nearly impractical on secondary storage for indexes consisting of only a few hundred keys, much less thousands of keys. We need to find a way to make insertions and deletions that have only local effects in the index, rather than requiring massive reorganization.

These were the two critical problems that confronted Bayer and Mc-Creight in 1970. They serve as guideposts for steering our discussion of the use of tree structures for secondary storage retrieval.

9.3 BINARY SEARCH TREES AS A SOLUTION

Let's begin by addressing the second of these two problems, looking at the cost of keeping a list in sorted order so we can perform binary searches. Given the sorted list in Fig. 9.1, we can express a binary search of this list as a *binary search tree*, as shown in Fig. 9.2.

Using elementary data structure techniques, it is a simple matter to create nodes that contain right and left link fields so that the binary search tree can be constructed as a linked structure. Figure 9.3 illustrates a linked representation of the first two levels of the binary search tree shown in Fig. 9.2. In each node, the left and right links point to the left and right *children* of the node.

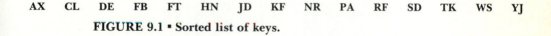

AX CL DE FB FT HN JD KF NR PA RF SD TK WS YJ

FIGURE 9.1 ▪ Sorted list of keys.

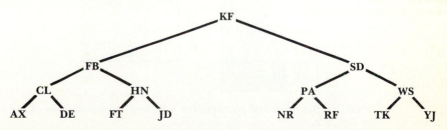

FIGURE 9.2 ▪ Binary search tree representation of the list of keys.

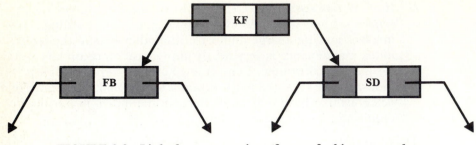

FIGURE 9.3 ▪ Linked representation of part of a binary search tree.

If each node is treated as a fixed length record in which the link fields contain relative record numbers (RRNs) pointing to other nodes, then it is possible to place such a tree structure on secondary storage. Figure 9.4 illustrates the contents of the 15 records that would be required to form the binary tree depicted in Fig. 9.2.

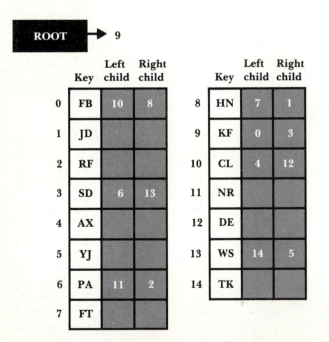

	Key	Left child	Right child		Key	Left child	Right child
0	FB	10	8	8	HN	7	1
1	JD			9	KF	0	3
2	RF			10	CL	4	12
3	SD	6	13	11	NR		
4	AX			12	DE		
5	YJ			13	WS	14	5
6	PA	11	2	14	TK		
7	FT						

ROOT → 9

FIGURE 9.4 ▪ Record contents for a linked representation of the binary tree in Fig. 9.2.

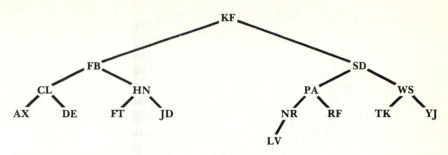

FIGURE 9.5 ▪ Binary search tree with LV added.

Note that over half of the link fields in the file are empty because they are leaf nodes, with no children. In practice, leaf nodes need to contain some special character, such as −1, to indicate that the search through the tree has reached the leaf level and that there are no more nodes on the search path. We leave the fields blank in this figure to make them more noticeable, illustrating the potentially substantial cost in terms of space utilization incurred by this kind of linked representation of a tree.

But to focus on the costs and not the advantages is to miss the important new capability that this tree structure gives us: We no longer have to sort the file to be able to perform a binary search. Note that the records in the file illustrated in Fig. 9.4 appear in random rather than sorted order. The sequence of the records in the file has no necessary relation to the structure of the tree; all the information about the logical structure is carried in the link fields. The very positive consequence that follows from this is that if we add a new key to the file, such as *LV, we need only link it to the appropriate leaf node to create a tree that provides search performance that is as good as we would get with a binary search on a sorted list.* The tree with LV added is illustrated in Fig. 9.5.

Search performance on this tree is still good because the tree is in a *balanced* state. By balanced we mean that the height of the shortest path to a leaf does not differ from the height of the longest path by more than one level. For the tree in Fig. 9.5, this difference of one is as close as we can get to *complete balance,* where all the paths from root to leaf are exactly the same length.

Consider what happens if we go on to enter the following eight keys to the tree in the sequence in which they appear.

NP   MB   TM   LA   UF   ND   TS   NK

Just searching down through the tree and adding each key at its correct position in the search tree results in the tree shown in Fig. 9.6.

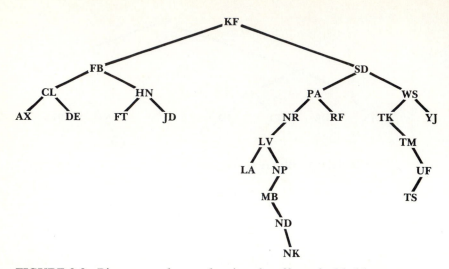

FIGURE 9.6 ▪ Binary search tree showing the effect of added keys.

The tree is now out of balance. This is a typical result for trees built by placing keys into the tree as they occur without rearrangement. The resulting disparity between the length of various search paths is undesirable in any binary search tree, but is especially troublesome if the nodes of the tree are being kept on secondary storage. There are now keys that require seven, eight, or nine seeks for retrieval. A binary search on a sorted list of these 24 keys requires only five seeks in the worst case. Although the use of a tree lets us avoid sorting, we are paying for this convenience in terms of extra seeks at retrieval time. For trees with hundreds of keys, in which an out-of-balance search path might extend to 30, 40, or more seeks, this price is too high.

9.4 AVL TREES

Earlier we said that there is no *necessary* relationship between the order in which keys are entered and the structure of the tree. We stress the word *necessary* because it is clear that order of entry is, in fact, important in determining the structure of the sample tree illustrated in Fig. 9.6. The reason for this sensitivity to the order of entry is that, so far, we have just been linking the newest nodes at the leaf levels of the tree. This approach can result in some very undesirable tree organizations.

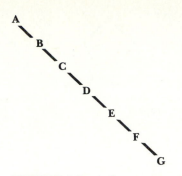

FIGURE 9.7 ▪ **A degenerate tree.**

Suppose, for example, that our keys consist of the letters A–G, and that we receive these keys in alphabetical order. Linking the nodes together as we receive them produces a degenerate tree that is, in fact, nothing more than a linked list, as illustrated in Fig. 9.7.

The solution to this problem is somehow to reorganize the nodes of the tree as we receive new keys, maintaining a near optimal tree structure. One elegant method for handling such reorganization results in a class of trees known as *AVL trees,* in honor of the pair of Russian mathematicians, G.M. Adel'son-Vel'skii and E.M. Landis, who first defined them. An AVL tree is a *height-balanced* tree. This means that there is a limit placed on the amount of difference that is allowed between the heights of any two subtrees sharing a common root. In an AVL tree the maximum allowable difference is 1. An AVL tree is therefore called a *height-balanced 1-tree* or *HB(1) tree.* It is a member of a more general class of height-balanced trees known as *HB(k)* trees, which are permitted to be *k* levels out of balance.

The trees illustrated in Fig. 9.8 have the AVL, or HB(1) property. Note that no two subtrees of any root differ by more than one level.

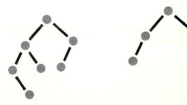

FIGURE 9.8 ▪ **AVL trees.**

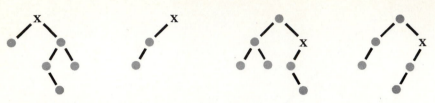

FIGURE 9.9 ▪ **Trees that are not AVL trees.**

The trees in Fig. 9.9 are *not* AVL trees. In each of these trees, the root of the subtree that is not in balance is marked with an X.

The two features that make AVL trees important are:

☐ By setting a maximum allowable difference in the height of any two subtrees, AVL trees guarantee a certain minimum level of performance in searching; and

☐ Maintaining a tree in AVL form as new nodes are inserted involves the use of one of a set of four possible rotations. Each of the rotations is confined to a single, local area of the tree. The most complex of the rotations requires only five pointer reassignments.

AVL trees are an important class of data structure. The operations used to build and maintain AVL trees are described in Knuth [1973b], Standish [1980], and elsewhere. AVL trees are not themselves directly applicable to most file structure problems because, like all strictly *binary* trees, they have too many levels—they are too *deep*. However, in the context of our general discussion of the problem of accessing and maintaining indexes that are too large to fit in memory, AVL trees are interesting because they suggest that it is possible to define procedures that maintain height balance.

The fact that an AVL tree is height balanced guarantees that search performance approximates that of a *completely balanced* tree. For exam-

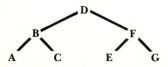

FIGURE 9.10 ▪ **A completely balanced search tree.**

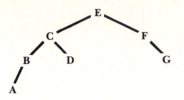

FIGURE 9.11 ▪ **A search tree constructed using AVL procedures.**

ple, the completely balanced form of a tree made up from the input keys

$$B \quad C \quad G \quad E \quad F \quad D \quad A$$

is illustrated in Fig. 9.10, and the AVL tree resulting from the same input keys, arriving in the same sequence, is illustrated in Fig. 9.11.

For a completely balanced tree, the worst-case search to find a key, given N possible keys, looks at

$$\log_2 (N + 1)$$

levels of the tree. For an AVL tree, the worst-case search could look at

$$1.44 \log_2 (N + 2)$$

levels. So, given 1,000,000 keys, a completely balanced tree requires seeking to 20 levels for some of the keys, but never to 21 levels. If the tree is an AVL tree, the maximum number of levels increases to only 28. This is a very interesting result, given that the AVL procedures guarantee that a single reorganization requires no more than five pointer reassignments. Empirical studies by VanDoren and Gray [1974], among others, have shown that such local reorganizations are required for approximately every other insertion into the tree and for approximately every fourth deletion. So height balancing using AVL methods guarantees that we will obtain a reasonable approximation to optimal binary tree performance at a cost that is acceptable in most applications using primary, random access memory.

When we are using secondary storage, a procedure that requires more than five or six seeks to find a key is less than desirable; 20 or 28 seeks is unacceptable. Returning to the two problems that we identified earlier in this chapter:

☐ Binary searching requires too many seeks; and
☐ Keeping an index in sorted order is expensive,

we can see that height balanced trees provide an acceptable solution to the second problem. Now we need to turn our attention to the first problem.

9.5
PAGED BINARY TREES

Once again we are confronting what is perhaps the most critical feature of secondary storage devices: It takes a relatively long time to seek to a specific location, but once the read head is positioned and ready, reading or writing a stream of contiguous bytes proceeds rapidly. This combination of slow seek and fast data transfer leads naturally to the notion of paging. In a paged system, you do not incur the cost of a disk seek just to get a few bytes. Instead, once you have taken the time to seek to an area of the disk, you read in an entire page from the file. This page might consist of a great many individual records. If the next bit of information you need from the disk is in the page that was just read in, you have saved the cost of a disk access.

Paging, then, is a potential solution to our searching problem. By dividing a binary tree into pages and then storing each page in a block of contiguous locations on disk, we should be able to reduce the number of seeks associated with any search. Figure 9.12 illustrates such a paged tree. In this tree we are able to locate any one of the 63 nodes in the tree with no more than two disk accesses. Note that every page holds seven nodes and can branch to eight new pages. If we extend the tree to one additional level of paging, we add 64 new pages; we can then find any one of 511 nodes in only three seeks. Adding yet another level of paging lets us find any one of 4095 nodes in only four seeks. A binary search of a list of 4095 items can take as many as 12 seeks.

Clearly, breaking the tree into pages has the potential to result in faster searching on secondary storage, providing us with much faster retrieval than any other form of keyed access that we have considered up to this point. Moreover, our use of a page size of seven in Fig. 9.12 is dictated more by the constraints of the printed page than by anything having to do with secondary storage devices. A more typical example of a page size might be 8 kilobytes capable of holding 511 key/reference field pairs. Given this page size, and assuming that each page contains a completely balanced, full tree, and that the pages themselves are organized as a completely balanced, full tree, it is then possible to find any one of 134,217,727 keys with only three seeks. That is the kind of performance we are looking for. Note that, while the number of seeks

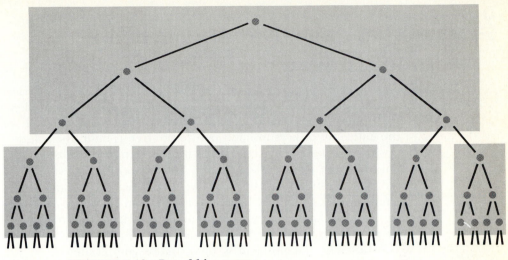

FIGURE 9.12 ▪ Paged binary tree.

required for a worst-case search of a completely full, balanced binary tree is

$$\log_2 (N + 1)$$

where N is the number of keys in the tree, the number of seeks required for the *paged* versions of a completely full, balanced tree is

$$\log_{k+1} (N + 1)$$

where N is, once again, the number of keys. The new variable, k, is the number of keys held in a single page. The second formula is actually a generalization of the first, since the number of keys in a page of a purely binary tree is 1. It is the logarithmic effect of the page size that makes the impact of paging so dramatic:

$$\log_2 (134{,}217{,}727 + 1) \quad = 27 \text{ seeks}$$

$$\log_{511+1} (134{,}217{,}727 + 1) = 3 \text{ seeks.}$$

The use of large pages does not come free. Every access to a page requires the transmission of a large amount of data, most of which is not used. This extra transmission time is well worth the cost, however, because it saves so many seeks, which are far more time consuming than the extra transmissions. A much more serious problem, which we look at next, has to do with keeping the paged tree organized.

9.6

THE PROBLEM WITH THE TOP-DOWN CONSTRUCTION OF PAGED TREES

Breaking a tree into pages is a strategy that is well suited to the physical characteristics of secondary storage devices such as disks. The problem, once we decide to implement a paged tree, is how to build it. If we have the entire set of keys in hand before the tree is built, the solution to the problem is relatively straightforward: We can sort the list of keys and build the tree from this sorted list. Most important, if we plan to start building the tree from the root, we know that the middle key in the sorted list of keys should be the *root key* within the *root page* of the tree. In short, we know where to begin and are assured that this beginning point will divide the set of keys in a balanced manner.

Unfortunately, the problem is much more complicated if we are receiving keys in random order and inserting them as soon as we receive them. Assume that we must build a paged tree as we receive the following sequence of single letter keys:

C S D T A M P I B W N G U R K E H O L J Y Q Z F X V

We will build a paged binary tree that contains a maximum of three keys per page. As we insert the keys, we rotate them within a page as necessary to keep each page as balanced as possible. The resulting tree is illustrated in Fig. 9.13. Evaluated in terms of the depth of the tree (measured in pages), this tree does not turn out too badly. (Consider, for example, what happens if the keys arrive in alphabetical order.)

Even though this tree is not dramatically misshapen, it clearly illustrates the difficulties inherent in building a paged binary tree from the top down. When you start from the root, the initial keys must, of necessity, go into the root. In this example at least two of these keys, *C* and *D,* are not keys that we want there. They are adjacent in sequence and tend toward the beginning of the total set of keys. Consequently they force the tree out of balance.

Once the wrong keys are placed in the root of the tree (or in the root of any subtree further down the tree), what can you do about it? Unfortunately, there is no easy answer to this. We cannot simply rotate entire pages of the tree in the same way that we would rotate individual keys in an unpaged tree. If we rotate the tree so that the initial root page moves down to the left, moving the *C* and *D* keys into a better position, then the *S* key is out of place. So we must break up the pages.

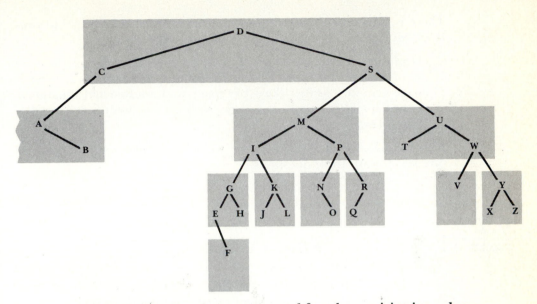

FIGURE 9.13 ▪ **Paged tree constructed from keys arriving in random input sequence.**

This opens up a whole world of possibilities, and difficulties. Breaking up the pages implies rearranging them to create new pages that are both internally balanced and well arranged relative to other pages. Try creating a page rearrangement algorithm for the simple, three-keys-per-page tree from Fig. 9.13. You will find it very difficult to create an algorithm that has only local effects, rearranging just a few pages. The tendency is for rearrangements and adjustments to spread out through a large part of the tree. This situation grows even more complex with larger page sizes.

So, although we have determined that the idea of collecting keys into pages is a very good one from the standpoint of reducing seeks to the disk, we have not yet found a way to collect the right keys. We are still confronting at least two unresolved questions:

☐ How do we ensure that the keys in the root page turn out to be good *separator* keys, dividing up the set of other keys more or less evenly?

☐ How do we avoid grouping keys, such as C, D, and S in our example, that should not share a page?

There is, in addition, a third question that we have not yet had to confront because of the small page size of our sample tree:

☐   How can we guarantee that each of the pages contains at least some minimum number of keys? If we are working with a larger page size, such as 8191 keys per page, we want to avoid situations in which a large number of pages each contains only a few dozen keys.

Bayer and McCreight's 1972 B-tree article provides a solution directed precisely toward these questions.

9.7 B-TREES: WORKING UP FROM THE BOTTOM

A number of the elegant, powerful ideas used in computer science have grown out of looking at a problem from a different viewpoint. B-trees are an example of this viewpoint-shift phenomenon.

The key insight required to make the leap from the kinds of trees we have been considering to a new solution, B-trees, is that we can choose to *build trees upwards from the bottom instead of downwards from the top*. So far, we have assumed the necessity of starting construction from the root as a given. Then, as we found that we had the wrong keys in the root, we tried to find ways to repair the problem with rearrangement algorithms. Bayer and McCreight recognized that the decision to work down from the root was, of itself, the problem. Rather than finding ways to undo a bad situation, they decided to avoid the difficulty altogether. With B-trees, you allow the root to *emerge*, rather than set it up and then find ways to change it.

9.8 SPLITTING AND PROMOTING

In a B-tree, a page, or *node*, consists of an ordered sequence of keys and a set of pointers. There is no explicit tree within a node, as with the paged trees shown previously; there is just an ordered list of keys and some pointers. The number of pointers always exceeds the number of keys by one. The maximum number of pointers that can be stored in a node is called the *order* of the B-tree. For example, suppose we

FIGURE 9.14 ▪ Initial leaf of a B-tree with a page size of seven.

have an order-eight B-tree. Each page can hold at most seven keys and eight pointers. Our initial *leaf* of the tree might have a structure like that illustrated in Fig. 9.14 after the insertion of the letters

> B C G E F D A

The starred (*) fields are the pointer fields. In this leaf, as in any other leaf node, the value of all the pointers is set to indicate end of list. By definition, a leaf node has no children in the tree; consequently the pointers do not lead to other pages in the tree. We assume that the pointers in the leaf pages usually contain an invalid pointer value, such as −1. Note, incidentally, that this *leaf* is also our *root*.

In a real-life application there is also usually some other information stored with the key, such as a reference to a record containing data that are associated with the key. Consequently, additional pointer fields in each page might actually lead to some associated data records that are stored elsewhere. But, paraphrasing Bayer and McCreight, for our present purposes, "the associated information is of no further interest."

Building the first page is easy enough. As we insert new keys, we use a single disk access to read the page into memory and, working in memory, insert the key into its place in the page. Since we are working in electronic memory, this insertion is relatively inexpensive compared to the cost of additional disk accesses.

But what happens as additional keys come in? Suppose we want to add the key *J* to the B-tree. When we try to insert the *J* we find that our leaf is full. We then *split* the leaf into two leaves, distributing the keys as evenly as we can between the old leaf node and the new one, as shown in Fig. 9.15.

Since we now have two leaves, we need to create a higher level in the tree to enable us to choose between the leaves when searching. In

FIGURE 9.15 ▪ Splitting the leaf to accommodate the new *J* key.

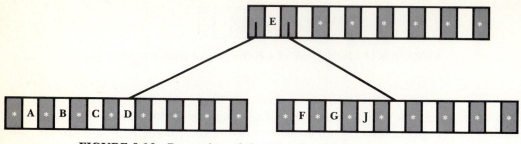

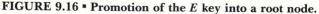

FIGURE 9.16 ▪ Promotion of the E key into a root node.

short, we need to create a new root. We do this by *promoting* a key that *separates* the leaves. In this case, we promote the *E* from the first position in the second leaf, as illustrated in Fig. 9.16.

In this example we describe the splitting and the promotion operations in two steps to make the procedure as clear as possible; in practice, splitting and promotion are handled in a single operation.

Let's see how a B-tree grows given the key sequence that produces the paged binary tree illustrated in Fig. 9.13. The sequence is

$$C \ S \ D \ T \ A \ M \ P \ I \ B \ W \ N \ G \ U \ R \ K \ E \ H \ O \ L \ J \ Y \ Q \ Z \ F \ X \ V$$

We use an order-four B-tree (four pointer fields and three key fields per page), since this corresponds to the page size of the paged binary tree. Using such a small page size has the additional advantage of causing pages to split more frequently, providing us with more examples of splitting and promotion. We omit explicit indication of the pointer fields so we can fit a larger tree on the printed page.

Figure 9.17 illustrates the growth of the tree up to the point at which the root node is about to split. Figure 9.18 shows the tree after the splitting of the root node. The figure also shows how the tree continues to grow as the remaining keys in the sequence are added. We number each of the tree's pages (upper left corner of each node) so you can distinguish the newly added pages from the ones already in the tree.

Note that the tree is always perfectly balanced with regard to height; the path from the root to any leaf is the same as the path from the root to any other leaf. Also note that the keys that are promoted upward into the tree are necessarily the kind of keys we want in a root: keys that are good separators. By working up from the leaf level, splitting and promoting as pages fill up, we overcome the problems that plague our earlier paged binary tree efforts.

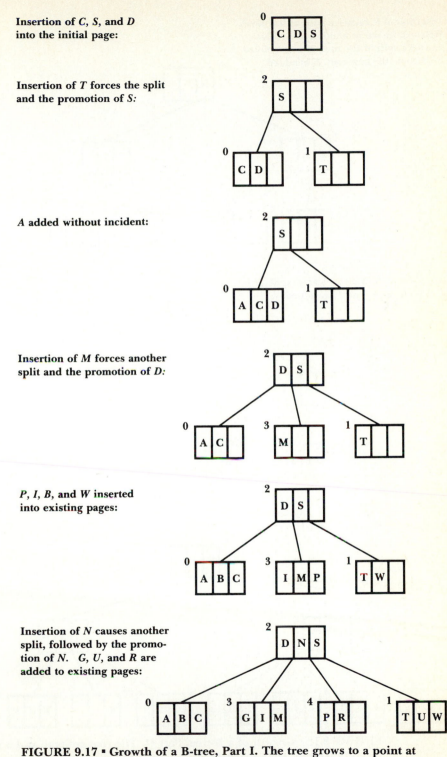

Insertion of *C, S,* and *D*
into the initial page:

Insertion of *T* forces the split
and the promotion of *S:*

A added without incident:

Insertion of *M* forces another
split and the promotion of *D:*

P, I, B, and *W* inserted
into existing pages:

Insertion of *N* causes another
split, followed by the promotion of *N. G, U,* and *R* are
added to existing pages:

FIGURE 9.17 ▪ Growth of a B-tree, Part I. The tree grows to a point at
which splitting of the root is imminent.

311

Insertion of *K* causes a split at leaf level,
followed by the promotion of *K*. This
causes a split of the root. *N* is promoted
to become the new root. *E* is added
to a leaf:

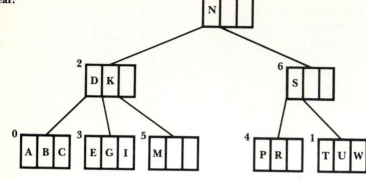

Insertion of *H* causes a leaf to split. *H* is
promoted. *O*, *L*, and *J* are added:

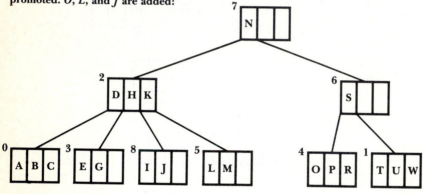

Insertion of *Y* and *Q* force two more leaf
splits and promotions. Remaining letters
are added:

FIGURE 9.18 ▪ Growth of a B-tree, Part II. The root splits to add a new
level; remaining keys are inserted.

<u>**9.9**</u>

ALGORITHMS FOR B-TREE SEARCHING AND INSERTION

Now that we have had a brief look at how B-trees work on paper, let's outline the structures and algorithms required to make them work in a computer. Most of the code that follows is pseudocode. C and Pascal implementations of the algorithms can be found at the end of the chapter.

PAGE STRUCTURE.   We begin by defining one possible form for the page used by a B-tree. As you see later in this chapter and in the following chapter, there are many different ways to construct the page of a B-tree. We start with a simple one in which each key is a single character. If the maximum number of keys and children allowed on a page is MAXKEYS and MAXCHILDREN, respectively, then the following structures expressed in C and Pascal describe a page called PAGE.

In C:
```
struct BTPAGE {
    short    KEYCOUNT;           /* number of keys stored in PAGE */
    char     KEY[MAXKEYS];       /* the actual keys               */
    short    CHILD[MAXKEYS+1];   /* RRNs of children              */
} PAGE;
```

In Pascal:
```
TYPE
    BTPAGE = RECORD
                KEYCOUNT: integer;
                KEY      : array[1..MAXKEYS] of char;
                CHILD    : array[1..MAXCHILDREN] of integer
             END;
VAR
    PAGE : BTPAGE;
```

Given this page structure, the file containing the B-tree consists of a set of fixed length records. Each record contains one page of the tree. Since the keys in the tree are single letters, this structure uses an array of *characters* to hold the keys. More typically, the key array is a vector of strings rather than just a vector of characters. The variable PAGE.KEYCOUNT is useful when the algorithms must determine whether a page is full or not. The PAGE.CHILD[] array contains the RRNs of PAGE's children, if there are any. When there is no descendent, the corresponding element of PAGE.CHILD[] is set to a nonaddress value, which we call NIL. Figure 9.19 shows two pages in a B-tree of order four.

Part of a B-tree:

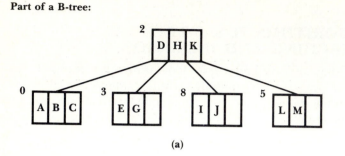

(a)

Contents of PAGE for pages 2 and 3:

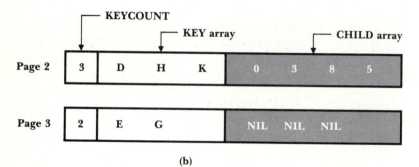

(b)

FIGURE 9.19 ▪ **A B-tree of order four. (a) An internal node and some leaf nodes. (b) Nodes 2 and 3, as we might envision them in the structure PAGE.**

SEARCHING. The first B-tree algorithms we examine are a tree-*searching* procedure. Searching is a good place to begin because it is relatively simple, yet still illustrates the characteristic aspects of most B-tree algorithms:

☐ They are recursive, and;
☐ They work in two stages, operating alternatively on entire pages and then *within* pages.

The searching procedure calls itself recursively, seeking to a page and then searching through the page, looking for the key at successively lower levels of the tree until it either finds the key or finds that it cannot descend further, having reached beyond the leaf level. Figure 9.20 contains a description of the searching procedure in pseudocode.

Let's work through the function by hand, searching for the key *K* in the tree illustrated in Fig. 9.21. We begin by calling the function with

```
FUNCTION: search (RRN, KEY, FOUND_RRN , FOUND_POS)

    if RRN == NIL then     /* stopping condition for the recursion */
        return NOT FOUND
    else
        read page RRN into PAGE
        look through PAGE for KEY, setting POS equal to the
            position where KEY occurs or should occur.
        if KEY was found then
            FOUND_RRN := RRN        /* current RRN contains the key */
            FOUND_POS := POS
            return FOUND
        else /* follow CHILD reference to next level down   */
            return(search(PAGE.CHILD[POS], KEY, FOUND_RRN, FOUND_POS))
        endif
    endif

end FUNCTION
```

FIGURE 9.20 ▪ Function *search (RRN, KEY, FOUND_RRN, FOUND_POS)*
searches recursively through the B-tree to find KEY. Each invocation
searches the page referenced by RRN. The arguments FOUND_RRN and
FOUND_POS identify the page and position of the key, if it is found. If
search() **finds the key, it returns FOUND. If it goes beyond the leaf level**
without finding the key, it returns NOT FOUND.

the RRN argument equal to the RRN of the root (2). This RRN is not
NIL, so the function reads the root into PAGE, then searches for *K*
among the elements of PAGE.KEY[]. The *K* is not found. Since *K*
should go between *D* and *N*, POS identifies position 1† in the root as
the position of the pointer to where the search should proceed. So
search() calls itself, this time using the RRN stored in PAGE.CHILD[1].
The value of this RRN is 3.

On the next call, *search()* reads the page containing the keys *G, I,*
and *M*. Once again the function searches for *K* among the keys in
PAGE.KEY[]. Again, *K* is not found. This time PAGE.CHILD[2] indicates where the search should proceed. *Search()* calls itself again, this
time using the RRN stored in PAGE.CHILD[2].

Since this call is from a leaf node, PAGE.CHILD[2] is NIL, so the
call to *search()* fails immediately. The value NOT FOUND is passed
back through the various levels of *return* statements until the program
that originally calls *search()* receives the information that the key is not
found.

†We will use zero origin indexing in these examples, so the leftmost key in a page is
PAGE.KEY[0], and the RRN of the leftmost child is PAGE.CHILD[0].

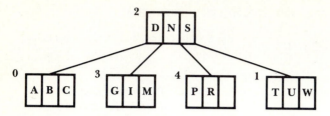

FIGURE 9.21 ▪ B-tree used for the search example.

Now let's use *search()* to look for *M*, which *is* in the tree. It follows the same downward path that it did for *K*, but this time it finds the *M* in position 2 of page 3. It stores the values 3 and 2 in *FOUND_RRN* and *FOUND_POS*, respectively, indicating that *M* can be found in the position 2 of page 3, and returns the value FOUND.

INSERTION, SPLITTING AND PROMOTION.   There are two important observations we can make about the insertion, splitting, and promotion process.

☐   It begins with a search that proceeds all the way down to the leaf level; and

☐   After finding the insertion location at the leaf level, the work of insertion, splitting and promotion proceeds upwards from the bottom.

Consequently, we can conceive of our recursive procedure as having three phases:

1. A search-page step that, as in the *search()* function, takes place before the recursive call;

2. The recursive call itself, which moves the operation down through the tree as it searches for either the key or the place to insert it; and

3. Insertion, splitting, and promotion logic that are executed after the recursive call, the action taking place on the upward return path following the recursive descent.

We need an example of an insertion so we can watch the insertion procedure work through these phases. Let's insert the $ character into the tree shown in the top half of Fig. 9.22, which contains all of the letters of the alphabet. Since the ASCII character sequence places the $ character ahead of the character *A*, the insertion is into the page with an RRN of 0. This page and its parent are both already full, so the insertion causes splitting and promotion that result in the tree shown in the bottom half of Fig. 9.22.

Now let's see how the *insert()* function performs this splitting and promotion. Since the function operates recursively, it is important to understand how the function arguments are used on successive calls. The *insert()* function that we are about to describe uses four arguments:

CURRENT_RRN	The RRN of the B-tree page that is currently in use. As the function recursively descends and ascends the tree, all the RRNS on the search and insertion path are used.
KEY	The key that is to be inserted.
PROMO_KEY	Argument used only to carry back the return value. If the insertion results in a split and the promotion of a key, PROMO_KEY contains the promoted key on the ascent back up the tree.
PROMO_R_CHILD	This is another return value argument. If there is a split, higher levels of the calling sequence must not only insert the promoted key value, but also the RRN of the new page created in the split. When PROMO_KEY is inserted, PROMO_R_CHILD is the right child pointer inserted with it.

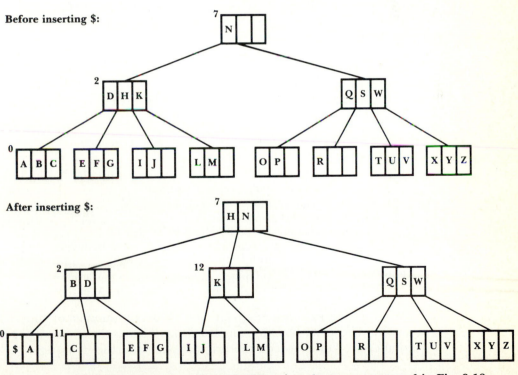

FIGURE 9.22 ▪ The effect of adding $ to the tree constructed in Fig. 9.18.

In addition to the values returned via the arguments PROMO_ KEY and PROMO_R_CHILD, *insert()* returns the value PROMOTION if it makes a promotion, NO PROMOTION if an insertion is done and nothing is promoted, and ERROR if the insertion cannot be made.

Figure 9.23 illustrates the way the values of these arguments change as the *insert()* function is called and calls itself to perform the insertion of the $ character. The figure makes a number of important points:

☐ During the search step part of the insertion, only CURRENT_ RRN changes as the function calls itself, descending the tree. This search path of successive calls includes every page of the tree that can be affected by splitting and promotion on the return path.

☐ The search step ends when CURRENT_RRN is NIL. There are no further levels to search.

☐ As each recursive call returns, we execute the insertion and splitting logic at that level. If the lower-level function returns the value PROMOTION, then we have a key to insert at this level. Otherwise, we have no work to do and can just return. For example, we are able to insert *H* at the highest (root) level of the tree without splitting, and therefore return NO PROMOTION from this level. That means that the PROMO_KEY and PROMO_ R_CHILD from this level have no meaning.

Given this introduction to the *insert()* function's operation, we are ready to look at an algorithm for the function shown in Fig. 9.24. We have already described *insert()*'s arguments. There are several important local variables as well:

PAGE	The page that *insert()* is currently examining.
NEWPAGE	New page created if a split occurs.
POS	The position in PAGE where the key occurs (if it is present) or would occur (if inserted).
P_B_RRN	The relative record number promoted *from below up to this level*. If a split occurs at the next lower level, P_B_RRN contains the relative record number of the new page created during the split. P_B_RRN is the right child that is inserted with P_B_KEY into PAGE.
P_B_KEY	The key promoted from below up to this level. This key, along with P_B_RRN is inserted into PAGE.

When coded in a real language, *insert()* uses a number of support functions. The most obvious one is *split()*, which creates a new page, distributes the keys between the original page and the new page, and

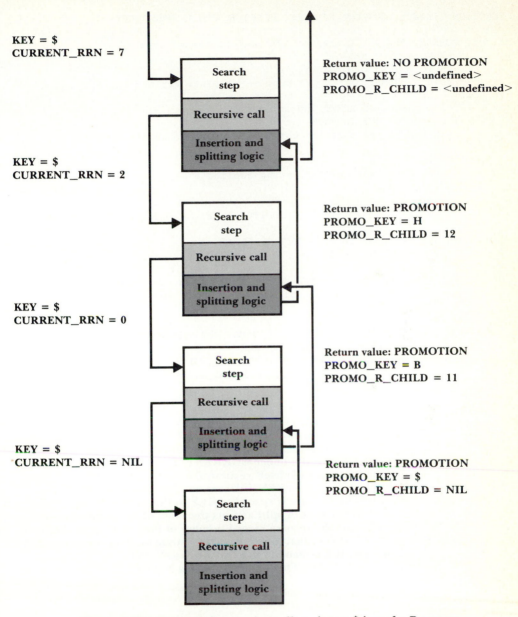

KEY = $
CURRENT_RRN = 7

Return value: NO PROMOTION
PROMO_KEY = <undefined>
PROMO_R_CHILD = <undefined>

KEY = $
CURRENT_RRN = 2

Return value: PROMOTION
PROMO_KEY = H
PROMO_R_CHILD = 12

KEY = $
CURRENT_RRN = 0

Return value: PROMOTION
PROMO_KEY = B
PROMO_R_CHILD = 11

KEY = $
CURRENT_RRN = NIL

Return value: PROMOTION
PROMO_KEY = $
PROMO_R_CHILD = NIL

Search step
Recursive call
Insertion and splitting logic

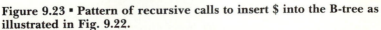

Figure 9.23 ▪ Pattern of recursive calls to insert $ into the B-tree as illustrated in Fig. 9.22.

```
FUNCTION: insert (CURRENT_RRN, KEY PROMO_R_CHILD, PROMO_KEY)

    if CURRENT_RRN = NIL then      /* past bottom of tree */
        PROMO_KEY := KEY
        PROMO_R_CHILD := NIL
        return PROMOTION        /* promote original key and NIL */
    else
        read page at CURRENT_RRN into PAGE
        search for KEY in PAGE.
        let POS := the position where KEY occurs or should occur.

    if KEY found then
        issue error message indicating duplicate key
        return ERROR

    RETURN_VALUE := insert(PAGE.CHILD[POS], KEY, P_B_RRN, P_B_KEY)

    if RETURN_VALUE == NO PROMOTION or ERROR then
        return RETURN_VALUE

    elseif there is space in PAGE for P_B_KEY then
        insert P_B_KEY and P_B_RRN (promoted from below) in PAGE
        return NO PROMOTION
    else
        split(P_B_KEY, P_B_RRN, PAGE,PROMO_KEY, PROMO_R_CHILD, NEWPAGE)
        write PAGE to file at CURRENT_RRN
        write NEWPAGE to file at rrn PROMO_R_CHILD
        return PROMOTION     /* promoting PROMO_KEY and PROMO_R_CHILD */
    endif

end FUNCTION
```

FIGURE 9.24 ▪ Function *insert (CURRENT_RRN, KEY, PROMO_R_CHILD, PROMO_KEY)* inserts a KEY in a B-tree. The insertion attempt starts at the page with relative record number CURRENT_RRN. If this page is not a leaf page, the function calls itself recursively until it finds KEY in a page or reaches a leaf. If it finds KEY, it issues an error message and quits, returning ERROR. If there is space for KEY in PAGE, KEY is inserted. Otherwise, PAGE is split. A split assigns the value of the middle key to PROMO_KEY and the relative record number of the newly created page to PROMO_R_CHILD so that insertion can continue on the recursive ascent back up the tree. If a promotion does occur, *insert()* indicates this by returning PROMOTION. Otherwise, it returns NO PROMOTION.

determines which key and RRN to promote. Figure 9.25 contains a description of a simple *split()* procedure, which is also encoded in C and Pascal at the end of the chapter.

You should pay careful attention to how *split()* moves data. Note that only the *key* is promoted from the working page—*all* of the CHILD

```
PROCEDURE: split (I_KEY, I_RRN, PAGE, PROMO_KEY, PROMO_R_CHILD, NEWPAGE)

    copy all keys and pointers from PAGE into a working page that
        can hold one extra key and child.

    insert I_KEY and I_RRN into their proper places in the working page.

    allocate and initialize a new page in the B-tree file to hold NEWPAGE.

    set PROMO_KEY to value of middle key, which will be promoted after
        the split.

    set PROMO_R_CHILD to RRN of NEWPAGE.

    copy keys and child pointers preceding PROMO_KEY from the working
        page to PAGE.

    copy keys and child pointers following PROMO_KEY from the working
        page to NEWPAGE.

end PROCEDURE
```

FIGURE 9.25 ▪ *Split (I_KEY, I_RRN, PAGE, PROMO_KEY, PROMO_R_CHILD, NEWPAGE)*, a procedure that inserts I_KEY and I_RRN, causing overflow, creates a new page called NEWPAGE, distributes the keys between the original PAGE and NEWPAGE, and determines which key and RRN to promote. The promoted key and RRN are returned via the arguments PROMO_KEY and PROMO_R_CHILD.

RRNs are transferred back to PAGE and NEWPAGE. The *RRN* that is promoted is the RRN of NEWPAGE, since NEWPAGE is the right descendent from the promoted key. Figure 9.26 illustrates the working page activity among PAGE, NEWPAGE, the working page, and the function arguments.

The version of *split()* described here is less efficient than might sometimes be desirable, since it moves more data than it needs to. In Exercise 16 you are asked to implement a more efficient version of *split()*.

THE TOP LEVEL. We need a routine to tie together our *insert()* and *split()* procedures and to do some things that are not done by the lower-level routines. Our driver must be able to do the following:

☐   Open or create the B-tree file, and identify or create the root page.
☐   Read in keys to be stored in the B-tree, and call *insert()* to put the keys in the tree.
☐   Create a new root node when *insert()* splits the current root page.

Contents of PAGE are copied to the working page.

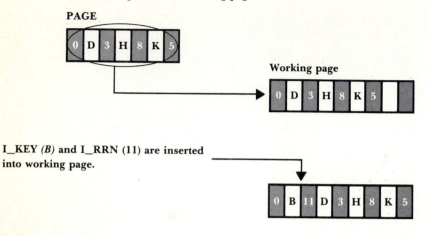

I_KEY *(B)* and I_RRN (11) are inserted into working page.

Contents of working page are divided between PAGE and NEWPAGE, except for the middle key *(H)*. *H* promoted, along with the RRN (12) of NEWPAGE.

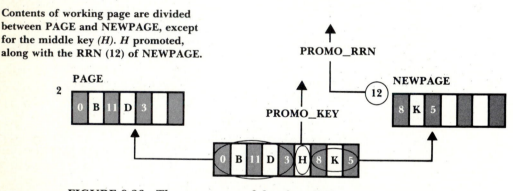

FIGURE 9.26 ▪ The movement of data in *split()*.

The routine *driver* shown in Fig. 9.27 carries out these top-level tasks. It is assumed that the RRN of the root node is stored in the B-tree file itself, if the file exists. If the file does exist, *driver* opens it and gets the RRN of the root node. If it does not exist, *driver* must create the file and build an original root page. Since a root must contain at least one key, this involves getting the first key to be inserted in the tree and placing it in the root. Next, *driver* reads in the keys to be inserted, one at a time, and calls *insert()* to insert the keys into the B-tree file. If *insert()* splits the root node, it promotes a key and right child in PROMO_KEY and PROMO_R_CHILD, and *driver* uses these to create a new root.

```
MAIN PROCEDURE: driver

    if the B-tree file exists, then
        open B-tree file
    else
        create a B-tree file and place the first key in the root

    get RRN of root page from file and store it in ROOT
    get a key and store it in KEY
    while keys exist
        if (insert(ROOT, KEY, PROMO_R_CHILD, PROMO_KEY) == PROMOTION) then
            create a new root page with key := PROMO_KEY, left
                child := ROOT, and right child := PROMO_R_CHILD
            set ROOT to RRN of new root page
        get next key and store it in KEY
    endwhile
    write RRN stored in ROOT back to B-tree file
    close B-tree file

end MAIN PROCEDURE
```

FIGURE 9.27 ▪ *Driver* for building a B-tree.

9.10
B-TREE NOMENCLATURE

Before moving on to discuss B-tree performance and variations on the basic B-tree algorithms, we need to formalize our B-tree terminology. Providing careful definitions of terms such as *order* and *leaf* enables us to state precisely the properties that must be present for a data structure to qualify as a B-tree. This definition of B-tree properties, in turn, informs our discussion of matters such as the procedure for deleting keys from a B-tree.

Unfortunately, the literature on B-trees is not uniform in its use of terms relating to B-trees. Reading that literature and keeping up with new developments therefore require some flexibility and some background: the reader needs to be aware of the different usages of some of the fundamental terms.

For example, Bayer and McCreight [1972], Comer [1979], and a few others refer to the *order* of a B-tree as the *minimum* number of *keys* that can be in a page of a tree. So, our initial sample B-tree (Fig. 9.16), which can hold a *maximum* of seven keys per page, has an *order* of three, using Bayer and McCreight's terminology. The problem with this definition of order is that it becomes clumsy when you try to account for pages that hold a maximum number of keys that is *odd*. For example, consider the following question: Within the Bayer and McCreight framework, is the page of an order three B-tree full when it contains six keys or when it contains seven keys?

Knuth [1973b] and others have addressed the odd/even confusion by defining the *order* of a B-tree to be the *maximum* number of *descendents* that a page can have. This is the definition of *order* that we use in this text. Note that this definition differs from Bayer and McCreight's in two ways: it references a *maximum*, not a *minimum*, and it counts *descendents* rather than *keys*.

Use of Knuth's definition must be coupled with the fact that the number of keys in a B-tree page is always one less than the number of descendents from the page. Consequently, a B-tree of order 8 has a maximum of seven keys per page. In general, given a B-tree of order m, the maximum number of keys per page is $m - 1$.

When you split the page of a B-tree, the descendents are divided as evenly as possible between the new page and the old page. Consequently, every page except the root and the leaves has at *least* $m/2$ descendents. Expressed in terms of a ceiling function, we can say that the minimum number of descendents is $\lceil m/2 \rceil$. It follows that the *minimum* number of *keys* per page is $\lceil m/2 \rceil - 1$, so our initial sample B-tree has an order of eight, which means that it can hold no more than seven keys per page and that all of the pages except the root contain at least three keys.

The other term that is used differently by different authors is *leaf*. Bayer and McCreight refer to the lowest level of keys in a B-tree as the leaf level. This is consistent with the nomenclature we have used in this text. Other authors, including Knuth, consider the leaves of a B-tree to be one level *below* the lowest level of keys. In other words, they consider the leaves to be the actual data records that might be pointed to by the lowest level of keys in the tree. We do *not* use this definition, sticking instead with the notion of leaf as the lowest level of keys in the B-tree.

9.11
FORMAL DEFINITION
OF B-TREE PROPERTIES

Given these definitions of order and leaf, we can formulate a precise statement of the properties of a B-tree of order m:

1. Every page has a maximum of m descendents.
2. Every page except for the root and the leaves has at least $\lceil m/2 \rceil$ descendents.

3. The root has at least two descendents (unless it is a leaf).
4. All the leaves appear on the same level.
5. A nonleaf page with k descendents contains $k - 1$ keys.
6. A leaf page contains at least $\lceil m/2 \rceil - 1$ keys and no more than $m - 1$ keys.

9.12 WORST-CASE SEARCH DEPTH

It is important to have a quantitative understanding of the relationship between the page size of a B-tree, the number of keys to be stored in the tree, and the number of levels that the tree can extend. For example, you might know that you need to store 1,000,000 keys and that, given the nature of your storage hardware and the size of your keys, it is reasonable to consider using a B-tree of order 512 (maximum of 511 keys per page). Given these two facts, you need to be able to answer the question, "In the worst case, what will be the maximum number of disk accesses required to locate a key in the tree?" This is the same as asking how deep the tree will be.

We can answer this question by beginning with the observation that the number of descendents from any level of a B-tree is one greater than the number of keys contained at that level and all the levels above it. Figure 9.28 illustrates this relation for the tree we construct earlier in the chapter. This tree contains 27 keys (all the letters of the alphabet and $). If you count the number of potential descendents trailing from the leaf level, you see that there are 28 of them.

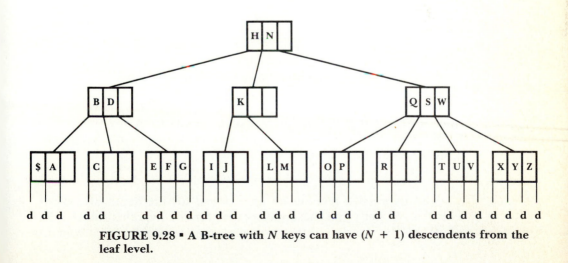

FIGURE 9.28 ▪ A B-tree with N keys can have $(N + 1)$ descendents from the leaf level.

Next we need to observe that we can use the formal definition of B-tree properties to calculate the *minimum* number of descendents that can extend from any level of a B-tree of some given order. This is of interest because we are interested in the *worst-case* depth of the tree. The worst case occurs when every page of the tree has only the minimum number of descendents. In such a case the keys are spread over a *maximal height* for the tree and a *minimal breadth*.

For a B-tree of order m, the minimum number of descendents from the root page is two, so the second level of the tree contains only two pages. Each of these pages, in turn, has at least $\lceil m/2 \rceil$ descendents. The third level, then, contains

$$2 \times \lceil m/2 \rceil$$

pages. Since each of these pages, once again, has a minimum of $\lceil m/2 \rceil$ descendents, the general pattern of the relation between depth and the minimum number of descendents takes the following form:

Level	Minimum number of descendents
1 (root)	2
2	$2 \times \lceil m/2 \rceil$
3	$2 \times \lceil m/2 \rceil \times \lceil m/2 \rceil$ or $2 \times \lceil m/2 \rceil^2$
4	$2 \times \lceil m/2 \rceil^3$
.	.
.	.
.	.
d	$2 \times \lceil m/2 \rceil^{d-1}$

So, in general, for any level d of a B-tree, the *minimum* number of descendents extending from that level is

$$2 \times \lceil m/2 \rceil^{d-1}$$

We know that a tree with N keys has $N + 1$ descendents from its leaf level. Let's call the depth of the tree at the leaf level d. We can express the relationship between the $N + 1$ descendents and the minimum number of descendents from a tree of height d as

$$N + 1 \geq 2 \times \lceil m/2 \rceil^{d-1}$$

since we know that the number of descendents from any tree cannot be less than the number for a worst-case tree of that depth. Solving for d, we arrive at the following expression:

$$d \leq 1 + \log_{\lceil m/2 \rceil} ((N + 1)/2).$$

This expression gives us an *upper bound* for the depth of a B-tree with N keys. Let's find the upper bound for the hypothetical tree that we describe at the start of this section: a tree of order 512 that contains

1,000,000 keys. Substituting these specific numbers into the expression, we find that

$$d \le 1 + \log_{256} 500000.5,$$

or

$$d \le 3.37.$$

So we can say that given 1,000,000 keys, a B-tree of order 512 has a depth of no more than three levels.

9.13 DELETION, REDISTRIBUTION, AND CONCATENATION

Indexing 1,000,000 keys in no more than three levels of a tree is precisely the kind of performance we are looking for. As we have just seen, this performance is predicated on the B-tree properties we describe earlier; in particular, the ability to guarantee that B-trees are broad and shallow rather than narrow and deep is coupled to the rules that state:

□ Every page except for the root and the leaves has at least $\lceil m/2 \rceil$ descendents;
□ A nonleaf page with k descendents contains $k - 1$ keys; and
□ A leaf page contains at least $\lceil m/2 \rceil - 1$ keys and no more than $m - 1$ keys.

We have already seen that the process of page splitting guarantees that these properties are maintained when new keys are inserted into the tree. We need to develop some kind of equally reliable guarantee that these properties are maintained when keys are *deleted* from the tree.

Working through some simple deletion situations by hand helps us demonstrate that the deletion of a key can result in several different situations. Figure 9.29 illustrates each of these situations and the associated response in the course of several deletions from an order six B-tree.

The simplest situation is illustrated in Case 1. Deleting the key *J* does not cause the contents of page 5 to drop below the minimum number of keys. Consequently, deletion involves nothing more than removing the key from the page and rearranging the keys *within* the page to close up the space.

Deleting the *M* (Case 2) is more complicated. If we simply remove the *M* from the root, it becomes very difficult to reorganize the tree to

$m=6 \quad \lceil \frac{m}{2} \rceil - 1 = 2$

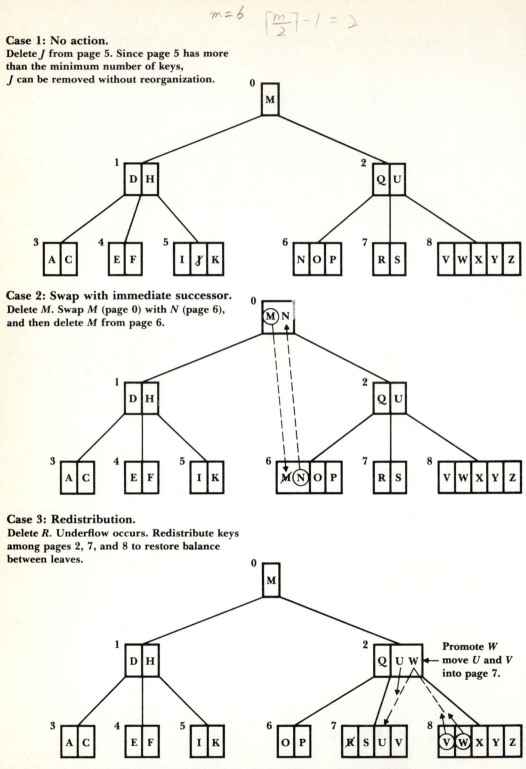

Case 1: No action.
Delete *J* from page 5. Since page 5 has more
than the minimum number of keys,
J can be removed without reorganization.

Case 2: Swap with immediate successor.
Delete *M*. Swap *M* (page 0) with *N* (page 6),
and then delete *M* from page 6.

Case 3: Redistribution.
Delete *R*. Underflow occurs. Redistribute keys
among pages 2, 7, and 8 to restore balance
between leaves.

Promote *W*
move *U* and *V*
into page 7.

FIGURE 9.29 ▪ Six situations that can occur during deletions.

328

Case 4: Concatenation.
Delete *A*. Underflow occurs, but it cannot be addressed by redistribution. Concatenate the keys from pages 3 and 4, plus the *D* from page 1 into one page.

Case 5: Underflow propagates upward.
Now page 1 has underflow. Again, we cannot redistribute, so we concatenate.

Case 6: Height of tree decreased.
Since the root contains only one key, it is absorbed into the new root.

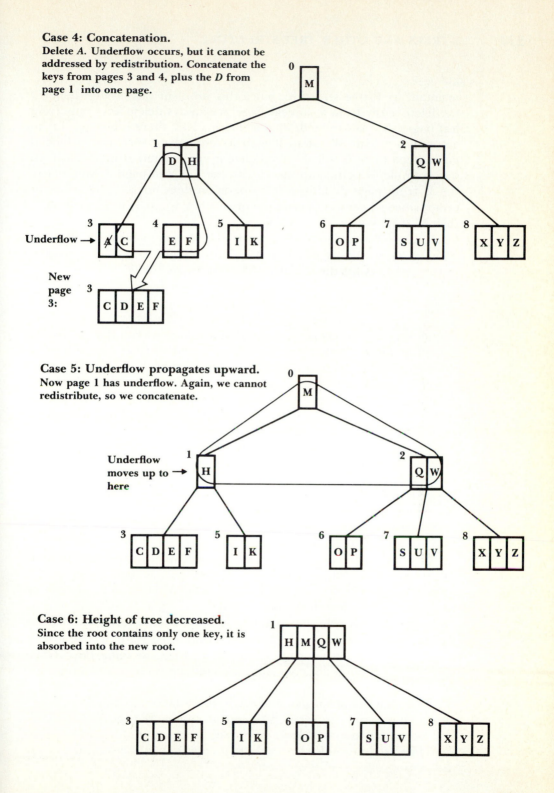

329

maintain its B-tree structure. Since this problem can occur whenever we delete a key from a nonleaf page, we always delete keys only from leaf pages. If a key to be deleted is not in a leaf, there is an easy way to get it into a leaf: We swap it with its immediate successor, which is guaranteed to be in a leaf, then delete it immediately from the leaf. In our example, we can swap the M with the the N in page 6, then delete the M from page 6. This simple operation does not put the N out of order, since all keys in the subtree of which N is a part must be greater than N. (Can you see why this is the case?)

In Case 3 we delete R from page 7. If we simply remove R and do nothing more, the page that it is in has only one key. The minimum number of keys for the leaf page of an order six tree is

$$\lceil 6/2 \rceil - 1 = 2.$$

Therefore we have to take some kind of action to correct this underflow condition. Since the neighboring page 8 (called a *sibling* since it has the same parent) has more than the minimum number of keys, the corrective action consists of redistributing the keys between the pages. *Redistribution* must also result in a change in the key that is in the parent page so that it continues to act as a separator between the lower-level pages. In the example, we move the U and V into page 7, and move W into the separator position in page 2.

The deletion of A in Case 4 results in a situation that cannot be resolved by redistribution. Addressing the underflow in page 3 by moving keys from page 4 only transfers the underflow condition. There are not enough keys to share between two pages. The solution to this is *concatenation*, combining the two pages and the key from the parent page to make a single full page.

Concatenation is essentially the reverse of splitting. Like splitting, it can propagate upwards through the B-tree. Just as splitting promotes a key, concatenation must involve demotion of keys, and this can in turn cause underflow in the parent page. This is just what happens in our example. Our concatenation of pages 3 and 4 pulls the key D from the parent page down to the leaf level, leading to Case 5: The loss of the D from the parent page causes it, in turn, to underflow. Once again, redistribution does not solve the problem, so concatenation must be used.

Note that the propagation of the underflow condition does not necessarily imply the propagation of concatenation. If page 2 (Q and W) had contained another key, then redistribution, not concatenation, would be used to resolve the underflow condition at the second level of the tree.

Case 6 shows what happens when concatenation propagates all the way to the root. The concatenation of pages 1 and 2 absorbs the only key in the root page, decreasing the height of the tree by one level.

The steps involved in deleting keys from a B-tree can be summarized as follows:

1. If the key to be deleted is not in a leaf, swap it with its immediate successor, which is in a leaf.
2. Delete the key.
3. If the leaf now contains at least the minimum number of keys, no further action is required.
4. If the leaf now contains one too few keys, look at the left and right siblings.
   a) If a sibling has more than the minimum number of keys, redistribute.
   b) If neither sibling has more than the minimum, concatenate the two leaves *and* the median key from the parent into one leaf.
5. If leaves are concatenated, apply Steps 3–6 to the *parent*.
6. If the last key from the root is removed, then the height of the tree decreases.

9.13.1 REDISTRIBUTION

Unlike concatenation, which is a kind of reverse split, redistribution is a new idea. Our insertion algorithm does not involve operations analogous to redistribution.

Redistribution differs from both splitting and concatenation in that it does not propagate. It is guaranteed to have strictly local effects. Note that the term *sibling* implies that the pages have the same parent page. If there are two nodes at the leaf level that are logically adjacent but do not have the same parent (for example, IJK and NOP in the tree at the top of fig. 9.29), these nodes are not siblings. Redistribution algorithms are generally written so that they do not consider moving keys between nodes that are not siblings, even when they are logically adjacent. Can you see the reasoning behind this restriction?

Another difference between redistribution on the one hand and concatenation and splitting on the other is that there is no necessary, fixed prescription for how the keys should be rearranged. A single deletion in a properly formed B-tree cannot cause an underflow of more than one key. Therefore, redistribution can restore the B-tree properties by moving only one key from a sibling into the page that has underflowed, even if the distribution of the keys between the pages is very uneven. Suppose, for example, that we are managing a B-tree of order 101. The minimum number of keys that can be in a page is 50, the maximum is 100. Suppose we have one page that contains the minimum and a sibling that contains the maximum. If a key is deleted from the page containing 50 keys, an underflow condition occurs. We can correct the condition through redistribution by moving one key, 50 keys, or any number of keys that falls between 1 and 50. The usual strategy is to divide the keys as evenly as possible between the pages. In this instance that means moving 25 keys.

9.14
REDISTRIBUTION DURING INSERTION: A WAY TO IMPROVE STORAGE UTILIZATION

As you may recall, B-tree insertion does not require an operation analogous to redistribution; splitting is able to account for all instances of overflow. This does not mean, however, that it is not *desirable* to use redistribution during insertion as an *option,* particularly since a set of B-tree maintenance algorithms must already include a redistribution procedure to support deletion. Given that a redistribution procedure is already present, what advantage might we gain by using it as an alternative to node splitting?

Redistribution during insertion is a way of avoiding, or at least postponing, the creation of new pages. Rather than splitting a full page and creating two approximately half-full pages, redistribution lets us place some of the overflowing keys into another page. The use of redistribution in place of splitting should therefore tend to make a B-tree more efficient in terms of its utilization of space.

It is possible to quantify this efficiency of space utilization by viewing the amount of space used to store information as a percentage of the total amount of space required to hold the B-tree. After a node splits, each of the two resulting pages is about half full. So, in the worst case, space utilization in a B-tree using two-way splitting is around 50 percent. Of course, the actual degree of space utilization is better than this worst-case figure. VanDoren [1975] and Yao [1978] have shown that, for large trees of relatively large order, space utilization approaches a theoretical average of about 69 percent if insertion is handled through two-way splitting.

The idea of using redistribution as an alternative to splitting when possible, splitting a page only when both of its siblings are full, is introduced in Bayer and McCreight's original paper [1972]. The paper includes some experimental results that show that two-way splitting results in a space utilization of 67 percent for a tree of order 121 after 5,000 random insertions. When the experiment was repeated, using redistribution when possible, space utilization increased to over 86 percent. Subsequent empirical testing by Davis [1974] (B-tree of order 49) and Crotzer [1975] (B-tree of order 303) also resulted in space utilization exceeding 85 percent when redistribution was used. These findings and others suggest that any serious application of B-trees to even moderately large files should implement insertion procedures that handle overflow through redistribution when possible.

9.15   B* TREES

In his review and amplification of work on B-trees in 1973, Knuth [1973] extends the notion of redistribution during insertion to include new rules for splitting. He calls the resulting variation on the fundamental B-tree form a *B* tree*.

Consider a system in which we are postponing splitting through redistribution, as outlined in the preceding section. If we are considering any page other than the root, we know that when it finally is time to split, the page has at least one sibling that is also full. This opens up the possibility of a two-to-three split rather than the usual one-to-two or two-way split. Figure 9.30 illustrates such a split.

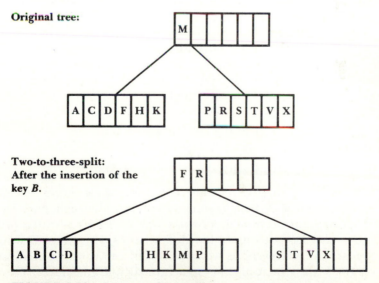

FIGURE 9.30 ▪ A two-to-three split.

The important aspect of this two-to-three split is that it results in pages that are each about two-thirds full rather than just half full. This makes it possible to define a new kind of B-tree, called a B* tree, which has the following properties:

1. Every page has a maximum of m descendents.
2. *Every page except for the root and the leaves has at least $(2m - 1)/3$ descendents.*
3. The root has at least two descendents (unless it is a leaf).
4. All the leaves appear on the same level.
5. A nonleaf page with k descendents contains $k - 1$ keys.
6. *A leaf page contains at least $\lfloor (2m - 1)/3 \rfloor$ keys and no more than $m - 1$ keys.*

The critical changes between this set of properties and the set we define for a conventional B-tree are in Rules 2 and 6: a B* tree has pages that contain a minimum of $\lfloor (2m - 1)/3 \rfloor$ keys. This new property, of course, affects procedures for deletion and redistribution.

To implement B* tree procedures one must also deal with the question of splitting the root, which, by definition, never has a sibling. If there is no sibling, no two-to-three split is possible. Knuth suggests allowing the root to grow to a size larger than the other pages so that, when it does split, it can produce two pages that are each about two-thirds full. This suggestion has the advantage of ensuring that all pages below the root level adhere to B* tree characteristics. However, it has the disadvantage of requiring that the procedures be able to handle a page that is larger than all the others. Another solution is to handle the splitting of the root as a conventional one-to-two split. This second solution avoids any special page-handling logic. On the other hand, it complicates deletion, redistribution, and other procedures that must be sensitive to the minimum number of keys allowed in a page. Such procedures would have to be able to recognize that pages descending from the root might legally be only half full.

9.16
BUFFERING OF PAGES: VIRTUAL B-TREES

We have seen that, given some additional refinements, the B-tree can be a very efficient, flexible storage structure that maintains its balanced properties after repeated deletions and insertions and that provides access to any key with just a few disk accesses. However, focusing on just the structural aspects, as we have so far, can cause us inadvertently to overlook ways of using this structure to full advantage. For example, the fact that a B-tree has a depth of three levels does not at all mean that we need to do three disk accesses to retrieve keys from pages at the leaf level. We can do much better than that.

Obtaining better performance from B-trees involves looking in a precise way at our original problem. We needed to find a way to make efficient use of indexes that are too large to be held *entirely* in RAM. Up to this point we have approached this problem in an all-or-nothing way: An index has been either held entirely in RAM, organized as a list or binary tree, or has been accessed entirely on secondary store, using a B-tree structure. But, stating that we cannot hold *all* of an index in RAM does not imply that we cannot hold *some* of it there.

For example, assume we have an index that contains a megabyte of records and that we cannot reasonably use more than 256K of RAM for index storage at any given time. Given a page size of 4K, holding around 64 keys per page, our B-tree can be contained in three levels. We can reach any one of our keys in no more than three disk accesses. That is certainly acceptable, but why should we settle for this kind of performance? Why not try to find a way to bring the average number of disk accesses per search down to one disk access or less?

Thinking of the problem strictly in terms of physical storage structures, retrieval averaging one disk access or less sounds impossible. But, remember, our objective was to find a way to manage our megabyte of index within 256K of RAM, not within the 4K required to hold a single page of our tree.

We know that every search through the tree requires access to the root page. Rather than accessing the root page again and again at the start of every search, we could read the root page into RAM and just keep it there. This strategy increases our RAM requirement from 4K to 8K, since we need 4K for the root and 4K for whatever other page we read in, but this is still much less than the 256K that are available. This very simple strategy reduces our worst-case search to two disk accesses, and the average search to under two accesses (keys in the root require *no* disk access; keys at the first level require one access).

This simple, keep-the-root strategy suggests an important, more general approach: Rather than just holding the root page in RAM, we can create a *page buffer* to hold some number of B-tree pages, perhaps 5, 10, or more. As we read pages in from the disk in response to user requests, we fill up the buffer. Then, when a page is requested, we access it from RAM if we can, thereby avoiding a disk access. If the page is not in RAM, then we read it into the buffer from secondary storage, replacing one of the pages that was previously there. A B-tree that uses a RAM buffer in this way is sometimes referred to as a *virtual B-tree*.

9.16.1 LRU REPLACEMENT

Clearly, such a buffering scheme works only if we are more likely to request a page that is in the buffer than one that is not. The process of accessing the disk to bring in a page that is *not* already in the buffer is called a *page fault*. There are two causes of page faults:

1. We have never used the page.
2. It was once in the buffer but has since been replaced with a new page.

The first cause of page faults is unavoidable: If we have not yet read in and used a page, there is no way it can already be in the buffer. But the second cause is one we can try to minimize through buffer management. The critical management decision arises when we need to read a new page into a buffer that is already full: Which page do we decide to replace?

One common approach is to replace the page that was least-recently used; this is called *LRU* replacement. Note that this is different from replacing the page that was *read into* the buffer least recently. Since the root page is always read in first, simply replacing the oldest page results in replacing the root, which is an undesirable outcome. Instead, the LRU method keeps track of the actual *requests* for pages. Since the root is requested on every search, it seldom, if ever, is selected for replacement. The page to be replaced is the one that has gone the longest time without a request for use.

Some research by Webster [1980] shows the effect of increasing the number of pages that can be held in the buffer area under an LRU replacement strategy. Table 9.1 summarizes a small but representative portion of Webster's results. It lists the average number of disk accesses per search given different numbers of page buffers. These results are obtained using a simple LRU replacement strategy without accounting for page height.

TABLE 9.1

Effect of using more buffers with a simple LRU replacement strategy

Buffer count	1	5	10	20
Average accesses per search	3.00	1.71	1.42	0.97

Number of keys = 2400
Total pages = 140
Tree height = 3 levels

Webster's study was conducted using B^+ trees rather than simple B-trees. In the next chapter, where we look closely at B^+ trees, you see that the nature of B^+ trees accounts for the fact that, given one buffer, the average search length is 3.00. With B^+ trees, all searches must go all the way to the leaf level every time. The fact that Webster used B^+ trees, however, does not detract from the usefulness of his results as an illustration of the positive impact of page buffering. Keeping less than 15 percent of the tree in RAM (20 pages out of the total 140) reduces the average number of accesses per search to less than one. The results are even more dramatic with a simple B-tree, since not all searches have to proceed to the leaf level.

Note that the decision to use LRU replacement is based on the assumption that we are more likely to need a page that we have used recently than we are to need a page that we have never used or one that we used some time ago. If this assumption is not valid, then there is absolutely no reason to preferentially retain pages that were used recently. The term for this kind of assumption is *temporal locality*. We are assuming that there is a kind of *clustering* of the use of certain pages over time. The hierarchical nature of a B-tree makes this kind of assumption reasonable.

For example, during redistribution after overflow or underflow, we access a page and then access its sibling. Because B-trees are hierarchical, accessing a set of sibling pages involves repeated access to the parent page in rapid succession. This is an instance of temporal locality; it is easy to see how it is related to the tree's hierarchy.

9.16.2 REPLACEMENT BASED ON PAGE HEIGHT

There is another, more direct way to use the hierarchical nature of the B-tree to guide decisions about page replacement in the buffers. Our simple, keep-the-root strategy exemplifies this alternative: Always retain the pages that occur at the highest levels of the tree. Given a larger amount of buffer space, it might be possible to retain not only the root, but also all of the pages at the second level of a tree.

Let's explore this notion by returning to a previous example in which we have access to 256K of RAM and a 1-megabyte index. Since our page size is 4K, we could build a buffer area that holds 64 pages within the RAM area. Assume that our 1 megabyte worth of index requires around 1.2 megabytes of storage on disk (storage utilization = 83 percent). Given the 4K page size, this 1.2 megabytes requires slightly more than 300 pages. We assume that, on the average, each of our pages has around 30 descendents. It follows that our three-level tree has, of course, a single page at the root level, followed by nine or ten pages at the second level, with all the remaining pages at the leaf level. Using a page replacement strategy that always retains the higher-level pages, it is clear that our 64-page buffer eventually contains the root page and all the pages at the second level. The approximately 50 remaining buffer slots are used to hold leaf level pages. Decisions about which of these pages to replace can be handled through an LRU strategy. For many searches, all of the pages required are already in the buffer; the search requires no disk accesses. It is easy to see how, given a sizable buffer, it is possible to bring the average number of disk accesses per search down to a number that is less than one.

Webster's research [1980] also investigates the effect of taking page height into account, giving preference to pages that are higher in the tree when it comes time to decide which pages to keep in the buffers. Augmenting the LRU strategy with a weighting factor that accounts for page height reduces the average number of accesses, given a ten-page buffer, from 1.42 accesses per search down to 1.12 accesses per search.

9.16.3 IMPORTANCE OF VIRTUAL B-TREES

It is difficult to overemphasize the importance of including a page buffering scheme into any implementation of a B-tree index structure. Because the B-tree structure itself is so interesting and powerful, it is easy to fall into the trap of thinking that the B-tree organization is itself a sufficient solution to the problem of accessing large indexes that must be maintained on secondary storage. As we have emphasized, to fall into that trap is to lose sight of the original problem: to find a way to *reduce* the amount of memory required to handle large indexes. We did not, however, need to reduce the amount of memory to the amount required for a single index page. It is usually possible to find enough memory to hold a number of pages. Doing so can dramatically increase system performance.

9.17
PLACEMENT OF INFORMATION ASSOCIATED WITH THE KEY

Early in this chapter we focus on the B-tree index itself, setting aside any consideration of the actual information associated with the keys. We paraphrase Bayer and McCreight and state that "the associated information is of no further interest."

But, of course, in any actual application the associated information is, in fact, the true object of interest. Rarely do we ever want to index keys just to be able to find the keys themselves. It is usually the information associated with the key that we really want to find. So, before closing our discussion of B-tree indexes, it is important to turn to the question of where and how to store the information indexed by the keys in the tree. Fundamentally, we have two choices. We can:

☐ Store the information in the B-tree along with the key; or
☐ Place the information in a separate file; within the index we couple the key with a relative record number or byte address pointer that references the location of the information in that separate file.

The distinct advantage that the first approach has over the second is that once the key is found, no more disk accesses are required. The information is right there with the key. However, if the amount of information associated with each key is relatively large, then storing the information with the key reduces the number of keys that can be placed in a page of the B-tree. As the number of keys per page is reduced, the order of the tree is reduced, and the tree tends to become taller since there are fewer descendents from each page. So, the advantage of the second method is that, given associated information that has a long length relative to the length of a key, placing the associated information elsewhere allows us to build a higher-order and therefore possibly shallower tree.

For example, assume we need to index 1000 keys and associated information records. Suppose that the length required to store a key and its associated information is 128 bytes. Furthermore, suppose that if we store the associated information elsewhere, we can store just the key and a pointer to the associated information in only 16 bytes. Given a B-tree page that had 512 bytes available for keys and associated information, the two fundamental storage alternatives translate into the following orders of B-trees:

☐ *Information stored with key:* four keys per page—order five tree; and
☐ *Pointer stored with key:* 32 keys per page—order 33 tree.

Using the formula for finding the worst-case depth of B-trees developed earlier:

$$d_{(info\ w/key)} \leq 1 + \log_3 500.5 = 6.66$$
$$d_{(info\ elsewhere)} \leq 1 + \log_{17} 500.5 = 3.19$$

So, if we store the information with the keys, the tree has a worst-case depth of six levels. If we store the information elsewhere, we end up reducing the height of the worst-case tree to three. Even though the additional indirection associated with the second method costs us one disk access, the second method still reduces the total number of accesses to find a record in the worst case.

In general, then, the decision about where to store the associated information should be guided by some calculations that compare the depths of the trees that result. The critical factor that influences these calculations is the ratio of overall record length to the length of just a key and pointer. If you can put many key/pointer pairs in the area required for a single, full key/record pair, it is probably advisable to remove the associated information from the B-tree and put it in a separate file.

9.18
VARIABLE LENGTH RECORDS AND KEYS

In many applications the information associated with a key varies in length. Secondary indexes referencing inverted lists are an excellent example of this. One way to handle this variability is to place the associated information in a separate, variable length record file; the B-tree would contain a reference to the information in this other file. Another approach is to allow a variable number of keys and records in a B-tree page.

Up to this point we have regarded B-trees as being of some order *m*. Each page has a fixed maximum and minimum number of keys that it can legally hold. The notion of a variable length record, and, therefore, a variable number of keys per page, is a significant departure from the point of view we have developed so far. A B-tree with a variable number of keys per page clearly has no single, fixed order.

The variability in length can also extend to the keys themselves as well as to entire records. For example, in a file in which people's names are the keys, we might choose to use only as much space as required for a name, rather than allocate a fixed-size field for each key. As we saw in earlier chapters, implementing a structure with variable length fields can allow us to put many more names in a given amount of space since it does away with internal fragmentation. If we can put more keys in a page, then we have a larger number of descendents from a page and, very probably, a tree with fewer levels.

Accommodating this variability in length means using a different kind of page structure. We look at page structures appropriate for use with variable length keys in detail in the next chapter, where we discuss

B^+ trees. We also need a different criterion for deciding when a page is full and when it is in an underflow condition. Rather than use a maximum and minimum number of keys per page, we need to use a maximum and minimum number of bytes.

Once the fundamental mechanisms for handling variable length keys or records are in place, interesting new possibilities emerge. For example, we might consider the notion of biasing the key promotion mechanism so that the shortest variable length keys (or key/record pairs) are promoted upwards in preference to longer keys. The idea is that we want to have pages with the largest numbers of descendents up high in the tree, rather than at the leaf level. Branching out as broadly as possible as high as possible in the tree tends to reduce the overall height of the tree. McCreight [1977] explores this notion in the article, "Pagination of B* Trees with Variable-Length Records."

The principal point we want to make with these examples of variations on B-tree structures is that this chapter introduces only the most basic forms of this very useful, flexible file structure. Actual implementations of B-trees do not slavishly follow the textbook form of B-trees. Instead, they use many of the other organizational techniques we study in this book, such as variable length record structures, in combination with the fundamental B-tree organization to make new, special-purpose file structures uniquely suited to the problems at hand.

SUMMARY

We begin this chapter by picking up the problem we left unsolved at the end of Chapter 7: Simple, linear indexes work well if they are held in electronic RAM memory, but are expensive to maintain and search if they are so big that they must be held on secondary storage. The expense of using secondary storage is most evident in two areas:

- Sorting of the index; and
- Searching, since even binary searching required more than just two or three disk accesses.

We first address the question of structuring an index so that it can be kept in order without sorting. We use tree structures to do this, discovering that we need a *balanced* tree to ensure that the tree does not become overly deep after repeated random insertions. We see that AVL trees provide a way of balancing a binary tree with only a small amount of overhead.

Next we turn to the problem of reducing the number of disk accesses required to search a tree. The solution to this problem involves dividing the tree into pages, so that a substantial portion of the tree can be retrieved with a single disk access. Paged indexes let us search through very large numbers of keys with only a few disk accesses.

Unfortunately, we find that it is difficult to combine the idea of *paging* of tree structures with the *balancing* of these trees by AVL methods. The most obvious evidence of this difficulty is associated with the problem of selecting the members of the root page of a tree or subtree when the tree is built in the conventional top-down manner. This sets the stage for introducing Bayer and McCreight's work on B-trees, which solves the paging and balancing dilemma by starting from the leaf level, promoting keys upward as the tree grows.

Our discussion of B-trees begins with examples of searching, insertion, splitting, and promotion to show how B-trees grow while maintaining balance in a paged structure. Next we formalize our description of B-trees. This formal definition permits us to develop a formula for estimating worst-case B-tree depth. The formal description also motivates our work on developing deletion procedures that maintain the B-tree properties when keys are removed from a tree.

Once the fundamental structure and procedures for B-trees are in place, we begin refining and improving on these ideas. The first set of improvements involves increasing the storage utilization within B-trees. Of course, increasing storage utilization can also result in a decrease in the height of the tree, and therefore in improvements in performance. We find that by sometimes redistributing keys during insertion, rather than splitting pages, we can improve storage utilization in B-trees so that it averages around 85 percent. Carrying our search for increased storage efficiency even farther, we find that we can combine redistribution during insertion with a different kind of splitting to ensure that the pages are about two-thirds full rather than only one-half full after the split. Trees using this combination of redistribution and two-to-three splitting are called *B* trees*.

Next we turn to the matter of buffering pages, creating a *virtual B-tree*. We note that the use of memory is not an all or nothing choice: indexes that are too large to fit into memory do not have to be accessed *entirely* from secondary storage. If we hold pages that are likely to be reused in RAM, then we can save the expense of reading these pages in from the disk again. We develop two methods of guessing which pages are to be reused. One method uses the height of the page in the tree to decide which pages to keep. Keeping the root has the highest priority, the root's descendents have the next priority, and so on. The second method for selecting pages to keep in RAM is based on recentness of use: we always replace the least-recently-used (LRU) page, retaining the pages used most recently. We see that it is possible to combine these methods, and that doing so can result in the ability to find keys while using an average of less than one disk access per search.

We then turn to the question of where to place the information associated with a key in the B-tree index. Storing it with the key is attractive because, in that case, finding the key is the same as finding the information; no additional disk accesses are required. However, if the associated information takes up a lot of space, it can reduce the order of the tree, thereby increasing the tree's height. In such cases it is often advantageous to store the associated information in a separate file.

We close the chapter with a brief look at the use of variable length records within the pages of a B-tree, noting that significant savings in space and consequent reduction in the height of the tree can result from the use of variable length records. The modification of the basic textbook B-tree definition to include the use of variable length records is just one example of the many variations on B-trees that are used in real-world implementations.

KEY TERMS

AVL tree. A height-balanced (HB(1)) binary tree in which insertions and deletions can be performed with minimal accesses to local nodes. AVL trees are interesting because they keep branches from getting overly long after many random insertions.

B-tree of order m. A multiway search tree with these properties:

1. Every node has a maximum of m descendents.
2. Every node except the root and the leaves has at least $\lceil m/2 \rceil$ descendents.
3. The root has at least two descendents (unless it is a leaf).
4. All of the leaves appear on the same level.
5. A nonleaf page with k descendents contains $k-1$ keys.
6. A leaf page contains at least $\lceil m/2 \rceil - 1$ keys and no more than $m-1$ keys.

B-trees are built upwards from the leaf level, so that creation of new pages always starts at the leaf level.

The power of B-trees lies in the facts that: they are balanced (no overly long branches); they are shallow (requiring few seeks);

they accommodate random deletions and insertions at a relatively low cost while remaining in balance; and they guarantee at least 50 percent storage utilization.

B* tree. A special B-tree in which each node is at least two-thirds full. B* trees generally provide better storage utilization than do B-trees.

Concatenation. When a B-tree node underflows (becomes less than 50 percent full), it sometimes becomes necessary to combine the node with an adjacent node, thus decreasing the total number of nodes in the tree. Since concatenation involves a change in the number of nodes in the tree, its effects can require reorganization at many levels of the tree.

Height-balanced tree. A tree structure with a special property: for each node there is a limit to the amount of difference that is allowed among the heights of any of the node's subtrees. An *HB(k)* tree allows subtrees to be *k* levels out of balance. (See *AVL tree*.)

Leaf of a B-tree. A page at the lowest level in a B-tree. All leaves in a B-tree occur at the same level.

Order of a B-tree. The maximum number of descendents that a node in the B-tree can have.

Paged index. An index that is divided into blocks, or pages, each of which can hold many keys. The use of paged indexes allows us to search through very large numbers of keys with only a few disk accesses.

Promotion of a key. The movement of a key from one node into a higher level node (creating the higher-level node, if necessary) when the original node becomes overfull and must be split.

Redistribution. When a B-tree node underflows (becomes less than 50 percent full), it may be possible to move keys into the node from an adjacent node with the same parent. This helps ensure that the 50-percent-full property is maintained. When keys are redistributed, it becomes necessary to alter the contents of the parent as well. Redistribution, as opposed to *concatenation,* does not involve creation or deletion of nodes—its effects are entirely local. Redistribution can also often be used as an alternative to splitting.

Splitting. Creation of two nodes out of one because the original node becomes overfull. Splitting results in the need to promote a key to a higher-level node to provide an index separating the two new nodes.

Virtual B-tree. A B-tree index in which several pages are kept in RAM in anticipation of the possibility that one or more of them will be needed by a later access. Many different strategies can be applied to replacing pages in RAM when virtual B-trees are used, including the least-recently-used strategy and height-weighted strategies.

EXERCISES

1. Balanced binary trees can be effective index structures for RAM-based indexing, but they have several drawbacks when they become so large that part or all of them must be kept on secondary storage. The following questions should help bring these drawbacks into focus, and thus reinforce the need for an alternative structure such as the B-tree.

a) There are two major problems with using binary search to search a simple sorted index on secondary storage: the number of disk accesses is larger than we would like; and the time it takes to keep the index sorted is substantial. Which of the problems does a binary search tree alleviate?

b) Why is it important to keep search trees balanced?

c) In what way is an AVL tree better than a simple binary search tree?

d) Suppose you have a file with 1,000,000 keys stored on disk in a completely full, balanced binary search tree. If the tree is not paged, what is the maximum number of accesses required to find a key? If the tree is paged in the manner illustrated in Fig. 9.12, but with each page able to hold 15 keys and to branch to 16 new pages, what is the maximum number of accesses required to find a key? If the page size is increased to hold 511 keys with branches to 512 nodes, how does the maximum number of accesses change?

e) Consider the problem of balancing the three-key-per-page tree in Fig. 9.13 by rearranging the pages. Why is it difficult to create a tree-balancing algorithm that has only local effects? When the page size increases to a more likely size (such as 512 keys), why does it become difficult to guarantee that each of the pages contains at least some minimum number of keys?

f) Explain the following statement: B-trees are built upwards from the bottom, whereas binary trees are built downwards from the top.

g) Although B-trees are generally considered superior to binary search trees for external searching, binary trees are still commonly used for internal searching. Why is this so?

2. Describe the *necessary* parts of a leaf node of a B-tree. How does a leaf node differ from an internal node?

3. Since leaf nodes never have children, it might be possible to use the pointer fields in a leaf node to point to data records. This could eliminate the need for pointer fields to data records in the internal nodes. Why? What are the implications of doing this in terms of storage utilization and retrieval time?

4. Show the B-trees of order four that result from loading the following sets of keys in order.
a) C G J X
b) C G J X N S U O A E B H I
c) C G J X N S U O A E B H I F
d) C G J X N S U O A E B H I F K L Q R T V U W Z

5. Figure 9.23 shows the pattern of recursive calls involved in inserting a $ into the B-tree in Fig. 9.22. Suppose that subsequent to this insertion, the character [is inserted *after* the Z. (The ASCII code for [is greater than the ASCII code for Z.) Draw a figure similar to Fig. 9.23, which shows the pattern of recursive calls required to perform this insertion.

6. Given a B-tree of order 256 that contains 100,000 keys,
a) What is the maximum number of descendents from a page?
b) What is the minimum number of descendents from a page (excluding the root and leaves)?
c) What is the minimum number of descendents from the root?
d) What is the minimum number of descendents from a leaf?
e) How many keys are there on a nonleaf page with 200 descendents?
f) What is the maximum depth of the tree?

7. Using a method similar to that used to derive the formula for worst-case depth, derive a formula for best case, or minimum depth, for an order m B-tree with N keys. What is the minimum depth of the tree described in the preceding question?

8. Suppose you have a B-tree index for an unsorted file containing N data records, where each key has stored with it the RRN of the corresponding record. The depth of the B-tree is d. What are the maximum and minimum numbers of disk accesses required to
a) Retrieve a record;
b) Add a record;
c) Delete a record; and
d) Retrieve all records from the file in sorted order.

Assume that page buffering is *not* used. In each case, indicate how you arrived at your answer.

9. Show the trees that result after each of the keys *A, B, Q,* and *R* is deleted from the following B-tree of order five.

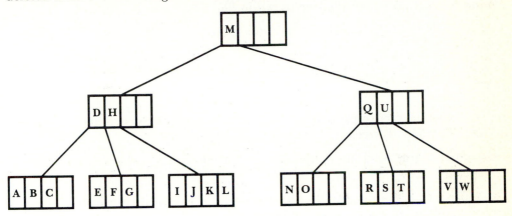

10. Suppose you want to delete a key from a node in a B-tree. You look at the right sibling and find that redistribution does not work; concatenation would be necessary. Look to the left and see that redistribution is an option here. Do you choose to concatenate or redistribute?

11. What is the difference between a B* tree and a B-tree? What improvement does a B* tree offer over a B-tree, and what complications does it introduce? How does the minimum depth of an order *m* B* tree compare with that of an order *m* B-tree?

12. What is a virtual B-tree? How can it be possible to average fewer than one access per key when retrieving keys from a three-level virtual B-tree? Write a pseudocode description for an LRU replacement scheme for a ten-page buffer used in implementing a virtual B-tree.

13. Discuss the trade-offs between storing the information indexed by the keys in a B-tree with the key and storing the information in a separate file.

14. We noted that, given variable length keys, it is possible to optimize a tree by building in a bias toward promoting shorter keys. With fixed order trees we promote the middle key. In a variable order, variable length key tree, what is the meaning of "middle key"? What are the trade-offs associated with building in a bias toward shorter keys in this selection of a key for promotion? Outline an implementation for this selection and promotion process.

PROGRAMMING EXERCISES

15. Implement the programs at the end of the chapter and add a recursive procedure that performs a parenthesized symmetric traversal of a B-tree created by the program. As an example, here is the result of a parenthesized traversal of the tree shown in Fig. 9.18:

$$(((A,B,C)D(E,F,G)H(I,J)K(L,M))N((O,P)Q(R)S(T,U,V)W(X,Y,Z)))$$

16. The *split()* routine in the B-tree programs is not very efficient. Rewrite it to make it more efficient.

17. Write a program that searches for a key in a B-tree.

18. Write an interactive program that allows a user to find, insert, and delete keys from a B-tree.

19. Write a B-tree program that uses keys that are strings, rather than single characters.

20. Write a program that builds a B-tree index for a data file in which records contain more information than just a key.

FURTHER READINGS

Currently available textbooks on file and data structures contain surprisingly brief discussions on B-trees. These discussions do not, in general, add substantially to the information presented in this chapter and the following chapter. Consequently, readers interested in more information about B-trees must turn to the articles that have appeared in journals over the past 15 years.

The article that introduced B-trees to the world is Bayer and McCreight's "Organization and Maintenance of Large Ordered Indexes" [1972]. It describes the theoretical properties of B-trees and includes empirical results concerning, among other things, the effect of using redistribution in addition to splitting during insertion. Readers should be aware that the notation and terminology used in this article differ from that used in this text in a number of important respects.

Comer's [1979] survey article, "The Ubiquitous B-tree," provides an excellent overview of some important variations on the basic B-tree form. Knuth's [1973b] discussion of B-trees, although brief, is an important resource, in part because many of the variant forms such as B* trees were first collected together in Knuth's discussion. McCreight [1977] looks specifically at operations on trees that use variable length records and that are therefore of variable order. Although this article speaks specifically about B* trees, the consideration of variable length records can be applied to many other B-tree forms. In "Time and Space Optimality on B-trees," Rosenberg and Snyder [1981] analyze the effects of initializing B-trees with the minimum number of nodes. In "Analysis of Design Alternatives for Virtual Memory Indexes," Murayama and Smith [1977] look at three factors that affect the cost of retrieval: choice of search strategy, whether or not pages in the index are structured, and whether or not keys are compressed. Zoellick [1986] discusses the use of B-tree–like structures on optical discs.

Since B-trees in various forms have become a standard file organization for databases, a good deal of interesting material on applications of B-trees can be found in the database literature. Ullman [1982], Held and Stonebraker [1978], and Snyder [1978] discuss the use of B-trees in database systems generally. Ullman [1982] covers the problem of dealing with applications in which several programs have access to the same database concurrently and identifies literature concerned with concurrent access to B-tree.

Uses of B-trees for secondary key access are covered in many of the previously cited references. There is also a growing literature on multidimensional dynamic indexes, including a B-tree-like structure called a *k-d* B-tree. *K-d* B-trees are described in papers by Ouskel and Scheuermann [1981] and Robinson [1981]. Other approaches to secondary indexing include the use of *tries* and *grid files*. Tries are covered in many texts on files and data structures, including Knuth [1973b], Claybrook [1983], and Loomis [1983]. Grid files are covered thoroughly in Nievergelt et al. [1984].

An interesting early paper on the use of dynamic tree structures for processing files is "The Use of Tree Structures for Processing Files," by Sussenguth [1963]. Wagner [1973] and Keehn and Lacy [1974] examine the index design considerations that led to the development of VSAM. VSAM uses an index structure very similar to a B-tree, but appears to have been developed independently of Bayer and McCreight's work. Readers interested in learning more about AVL trees will find a good, approachable discussion of the algorithms associated with these trees in Standish [1980]. Knuth [1973b] takes a more rigorous, mathematical look at AVL tree operations and properties.

C PROGRAM TO INSERT KEYS INTO A B-TREE

The C program that follows implements the insert program described in the text. The only difference between this program and the one in the text is that this program builds a B-tree of order five, whereas the one in the text builds a B-tree of order four. Input characters are taken from standard I/O, with *q* indicating end of data.

The program requires the use of functions from several files:

driver.c   Contains the main program, which parallels the driver program described in the text very closely.

insert.c   Contains *insert()*, the recursive function that finds the proper place for a key, inserts it, and supervises splitting and promotions.

btio.c   Contains all support functions that directly perform I/O. The header files *fileio.h* and *stdio.h* must be available for inclusion in *btio.c*.

btutil.c   Contains the rest of the support functions, including the function *split()* described in the text.

All the programs include the header file called *bt.h*.

```
/* bt.h...
       header file for B-tree programs
*/
#define  MAXKEYS  4
#define  MINKEYS  MAXKEYS/2
#define  NIL      (-1)
#define  NOKEY    '@'

typedef struct {
    short keycount;              /* number of keys in page     */
    char  key[MAXKEYS];          /* the actual keys            */
    short child[MAXKEYS+1];      /* ptrs to RRNs of descendents */
} BTPAGE;

#define PAGESIZE  sizeof(BTPAGE)
```

▇▇▇ DRIVER.C

```
/* driver.c...
        Driver for btree tests:

                Opens or creates btree file.
                Gets next key and calls insert to insert key in tree.
                If necessary, creates a new root.
*/
#include "stdio.h"
#include "bt.h"

main()
{
    int    promoted;      /* boolean: tells if a promotion from below */
    short root,           /* RRN of root page                         */
          promo_rrn;      /* RRN promoted from below                  */
    char   promo_key,     /* key promoted from below                  */
          key;            /* next key to insert in tree               */

    if (btopen())    -               /* try to open btree.dat and get root   */
        root = getroot();
    else                             /* if btree.dat not there, create it    */
        root = create_tree();

    while ((key = getchar()) != 'q') {
        promoted = insert(root, key, &promo_rrn, &promo_key);
        if (promoted)
            root = create_root(promo_key, root, promo_rrn);
    }
    btclose();
}
```

▇▇▇ INSERT.C

```
/* insert.c...
        Contains insert() -- function to insert a key into a B-tree:
                Calls itself recursively until bottom of tree is reached.
                Then inserts key in node.
                If node is out of room,
                    - calls split() to split node
                    - promotes middle key and RRN of new node
*/
#include "bt.h"

insert (rrn, key, promo_r_child, promo_key)
short rrn,              /* RRN of page to make insertion in          */
      *promo_r_child;   /* child promoted up from here to next level */
char key,               /* key to be inserted here or lower          */
      *promo_key;       /* key promoted up from here to next level   */
```
                                                              (continued)

```
{
    BTPAGE page,            /* current page                        */
            newpage;        /* new page created if split occurs    */
    int found, promoted;    /* boolean values                      */
    short  pos,
            p_b_rrn;        /* RRN promoted from below             */
    char   p_b_key;         /* key promoted from below             */

    if (rrn == NIL) {            /* past bottom of tree... "promote" */
        *promo_key = key;       /* original key so that it will be  */
        *promo_r_child = NIL;   /* inserted at leaf level           */
        return (YES);
    }
    btread(rrn, &page);
    found = search_node(key, &page, &pos);
    if (found) {
        printf("Error: attempt to insert duplicate key: %c \n\007", key);
        return (0);
    }
    promoted = insert(page.child[pos], key, &p_b_rrn, &p_b_key);
    if (!promoted)
        return (NO);  /* no promotion */
    if (page.keycount < MAXKEYS) {
        ins_in_page(p_b_key, p_b_rrn, &page);   /* OK to insert key and  */
        btwrite(rrn, &page);                    /* pointer in this page. */
        return (NO);  /* no promotion */
    }
    else {
        split(p_b_key, p_b_rrn, &page, promo_key, promo_r_child, &newpage);
        btwrite(rrn, &page);
        btwrite(*promo_r_child, &newpage);
        return (YES);   /* promotion */
    }
}
```

▬▬▬ BTIO.C

```
/* btio.c...
        Contains B-tree functions that directly involve file i/o:

        btopen() -- open file "btree.dat" to hold the btree
        btclose() -- close "btree.dat"
        getroot() -- get rrn of root node from first two bytes of btree.dat
        putroot() -- put rrn of root node in first two bytes of btree.dat
        create_tree() -- create "btree.dat" and root node
        getpage() -- get next available block in "btree.dat" for a new page
        btread() -- read page number RRN from "btree.dat"
        btwrite() -- write page number RRN to "btree.dat"
*/
```

```c
#include <stdio.h>
#include "bt.h"
#include "fileio.h"

int btfd;      /* global file descriptor for "btree.dat"  */

btopen()
{
    btfd = open("btree.dat", READWRITE);
    return(btfd > 0);
}

btclose()
{
    close(btfd);
}

short getroot()
{
    short root;
    long lseek();

    lseek(btfd, 0L, 0);
    if (read(btfd, &root, 2) == 0) {
        printf("Error: Unable to get root.\007\n");
        exit(1);
    }
    return (root);
}

putroot(root)
short root;
{
    long lseek();

    lseek(btfd, 0L, 0);
    write(btfd, &root, 2);
}

short create_tree()
{
    char key;

    btfd = creat("btree.dat",PMODE);
    close(btfd);          /* Have to close and reopen to ensure  */
    btopen();             /* read/write access on many systems.  */
    key = getchar();    /* Get first key.  */
    return (create_root(key, NIL, NIL));
}
```

(continued)

```
short getpage()
{
    long lseek(), addr;
    addr = lseek(btfd, 0L, 2) - 2L;
    return ((short) addr / PAGESIZE);
}


btread(rrn, page_ptr)
short rrn;
BTPAGE *page_ptr;
{
    long lseek(), addr;

    addr = (long)rrn * (long)PAGESIZE + 2L;
    lseek(btfd, addr, 0);
    return ( read(btfd, page_ptr, PAGESIZE) );
}

btwrite(rrn, page_ptr)
short rrn;
BTPAGE *page_ptr;
{
    long lseek(), addr;
    addr = (long) rrn * (long) PAGESIZE + 2L;
    lseek(btfd, addr, 0);
    return (write(btfd, page_ptr, PAGESIZE));
}
```

≡≡≡ BTUTIL.C

```
/* btutil.c...
        Contains utility functions for btree program:

        create_root() -- get and initialize root node and insert one key
        pageinit() -- put NOKEY in all "key" slots and NIL in "child" slots
        search_node() -- return YES if key in node, else NO. In either case,
                        put key's correct position in pos.
        ins_in_page() -- insert key and right child in page
        split() -- split node by creating new node and moving half of keys to
                        new node. Promote middle key and RRN of new node.
*/
#include "bt.h"

create_root(key, left, right)
char key;
short left, right;
{
    BTPAGE page;
    short rrn;
```

```
    rrn = getpage();
    pageinit(&page);
    page.key[0] = key;
    page.child[0] = left;
    page.child[1] = right;
    page.keycount = 1;
    btwrite(rrn,&page);
    putroot(rrn);
    return(rrn);
}


pageinit(p_page)
BTPAGE *p_page;         /* p_page: pointer to a page  */
{
    int j;

    for (j = 0; j < MAXKEYS; j++) {
        p_page->key[j] = NOKEY;
        p_page->child[j] = NIL;
    }
    p_page->child[MAXKEYS] = NIL;
}


search_node(key, p_page, pos)
char key;
BTPAGE *p_page;
short *pos;              /* position where key is or should be inserted  */
{
    int i;
    for (i = 0;  i < p_page->keycount  &&   key > p_page->key[i] ; i++ )
        ;
    *pos = i;
    if (  *pos < p_page->keycount  &&  key == p_page->key[*pos] )
        return (YES);   /* key is in page */
    else
        return (NO);    /* key is not in page */
}


ins_in_page(key, r_child, p_page)
char key;
short r_child;
BTPAGE *p_page;
{
    int i;

    for (i = p_page->keycount; key < p_page->key[i-1] && i > 0; i--) {
        p_page->key[i] = p_page->key[i-1];
        p_page->child[i+1] = p_page->child[i];
    }
    p_page->keycount++;
    p_page->key[i] = key;
    p_page->child[i+1] = r_child;
}
```

(continued)

```
split(key, r_child, p_oldpage, promo_key, promo_r_child, p_newpage)
char    key,            /* key to be inserted              */
        *promo_key;     /* key to be promoted up from here */
short   r_child,        /* child RRN to be inserted        */
        *promo_r_child; /* RRN to be promoted up from here */
BTPAGE *p_oldpage,      /* pointers to old and new page structures */
        *p_newpage;
{
    int   i;
    short mid;                  /* tells where split is to occur        */
    char  workkeys[MAXKEYS+1];  /* temporarily holds keys, before split */
    short workch[MAXKEYS+2];    /* temporarily holds children, before split */

    for (i=0; i < MAXKEYS; i++) {           /* move keys and children from */
        workkeys[i] = p_oldpage->key[i];    /* old page into work arrays   */
        workch[i] = p_oldpage->child[i];
    }
    workch[i] = p_oldpage->child[i];
    for (i=MAXKEYS; key < workkeys[i-1] && i > 0; i--) {  /* insert new key */
        workkeys[i] = workkeys[i-1];
        workch[i+1] = workch[i];
    }
    workkeys[i] = key;
    workch[i+1] = r_child;

    *promo_r_child = getpage();             /* create new page for split,  */
    pageinit(p_newpage);                    /* and promote RRN of new page */

    for (i = 0; i < MINKEYS; i++) {         /* move first half of keys and */
        p_oldpage->key[i] = workkeys[i];    /* children to old page, second */
        p_oldpage->child[i] = workch[i];    /*  half to new page            */
        p_newpage->key[i] = workkeys[i+1+MINKEYS];
        p_newpage->child[i] = workch[i+1+MINKEYS];
        p_oldpage->key[i+MINKEYS] = NOKEY;    /* mark second half of old */
        p_oldpage->child[i+1+MINKEYS] = NIL;  /* page as empty           */
    }

    p_oldpage->child[MINKEYS] = workch[MINKEYS];
    p_newpage->child[MINKEYS] = workch[i+1+MINKEYS];
    p_newpage->keycount = MAXKEYS - MINKEYS;
    p_oldpage->keycount = MINKEYS;

    *promo_key = workkeys[MINKEYS];         /* promote middle key */
}
```

PASCAL PROGRAM TO INSERT KEYS INTO A B-TREE

The Pascal program that follows implements the insert program described in the text. The only difference between this program and the one in the text is that this program builds a B-tree of order five, whereas the one in the text builds a B-tree of order four. Input characters are taken from standard I/O, with q indicating end of data.

The main program includes three nonstandard compiler directives:

{$B-}

{$I btutil.prc}

{$I insert.prc}

The $B − instructs the Turbo Pascal compiler to handle keyboard input as a standard Pascal file.

The $I directives instruct the compiler to include the files *btutil.prc* and *insert.prc* in the main program. These two files contain functions needed by the main program. So the B-tree program requires the use of functions from three files:

driver.pas	Contains the main program, which closely parallels the driver program described in the text.
insert.prc	Contains *insert()*, the recursive function that finds the proper place for a key, inserts it, and supervises splitting and promotions.
btutil.prc	Contains all other support functions, including the function *split()* described in the text.

▬▬▬ DRIVER.PAS

```
PROGRAM btree (INPUT,OUTPUT);
{
        Driver for B-tree tests:

                Opens or creates btree file.
                Gets next key and calls insert to insert key in tree.
                If necessary, creates a new root.
}
```

(continued)

```
{$B-}

CONST
    MAXKEYS = 4;        {maximum number of keys in page}
    MAXCHLD = 5;        {maximum number of children in page}
    MAXWKEYS = 5;       {maximum number of keys in working space}
    MAXWCHLD = 6;       {maximum number of children in working space}
    NOKEY = '@'         {symbol to indicate no key }
    NO = FALSE;
    YES = TRUE;
    NULL = -1;

TYPE
    BTPAGE = RECORD
        keycount : integer;                      {number of keys in page      }
        key : array [1..MAXKEYS] of char;        {the actual keys             }
        child : array [1..MAXCHLD] of integer;   {ptrs to RRNs of descendents}
    END;

VAR
    promoted   : boolean;               {tells if a promotion from below}
    root,                               {RRN of root                    }
    promo_rrn  : integer;               {RRN promoted from below         }
    promo_key,                          {key promoted from below         }
    key        : char;                  {next key to insert in tree      }
    btfd       : file of BTPAGE;        {global file descriptor for      }
                                        {"btree.dat"                     }
    MINKEYS    : integer;               {min. number of keys in a page   }
    PAGESIZE   : integer;               {size of a page                  }

{$I btutil.prc}
{$I insert.prc}

BEGIN {main}
    MINKEYS := MAXKEYS DIV 2;
    PAGESIZE := sizeof(BTPAGE);

    if btopen then                  {try to open btree.dat and get root}
        root := getroot
    else                            {if btree.dat not there, create it }
        root := create_tree;

    read(key);
    WHILE (key <> 'q') DO
        BEGIN
        promoted := insert(root,key,promo_rrn,promo_key);
        if promoted then
            root := create_root(promo_key,root,promo_rrn);
        read(key)
        END;

    btclose
END.
```

▆▆▆ INSERT.PRC

```
FUNCTION insert (rrn: integer;key: char;VAR promo_r_child: integer;
                 VAR promo_key: char): boolean;

{   Function to insert a key into a B-tree:

        Calls itself recursively until the bottom of the tree is reached.
        Then inserts the key in the node.
        If node is out of room, then it calls split() to split the node and
            promotes the middle key and RRN of new node.
}

VAR
    page,                      {current page                          }
    newpage : BTPAGE;          {new page created if split occurs      }
    found,                     {tells if key is already in B-tree     }
    promoted : boolean;        {tells if key is promoted              }
    pos,                       {position that key is to go in          }
    p_b_rrn : integer;         {RRN promoted from below                }
    p_b_key : char;            {key promoted from below                }

BEGIN
    if (rrn = NULL) then            {past bottom of tree... "promote" }
        BEGIN                       {original key so that it will be  }
        promo_key := key;           {inserted at leaf level           }
        promo_r_child := NULL;
        insert := YES
        END
    else
        BEGIN
        btread(rrn,page);
        found := search_node(key,page,pos);
        if (found) then
            BEGIN
            writeln('Error: attempt to insert duplicate key: ',key);
            insert := NO
            END
        else          {insert key at lower level}
            BEGIN
            promoted := insert(page.child[pos],key,p_b_rrn,p_b_key);
            if (NOT promoted) then
                insert := NO        {no promotion}
            else
                BEGIN
                if (page.keycount < MAXKEYS) then
                    BEGIN                               {OK to insert key    }
                    ins_in_page(p_b_key,p_b_rrn,page); {and pointer in this }
                    btwrite(rrn,page);                  {page.               }
                    insert := NO     {no promotion}
                    END
```

(continued)

```
                else
                    BEGIN
                    split(p_b_key,p_b_rrn,page,promo_key,
                        promo_r_child,newpage);
                    btwrite(rrn,page);
                    btwrite(promo_r_child,newpage);
                    insert := YES          {promotion}
                    END
                END
            END
        END
END;
```

≡≡≡ BTUTIL.PRC

```
FUNCTION btopen : BOOLEAN;
{Function to open "btree.dat" if it already exists.  Otherwise
 it returns false }
VAR
    response : char;
BEGIN
    assign(btfd,'btree.dat');
    write('Does btree.dat already exist? (respond Y or N): ');
    readln(response);
    writeln;
    if (response = 'Y') OR (response = 'y') then
        BEGIN
        reset(btfd);
        btopen := TRUE
        END
    else
        btopen := FALSE
END;


PROCEDURE btclose;
{Procedure to close "btree.dat"}
BEGIN
    close (btfd);
END;
```

```pascal
FUNCTION getroot : integer;
{Function to get the RRN of the root node from first record of btree.dat}
VAR
    root : BTPAGE;
BEGIN
    seek(btfd,0);
    if (not EOF) then
        BEGIN
        read(btfd,root);
        getroot := root.keycount
        END
    else
        writeln('Error: Unable to get root.')
END;


FUNCTION getpage : integer;
{Function that gets the next available block in "btree.dat" for a new page}
BEGIN
    getpage := filesize(btfd)
END;

PROCEDURE pageinit (VAR p_page : BTPAGE);
{puts NOKEY in all "key" slots and NULL in "child" slots}
VAR
    j : integer;
BEGIN
    for j := 1 TO MAXKEYS  DO
        BEGIN
        p_page.key[j] := NOKEY;
        p_page.child[j] := NULL;
        END;
    p_page.child[MAXKEYS+1] := NULL
END;


PROCEDURE putroot (root: integer);
{Puts RRN of root node in the keycount of the first record of btree.dat }
VAR
    rootrrn : BTPAGE;
BEGIN
    seek(btfd,0);
    rootrrn.keycount := root;
    pageinit (rootrrn);
    write(btfd,rootrrn)
END;

PROCEDURE btread (rrn : integer; VAR page_ptr : BTPAGE);
{reads page number RRN from btree.dat}
BEGIN
    seek (btfd,rrn);
    read(btfd,page_ptr);
END;
```

(continued)

```
PROCEDURE btwrite (rrn : integer; page_ptr : BTPAGE);
{writes page number RRN to btree.dat}
BEGIN
    seek(btfd,rrn);
    write(btfd,page_ptr);
END;

FUNCTION create_root (key :char; left,right : integer): integer;
{get and initialize root node and insert one key}
VAR
    page : BTPAGE;
    rrn : integer;
BEGIN
    rrn := getpage;
    pageinit(page);
    page.key[1] := key;
    page.child[1] := left;
    page.child[2] := right;
    page.keycount := 1;
    btwrite(rrn,page);
    putroot(rrn);
    create_root := rrn
END;

FUNCTION create_tree : integer;
{creates "btree.dat" and the root node}
VAR
    rootrrn : integer;
BEGIN
    rewrite(btfd);
    read(key);
    rootrrn := getpage;
    putroot(rootrrn);
    create_tree := create_root(key,NULL,NULL);
END;


FUNCTION search_node(key : char; p_page : BTPAGE; VAR pos : integer): boolean;
{returns YES if key in node, else NO.  In either case, put key's correct
 position in pos }
VAR
    i : integer;
BEGIN
    i := 1;
    while ((i <= p_page.keycount) AND (key > p_page.key[i])) DO
        i := i + 1;
    pos := i;
    if ((pos <= p_page.keycount) AND (key = p_page.key[pos])) then
        search_node := YES
    else
        search_node := NO
END;
```

```
PROCEDURE ins_in_page (key: char;r_child: integer; VAR p_page: BTPAGE);
{insert key and right child in page}
VAR
    i : integer;
BEGIN
    i := p_page.keycount + 1;
    while ((key < p_page.key[i-1]) AND (i > 1)) DO
        BEGIN
        p_page.key[i] := p_page.key[i-1];
        p_page.child[i+1] := p_page.child[i];
        i := i - 1
        END;
    p_page.keycount := p_page.keycount + 1;
    p_page.key[i] := key;
    p_page.child[i+1] := r_child
END;


PROCEDURE split (key: char; r_child: integer; VAR p_oldpage: BTPAGE;
                 VAR promo_key: char; VAR promo_r_child: integer;
                 VAR p_newpage: BTPAGE);

{split node by creating new node and moving half of keys to new node.
 Promote middle key and RRN of new node.}
VAR
    i : integer;
    workkeys : array [1..MAXWKEYS] of char;    {temporarily holds keys,}
                                               { before split}
    workch : array [1..MAXWCHLD] of integer;   {temporarily holds children, }
                                               { before split }
BEGIN
    for i := 1 TO MAXKEYS  DO                   {move keys and children from }
        BEGIN                                  {old page into work arrays   }
        workkeys[i] := p_oldpage.key[i];
        workch[i] := p_oldpage.child[i]
        END;
    workch[MAXKEYS+1] := p_oldpage.child[MAXKEYS+1];


    i := MAXKEYS + 1;
    while ((key < workkeys[i-1])  AND  (i > 1)) DO
        BEGIN
        workkeys[i] := workkeys[i-1];          {insert new key }
        workch[i+1] := workch[i];
        i := i - 1
        END;
    workkeys[i] := key;
    workch[i+1] := r_child;


    promo_r_child := getpage;                  {create new page for split  }
    pageinit(p_newpage);                       {and promote RRN of new page}
```
                                                          (continued)

```
for i := 1 TO MINKEYS DO              {move first half of keys and }
    BEGIN                             {children to old page,       }
    p_oldpage.key[i] := workkeys[i];  {second half to new page.    }
    p_oldpage.child[i] := workch[i];
    p_newpage.key[i] := workkeys[i+1+MINKEYS];
    p_newpage.child[i] := workch[i+1+MINKEYS];
    p_oldpage.key[i+MINKEYS] := NOKEY;        {mark second half of old }
    p_oldpage.child[i+1+MINKEYS] := NULL      {page as empty           }
    END;
p_oldpage.child[MINKEYS+1] := workch[MINKEYS+1];
p_newpage.child[MINKEYS+1] := workch[i+2+MINKEYS];
p_newpage.keycount := MAXKEYS - MINKEYS;
p_oldpage.keycount := MINKEYS;
promo_key := workkeys[MINKEYS+1]                       {promote middle key }
END;
```

CHAPTER

OBJECTIVES

Introduce *indexed sequential* files.

Describe operations on a *sequence set* of blocks that maintains records in order by key.

Show how an *index set* can be built on top of the sequence set to produce an indexed sequential file structure.

Introduce the use of a B-tree to maintain the index set, thereby introducing B^+ *trees* and *simple prefix B^+ trees*.

Illustrate how the B-tree index set in a simple prefix B^+ tree can be of variable order, holding a variable number of separators.

Compare the strengths and weaknesses of B^+ trees, simple prefix B^+ trees, and B-trees.

10 THE B^+ TREE FAMILY AND INDEXED SEQUENTIAL FILE ACCESS

CHAPTER OUTLINE

10.1

INDEXED SEQUENTIAL ACCESS

Indexed sequential file structures provide a choice between two alternative views of a file:

□ *Indexed*: The file can be seen as a set of records that is *indexed* by key; or

□ *Sequential*: The file can be accessed sequentially (physically contiguous records—no seeking), returning records in order by key.

The idea of having a single organizational method that provides both of these views is a new one. Up to this point we have had to choose between them. As a somewhat extreme, though instructive, example of the potential divergence of these two choices, suppose that we have developed a file structure consisting of a set of entry sequenced records indexed by a separate B-tree. This structure can provide excellent *indexed* access to any individual record by key, even as records are added and deleted. Now let's suppose that we also want to use this file as part of a cosequential merge. In cosequential processing we want to retrieve all the records in order by key. Since the actual records in this file system are *entry sequenced,* rather than physically sorted by key, the only way to retrieve them in order by key is through the index. For a file of N records, following the N pointers from the index into the entry sequenced set requires N essentially random seeks into the record file. This is a *much* less efficient process than the sequential reading of physically adjacent records—so much so that it is unacceptable for any situation in which cosequential processing is a frequent occurrence.

On the other hand, our discussions of indexing show us that a file consisting of a set of records sorted by key, though ideal for cosequential processing, is an unacceptable structure when we want to access, insert, and delete records by key in random order.

What if an application involves both interactive random access and cosequential batch processing? There are many examples of such dual-mode applications. Student record systems at universities, for example, require keyed access to individual records while also requiring a large amount of batch processing, as when grades are posted or when fees are paid during registration. Similarly, credit card systems require both batch processing of charge slips and interactive checks of account status. Indexed sequential access methods were developed in response to these kinds of needs.

10.2

MAINTAINING A SEQUENCE SET

We set aside, for the moment, the indexed part of indexed sequential access, focusing on the problem of keeping a set of records in physical order by key as records are added and deleted. We refer to this ordered set of records as a *sequence set.* We will assume that once we have a good way of maintaining a sequence set, we will find some way to index it as well.

10.2.1 THE USE OF BLOCKS

We can immediately rule out the idea of sorting and resorting the entire sequence set as records are added and deleted, since we know that sorting an entire file is an expensive process. We need instead to find a way to *localize* the changes. One of the best ways to restrict the effects of an insertion or deletion to just a part of the sequence set involves a tool we first encountered in Chapters 3 and 4: We can collect the records into *blocks*.

When we block records, the block becomes the basic unit of input and output. We read and write entire blocks at once. Consequently, the size of the buffers we use in a program is such that they can hold an entire block. After reading in a block, all the records in a block are in RAM, where we can work on them or rearrange them much more rapidly.

An example helps illustrate how the use of blocks can help us keep a sequence set in order. Suppose we have records that are keyed on last name and collected together so that there are four records in a block. We also include *link fields* in each block that point to the preceding block and the following block. We need these fields because, as you will see, consecutive blocks are not necessarily physically adjacent.

As with B-trees, the insertion of new records into a block can cause the block to *overflow*. The overflow condition can be handled by a block splitting process that is analogous to, but not the same as, the block splitting process used in a B-tree. For example, Fig. 10.1(a) shows what our blocked sequence set looks like before any insertions or deletions take place. We show only the forward links. In Fig. 10.1(b) we have inserted a new record with the key CARTER. This insertion causes Block 2 to split. The second half of what was originally Block 2 is found in Block 4 after the split. Note that this block-splitting process operates differently than the splitting we encountered in B-trees. In a B-tree a split results in the *promotion* of a record. Here things are simpler: we just divide the records between two blocks and rearrange the links so we can still move through the file in order by key, block after block.

Deletion of records can cause a block to be less than half full and therefore to *underflow*. Once again, this problem and its solutions are analogous to what we encounter when working with B-trees. Underflow in a B-tree can lead to either of two solutions:

☐ If a neighboring node is also half full, we can *concatenate* the two nodes, freeing one up for reuse.
☐ If the neighboring nodes are more than half full, we can *redistribute* records between the nodes to make the distribution more nearly even.

Underflow within a block of our sequence set can be handled through the same kinds of processes. As with insertion, the process for the sequence set is simpler than the process for B-trees since the sequence set is *not* a tree and there are therefore no keys and records in

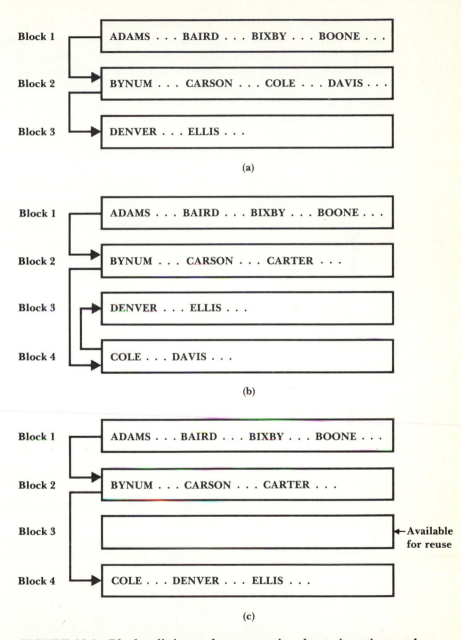

FIGURE 10.1 ▪ Block splitting and concatenation due to insertions and deletions in the sequence set. (a) Initial blocked sequence set. (b) Sequence set after insertion of CARTER record—Block 2 splits, and the contents are divided between Blocks 2 and 4. (c) Sequence set after deletion of DAVIS record—Block 4 is less than half full, so it is concatenated with Block 3.

a parent node. In Fig. 10.1(c) we show the effects of deleting the record for DAVIS. Block 4 underflows and is then concatenated with its successor in *logical* sequence, which is Block 3. The concatenation process frees up Block 3 for reuse. We do not show an example in which underflow leads to redistribution, rather than concatenation, since it is easy to see how the redistribution process works. Records are simply moved between logically adjacent blocks.

Given the separation of records into blocks, along with these fundamental block splitting, concatenation, and redistribution operations, we can keep a sequence set in order by key without ever having to sort the entire set of records. As always, nothing comes free; consequently, there are costs associated with this avoidance of sorting:

☐   Once insertions are made, our file takes up more space than an unblocked file of sorted records because of internal fragmentation within a block. However, we can apply the same kinds of strategies used to increase space utilization in a B-tree (e.g., the use of redistribution in place of splitting during insertion, two-to-three splitting, and so on). Once again, the implementation of any of these strategies must account for the fact that the sequence set *is not a tree* and that there is therefore no promotion of records.

☐   The order of the records is not necessarily *physically* sequential throughout the file. The maximum guaranteed extent of physical sequentiality is within a block.

This last point leads us to the important question of selecting a block size.

10.2.2 CHOICE OF BLOCK SIZE

As we work with our sequence set, a block is the basic unit for our I/O operations. When we read data from the disk, we never read less than a block; when we write data, we always write at least one block. A block is also, as we have said, the maximum *guaranteed* extent of physical sequentiality. It follows that we should think in terms of *large* blocks, with each block holding many records. So the question of block size becomes one of identifying the *limits* on block size: Why not make the block size so big we can fit the entire file in a single block?

One answer to this is the same as the reason why we cannot always use a RAM sort on a file: We usually do not have enough RAM available. So our first consideration regarding an upper bound for block size is as follows.

Consideration 1:   The block size should be such that we can hold several
                           blocks in RAM at once. For example, in performing a
                           block split or concatenation, we want to be able to hold
                           at least two blocks in RAM at a time. If we are
                           implementing two-to-three splitting to conserve disk
                           space, we need to hold at least three blocks in RAM at
                           a time.

Although we are presently focusing on the ability to access our sequence set *sequentially,* we eventually want to consider the problem of
randomly accessing a single record from our sequence set. We have to
read in an entire block to get at any one record within that block. We
can therefore state a second consideration:

Consideration 2:   Reading in or writing out a block should not take very
                           long. Even if we had an unlimited amount of RAM, we
                           would want to place an upper limit on the block size so
                           that we would not end up reading in the entire file just
                           to get at a single record.

This second consideration is more than a little imprecise: How long
is very long? We can refine this consideration by factoring in some of
our knowledge of the performance characteristics of disk drives:

Consideration 2   The block size should be such that we can access a block
(redefined):   without having to bear the cost of a disk seek within the
                           block read or block write operation.

This is not a *mandatory* limitation, but it is a sensible one: We are
interested in a block because it contains records that are physically adjacent, so let's not extend blocks beyond the point at which we can
guarantee such adjacency. And where is that?

When we discussed sector formatted disks back in Chapter 3, we
introduced the term *cluster*. A cluster is the minimum number of sectors
allocated at a time. If a cluster consists of eight sectors, as it does on a
typical fixed disk on an IBM PC/XT, then a file containing only one
byte still uses up eight sectors (4096 bytes) on the disk. The reason for
clustering is that it guarantees a minimum amount of physical sequentiality. As we move from cluster to cluster in reading a file, we may
incur a disk seek, but within a cluster the data can be accessed without
seeking.

One reasonable suggestion for deciding on a block size, then, is to
make each block equal to the size of a cluster. Often the cluster size on
a disk system has already been determined by the system administrator.
But what if you are configuring a disk system for a particular application and can therefore choose your own cluster size? Then you need to

consider the issues relating to cluster size raised in Chapter 3, along with the constraints imposed by the amount of RAM available and the number of blocks you want to hold in RAM at once. As is so often the case, the final decision will probably be a compromise between a number of divergent considerations. The important thing is that the compromise be a truly *informed* decision, based on knowledge of how I/O devices and file structures work, rather than just a guess.

If you are working with a disk system that is not sector oriented, but that allows you to choose the block size for a particular file, a good starting point is to think of a block as an entire track of the disk. You may want to revise this downward, to half a track, for instance, depending on memory constraints, record size, and other factors.

10.3 ADDING A SIMPLE INDEX TO THE SEQUENCE SET

We have created a mechanism for maintaining a set of records so that we can access them sequentially in order by key. It is based on the idea of grouping the records into blocks and then maintaining the blocks, as records are added and deleted, through splitting, concatenation, and redistribution. Now let's see whether we can find an efficient way to locate some specific block containing a particular record, given the record's key.

We can view each of our blocks as containing a *range* of records, as illustrated in Fig. 10.2. This is an outside view of the blocks (we have not actually read any blocks and so do not know *exactly* what they contain), but it is sufficiently informative to allow us to choose which block *might* have the record we are seeking. We can see, for example that if we are looking for a record with the key BURNS, we want to retrieve and inspect the second block.

It is easy to see how we could construct a simple, single-level index for these blocks. We might choose, for example, to build an index of

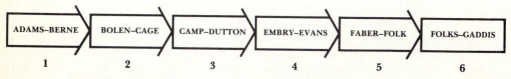

ADAMS–BERNE	BOLEN–CAGE	CAMP–DUTTON	EMBRY–EVANS	FABER–FOLK	FOLKS–GADDIS
1	2	3	4	5	6

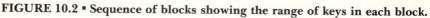

FIGURE 10.2 ▪ Sequence of blocks showing the range of keys in each block.

Key	Block number
BERNE	1
CAGE	2
DUTTON	3
EVANS	4
FOLK	5
GADDIS	6

FIGURE 10.3 ▪ Simple index for the sequence set illustrated in Fig. 10.2.

fixed length records that contain the key for the last record in each block, as shown in Fig. 10.3.

The combination of this kind of index with the sequence set of blocks provides complete indexed sequential access. If we need to retrieve a specific record, we consult the index and then retrieve the correct block; if we need sequential access we start at the first block and read through the linked list of blocks until we have read them all. As simple as this approach is, it is in fact a very workable one as long as the entire index can be held in electronic RAM memory. The requirement that the index be held in RAM is important for two reasons:

☐ Since this is a simple index of the kind we discuss in Chapter 7, we find specific records by means of a binary search of the index. Binary searching works well if the searching takes place in RAM, but, as we saw in the previous chapter on B-trees, it requires too many seeks if the file is on a secondary storage device.

☐ As the blocks in the sequence set are changed through splitting, concatenation, and redistribution, the index has to be updated. Updating a simple, fixed length record index of this kind works well if the index is relatively small and contained in RAM. If, however, the updating requires seeking to individual index records on disk, the process can become very expensive. Once again, this is a point we discuss more completely in earlier chapters.

What do we do, then, if the file contains so many blocks that the block index does not conveniently fit into RAM? In the preceding chapter we found that we could divide the index structure into *pages*, much like the *blocks* we are discussing here, handling several pages, or blocks, of the index in RAM at a time. More specifically, we found that B-trees are an excellent file structure for handling indexes that are too large to fit entirely in RAM. This suggests that we might organize the index to our sequence set as a B-tree.

The use of a B-tree index for our sequence set of blocks is, in fact, a very powerful notion. The resulting hybrid structure is known as a *B⁺ tree,* which is appropriate since it is a B-tree index *plus* a sequence set that holds the actual records. Before we can fully develop the notion of a B⁺ tree, we need to think more carefully about what it is we need to keep in the index.

10.4   THE CONTENT OF THE INDEX: SEPARATORS INSTEAD OF KEYS

The purpose of the index we are building is to assist us when we are searching for a record with a specific key. The index must guide us to the block in the sequence set that contains the record, if it exists in the sequence set at all. The index serves as a kind of roadmap for the sequence set. We are interested in the content of the index only insofar as it can assist us in getting to the correct block in the sequence set; the index set does not itself contain answers, it contains only information about where to go to get answers.

Given this view of the index set as a roadmap, we can take the very important step of recognizing that *we do not need to have actual keys in the index set.* Our real need is for *separators.* Figure 10.4 shows one possible set of separators for the sequence set in Fig. 10.2.

Note that there are many potential separators capable of distinguishing between two blocks. For example, all of the strings shown between Blocks 3 and 4 in Fig. 10.5 are capable of guiding us in our choice between the blocks as we search for a particular key. If a string comparison between the key and any of these separators shows that the key precedes the separator, we look for the key in Block 3. If the key follows the separator, we look in Block 4.

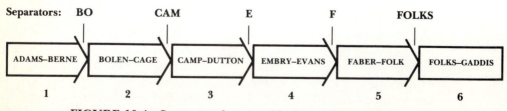

FIGURE 10.4 ▪ Separators between blocks in the sequence set.

DUTU
DVXGHESJF
DZ
E
EBQX
ELEEMOSYNARY

CAMP–DUTTON

EMBRY–EVANS

3

4

FIGURE 10.5 ▪ A list of potential separators.

If we are willing to treat the separators as variable length entities within our index structure (we talk about how to do this later), we can save space by placing the *shortest separator* in the index structure. Consequently, we use E as the separator to guide our choice between Blocks 3 and 4. Note that there is not always a unique shortest separator. For example, BK, BN, and BO are separators that are all the same length and that are equally effective as separators between Blocks 1 and 2 in Fig. 10.4. We choose BO and all of the other separators contained in Fig. 10.4 by using the logic embodied in the C function shown in Fig. 10.6 and in the Pascal procedure listed in Fig. 10.7.

Note that these functions can produce a separator that is the same as the second key. This situation is illustrated in Fig. 10.4 by the separator between Blocks 5 and 6, which is the same as the first key contained in Block 6. It follows that, as we use the separators as a roadmap to the sequence set, we must decide to retrieve the block that is to the

```
/* find_sep(key1,key2,sep) ...

        finds shortest string that serves as a separator between key1 and
        key2.  Returns this separator through the address provided by
        the "sep" parameter

        the function assumes that key2 follows key1 in collating sequence
*/

find_sep(key1,key2,sep)
        char key1[], key2[], sep[];
{
        while ( (*sep++ = *key2++) == *key1++)
                ;
        *sep='\0';    /* ensure that separator string is null terminated */
}
```

FIGURE 10.6 ▪ C function to find a shortest separator.

```
PROCEDURE find_sep (key1, key2 : strng ; VAR sep : strng);
{ finds the shortest string that serves as a separator between key1 and
  key2.  Returns the separator through the variable sep.  Strings are
  handled as character arrays in which the length of the string is stored
  in the 0th position of the array.  The type "strng" is used for strings.

  Assumes that key2 follows key1 in collating sequence.

  Uses two functions defined in the Appendix:
     len_str(s) -- returns the length of the string s.
     min(i,j)   -- compares i and j and returns the smallest value
}
VAR
    i, minlgth  : integer;
BEGIN
    minlgth := min(len_str(key1),len_str(key2));
    i := 1;
    while (key1[i] = key2[i]) and (i <= minlgth) DO
    BEGIN
        sep[i] := key2[i];
        i := i + 1
    END;
    sep[i] := key2[i];
    sep[0] := CHR(i)              { set length indicator in separator array }
END;
```

FIGURE 10.7 ▪ Pascal procedure to find a shortest separator.

right of the separator or the one that is to the left of the separator
according to the following rule:

Relation of search key and separator	Decision
Key < separator	Go left
Key = = separator	Go right
Key > separator	Go right

10.5

THE SIMPLE PREFIX B$^+$ TREE

Figure 10.8 shows how we can form the separators identified in Fig.
10.4 into a B-tree index of the sequence set blocks. The B-tree index is
called the *index set*. Taken together with the sequence set, it forms a file
structure called a *simple prefix B$^+$ tree*. The modifier *simple prefix* indi-

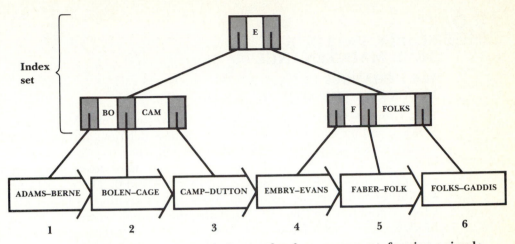

FIGURE 10.8 ▪ A B-tree index set for the sequence set, forming a simple prefix B+ tree.

cates that the index set contains shortest separators, or *prefixes* of the keys rather than copies of the actual keys. Our separators are simple because they are, simply, prefixes: they are actually just the initial letters within the keys. More complicated (not simple) methods of creating separators from key prefixes remove unnecessary characters from the front of the separator as well as from the rear. (See Bayer and Unterauer [1977] for a more complete discussion of prefix B⁺ trees.)†

Note that since the index set is a B-tree, a node containing N separators branches to $N + 1$ children. If we are searching for the record with the key EMBRY, we start at the root of the index set, comparing EMBRY to the separator E. Since EMBRY comes after E, we branch to the right, retrieving the node containing the separators F and FOLKS. Since EMBRY comes before even the first of these separators, we follow the branch that is to the left of the F separator, which leads us to Block 4, the correct block in the sequence set.

---

†The literature on B⁺ trees and simple prefix B⁺ trees is remarkably inconsistent in the nomenclature used for these structures. B⁺ trees are sometimes called B* trees; simple prefix B⁺ trees are sometimes called simple prefix B-trees. Comer's important article in *Computing Surveys* in 1979 has reduced some of the confusion by providing a consistent, standard nomenclature which we use here.

10.6

SIMPLE PREFIX B⁺ TREE MAINTENANCE

10.6.1 CHANGES LOCALIZED TO SINGLE BLOCKS IN THE SEQUENCE SET

Let's suppose that we want to delete the records for EMBRY and FOLKS, and let's suppose that neither of these deletions results in any concatenation or redistribution within the sequence set. Since there is no concatenation or redistribution, the effect of these deletions on the *sequence set* is limited to changes *within* Blocks 4 and 6. The record that was formerly the second record in Block 4 (let's say that its key is ERVIN) is now the first record. Similarly, the former second record in Block 6 (we assume it has a key of FROST) now starts that block. These changes can be seen in Fig. 10.9.

The more interesting question is what effect, if any, these deletions have on the *index set*. The answer is that since the number of sequence set blocks is unchanged, and since no records are moved between blocks, the index set can also remain unchanged. This is easy to see in the case of the EMBRY deletion: E is still a perfectly good separator for sequence set Blocks 3 and 4, so there is no reason to change it in the index set. The case of the FOLKS deletion is a little more confusing

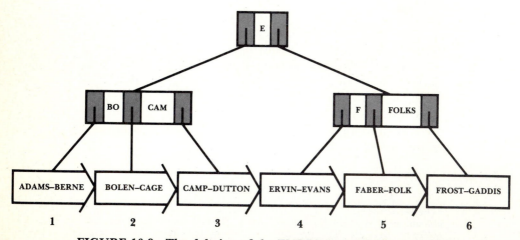

FIGURE 10.9 ▪ The deletion of the EMBRY and FOLKS records from the sequence set leaves the index set unchanged.

since the string FOLKS appears both as a key in the deleted record and as a separator within the index set. To avoid confusion, remember to distinguish clearly between these two uses of the string FOLKS: FOLKS can continue to serve as a separator between Blocks 5 and 6 even though the FOLKS record is deleted. (One could argue that although we do not *need* to replace the FOLKS separator, we should do so anyway because it is now possible to construct a *shorter* separator. However, the cost of making such a change in the index set usually outweighs the benefits associated with saving a few bytes of space.)

The effect of inserting into the sequence set new records that do not cause block splitting is much the same as the effect of these deletions that do not result in concatenation: The index set remains unchanged. Suppose, for example, that we insert a record for EATON. Following the path indicated by the separators in the index set, we find that we will insert the new record into Block 4 of the sequence set. We assume, for the moment, that there is room for the record in the block. The new record becomes the first record in Block 4, but no change in the index set is necessary. This is not surprising since we decided to insert the record into Block 4 on the basis of the existing information in the index set. It follows that the existing information in the index set is sufficient to allow us to find the record again.

10.6.2 CHANGES INVOLVING MULTIPLE BLOCKS IN THE SEQUENCE SET

What happens when the addition and deletion of records to and from the sequence set *does* change the number of blocks in the sequence set? Clearly, if we have more blocks, we need additional separators in the index set, and if we have fewer blocks, we need fewer separators. Changing the number of separators certainly has an effect on the index set, where the separators are stored.

Since the index set for a simple prefix B⁺ tree is actually just a normal B-tree, the changes to the index set are handled according to the familiar rules for B-tree insertion and deletion.† In the following examples we assume that the index set is a B-tree of order three, which means that the maximum number of separators we can store in a node is two. We use this small node size for the index set to illustrate node

---

†As you study the material here, you may find it helpful to refer back to Chapter 9, where we discuss B-tree operations in much more detail.

splitting and concatenation while using only a few separators. As you will see later, actual implementations of simple prefix B⁺ trees place a much larger number of separators in a node of the index set.

We begin with an insertion into the sequence set shown in Fig. 10.9. Specifically, let's assume that there is an insertion into the first block, and that this insertion causes the block to split. A new block (Block 7) is brought in to hold the second half of what was originally the first block. This new block is linked into the correct position in the sequence set, following Block 1 and preceding Block 2 (these are the *physical* block numbers). These changes to the sequence set are illustrated in Fig. 10.10.

Note that the separator that formerly distinguished between Blocks 1 and 2, the string BO, is now the separator for Blocks 7 and 2. We need a new separator, with a value of AY, to distinguish between Blocks 1 and 7. As we go to place this separator into the index set, we find that the node into which we want to insert it, containing BO and CAM, is already full. Consequently, insertion of the new separator causes a split and promotion, according to the usual rules for B-trees. The promoted separator, BO, is placed in the root of the index set.

Now let's suppose we delete a record from Block 2 of the sequence set that causes an underflow condition and consequent concatenation

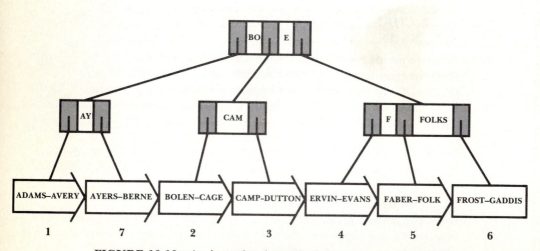

FIGURE 10.10 ▪ An insertion into Block 1 causes a split and the consequent addition of Block 7. The addition of a block in the sequence set requires a new separator in the index set. Insertion of the AY separator into the node containing BO and CAM causes a node split in the index set B-tree and consequent promotion of BO to the root.

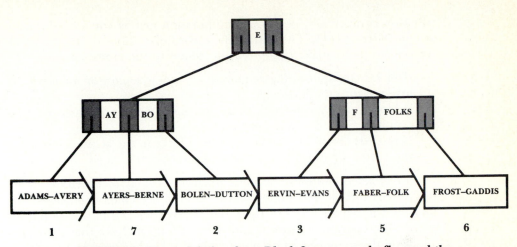

FIGURE 10.11 ▪ A deletion from Block 2 causes underflow and the consequent concatenation of Blocks 2 and 3. After the concatenation, Block 3 is no longer needed and can be placed on an avail list. Consequently, the separator CAM is no longer needed. Removing CAM from its node in the index set forces a concatenation of index set nodes, bringing BO back down from the root.

of Blocks 2 and 3. Once the concatenation is complete, Block 3 is no longer needed in the sequence set, and the separator that once distinguished between Blocks 2 and 3 must be removed from the index set. Removing this separator, CAM, causes an underflow in an index set node. Consequently, there is another concatenation, this time in the index set, that results in the demotion of the BO separator from the root, bringing it back down into a node with the AY separator. Once these changes are complete, the simple prefix B⁺ tree has the structure illustrated in Fig. 10.11.

Although in these examples a block split in the sequence set results in a node split in the index set, and a concatenation in the sequence set results in a concatenation in the index set, there is not always this correspondence of action. Insertions and deletions in the index set are handled as standard B-tree operations; whether there is splitting or a simple insertion, concatenation or a simple deletion, depends entirely upon how full the index set node is.

Writing procedures to handle these kinds of operations is straightforward if you remember that the changes take place *from the bottom up.* Record insertion and deletion *always* take place in the sequence set, since that is where the records are. If splitting, concatenation, or redistribution is necessary, perform the operation just as you would *if there were no index set at all*. Then, after the record operations in the sequence set are complete, make changes as necessary in the index set:

☐ If blocks are split in the sequence set, a new separator must be inserted into the index set;

☐ If blocks are concatenated in the sequence set, a separator must be removed from the index set; and

☐ If records are redistributed between blocks in the sequence set, the value of a separator in the index set must be changed.

Index set operations are performed according to the rules for B-trees. This means that node splitting and concatenation *propagate* up through the higher levels of the index set. We see this in our examples as the BO separator moves in and out of the root. Note that the operations on the sequence set do not involve this kind of propagation. That is because the sequence set is a linear, linked list, whereas the index set is a tree. It is easy to lose sight of this distinction and think of an insertion or deletion in terms of a *single* operation on the *entire* simple prefix B⁺ tree. This is a good way to become confused. Remember: insertions and deletions happen in the *sequence set* since that is where the records are. Changes to the index set are secondary; they are a by-product of the fundamental operations on the sequence set.

10.7   INDEX SET BLOCK SIZE

Up to this point we have ignored the important issues of the size and structure of the index set nodes. Our examples have used extremely small index set nodes and have treated them as fixed-order B-tree nodes, even though the separators are variable in length. We need to develop more realistic, useful ideas about the size and structure of index set nodes.

The physical size of a node for the index set is usually the same as the physical size of a block in the sequence set. When this is the case we speak of index set *blocks,* rather than *nodes,* just as we speak of sequence set blocks. There are a number of reasons for using a common block size for the index and sequence sets:

☐ The block size for the sequence set is usually chosen because there is a good fit between this block size, the characteristics of the disk drive, and the amount of memory available. The choice of an index set block size is governed by consideration of the same factors; therefore, the block size that is best for the sequence set is usually best for the index set.

☐ A common block size makes it easier to implement a buffering scheme to create a *virtual* simple prefix B^+ tree, similar to the virtual B-trees discussed in the preceding chapter.

☐ The index set blocks and sequence set blocks are often mingled within the same file to avoid seeking between two separate files while accessing the simple prefix B^+ tree. Use of one file for both kinds of blocks is simpler if the block sizes are the same.

10.8
INTERNAL STRUCTURE OF INDEX SET BLOCKS: A VARIABLE ORDER B-TREE

Given a large, fixed-size block for the index set, how do we store the separators within it? In the examples considered so far, the block structure is such that it can contain only a fixed number of separators. The entire motivation behind the use of *shortest* separators is the possibility of packing more of them into a node. This motivation disappears completely if the index set uses a fixed-order B-tree in which there is a fixed number of separators per node.

We want each index set block to hold a variable number of variable length separators. How should we go about searching through these separators? Since the blocks are probably large, any single block can hold a large number of separators. Once we read a block into RAM for use, we want to be able to do a binary rather than sequential search on its list of separators. We therefore need to structure the block so that it can support a binary search, despite the fact that the separators are of variable length.

In Chapter 7, which covers indexing, we see that the use of a separate index can provide a means of performing binary searches on a list of variable length entities. If the index itself consists of fixed length references, we can use binary searching on the index, retrieving the actual variable length records or fields through indirection. For example, suppose we are going to place the following set of separators into an index block:

As, Ba, Bro, C, Ch, Cra, Dele, Edi, Err, Fa, Fle.

(We are using lowercase letters, rather than all uppercase letters, so you can find the separators more easily when we concatenate them.) We could concatenate these separators and build an index for them, as shown in Fig. 10.12.

If we are using this block of the index set as a roadmap to help us find the record in the sequence set for "Beck", we perform a binary

FIGURE 10.12 ▪ Variable length separators and corresponding index.

search on the index to the separators, retrieving first the middle separator, "Cra", which starts in position 10. Note that we can find the length of this separator by looking at the starting position of the separator that follows. Our binary search eventually tells us that "Beck" falls between the separators "Ba" and "Bro". Then what do we do?

The purpose of the index set roadmap is to guide us downward through the levels of the simple prefix B$^+$ tree, leading us to the sequence set block we want to retrieve. Consequently, the index set block needs some way to store references to its children, to the blocks descending from it in the next lower level of the tree. We assume that the references are made in terms of a relative block number (RBN), which is analogous to a relative record number except that it references a fixed length block rather than a record. If there are N separators within a block, the block has $N + 1$ children, and therefore needs space to store $N + 1$ RBNs in addition to the separators and the index to the separators.

There are many ways to combine the list of separators, index to separators, and list of RBNs into a single index set block. One possible approach is illustrated in Fig. 10.13. In addition to the vector of separators, the index to these separators, and the list of associated block numbers, this block structure includes:

☐ *Separator count*: We need this to help us find the middle element in the index to the separators so we can begin our binary search.

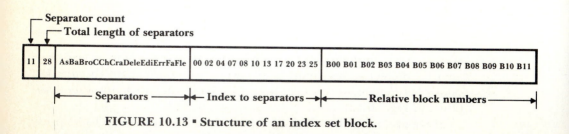

FIGURE 10.13 ▪ Structure of an index set block.

☐ *Total length of separators*: The list of concatenated separators varies in length from block to block. Since the index to the separators begins at the end of this variable length list, we need to know how long the list is so we can find the beginning of our index.

Let's suppose, once again, that we are looking for a record with the key "Beck" and that the search has brought us to the index set block pictured in Fig. 10.13. The total length of the separators and the separator count allows us to find the beginning, the end, and consequently the middle of the index to the separators. As in the preceding example, we perform a binary search of the separators through this index, finally concluding that the key "Beck" falls between the separators "Ba" and "Bro". *Conceptually*, the relation between the keys and the RBNs is as illustrated in Fig. 10.14. (Why isn't this a good *physical* arrangement?)

As Fig. 10.14 makes clear, discovering that the key falls between "Ba" and "Bro" allows us to decide that the *next* block we need to retrieve has the RBN stored in the B02 position of the RBN vector. This next block could be another index set block, and thus another block of the roadmap, or it could be the sequence set block that we are looking for. In either case, the quantity and arrangement of information in the current index set block is sufficient to let us conduct our binary search *within* the index block and then proceed to the next block in the simple prefix B^+ tree.

There are many alternate ways to arrange the fundamental components of this index block. (For example, would it be easier to build the block if the vector of keys were placed at the end of the block? How would you handle the fact that the block consists of both *character* and *integer* entities with no constant, fixed dividing point between them?) For our purposes here, the specific implementation details for this particular index block structure are not nearly as important as the block's *conceptual structure*. This kind of index block structure illustrates two important points.

Separator subscript:	0	1	2	3	4	5	6	7	8	9	10

B00	As	B01	Ba	B02	Bro	B03	C	B04	Ch	B05	Cra	B06	Dele	B07	Edi	B08	Err	B09	Fa	B10	Fle	B11

FIGURE 10.14 ▪ Conceptual relationship of separators and relative block numbers.

The first point is that a block is not just an arbitrary chunk cut out of a homogeneous file; it can be more than just a set of records. A block can have a sophisticated internal structure all its own, including its own internal index, a collection of variable length records, separate sets of fixed length records, and so forth. This idea of building more sophisticated data structures inside of each block becomes increasingly attractive as the block size increases. With very large blocks it becomes imperative that we have an efficient way of processing all of the data within a block once it has been read into RAM. This point applies not only to simple prefix B$^+$ trees, but to any file structure using a large block size.

The second point is that a node within the B-tree index set of our simple prefix B$^+$ tree is of variable order, since each index set block contains a variable number of separators. This variability has interesting implications:

☐ The number of separators in a block is directly limited by block size rather than by some predetermined *order* (as in an *order M* B-tree). The index set will have the maximum *order,* and therefore the minimum depth, that is possible given the degree of compression used to form the separators.

☐ Since the tree is of *variable order,* operations such as determining when a block is full, or half full, are no longer a simple matter of comparing a separator count against some fixed maximum or minimum. Decisions about when to split, concatenate, or redistribute become more complicated.

The exercises at the end of the chapter provide opportunities for exploring variable order trees more thoroughly.

10.9
LOADING A SIMPLE PREFIX B$^+$ TREE

In the previous description of the simple prefix B$^+$ tree, we focus first on building a sequence set, and subsequently present the index set as something that is added or built on top of the sequence set. It is not only possible to *conceive* of simple prefix B$^+$ trees this way, as a sequence set with an added index, but one can also *build* them this way.

One way of building a simple prefix B$^+$ tree, of course, is through a series of successive insertions. We would use the procedures outlined in Section 10.6, where we discuss the maintenance of simple prefix B$^+$ trees, to split or redistribute blocks in the sequence set and in the index set as we added blocks to the sequence set. The difficulty with this approach is that splitting and redistribution are relatively expensive. They involve searching down through the tree for each insertion and then reorganizing the tree as necessary on the way back up. These operations are fine for tree *maintenance* as the tree is updated, but when we are loading the tree we do not have to contend with a *random order* insertion and therefore do not need procedures that are so powerful, flexible, and expensive. Instead, we can begin by sorting the records that are to be loaded. Then we can guarantee that the next record we encounter is the next record we need to load.

Working from a sorted file, we can place the records into sequence set blocks, one by one, starting a new block when the one we are working with fills up. As we make the transition between two sequence set blocks, we can determine the shortest separator for the blocks. We can collect these separators into an index set block that we build and hold in RAM until it is full.

To develop an example of how this works, let's assume that we have sets of records associated with terms that are being compiled for a book index. The records might consist of a list of the occurrences of each term. In Fig. 10.15 we show four sequence set blocks that have been written out to the disk and one index set block that has been built in RAM from the shortest separators derived from the sequence set block keys. As you can see, the next sequence set block consists of a set of terms ranging from CATCH through CHECK, and therefore the next separator is CAT. Let's suppose that the index set block is now full. We write it out to disk. Now what do we do with the separator CAT?

Clearly we need to start a new index block. But we cannot place CAT into another index block at the same level as the one containing the separators ALW, ASP, and BET since we cannot have two blocks at the same level without having a parent block. Instead, we promote the CAT separator to a higher-level block. However, the higher-level block

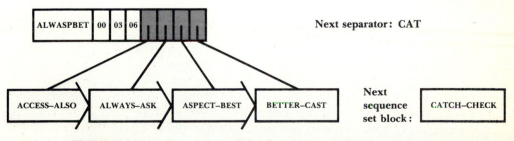

FIGURE 10.15 ▪ Formation of the first index set block as the sequence set is loaded.

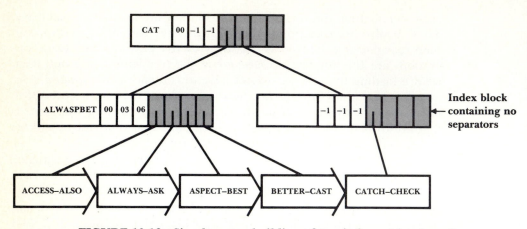

FIGURE 10.16 ▪ Simultaneous building of two index set levels as the sequence set continues to grow.

cannot point directly to the sequence set; it must point to the lower-level index blocks. This means that we will now be building *two* levels of the index set in RAM as we build the sequence set. Figure 10.16 illustrates this working-on-two-levels phenomenon: The addition of the CAT separator requires us to start a new, root-level index block as well as a lower-level index block. (Actually, we are working on *three* levels at once since we are also constructing the sequence set blocks in RAM.) Figure 10.17 shows what the index looks like after even more sequence set blocks are added. As you can see, the lower-level index block that contained no separators when we added CAT to the root has now filled up. To establish that the tree works, do a search for the term CATCH. Then search for the two terms CASUAL and CATALOG. How can you tell that these terms are not in the sequence set?

It is instructive to ask what would happen if the last record were CHECK, so that the construction of the sequence sets and index sets would stop with the configuration shown in Fig. 10.16. The resulting simple prefix B⁺ tree would contain an index set node that holds no separators. This is not an isolated, one-time possibility. If we use this sequential loading method to build the tree, there will be many points during the loading process at which there is an empty or nearly empty index set node. If the index set grows to more than two levels, this empty node problem can occur at even higher levels of the tree, creating a potentially severe out-of-balance problem. Clearly, these empty node and nearly empty node conditions violate the B-tree rules that apply to the index set. However, once a tree is loaded and goes into regular use, the very fact that a node is violating B-tree conditions can be used to guarantee that the node will be corrected through the action of normal B-tree maintenance operations. It is easy to write the procedures for insertion and deletion so that a redistribution procedure is invoked when an underfull node is encountered.

The advantages of loading a simple prefix B⁺ tree in this way, as a sequential operation following a sort of the records, almost always outweigh the disadvantages associated with the possibility of creating

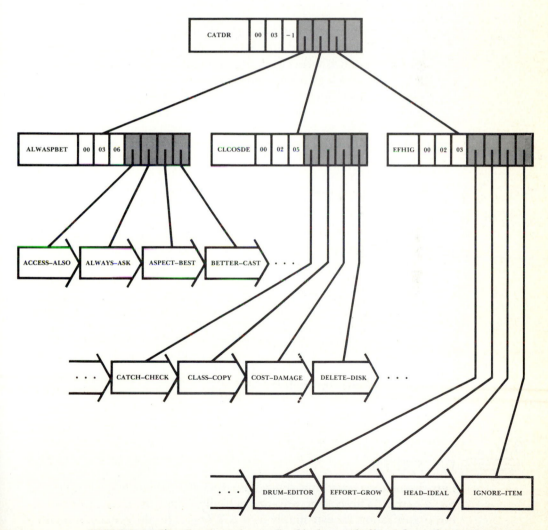

FIGURE 10.17 ▪ **Continued growth of index set built up from the sequence set.**

blocks that contain too few records or too few separators. The principal advantage is that the loading process goes more quickly since:

- ☐ The output can be written sequentially;
- ☐ We make only one pass over the data, rather than the many passes associated with random order insertions; and
- ☐ No blocks need to be reorganized as we proceed.

There are two additional advantages to using a separate loading process such as the one we have described. These advantages are related to performance *after* the tree is loaded rather than performance during loading:

- ☐ Random insertion produces blocks that are, on the average, between 67 percent and 80 percent full. In the preceding chapter, as we discussed B-trees, we increased this storage utilization by mechanisms such as using redistribution during insertion rather than using just block splitting. But, still, we never had the option of filling the blocks completely so that we had 100 percent utilization. The sequential loading process changes this. If we want, we can load the tree so that it starts out with 100 percent utilization. This is an attractive option if we do not expect to add very many records to the tree. On the other hand, if we do anticipate many insertions, sequential loading allows us to select any other degree of utilization that we want. Sequential loading gives us much more control over the amount and placement of empty space in the newly loaded tree.
- ☐ In the loading example presented in Fig. 10.16, we write out the first four sequence set blocks, then write out the index set block containing the separators for these sequence set blocks. If we use the same file for both sequence set and index set blocks, this process guarantees that an index set block starts out in *physical proximity* to the sequence set blocks that are its descendents. In other words, our sequential loading process is creating a degree of *spatial locality* within our file. This locality can minimize seeking as we search down through the tree.

10.10 B$^+$ TREES

Our discussions up to this point have focused primarily on simple prefix B$^+$ trees. These structures are actually a variant of an approach to file organization known simply as a *B$^+$ Tree*. The difference between a

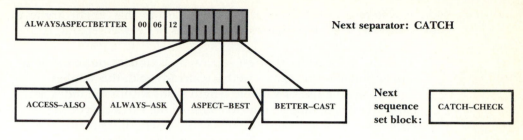

FIGURE 10.18 ▪ Formation of the first index set block in a B⁺ tree without the use of shortest separators.

simple prefix B⁺ tree and a plain B⁺ tree is that the latter structure does not involve the use of prefixes as separators. Instead, the separators in the index set are simply copies of the actual keys. Contrast the index set block shown in Fig. 10.18, which illustrates the initial loading steps for a B⁺ tree, with the index block that is illustrated in Fig. 10.15, where we are building a simple prefix B⁺ tree.

The operations performed on B⁺ trees are essentially the same as those discussed for simple prefix B⁺ trees. Both B⁺ trees and simple prefix B⁺ trees consist of a set of records arranged in key order in a sequence set, coupled with an index set that provides rapid access to the block containing any particular key/record combination. The only difference is that in the simple prefix B⁺ tree we build an index set of shortest separators formed from key prefixes.

One of the reasons behind our decision to focus first on simple prefix B⁺ trees, rather than on the more general notion of a B⁺ tree, is that we want to distinguish between the role of the *separators* in the index set and *keys* in the sequence set. It is much more difficult to make this distinction when the separators are exact copies of the keys. By beginning with simple prefix B⁺ trees we have the pedagogical advantage of working with separators that are clearly different than the keys in the sequence set.

But another reason for starting with simple prefix B⁺ trees revolves around the fact that they are quite often a more desirable alternative than the plain B⁺ tree. We want the index set to be as shallow as possible, which implies that we want to place as many separators into an index set block as we can. Why use anything longer than the simple prefix in the index set? In general, the answer to this question is that we do not, in fact, want to use anything longer than a simple prefix as a separator; consequently simple prefix B⁺ trees are often a good solution. There are, however, at least two factors that might argue in favor of using a B$^+$ tree that uses full copies of keys as separators:

- ☐ The reason for using shortest separators is to pack more of them into an index set block. As we have already said, this implies, ineluctably, the use of variable length fields within the index set blocks. For some applications the cost of the extra overhead required to maintain and use this variable length structure outweighs the benefits of shorter separators. In these cases one might choose to build a straightforward B$^+$ tree using fixed length copies of the keys from the sequence set as separators.
- ☐ Some key sets do not show much compression when the simple prefix method is used to produce separators. For example, suppose the keys consist of large, consecutive alphanumeric sequences such as 34C18K756, 34C18K757, 34C18K758, and so on. In this case, to enjoy appreciable compression, we need to use compression techniques that remove redundancy from the *front* of the key. Bayer and Unterauer [1977] describe such compression methods. Unfortunately, they are more expensive and complicated than simple prefix compression. If we calculate that tree height remains acceptable with the use of full copies of the keys as separators, we might elect to use the no-compression option.

10.11
B-TREES, B$^+$ TREES, AND SIMPLE PREFIX B$^+$ TREES IN PERSPECTIVE

In this chapter and the preceding chapter we have looked at a number of "tools" used in building file structures. These tools, B-trees, B$^+$ trees, and simple prefix B$^+$ trees, have similar sounding names and a number of common features. We need a way to differentiate these tools so we can reliably choose the most appropriate one for a given file structure job.

Before addressing this problem of differentiation, however, we should point out that these are not the only tools in the toolbox. Because B-trees, B$^+$ trees, and their relatives are such powerful, flexible file structures, it is easy to fall into the trap of regarding them as the answer to all problems. This is a serious mistake. Simple index structures of the kind discussed in Chapter 7, which are maintained wholly in RAM, are a much simpler, neater solution when they suffice for the job at hand. As we see at the beginning of this chapter, simple RAM indexes are not limited to direct access situations. This kind of index can be coupled with a sequence set of blocks to provide effective indexed sequential access as well. It is only when the index grows so large that we cannot economically hold it in RAM that we need to turn to paged index structures such as B-trees and B⁺ trees.

In the chapter that follows we encounter yet another tool, known as *hashing*. Like simple RAM-based indexes, hashing is an important alternative to B-trees, B⁺ trees, and so on. In many situations, hashing can provide faster access to a very large number of records than can the use of a member of the B-tree family.

So, B-trees, B⁺ trees, and simple prefix B⁺ trees are not a panacea. However, they do have broad applicability, particularly for situations that require the ability to access a large file both sequentially, in order by key, and through an index. All three of these different tools share the following characteristics:

- ☐ They are all paged index structures, which means that they bring entire blocks of information into RAM at once. As a consequence, it is possible to choose between a great many alternatives (e.g., the keys for hundreds of thousands of records) with just a few seeks out to disk storage. The shape of these trees tends to be broad and shallow.
- ☐ All three approaches maintain height-balanced trees. The trees do not grow in an uneven way which would result in some potentially long searches for certain keys.
- ☐ In all cases the trees grow from the bottom up. Balance is maintained through block splitting, concatenation, and redistribution.
- ☐ With all three structures it is possible to obtain greater storage efficiency through the use of two-to-three splitting and of redistribution in place of block splitting when possible. These techniques are described in Chapter 9.
- ☐ All three approaches can be implemented as virtual tree structures in which the most recently used blocks are held in RAM. The advantages of virtual trees are described in Chapter 9.
- ☐ Any of these approaches can be adapted for use with variable length records using structures inside a block similar to those outlined in this chapter.

For all of this similarity, there are some important differences. These differences are brought into focus through a review of the strengths and unique characteristics of each of these three file structures:

B-trees. B-trees contain information that is grouped as a set of *pairs*. One member of each pair is the *key,* the other member is the *associated information*. These pairs are distributed over *all* the nodes of the B-tree. Consequently, we might find the information we are seeking at any level of the B-tree. This differs from B$^+$ trees and simple prefix B$^+$ trees, which require all searches to proceed all the way down to the lowest, sequence set level of the tree. Because the B-tree itself contains the actual keys and associated information, and there is therefore no need for additional storage to hold separators, a B-tree can take up less space than does a B$^+$ tree.

Given a large enough block size and an implementation that treats the tree as a virtual B-tree, it is possible to use a B-tree for ordered sequential access as well as for indexed access. The ordered sequential access is obtained through an in-order traversal of the tree. The implementation as a virtual tree is necessary so that this traversal does not involve seeking as it returns to the next highest level of the tree. This use of a B-tree for indexed sequential access works only when the record information is actually stored within the B-tree. If the B-tree merely contains pointers to records that are in entry sequence off in some other file, then indexed sequential access is not workable because of all the seeking required to retrieve the actual record information.

B-trees are most attractive when the key itself comprises a large part of each record stored in the tree. When the key is only a small part of the record, it is possible to build a broader, shallower tree using B$^+$ tree methods.

B$^+$ trees.   The primary difference between the B$^+$ tree and the B-tree is that in the B$^+$ tree all the key and record information is contained in a linked set of blocks known as the *sequence set*. The key and record information is *not* in the upper-level, tree-like portion of the B$^+$ tree. Indexed access to this sequence set is provided through a conceptually (though not necessarily physically) separate structure called the *index set*. In a B$^+$ tree the index set consists of copies of the keys that represent the boundaries between sequence set blocks. These copies of keys are called *separators* since they separate a sequence set block from its predecessor.

There are two significant advantages that the B$^+$ tree structure provides over the B-tree:

☐   The sequence set can be processed in a truly linear, sequential way, providing efficient access to records in order by key; and

☐   The use of separators, rather than entire records, in the index set often means that the number of *separators* that can be placed in a single index set block in a B$^+$ tree substantially exceeds the number of *records* that could be placed in an equal-sized block in a B-tree. Separators (copies of keys) are simply smaller than the key/record pairs stored in a B-tree.

Since you can put more of them in a block of given size, it follows that the number of other blocks descending from that block can be greater. As a consequence, a B^+ tree approach can often result in a shallower tree than would a B-tree approach.

In practice, the latter of these two advantages is often the more important one. The impact of the first advantage is lessened by the fact that it is often possible to obtain acceptable performance during an in-order traversal of a B-tree through the page-buffering mechanism of a virtual B-tree.

Simple prefix B^+ trees. We just indicated that the primary advantage of using a B^+ tree instead of a B-tree is that a B^+ tree sometimes allows us to build a shallower tree because we can obtain a higher branching factor out of the upper-level blocks of the tree. The simple prefix B^+ tree builds on this advantage by making the separators in the index set *smaller* than the keys in the sequence set, rather than just using copies of these keys. If the separators are smaller, then we can fit more of them into a block to obtain an even higher branching factor out of the block. In a sense, the simple prefix B^+ tree takes one of the strongest features of the B^+ tree one step farther.

The price we have to pay to obtain this separator compression and consequent increase in branching factor is that we must use an index set block structure that supports variable length fields. The question of whether this price is worth the gain is one that has to be considered on a case-by-case basis.

SUMMARY

We begin this chapter by presenting a new problem. In the previous chapters we provide either indexed access or sequential access in order by key, but without finding an efficient way to provide both of these kinds of access. This chapter explores one class of solutions to this problem, a class based on the use of a blocked sequence set and an associated index set.

The sequence set holds all of the file's data records in order by key. Since all insertion or deletion operations on the file begin with modifications to the sequence set, we start our study of indexed sequential file structures with an examination of a method for managing sequence set changes. The fundamental tools used to insert and delete records while still keeping everything in order within the sequence set are ones that we encounter in Chapter 9: block splitting, block concatenation, and redistribution of records between blocks. The critical difference between the use made of these tools for B-trees and the use made here is that there is no promotion of records or keys during block splitting in a sequence set. A sequence set is just a linked list of blocks, not a tree, therefore there is no place to promote anything to. So, when a block splits, *all* the records are divided between blocks at the same level; when blocks are concatenated there is no need to bring anything down from a parent node.

In this chapter, we also discuss the question of how large to make sequence set blocks. There is no precise answer we can give to this question since conditions vary between applications and environments. In general a block should be large, but not so large that we cannot hold several blocks in RAM or cannot read in a block without incurring the cost of a seek. In practice, blocks are often the size of a cluster (on sector-formatted disks) or the size of a single disk track.

Once we are able to build and maintain a sequence set, we turn to the matter of building an index for the blocks in the sequence set. If the index is small enough to fit in RAM, one very satisfactory solution is to use a simple index that might contain, for example, the key for the last record in every block of the sequence set.

If the index set turns out to be too large to fit in RAM, we recommend the use of the same strategy we develop in the preceding chapter when a simple index outgrows the available RAM space: We turn the index into a B-tree. This combination of a sequence set with a B-tree index set is our first encounter with the structure known as a *B$^+$ tree.*

Before looking at B$^+$ trees as complete entities, we take a closer look at the makeup of the index set. The index set does not hold any information that we would ever seek for its own sake. Instead, an index set is used only as a roadmap to guide searches into the sequence set. The index set consists of *separators* that allow us to choose between sequence set blocks. There are many possible separators for any two sequence set blocks, so we might as well choose the *shortest separator.* The scheme we use to find this shortest separator consists of finding the common prefix of the two keys on either side of a block boundary in the sequence set, and then going one letter beyond this common prefix to define a true separator. A B$^+$ tree with an index set made up of separators formed in this way is called a *simple prefix B$^+$ tree.*

We study the mechanism used to maintain the index set as insertions and deletions are made in the sequence set of a B$^+$ tree. The principal observation we make about all of these operations is that the primary action is within the *sequence set,* since that is where the records are. Changes to the index set are secondary; they are a by-product of the fundamental operations on the sequence set. We add a new separator to the index set only if we form a new block in the sequence set; we delete a separator from the index set only if we remove a block from the sequence set through concatenation. Block overflow and underflow in the index set differ from the operations on the sequence set in that the index set is potentially a *multilevel* structure and is therefore handled as a B-tree.

The size of blocks in the index set is usually the same as the size chosen for the sequence set. To create blocks containing variable numbers of variable length separators while at the same time supporting binary searching, we develop an internal structure for the block that consists of block header fields (for the separator count and total separator length), the variable length separators themselves, an index to these separators, and a vector of relative block numbers (RBNs) for the blocks descending from the index set block. This illustrates an important general principle about large blocks within file structures: They are more than just a slice out of a homogeneous set of records; blocks often have a sophisticated internal structure of their own, apart from the larger structure of the file.

We turn next to the problem of loading a B$^+$ tree. We find that if we start with a set of records sorted by key, we can use a single-pass, sequential process to place these records into the sequence set. As we move from block to block in building the sequence set, we can extract separators and build the blocks of the index set. Compared to a series of successive insertions that work down from the top of the tree, this sequential loading process is much more efficient. Sequential loading also lets us choose the percentage of space utilized, right up to a goal of 100 percent.

The chapter closes with a comparison of B-trees, B$^+$ trees, and simple prefix B$^+$ trees. The primary advantages that B$^+$ trees offer over B-trees are:

- They support true indexed sequential access; and
- The index set contains only separators, rather than full keys and records, so it is often possible to create a B$^+$ tree that is shallower than a B-tree.

We suggest that the second of these advantages is often the more important one, since treating a B-tree as a virtual tree provides acceptable indexed sequential access in many circumstances. The simple prefix B$^+$ tree takes this second advantage and carries it farther, compressing the separators and potentially producing an even shallower tree. The price for this extra compression in a simple prefix B$^+$ tree is that we must deal with variable length fields and a variable order tree.

KEY TERMS

B⁺ tree. A B⁺ tree consists of a *sequence set* of records that are ordered sequentially by key, along with an *index set* that provides indexed access to the records. All of the records are stored in the sequence set. Insertions and deletions of records are handled by splitting, concatenating, and redistributing blocks in the sequence set. The index set, which is used only as a finding aid to the blocks in the sequence set, is managed as a B-tree.

Index set. The index set consists of *separators* that provide information about the boundaries between the blocks in the sequence set of a B⁺ tree. The index set can locate the block in the sequence set that contains the record corresponding to a certain key.

Indexed sequential access. Indexed sequential access is not actually a single access method, but rather a term used to describe situations in which a user wants both sequential access to records, ordered by key, and indexed access to those same records. B⁺ trees are just one method for providing indexed sequential access.

Separator. Separators are derived from the keys of the records on either side of a block boundary in the sequence set. If a given key is in one of the two blocks on either side of a separator, the separator reliably tells the user which of the two blocks holds the key.

Sequence set. The sequence set is the base level of an indexed sequential file structure, such as B⁺ tree. It contains all of the records in the file. When read in logical order, block after block, the sequence set lists all of the records in order by key.

Shortest separator. Many possible separators can be used to distinguish between any two blocks in the sequence set. The class of shortest separators consists of those separators that take the least space, given a particular compression strategy. We looked carefully at a compression strategy that consists of removing as many letters as possible from the rear of the separators, forming the shortest simple prefix that can still serve as a separator.

Simple prefix B⁺ tree. A B⁺ tree in which the index set is made up of *shortest separators* that are simple prefixes, as described in the definition for *shortest separator*.

Variable order. A B-tree is of variable order when the number of direct descendents from any given node of the tree is variable. This occurs when the B-tree nodes contain a variable number of keys or separators. This form is most often used when there is variability in the *lengths* of the keys or separators. Simple prefix B⁺ trees always make use of a variable order B-tree as an index set so that it is possible to take advantage of the compression of separators and place more of them in a block.

EXERCISES

1. Describe file structures that permit each of the following types of access: (a) Sequential access only; (b) Direct access only; (c) Indexed sequential access.

2. A B^+ tree structure is generally superior to a B-tree for indexed sequential access. Since B^+ trees incorporate B-trees, why not use a B^+ tree whenever a hierarchical indexed structure is called for?

3. Consider the sequence set shown in Fig. 10.1(b). Show the sequence set after the keys DOVER and EARNEST are added, then show the sequence set after the key DAVIS is deleted. Did you use concatenation or redistribution for handling the underflow?

4. What considerations affect your choice of a block size for constructing a sequence set? If you know something about expected patterns of access (primarily sequential versus primarily random versus an even division between the two), how might this affect your choice of block size? On a sector-oriented drive, how might sector size and cluster size affect your choice of a block size?

5. It is possible to construct an indexed sequential file without using a tree-structured index. A simple index like the one developed in Chapter 7 could be used. Under what conditions might one consider using such an index? Under what conditions might it be reasonable to use a binary tree (such as an AVL tree) rather than a B-tree for the index?

6. The index set of a B^+ tree is just a B-tree, but unlike the B-trees discussed in Chapter 9, the separators do not have to be keys. Why the difference?

7. How does block splitting in the sequence set of a simple prefix B^+ tree differ from block splitting in the index set?

8. If the key BOLEN in the simple prefix B^+ tree in Fig. 10.8 is deleted from the sequence set node, how is the separator BO in the parent node affected?

9. Consider the simple prefix B^+ tree shown in Fig. 10.8. Suppose a key added to Block 5 results in a split of Block 5 and the consequent addition of Block 8, so that Blocks 5 and 8 appear as follows:

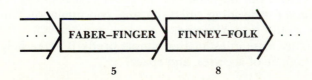

5   8

a) What does the tree look like after the insertion?
b) Suppose that, subsequent to the insertion, a deletion causes underflow and the consequent concatenation of Blocks 4 and 5. What
does the tree look like after the deletion?
c) Describe a case in which a deletion results in redistribution, rather
than concatenation, and show the effect it has on the tree.

10. Why is it often a good idea to use the same block size for the index
set and the sequence set in a simple prefix B⁺ tree? Why should the
index set nodes and the sequence set nodes usually be kept in the same
file?

11. Show a conceptual view of an index set block, similar to the one
illustrated in Fig. 10.12, that is loaded with the separators

Ab Arch Astron B Bea

Also show a more detailed view of the index block, as illustrated in
Fig. 10.13.

12. If the initial set of records is sorted by key, the process of loading
a B+ tree can be handled by using a single-pass sequential process,
instead of randomly inserting new records into the tree. What are the
advantages of this approach?

13. Show how the simple prefix B⁺ tree in Fig. 10.17 changes after the
addition of the node

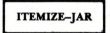

ITEMIZE–JAR

Assume that the index set node containing the separators EF, H, and
IG does not have room for the new separator, but that there is room in
the root.

14. Use the data stored in the simple prefix B⁺ tree in Fig. 10.17 to
construct a B⁺ tree. Assume that the index set of the B⁺ tree is of
order four. Compare the resulting B⁺ tree with the simple prefix B⁺
tree.

15. The use of variable length separators and/or key compression
changes some of the rules about how we define and use a B-tree and
how we measure B-tree performance.
a) How does it affect our definition of the order of a B-tree?
b) Suggest criteria for deciding when splitting, concatenation, and redistribution should be performed.
c) What difficulties arise in estimating simple prefix B⁺ tree height,
maximum number of accesses, and space?

16. Make a table comparing B-trees, B^+ trees and simple prefix B^+ trees in terms of the criteria listed below. Assume that the B-tree nodes do not contain data records, but only keys and corresponding RRNs of data records. In some cases you will be able to give specific answers based on a tree's height or the number of keys in the tree. In other cases, the answers will depend on unknown factors, such as patterns of access or average separator length.

  a) The number of accesses required to retrieve a record from a tree of height h (average, best case, and worst case).
  b) The number of accesses required to insert a record (best and worst cases).
  c) The number of accesses required to delete a record (best and worst cases).
  d) The number of accesses required to process a file of n keys sequentially, assuming that each node can hold a maximum of k keys and a minimum of $k/2$ keys. (best and worst cases.)
  e) The number of accesses required to process a file of n keys sequentially, assuming that there are $h + 1$ node-sized buffers available.

17. Some commercially available indexed sequential file organizations are based on block interval splitting approaches very similar to those used with B^+ trees. IBM's VSAM offers the user several file access modes, one of which is called *key-sequenced* access and which results in a file being organized much like a B^+ tree. Look up a description of VSAM and report on how its key-sequenced organization relates to a B^+ tree, and also how it offers the user file-handling capabilities well beyond those of a straightforward B^+ tree implementation. (See the Further Readings section of this chapter for articles and books on VSAM.)

18. Although B^+ trees provide the basis for most indexed sequential access methods now in use, this was not always the case. A method called ISAM (see Further Readings for this chapter) was once very common, especially on large computers. ISAM uses a rigid tree-structured index consisting of at least two and at most three levels. Indexes at these levels are tailored to the specific disk drive being used. Data records are organized by track, so the lowest level of an ISAM index is called the *track index*. Since the track index points to the track on which a data record can be found, there is one track index for each cylinder. When the addition of data records causes a track to overflow, the track is not split. Instead, the extra records are put into a separate overflow area and chained together in logical order. Hence, every entry in a track index may contain a pointer to the overflow area, in addition to its pointer to the home track.

The essential difference between the ISAM organization and B$^+$ tree–like organizations is in the way overflow records are handled. In the case of ISAM, overflow records are simply added to a chain of overflow records—the index structure is not altered. In the B$^+$ tree case, overflow records are not tolerated. When overflow occurs, a block is split and the index structure is altered to accommodate the extra data block.

Can you think of any advantages of using the more rigid index structure of ISAM, with separate overflow areas to handle overflow records? Why do you think B$^+$ tree–like approaches are replacing those that use overflow chains to hold overflow records? Consider the two approaches in terms of both sequential and direct access, as well as addition and deletion of records.

PROGRAMMING EXERCISES

[We begin this chapter by discussing operations on a sequence set, which is just a linked list of blocks containing records. Only later do we add the concept of an index set to provide faster access to the blocks in the sequence set. The following programming problems echo this approach, requiring you first to write a program that builds a sequence set, then to write functions that maintain the sequence set, and finally to write programs and functions to add an index set to the sequence set, creating a B$^+$ tree. These programs can be implemented in either C or Pascal.]

19. Write a program that accepts a file of strings as input. The input file should be sorted so that the strings are in ascending order. Your program should use this input file to build a sequence set with the following characteristics:

- The strings are stored in 15-byte records;
- A sequence set block is 128 bytes long;
- Sequence set blocks are doubly linked;
- The first block in the output file is a header block containing, among other things, a reference to the RRN of the first block in the sequence set;
- Sequence set blocks are loaded so that they are as full as possible; and
- Sequence set blocks contain other fields (other than the actual records containing the strings) as needed.

20. Write an update program that accepts strings input from the keyboard, along with an instruction either to search, add, or delete the string from the sequence set. The program should have the following characteristics:

- Strings in the sequence set must, of course, be kept in order;

- Response to the search instruction should be either found or not found;
- A string should not be added if it is already in the sequence set;
- Blocks in the sequence set should never be allowed to be less than half full; and
- Splitting, redistribution, and concatenation operations should be written as separate procedures so that they can be used in subsequent program development.

21. Write a program that traverses the sequence set created in the preceding exercises and that builds an index set in the form of a B-tree. You may assume that the B-tree index will never be deeper than two levels. The resulting file should have the following characteristics:

- The index set and the sequence set, taken together, should constitute a B^+ tree;
- Do not compress the keys as you form the separators for the index set;
- Index set blocks, like sequence set blocks, should be 128 bytes long; and
- Index set blocks should be kept in the same file as the sequence set blocks. The header block should contain a reference to the root of the index set as well as the already existing reference to the beginning of the sequence set.

22. Write a new version of the update program that acts on the entire B^+ tree that you created in the preceding exercise. Search, add, and delete capabilities should be supported, as they are in the earlier update program. B-tree characteristics should be maintained in the index set; the sequence set should, as before, be maintained so that blocks are always at least half full.

23. Consider the block structure illustrated in Fig. 10.13, in which an index to separators is used to permit binary searching for a key in an index page. Each index set block contains three variable length sets of items: a set of separators, an index to the separators, and a set of relative block numbers. Develop code in Pascal or C for storing these items in an index block and for searching the block for a separator. You need to answer such questions as:

- Where should the three sets be placed relative to one another?
- Given the data types permitted by the language you are using, how can you handle the fact that the block consists of *both* character and integer data with no fixed dividing point between them?
- As items are added to a block, how do you decide when a block is too full to insert another separator?

FURTHER READINGS

The initial suggestion for the B$^+$ tree structure appears to have come from Knuth [1973b], although he did not name or develop the approach. Most of the literature that discusses B$^+$ trees in detail (as opposed to describing specific implementations such as VSAM) is in the form of articles rather than textbooks. Comer [1979] provides what is perhaps the best brief overview of B$^+$ trees. Bayer and Unterauer [1977] offer a definitive article describing techniques for compressing separators. The article includes consideration of simple prefix B$^+$ trees as well as a more general approach called a *prefix B$^+$ tree*. McCreight [1977] describes an algorithm for taking advantage of the variation in the lengths of separators in the index set of a B$^+$ tree. McCreight's algorithm attempts to ensure that short separators, rather than longer ones, are promoted as blocks split. The intent is to shape the tree so that blocks higher up in the tree have a greater number of immediate descendents, thereby creating a shallower tree.

Rosenberg and Snyder [1981] study the effects of initializing a compact B-tree on later insertions and deletions. The use of batch insertions and deletions to B-Trees, rather than individual updates, is proposed and analyzed in Lang et al. [1985]. B$^+$ trees are compared with more rigid indexed sequential file organizations (such as ISAM) in Batory [1981] and in IBM's *VSAM Planning Guide*.

There are many commercial products that use methods related to the B$^+$ tree operations described in this chapter, but detailed descriptions of their underlying file structures are scarce. An exception to this is IBM's Virtual Storage Access Method (VSAM), one of the most widely used commercial products providing indexed sequential access. Wagner [1973] and Keehn and Lacy [1974] provide interesting insights into the early thinking behind VSAM. They also include considerations of key maintenance, key compression, secondary indexes, and indexes to multiple data sets. Good descriptions of VSAM can be found in several sources, and from a variety of perspectives, in IBM's *VSAM Planning Guide*, Bohl [1981], Comer [1979] (VSAM as an example of a B$^+$ tree), Bradley [1981] (emphasis on implementation in a PL/I environment), and Loomis [1983] (with examples from COBOL).

VAX-11 Record Management Services (RMS), Digital's file and record access subsystem of the VAX/VMS operating system, uses a B$^+$ tree–like structure to support indexed sequential access (Digital, 1979). Many microcomputer implementations of B$^+$ Trees can be found, including dBase III and Borland's Turbo Toolbox (Borland, 1984).

CHAPTER

OBJECTIVES

Introduce the concept of *hashing*.

Examine the problem of choosing a good *hashing algorithm,* present a reasonable one in detail, and describe some others.

Explore three approaches for *reducing collisions:* randomization of addresses, use of extra memory, and storage of several records per address.

Develop and use mathematical tools for analyzing performance differences resulting from the use of different hashing techniques.

Examine problems associated with *file deterioration* and discuss some solutions.

Examine effects of *patterns of record access* on performance.

11 HASHING

CHAPTER OUTLINE

11.1

INTRODUCTION

It has been a long time since we considered the possibility of having really direct access to records. As we have increased the demand for features and improved performance in our file organizations, we have always been able to find *indirect* accessing methods, in the form of a variety of types of indexes, that could satisfy our needs. It is probably

406

safe to say that indexing in its various forms provides the most powerful and flexible set of tools for organizing files. Of course, the use of indexes does introduce certain extra costs—indexes take up space, take time to keep organized, and, unless they are small enough to be kept in primary memory, require at least two accesses to find a record on secondary storage, and often more.

Usually the extra costs associated with the use of indexes can be made small enough that they are well worth the benefits, but there are times when the demands on a file system are so extreme that one or more of these costs becomes intolerable. Suppose, for example, that a file is used exclusively for primary key random accessing of records (including retrievals, additions, deletions, and updates), that queries occur at a rate of 500 per minute, and that a disk access takes 100 msec, on average. A two-level index, with only the root node kept in RAM, requires two disk accesses per record access, plus extra time occasionally to reorganize the index. Hence, indexed access requires

$$2 \times 100 \text{ msec/access} \times 500 \text{ accesses} = 100,000 \text{ msec} = 100 \text{ seconds}$$

for performing accesses, not including time needed for reorganization. Since there are not 100 seconds in a minute, this presents a real problem. Short of finding faster hardware or system software, a form of access requiring fewer than an average of two disk accesses per record operation becomes absolutely necessary.

It is in situations such as this that the need for rapid access to records surpasses all other design considerations. Direct keyed access, if it can be achieved, is the overriding goal. By far the most effective method used to approach this goal is a technique called *hashing*. In this chapter we describe these attributes of hashing:

☐ Hashing, unlike indexing, requires no extra storage for holding an index (though it normally does require some extra external storage);

☐ Hashing facilitates very rapid insertion and deletion of records; and

☐ Hashing makes it possible to find a record with very few disk accesses on the average—usually less than two.

Of course, these dramatic improvements in performance don't come free. Variable length records cannot be used with hashing nearly as easily as they can with indexing. Whereas indexed files can be considered as sorted (albeit indirectly, through the index), hashed files are by definition not sorted. Hashing does not permit duplicate keys. Finally, we see that hashed files are organized according to one key only, so multiple key access can be provided only by imposing extra file structures (such as indexes) on top of hashing.

11.1.1 WHAT IS HASHING?

A *hash function*, *h(K)*, transforms a key *K* into an address. The resulting address is used as the basis for searching for and storing records.

A hash function is like a black box into which you drop a key and out of which comes an address. In Fig. 11.1, the key LOWELL is transformed by the hash function to the address 4. That is, *h*(LOWELL) = 4. Address 4 is said to be the *home address* of LOWELL.

Hashing is like indexing in that it involves associating a key with a relative record address. Hashing differs from indexing in two important ways:

☐   With hashing, the addresses generated appear to be random— there is no immediately obvious connection between the key and the location of the corresponding record, even though the key is used to determine the location of the record. For this reason, hashing is sometimes referred to as *randomizing*.

☐   With hashing, two different keys may be transformed to the same address so that two records may be sent to the same place in the file. When this occurs, it is called a *collision* and some means has to be found to deal with it.

Consider the following simple example. Suppose you want to store 75 records in a file, where the key to each record is a person's name. Suppose also that you set aside space for 1000 records. The key can be hashed by taking two numbers from the ASCII representations of the

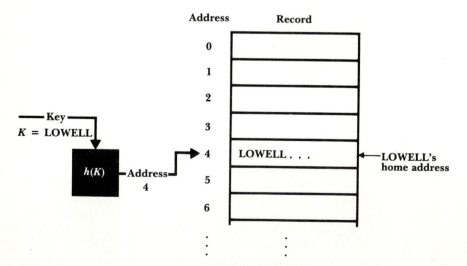

FIGURE 11.1 ▪ Hashing the key LOWELL to address 4.

	TABLE 11.1		

A simple hashing scheme

Name	ASCII code for first two letters	Product	Home address
BALL	66 65	$66 \times 65 = 4290$	290
LOWELL	76 79	$76 \times 79 = 6004$	004
TREE	84 82	$84 \times 82 = 6888$	888

first two characters of the name, multiplying these together, then using the rightmost three digits of the result for the address. Table 11.1 shows how three names would produce three addresses. Note that even though the names are listed in alphabetical order, there is no apparent order to the addresses. They appear to be in *random* order.

11.1.2 COLLISIONS

Now suppose there is a key in the sample file with the name OLIVIER. Since the name OLIVIER starts with the same two letters as the name LOWELL, they produce the same address (004). There is a *collision* between the record for OLIVIER and the record for LOWELL. We refer to keys that hash to the same address as *synonyms*.

Collisions obviously cause problems. We cannot put two records in the same space, so we need to attend to the problem of resolving collisions. We do this in two ways: by choosing hashing algorithms partly on the basis of how few collisions they are likely to produce, and by playing some tricks with the ways we store records.

At first one hopes to find a transformation algorithm that avoids collisions altogether. Such an algorithm is called a *perfect hashing algorithm*. It turns out to be much more difficult to find a perfect hashing algorithm than one might expect, however. Suppose, for example, that you want to store 4000 records among 5000 available addresses. It can be shown (Hanson, 1982) that of the huge number of possible hashing algorithms for doing this, only one out of $10^{120,000}$ avoids collisions altogether. Hence, it is usually not worth trying.†

---

†It is not unreasonable to try to generate perfect hashing functions for small (less than 500), stable sets of keys, such as might be used to look up reserved words in a programming language. But files generally contain more than a few hundred keys, or they contain sets of keys that change frequently, so they are not normally considered candidates for perfect hashing functions. See Knuth [1973b], Sager [1985], Chang [1984], and Chichelli [1980] for more on perfect hashing functions.

Next one wants to reduce the number of collisions to an acceptable number. For example, if only one out of ten searches for a record results in a collision, then the *average* number of disk accesses required to retrieve a record remains quite low. There are several different ways to reduce the number of collisions, including the following three.

☐ *Spread out the records.* Collisions occur when two or more records compete for the same address. If we could find a hashing algorithm that distributes the records fairly randomly among the available addresses, then we would not have large numbers of records clustering around certain addresses. Our sample hash algorithm, which uses only two letters from the key, is not good on this account because certain combinations of two letters are quite common in starting names, while others are uncommon (e.g., compare the number of names that start with "JO" with the number that start with "XZ"). We need to find a hashing algorithm that distributes records more randomly.

☐ *Use extra memory.* It is easier to find a hash algorithm that avoids collisions if we have only a few records to distribute among many addresses than if we have about the same number of records as addresses. Our sample hashing algorithm is very good on this account since there are 1000 possible addresses and only 75 addresses (corresponding to the 75 records) will be generated. The obvious disadvantage to spreading out the records is that storage space is wasted. (In the example, 7.5 percent of the available record space is used, and the remaining 92.5 percent is wasted.) There is no simple answer to the question of how much empty space should be tolerated to get the best hashing performance, but some techniques are provided later in the chapter for measuring the relative gains in performance for different amounts of free space.

☐ *Put more than one record at a single address.* Up to now we have assumed tacitly that each physical record location in a file could hold exactly one record, but there is usually no reason why we cannot create our file in such a way that every file address is big enough to hold several records. If, for example, each record is 80 bytes long, and we create a file with 512-byte physical records, we can store up to six records at each file address. Each address is able to tolerate five synonyms. Addresses that can hold several records in this way are sometimes called *buckets*.

In the following sections we elaborate on these collision-reducing methods, and as we do so we present some programs for managing hashed files.

11.2

A SIMPLE HASHING ALGORITHM

One goal in choosing any hashing algorithm should be to spread out records as uniformly as possible over the range of addresses available. The use of the term *hash* for this technique suggests what is done to achieve this. Our dictionary reminds us that the verb *to hash* means "to chop into small pieces . . . muddle or confuse." The algorithm used previously chops off the first two letters and then uses the resulting ASCII codes to produce a number that is in turn chopped to produce the address. It is not very good at avoiding clusters of synonyms because so many names begin with the same two letters. (A different set of keys might produce a decent set of addresses using this algorithm, but chances are it is just too simple to produce much randomization.)

One problem with the algorithm used previously is that it does not really do very much hashing. It uses only two letters of the key, for example, and it does not do much with the two letters. Now let us look at a hash function that does much more randomizing, primarily because it uses more of the key. It is a reasonably good basic algorithm, and is likely to give good results no matter what kinds of keys are used. It is also an algorithm that is not too difficult to alter in case a specific instance of the algorithm does not work well.

This algorithm has three steps:

1. Represent the key in numerical form.
2. Fold and add.
3. Divide by a prime number and use the remainder as the address.

STEP 1. REPRESENT THE KEY IN NUMERICAL FORM. If the key is already a number, then this step is already accomplished. If it is a string of characters, we take the ASCII code of each character and use it to form a number. For example,

$$\text{LOWELL} = \begin{array}{cccccccccccc} 76 & 79 & 87 & 69 & 76 & 76 & 32 & 32 & 32 & 32 & 32 & 32 \\ \text{L} & \text{O} & \text{W} & \text{E} & \text{L} & \text{L} & \vert\!\!\leftarrow & & \text{Blanks} & & \longrightarrow\vert \end{array}$$

In this algorithm we use the entire key, rather than just the first two letters. By using more parts of a key we increase the likelihood that differences among the keys cause differences in addresses produced. The extra processing time required to do this is usually insignificant when compared to the potential improvement in performance.

STEP 2. FOLD AND ADD. *Folding and adding* means chopping off pieces of the number and adding them together. In our algorithm we chop off pieces with two ASCII numbers each:

$$76\ 79 \mathbin{\vert} 87\ 69 \mathbin{\vert} 76\ 76 \mathbin{\vert} 32\ 32 \mathbin{\vert} 32\ 32 \mathbin{\vert} 32\ 32$$

These number pairs can be thought of as integer variables (rather than character variables, which is how they started out), so that we can do arithmetic on them. If we can treat them as integer variables, then we can add them. This is easy to do in C because C allows us to do arithmetic on characters. In Pascal, we can use the *ord()* function to obtain the integer position of a character within the computer's character set.

Before we add the numbers, we have to mention a problem caused by the fact that in most cases the sizes of numbers we can add together are limited. On some microcomputers, for example, integer values that exceed 32,767 (16 bits) cause overflow errors. For example, adding the first five of the numbers shown above gives

$$7679 + 8787 + 7676 + 3232 + 3232 + 30588.$$

Adding in the last 3,232 would, unfortunately, push the result over the maximum 32,767 (30,588 + 3,232 = 33,820), causing an overflow error. Since overflow errors generally should be avoided, we need to make sure that each successive sum is less than 32,767. We can do this by first identifying the largest single value we will ever add in our summation, then making sure after each step that our intermediate result differs from 32,767 by that amount.

In our case, let us assume that keys consist only of blanks and uppercase alphabetic characters, so that the largest addend is 9,090, corresponding to ZZ. Suppose we choose 20,000 as our largest allowable intermediate result. This differs from 32,767 by much more than 9,090, so we can be confident (in this example) that no new addition will cause overflow. We can ensure in our algorithm that no intermediate sum exceeds 20,000 by using the *mod* operator, which returns the remainder when one integer is divided by another:

$$
\begin{aligned}
7679 + 8769 &\longrightarrow 16448 \longrightarrow 16448 \bmod 20000 \longrightarrow 16448 \\
16448 + 7676 &\longrightarrow 24124 \longrightarrow 24124 \bmod 20000 \longrightarrow 4124 \\
4124 + 3232 &\longrightarrow 7356 \longrightarrow 7356 \bmod 20000 \longrightarrow 7356 \\
7356 + 3232 &\longrightarrow 10588 \longrightarrow 10588 \bmod 20000 \longrightarrow 10588 \\
10588 + 3232 &\longrightarrow 13820 \longrightarrow 13820 \bmod 20000 \longrightarrow 13820
\end{aligned}
$$

The number 13,820 is the result of the fold-and-add operation.

STEP 3. DIVIDE BY THE SIZE OF THE ADDRESS SPACE.   The purpose of this step is to cut down to size the number produced in Step 2 so that it falls within the range of addresses of records in the file. This can be done by dividing that number by a number that is the address size of the file, and then taking the remainder. The remainder will be the home address of the record.

We can represent this operation symbolically as follows: if s represents the sum produced in Step 2 (13,820 in the example), n represents the divisor (the number of addresses in the file), and a represents the address we are trying to produce, we apply the formula

$$a = s \bmod n.$$

The remainder produced by the mod operator will be a number between 0 and $n - 1$.

Suppose, for example, that we decide to use the 100 addresses 0–99 for our file. In terms of the preceding formula,

$$a = 13820 \bmod 100$$
$$= 12.$$

Since the number of addresses allocated for the file does not have to be any specific size (as long as it is big enough to hold all of the actual records to be stored in the file), we have a great deal of freedom in choosing the divisor n. It is a good thing that we do, because the choice of n can have a major effect on how well the records are spread out.

A *prime* number is usually used for the divisor because primes tend to distribute remainders much more uniformly than do nonprimes. A nonprime can work well in many cases, however, especially if it has no prime divisors less than 20 (Hanson, 1982). Since the remainder is going to be the address of a record, we choose a number as close as possible to the desired size of the address space. This number actually determines the size of the address space. For a file with 75 records, a good choice might be 101, which would leave the file 74.3 percent full ($74/101 = 0.743$).

If 101 is the size of the address space, the home address of the record in the example becomes

$$a = 13820 \bmod 101$$
$$= 84.$$

Hence, *the record whose key is LOWELL is assigned to record number 84 in the file*.

The procedure described previously can be carried out with a function that we call *hash()*, described mostly in pseudocode in Fig. 11.2. Procedure *hash()* takes two inputs: *KEY*, which must be an array of ASCII codes for at least 12 characters, and *MAXAD*, which has the address size. The value returned by *hash()* is the address.

```
FUNCTION hash(KEY,MAXAD)

    set SUM to 0
    set J to 0

    while (J < 12 )
        set SUM to (SUM + 100*KEY[J] + KEY[J+1]) mod 20000;
        increment J by 2
    endwhile

    return (SUM mod MAXAD)

end FUNCTION
```

FIGURE 11.2 ▪ **Function** *hash(KEY,MAXAD)* **uses folding and prime number division to compute a hash address.**

11.3
HASHING FUNCTIONS AND RECORD DISTRIBUTIONS

Of the two hash functions we have so far examined, one spreads out records pretty well, and one does not spread them out well at all. In this section we look at ways to describe distributions of records in files. Understanding distributions makes it easier to discuss other hashing methods.

11.3.1 DISTRIBUTING RECORDS AMONG ADDRESSES

Figure 11.3 illustrates three different distributions of seven records among ten addresses. Ideally, a hash function should distribute records in a file so that there are no collisions, as illustrated by distribution (a). Such a distribution is called *uniform* because the records are spread out uniformly among the addresses. We point out earlier that completely uniform distributions are so hard to find that it is generally not considered worth trying to find them.

Distribution (b) illustrates the worst possible kind of distribution. All records share the same home address, resulting in the maximum number of collisions. The more a distribution looks like this one, the more collisions will be a problem.

Distribution (c) illustrates a distribution in which the records are somewhat spread out, but with a few collisions. This is the most likely

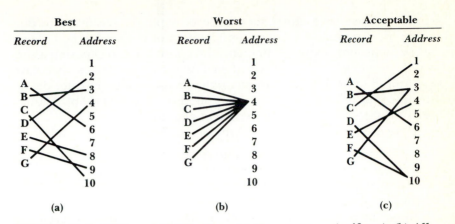

FIGURE 11.3 ▪ Different distributions. (a) No synonyms (uniform). (b) All synonyms (worst case). (c) A few synonyms.

case if we have a function that distributes keys *randomly*. If a hash function is random, then for a given key every address has the same likelihood of being chosen as every other address. The fact that a certain address is chosen for one key neither diminishes nor increases the likelihood that the same address will be chosen for another key.

It should be clear that if a random hash function is used to generate a large number of addresses from a large number of keys, then simply *by chance* some addresses are going to be generated more often than others. If you have, for example, a random hash function that generates addresses between 0 and 99, and you give the function 100 keys, you would expect some of the 100 addresses to be chosen more than once and some to be chosen not at all.

Although a random distribution of records among available addresses is not ideal, it is an acceptable alternative, given that it is practically impossible to find a function that gives a uniform distribution. Uniform distributions may be out of the question, but there are times when we can find distributions that are better than random in the sense that, while they do generate a fair number of synonyms, they spread out records among addresses more uniformly than does a random distribution.

11.3.2 SOME OTHER HASHING METHODS

It would be nice if there were a hash function that guaranteed a better-than-random distribution in all cases, but there is not. The distribution generated by a hashing function depends on the set of keys that are actually hashed. Therefore, the choice of a proper hashing function should involve some intelligent consideration of the keys to be hashed, and perhaps some experimentation. The approaches to choosing a reasonable hashing function covered in this section are ones that have been found to work well, given the right circumstances. Further details on these and other methods can be found in Knuth [1973b], Maurer [1975], Hanson [1982], and Sorenson et al. [1978].

Here are some methods that are potentially better than random:

☐ *Examine keys for a pattern.* Sometimes keys fall in patterns that naturally spread themselves out. This is more likely to be true of numeric keys than of alphabetic keys. For example, a set of employee identification numbers might be ordered according to when the employees entered an organization. This might even lead to *no* synonyms. If some *part* of a key shows a usable underlying pattern, a hash function that extracts that part of the key can also be used.

☐ *Fold parts of the key.* Folding is one stage in the method discussed earlier. It involves extracting digits from part of a key and adding the extracted parts together. This method destroys the original key patterns, but in some circumstances may preserve the separation between certain *subsets* of keys that naturally spread themselves out.

☐ *Divide the key by a number.* Division by the address size and use of the remainder usually is involved somewhere in a hash function since the purpose of the function is to produce an address within a certain range. Division preserves consecutive key sequences, so you can take advantage of sequences that effectively spread out keys. However, if there are *several* consecutive key sequences, division by a number that has many small factors can result in many collisions. Research has shown that numbers with no divisors less than 19 generally avoid this problem. Division by a *prime* is even more likely than division by a nonprime to generate different results from different consecutive sequences.

The preceding methods are designed to take advantage of natural orderings among the keys. The next two methods should be tried when, for some reason, the better-than-random methods do not work. In these cases, randomization is the goal.

☐ *Square the key and take the middle.* This popular method (often called the *mid-square* method) involves treating the key as a single large number, squaring the number, and extracting whatever number of digits is needed from the middle of the result. For example, suppose you want to generate addresses between 0 and 99. If the key is the number 453, its square is 205,209. Extracting the middle two digits yields a number between 0 and 99, in this case 52.

As long as the keys do not contain many leading or trailing zeros, this method usually produces fairly random results. One unattractive feature of this method is that it often requires multiple precision arithmetic.

☐ *Radix transformation.* This method involves converting the key to some number base other than the one you are working in, then taking the result modulo the maximum address as the hash address. For example, suppose you want to generate addresses between 0 and 99. If the key is the decimal number 453, its base 11 equivalent is 382; 382 mod 99 = 85, so 85 is the hash address.

Radix transformation is generally more reliable than the mid-square method for approaching true randomization, though mid-square has been found to give good results when applied to some sets of keys.

11.3.3 PREDICTING THE DISTRIBUTION OF RECORDS

Given that it is nearly impossible to achieve a uniform distribution of records among the available addresses in a file, it is important to be able to predict how records are likely to be distributed. If we know, for example, that a large number of addresses is likely to have far more records assigned to them than they can hold, then we know that there are going to be a lot of collisions.

Although there are no nice mathematical tools available for predicting collisions among distributions that are better than random, there are mathematical tools for understanding just this kind of behavior when records are distributed randomly. If we assume a random distribution (knowing that very likely it will be better than random), we can use these tools to obtain conservative estimates of how our hashing method is likely to behave.

THE POISSON DISTRIBUTION.† We want to predict the number of collisions that are likely to occur in a file that can hold only one record at an address. We begin by concentrating on what happens to a single

---

†This section develops a formula for predicting the ways in which records will be distributed among addresses in a file if a random hashing function is used. The discussion assumes knowledge of some elementary concepts of probability and combinatorics. You may want to skip the development and go straight to the formula, which is introduced in the next section.

given address when a hash function is applied to a key. We would like to answer the following questions. When all of the keys in a file are hashed, what is the likelihood that

☐ None will hash to the given address?
☐ Exactly one key will hash to the address?
☐ Exactly two keys will hash to the address (two synonyms)?
☐ Exactly three, four (and so on) keys will hash to the address?
☐ All keys in the file will hash to the same given address?

Which of these outcomes would you expect to be fairly likely, and which quite unlikely? Suppose there are N addresses in a file. When a single key is hashed, there are two possible outcomes with respect to the given address:

A — The address is not chosen; or

B — The address is chosen.

How do we express the probabilities of the two outcomes? If we let both $p(A)$ and a stand for the probability that the address is not chosen, and $p(B)$ and b stand for the probability that the address is chosen, then

$$p(B) = b = 1/N,$$

since the address has one chance in N of being chosen, and

$$p(A) = a = (N-1)/N = N - 1/N$$

since the address has $N-1$ chances in N of not being chosen. If there are ten addresses ($N = 10$), the probability of our address being chosen is $b = 1/10 = 0.1$, and the probability of the address not being chosen is $a = 1 - 0.1 = 0.9$.

Now suppose *two* keys are hashed. What is the probability that both keys hash to our given address? Since the two applications of the hashing function are independent of one another, the probability that both will produce the given address is a *product*:

$$p(BB) = b \times b = 1/N \times 1/N \qquad \text{for } N = 10: b \times b = 0.1 \times 0.1 = 0.01.$$

Of course, other outcomes are possible when two keys are hashed. For example, the second key could hash to an address other than the given address. The probability of this is the product

$$p(BA) = b \times a = 1/N \times (1 - 1/N) \text{ for } N = 10: b \times a = 0.1 \times 0.9 = 0.09.$$

In general, when we want to know the probability of a certain sequence of outcomes, such as *BABBA*, we can replace each A and B by a and b, respectively, and compute the indicated product:

$$p(BABBA) = b \times a \times b \times b \times a = a^2b^3 \qquad \text{for } N = 10: a^2b^3 = (0.9)^2(0.1)^3.$$

This example shows how to find the probability of three Bs and two As, where the Bs and As occur in the order shown. We want to know the probability that there are a certain number of Bs and As, but *without regard to order*. For example, suppose we are hashing four keys and we want to know how likely it is that exactly two of the keys hash to our given address. This can occur in six ways, all six ways having the same probability:

Outcome	Probability	For $N = 10$
BBAA	$bbaa = b^2a^2$	$(0.1)^2(0.9)^2 = 0.0036$
BABA	$baba = b^2a^2$	$(0.1)^2(0.9)^2 = 0.0036$
BAAB	$baab = b^2a^2$	$(0.1)^2(0.9)^2 = 0.0036$
ABBA	$abba = b^2a^2$	$(0.1)^2(0.9)^2 = 0.0036$
ABAB	$abab = b^2a^2$	$(0.1)^2(0.9)^2 = 0.0036$
AABB	$aabb = b^2a^2$	$(0.1)^2(0.9)^2 = 0.0036$

Since these six sequences are independent of one another, the probability of two Bs and two As is the sum of the probabilities of the individual outcomes:

$$p(BBAA) + p(BABA) + ... + p(AABB) = 6b^2a^2 = 6 \times 0.0036 = 0.0216.$$

The 6 in the expression $6b^2a^2$ represents the number of ways two Bs and two As can be distributed among four places.

In general, the event "r trials result in $r-x$ As and x Bs" can happen in as many ways as $r-x$ letters A can be distributed among r places. The probability of each such way is

$$a^{r-x}b^x.$$

and the number of such ways is given by the formula

$$C = \frac{r!}{(r-x)!\,x!}.$$

This is the well-known formula for the number of ways of selecting x items out of a set of r items. It follows that when r keys are hashed, the probability that an address will be chosen x times and not chosen $r-x$ times can be expressed as

$$p(x) = Ca^{r-x}b^x.$$

Furthermore, if we know that there are N addresses available, we can be precise about the individual probabilities of A and B, and the formula becomes

$$p(x) = C(1 - 1/N)^{r-x}(1/N)^x,$$

where C has the definition given previously.

What does this *mean?* It means that if, for example, $x = 0$, we can compute the probability that a given address will have 0 records assigned to it by the hashing function using the formula

$$p(0) = C(1 - 1/N)^{r-0}(1/N)^0.$$

If $x = 1$, this formula gives the probability that *one* record will be assigned to a given address:

$$p(1) = C(1 - 1/N)^{r-1}(1/N)^1.$$

This expression has the disadvantage that it is awkward to compute. (Try it for 1000 addresses and 1000 records: $N = r = 1000$.) Fortunately, for large values of N and r, there is a function that is a very good approximation for $p(x)$ and is much easier to compute. It is called the *Poisson function.*

THE POISSON FUNCTION APPLIED TO HASHING.   The Poisson function, which we also denote by $p(x)$, is given by

$$p(x) = \frac{(r/N)^x e^{-(r/N)}}{x!},$$

where N, r, x, and $p(x)$ have exactly the same meaning they have in the previous section. That is, if

$N = $ the number of available addresses;

$r = $ the number of records to be stored; and

$x = $ the number of records assigned to a given address;

then $p(x)$ *gives the probability that a given address will have had* x *records assigned to it after the hashing function has been applied to all* n *records.*

Suppose, for example, that there are 1000 addresses ($N = 1000$) and 1000 records whose keys are to be hashed to the addresses ($r = 1000$). Since $r/N = 1$, the probability that a given address will have *no* keys hashed to it ($x = 0$) becomes

$$p(0) = \frac{1^0 e^{-1}}{0!} = 0.368.$$

The probabilities that a given address will have exactly one, two, or three keys, respectively, hashed to it are

$$p(1) = \frac{1^1 e^{-1}}{1!} = 0.368$$

$$p(2) = \frac{1^2 e^{-1}}{2!} = 0.184$$

$$p(3) = \frac{1^3 e^{-1}}{3!} = 0.061.$$

If we can use the Poisson function to estimate the probability that a given address will have a certain number of records, we can also use it to predict the number of addresses that will have a certain number of records assigned.

For example, suppose there are 1000 addresses ($N = 1000$) and 1000 records ($r = 1000$). Multiplying 1000 by the probability that a *given* address will have x records assigned to it gives the expected *total* number of addresses with x records assigned to them. That is, $1000p(x)$ gives the number of addresses with x records assigned to them.

> **In general, if there are N addresses, then the expected number of addresses with x records assigned to them is**
>
> $$Np(x).$$

This suggests another way of thinking about $p(x)$. Rather than thinking about $p(x)$ as a measure of probability, *we can think of* p(x) *as giving the proportion of addresses having* x *logical records assigned by hashing.*

Now that we have a tool for predicting the expected proportion of addresses that will have zero, one, two, etc., records assigned to them by a random hashing function, we can apply this tool to predicting numbers of collisions.

11.3.4 PREDICTING COLLISIONS FOR A FULL FILE

Suppose you have a hashing function that you believe will distribute records randomly, and you want to store 10,000 records in 10,000 addresses. How many addresses do you expect to have no records assigned to them?

Since $r = 10,000$ and $N = 10,000$, $r/N = 1$. Hence the proportion of addresses with 0 records assigned should be

$$p(0) = \frac{1^0 e^{-1}}{0!} = 0.3679.$$

The *number* of addresses with no records assigned is

$$10,000 \times p(0) = 3679.$$

How many addresses should have one, two, and three records assigned, respectively?

$$10,000 \times p(1) = 0.3679 \times 10,000 = 3679$$

$$10,000 \times p(2) = 0.1839 \times 10,000 = 1839$$

$$10,000 \times p(3) = 0.0613 \times 10,000 = 613.$$

Since the 3679 addresses corresponding to $x = 1$ have exactly one record assigned to them, their records have no synonyms. The 1839 addresses with two records apiece, however, represent potential trouble. If each such address has space only for one record, and two records are assigned to them, there is a collision. This means that 1839 records will fit into the addresses, but another 1839 will not fit. There will be 1839 *overflow* records.

Each of the 613 addresses with three records apiece has an even bigger problem. If each address has space for only one record, there will be two overflow records per address. Corresponding to these addresses will be a total of $2 \times 613 = 1226$ overflow records. This is a bad situation. We have thousands of records that do not fit into the addresses assigned by the hashing function. We need to develop a method for handling these overflow records. But first, let's try to reduce the *number* of overflow records.

11.4
HOW MUCH EXTRA MEMORY SHOULD BE USED?

We have seen the importance of choosing a good hashing algorithm to reduce collisions. A second way to decrease the number of collisions (and thereby decrease the average search length) is to use extra memory. The tools developed in the previous section can be used to help us determine the effect of the use of extra memory on performance.

11.4.1 PACKING DENSITY

The term *packing density* refers to the ratio of the number of records to be stored (r) to the number of available spaces (N):†

$$\frac{\text{Number of records}}{\text{Number of spaces}} = \frac{r}{N} = \text{Packing density.}$$

For example, if there are 75 records ($n = 75$) and 100 addresses ($N = 100$), the packing density is

$$75/100 = 0.75 = 75\%.$$

---

†We assume here that only one record can be stored at each address. In fact, that is not necessarily the case, as we see later.

The packing density gives a measure of the amount of space in a file that is actually used, and it is the only such value needed to assess performance in a hashing environment, assuming that the hash method used gives a reasonably random distribution of records. The raw size of a file and its address space do not matter; what is important is the relative sizes of the two, which are given by the packing density.

Think of packing density in terms of tin cans lined up on a ten-foot length of fence. If there are ten tin cans and you throw a rock, there is a certain likelihood that you will hit a can. If there are 20 cans on the same length of fence, the fence has a higher packing density and your rock is more likely to hit a can. So it is with records in a file. The more records there are packed into a given file space, the more likely it is that a collision will occur when a new record is added.

We need to decide how much space we are willing to waste to reduce the number of collisions. The answer depends in large measure on particular circumstances. We want to have as few collisions as possible, but not, for example at the expense of requiring the file to use two disks instead of one.

11.4.2 PREDICTING COLLISIONS FOR DIFFERENT PACKING DENSITIES

We need a quantitative description of the effects of changing the packing density. In particular, we need to be able to predict the number of collisions that are likely to occur for a given packing density. Fortunately, the Poisson function provides us with just the tool to do this.

You may have noted already that the formula for packing density (r/N) occurs twice in the Poisson formula

$$p(x) = \frac{(r/N)^x e^{-r/N}}{x!}.$$

Indeed the numbers of records (r) and addresses (N) always occur together as the *ratio r/N*. They never occur independently. An obvious implication of this is that the way records are distributed depends partly on the ratio of the number of records to the number of available addresses, and *not* on the absolute numbers of records or addresses. The same behavior is exhibited by 500 records distributed among 1000 addresses as by 500,000 records distributed among 1,000,000 addresses.

Suppose that 1000 addresses are allocated to hold 500 records in a randomly hashed file, and that each address can hold one record. The packing density for the file is

$$r/N = 500/1000 = 0.5.$$

Let us answer the following questions about the distribution of records among the available addresses in the file:

☐ How many addresses should have no records assigned to them?
☐ How many addresses should have exactly one record assigned (no synonyms)?
☐ How many addresses should have one record *plus* one or more synonyms?
☐ Assuming that only one record can be assigned to each home address, how many overflow records can be expected?
☐ What percentage of records should be overflow records?

1. *How many addresses should have no records assigned to them?*
   Since $p(0)$ gives the *proportion* of addresses with no records assigned, the number of such addresses is

   $$Np(0) = 1000 \times \frac{(0.5)^0 e^{-0.5}}{0!}$$

   $$= 1000 \times 0.607$$

   $$= 607.$$

2. *How many addresses should have exactly one record assigned (no synonyms)?*

   $$Np(1) = 1000 \times \frac{(0.5)^1 e^{-0.5}}{1!}$$

   $$= 1000 \times 0.303$$

   $$= 303.$$

3. *How many addresses should have one record plus one or more synonyms?*
   The values of $p(2)$, $p(3)$, $p(4)$, and so on, give the proportions of addresses with one, two, three, and so on, synonyms assigned to them. Hence the sum

   $$p(2) + p(3) + p(4) + \ldots$$

   gives the proportion of all addresses with at least one synonym. This may appear to require a great deal of computation, but it doesn't since the values of $p(x)$ grow quite small for x larger than 3. This should make intuitive sense. Since the file is only 50 percent loaded, one would not expect very many keys to hash to any one address. Therefore, the number of addresses with more than about three keys hashed to them should be quite small. We need only compute the results up to $p(5)$ before they become insignificantly small:

$$p(2) + p(3) + p(4) + \text{p}(5) = 0.0758 + 0.0126 + 0.0016 + 0.0002$$

$$= 0.0902.$$

The *number* of addresses with one or more synonyms is just the product of N and this result:

$$N[p(2) + p(3) + \ldots] = 1000 \times 0.0902$$

$$= 90.$$

4. *Assuming that only one record can be assigned to each home address, how many overflow records could be expected?*
   For each of the addresses represented by $p(2)$, one record can be stored at the address and one must be an overflow record. For each address represented by $p(3)$, one record can be stored at the address, and *two* are overflow records, and so on. Hence, the expected number of overflow records is given by

$$1 \times N \times p(2) + 2 \times N \times p(3) + 3 \times N \times p(4) + 4 \times N \times p(5)$$

$$= N \times [1 \times p(2) + 2 \times p(3) + 3 \times p(4) + 4 \times p(5)]$$

$$= 1000 \times [1 \times 0.0758 + 2 \times 0.0126 + 3 \times 0.0016 + 4 \times 0.0002]$$

$$= 107.$$

5. *What percentage of records should be overflow records?*
   If there are 107 overflow records and 500 records in all, then the proportion of overflow records is

$$107/500 = 0.214 = 21.4\%.$$

Conclusion: if the packing density is 50 percent and each address can hold only one record, we can expect about 21 percent of all records to be stored somewhere other than at their home addresses.

Table 11.2 shows the proportion of records that are not stored in their home addresses for several different packing densities. The table shows that if the packing density is 10 percent, then about 5 percent of the time we try to access a record, there is already another record there. If the density is 100 percent, then about 37 percent of all records collide with other records at their home addresses. The 4.8 percent collision rate that results when the packing density is 10 percent looks very good until you realize that for every record in your file there will be nine unused spaces!

TABLE 11.2

Effect of packing density on the proportion of records not stored at their home addresses

Packing density (%)	Synonyms as % of records
10	4.8
20	9.4
30	13.6
40	17.6
50	21.4
60	24.8
70	28.1
80	31.2
90	34.1
100	36.8

The 36.8 percent that results from 100 percent usage looks good when viewed in terms of 0 percent unused space. Unfortunately, 36.8 percent doesn't tell the whole story. If 36.8 percent of the records are not at their home addresses, then they are somewhere else, probably in many cases using addresses that are home addresses for other records. The more homeless records there are, the more contention there is for space with other homeless records. After a while, clusters of overflow records can form, leading in some cases to extremely long searches for some of the records. Clearly the placement of records that collide is an important matter. Let us now look at one simple approach to placing overflow records.

11.5 COLLISION RESOLUTION BY PROGRESSIVE OVERFLOW

Even if a hashing algorithm is very good, it is likely that collisions will occur. Therefore, any hashing program must incorporate some method for dealing with records that cannot fit into their home addresses. There are a number of techniques for handling overflow records, and the search for ever-better techniques continues to be a lively area of research. We examine several approaches, but we concentrate on a very simple one that often works well. The technique has various names, including *progressive overflow,* and *linear probing.*

11.5.1 HOW PROGRESSIVE OVERFLOW WORKS

An example of a situation in which a collision occurs is shown in Fig. 11.4. In the example, we want to store the record whose key is York in the file. Unfortunately, the name York hashes to the same address as the name Rosen, whose record is already stored there. Since York cannot fit in its home address, it is an overflow record. If progressive overflow is used, the next several addresses are searched in sequence until an empty one is found. The first free address becomes the address of the record. In the example, address 9 is the first record found empty, so the record pertaining to York is stored in address 9.
so the record pertaining to York is stored in address 9.

Eventually we need to find York's record in the file. Since York still hashes to 6, the search for the record begins at address 6. It does not find York's record there, so it proceeds to look at successive records until it gets to address 9, where it finds York.

An interesting problem occurs when there is a search for an open space or for a record at the *end* of the file. This is illustrated in Fig. 11.5, in which it is assumed that the file can hold 100 records in addresses 0–99. Blue is hashed to record number 99, which is already occupied by Jello. Since the file holds only 100 records, it is not possible to use 100 as the next address. The way this is handled in progressive

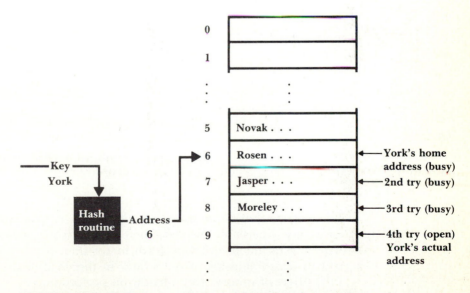

FIGURE 11.4 ▪ Collision resolution with progressive overflow.

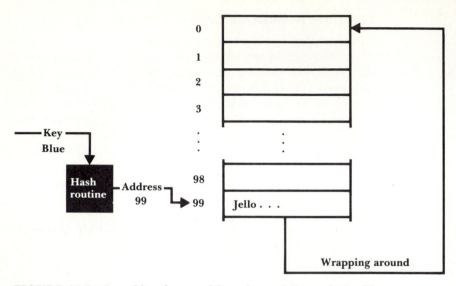

FIGURE 11.5 ▪ Searching for an address beyond the end of a file.

overflow is to wrap around the address space of the file by choosing address 0 as the next address. Since, in this case, address 0 is not occupied, Blue gets stored in address 0.

What happens if there is a search for a record, but the record was never placed in the file? The search begins, as before, at the record's home address, then proceeds to look for it in successive locations. Two things can happen:

☐ If an open address is encountered, the searching routine might assume this means that the recoed is not in the file; or
☐ If the file is full, the search comes back to where it began. Only then is it clear that the record is not in the file. When this occurs, or even when we approach filling our file, searching can become intolerably slow, whether or not the record being sought is in the file.

The greatest strength of progressive overflow is its simplicity. In many cases, it is a perfectly adequate method. There are, however, collision-handling techniques that perform better than progressive overflow, and we examine some of them later in the chapter. Now let us look at the effect of progressive overflow on performance.

11.5.2 SEARCH LENGTH

The reason to avoid overflow is, of course, that extra searches (hence, extra disk accesses) have to occur when a record is not found in its home address. If there are a lot of collisions, there are going to be a lot of overflow records taking up spaces where they ought not to be. Clusters of records can form, resulting in the placement of records a long way from home, so that many disk accesses are required to retrieve them.

Consider the following set of keys and the corresponding addresses produced by some hash function.

Key	Home address
Adams	20
Bates	21
Cole	21
Dean	22
Evans	20

If these records are loaded into an empty file, and progressive overflow is used to resolve collisions, only two of the records will be at their home addresses. All the others require extra accesses to retrieve. Figure 11.6 shows where each key is stored, together with information on how many accesses are required to retrieve it.

The term *search length* refers to the number of accesses required to retrieve a record from secondary memory. In the context of hashing, the search length for a record increases every time there is a collision. If a record is a long way from its home address, the search length may be unacceptable. A good measure of the extent of the overflow problem is *average search length*. The average search length is just the average number of times you can expect to have to access the disk to retrieve a record. A rough estimate of average search length may be computed by finding the *total search length* (the sum of the search lengths of the individual records) and dividing this by the number of records:

$$\text{Average search length} = \frac{\text{Total search length}}{\text{Total number of records}}.$$

In the example, the average search length for the five records is

$$\frac{1 + 1 + 2 + 2 + 5}{5} = 2.2.$$

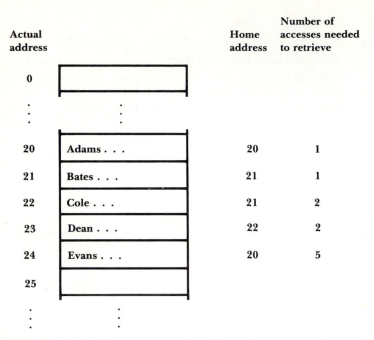

FIGURE 11.6 ▪ **Illustration of the effects of clustering of records. As keys are clustered, the number of accesses required to access later keys can become large.**

With no collisions at all, the average search length is 1, since only one access is needed to retrieve any record. (We indicated earlier that an algorithm that distributes records so evenly that no collisions occur is appropriately called a *perfect* hashing algorithm, and that, unfortunately, such an algorithm is almost impossible to construct.) On the other hand, if a large number of the records in a file results in collisions, the average search length becomes quite long. There are ways to estimate the expected average search length, given various file specifications, and we discuss them in a later section.

It turns out that, using progressive overflow, the average search length goes up very rapidly as the packing density increases. The curve in Fig. 11.7, adapted from Peterson [1957], illustrates the problem. If the packing density is kept as low as 60 percent, the average record takes fewer than two tries to access, but for a much more desirable packing density of 80 percent or more, it increases very rapidly.

Average search lengths of greater than 2.0 are generally considered unacceptable, so it appears that it is usually necessary to use less than

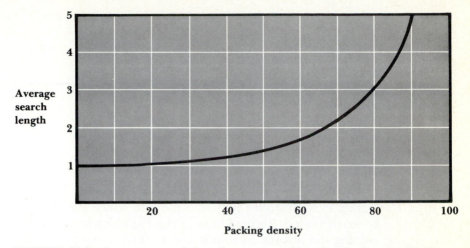

FIGURE 11.7 ▪ **Average search length versus packing density in a hashed file in which one record can be stored per address, progressive overflow is used to resolve collisions, and the file has just been loaded.**

40 percent of your storage space to get tolerable performance. Fortunately, we can improve on this situation substantially by making one small change to our hashing program. The change involves putting more than one record at a single address.

11.6
STORING MORE THAN ONE RECORD PER ADDRESS—BUCKETS

Recall that when a computer receives information from a disk, it is just about as easy for the I/O system to transfer several records as it is to transfer a single record. Recall too that sometimes it might be advantageous to think of records as being grouped together in *blocks* rather than stored individually. Therefore, why not extend the idea of a record address in a file to an address of a *group* of records? The word *bucket* is sometimes used to describe a block of records that is retrieved in one disk access, especially when those records are seen as sharing the same address. On sector-addressing disks, a bucket typically consists of one or more sectors; on block-addressing disks a bucket might be a block.

Consider the following set of keys, which is to be loaded into a hash file.

Key	Home address
Green	30
Hall	30
Jenks	32
King	33
Land	33
Marx	33
Nutt	33

Figure 11.8 illustrates part of a file into which the records with these keys are loaded. Each address in the file identifies a bucket capable of holding the records corresponding to three synonyms. Only the record corresponding to Nutt cannot be accommodated in a home address.

When a record is to be stored or retrieved, its home *bucket address* is determined by hashing. The entire bucket is loaded into primary memory. An in-RAM search through successive records in the bucket can then be used to find the desired record. When a bucket is filled, we still have to worry about the record overflow problem (as in the case of Nutt), but this occurs much less often when buckets are used than when each address can hold only one record.

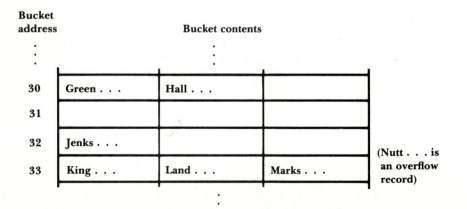

FIGURE 11.8 ▪ An illustration of buckets. Each bucket can hold up to three records. Only one synonym (Nutt) results in overflow.

11.6.1 EFFECTS OF BUCKETS ON PERFORMANCE

When buckets are used, the formula used to compute packing density is changed slightly since each bucket address can hold more than one record. To compute how densely packed a file is, we need to consider both the number of addresses (buckets) and the number or records we can put at each address (bucket size). If N is the number of addresses and b is the number of records that fit in a bucket, then bN is the number of available locations for records. If r is still the number of records in the file, then

$$\text{Packing density} = r/bN.$$

Suppose we have a file in which 750 records are to be stored. Consider the following two ways we might organize the file.

☐ We can store the 750 data records among 1000 locations, where each location can hold one record. The packing density in this case is

$$750/1000 = 75\%.$$

☐ We can store the 750 records among 500 locations, where each location has a bucket size of 2. There are still 1000 places (2×500) to store the 750 records, so the packing density is still

$$r/bN = 0.75 = 75\%.$$

Since the packing density is not changed, we might at first not expect the use of buckets in this way to improve performance, but in fact it does improve performance dramatically. The key to the improvement is that, although there are fewer addresses, each individual address has more room for variation in the number of records assigned to it.

Let's calculate the difference in performance for these two ways of storing the same number of records in the same amount of space. The starting point for our calculations is the fundamental description of each file structure.

	File without buckets	File with buckets
Number of records:	$r = 750$	$r = 750$
Number of addresses:	$N = 1000$	$N = 500$
Bucket size:	$b = 1$	$b = 2$
Packing density:	0.75	0.75
Ratio of records to addresses:	$r/N = 0.75$	$r/N = 1.5$

To determine the number of overflow records that are expected in the case of each file, recall that when a random hashing function is used, the Poisson function

$$p(x) = \frac{(r/N)^x \, e^{-r/N}}{x!}$$

gives the expected proportion of addresses assigned x records. Evaluating the function for the two different file organizations, we find that records are assigned to addresses according to the distributions shown in Table 11.3.

We see from the table that when buckets are not used, 42.3 percent of the addresses have no records assigned, whereas when two-record buckets are used, only 22.3 percent of the addresses have no records assigned. This should make intuitive sense—since in the two-record case there are only half as many addresses to choose from, it stands to reason that a greater proportion of the addresses are chosen to contain at least one record.

Note that the bucket column in Table 11.3 is longer than the non-bucket column. Does this mean that there are more synonyms in the bucket case than in the nonbucket case? Indeed it does, but half of those synonyms do not result in overflow records because each bucket can hold two records. Let us examine this further by computing the exact number of overflow records likely to occur in the two cases.

TABLE 11.3

Poisson distributions for two different file organizations

$p(x)$	File without buckets ($r/N = 0.75$)	File with buckets ($r/N = 1.5$)
$p(0)$	0.423	0.223
$p(1)$	0.354	0.335
$p(2)$	0.133	0.251
$p(3)$	0.033	0.126
$p(4)$	0.006	0.047
$p(5)$	0.001	0.014
$p(6)$	—	0.004
$p(7)$	—	0.001

In the case of the file with bucket size one, any address that is assigned exactly one record does not have any overflow. Any address with more than one record does have overflow. Recall that the expected number of overflow records is given by

$$N \times [1 \times p(2) + 2 \times p(3) + 3 \times p(4) + 4 \times p(5) + \dots]$$

which, for $r/N = 0.75$ and $N = 1000$, is approximately

$$1000 \times [1 \times 0.1328 + 2 \times 0.0332 + 3 \times 0.0062 + 4 \times 0.0009 + 5 \times 0.0001]$$
$$= 222.$$

The 222 overflow records represent 29.6 percent overflow.

In the case of the bucket file, any address that is assigned either one *or* two records does not have overflow. The value of $p(1)$ (with $r/N = 1.5$) gives the proportion of addresses assigned exactly one record, and $p(2)$ (with $r/N = 1.5$) gives the proportion of addresses assigned exactly two records. It is not until we get to $p(3)$ that we encounter addresses for which there are overflow records. For each address represented by $p(3)$, two records can be stored at the address, and one must be an overflow record. Similarly, for each address represented by $p(4)$, there are two overflow records, and so forth. Hence, the expected number of overflow records in the bucket file is

$$N \times [1 \times p(3) + 2 \times p(4) + 3 \times p(5) + 4 \times p(6) + \dots],$$

which for $r/N = 1.5$ and $N = 500$ is approximately

$$500 \times [1 \times 0.1255 + 2 \times 0.0471 + 3 \times 0.0141 + 4 \times 0.0035 + 5 \times 0.0008]$$
$$= 140.$$

The 140 overflow records represent 18.7 percent overflow.

We have shown that with one record per address and a packing density of 75 percent the expected number of overflow records is 29.6 percent. When 500 buckets are used, each capable of holding two records, the packing density remains 75 percent, but the expected number of overflow records drops to 18.7 percent. That is about a 37 percent decrease in the number of times the program is going to have to look elsewhere for a record. As the bucket size gets larger, performance continues to improve.

Table 11.4 shows the proportions of collisions that occur for different packing densities and for different bucket sizes. We see from the table, for example, that if we keep the packing density at 75 percent and increase the bucket size to ten, record accesses result in overflow only 4 percent of the time.

It should be clear that the use of buckets can improve hashing performance substantially. One might ask, "How big should buckets be?"

TABLE 11.4

Synonyms causing collisions as a percent of records for
different packing densities and different bucket sizes

Packing density (%)	Bucket size				
	1	*2*	*5*	*10*	*100*
10	4.8	0.6	0.0	0.0	0.0
20	9.4	2.2	0.1	0.0	0.0
30	13.6	4.5	0.4	0.0	0.0
40	17.6	7.3	1.1	0.1	0.0
50	21.3	10.4	2.5	0.4	0.0
60	24.8	13.7	4.5	1.3	0.0
70	28.1	17.0	7.1	2.9	0.0
75	*29.6*	*18.7*	*8.6*	*4.0*	*0.0*
80	31.2	20.4	10.3	5.3	0.1
90	34.1	23.8	13.8	8.6	0.8
100	36.8	27.1	17.6	12.5	4.0

Unfortunately, there is no simple answer to this question because it
depends very much on a number of different characteristics of the system, including the sizes of buffers the operating system can manage,
sector and track capacities on disks, and access times of the hardware
(seek, rotation, and data transfer times).

As a rule, it is probably not a good idea to use buckets larger than
a track (unless records are very large). Even a track, however, can sometimes be too large when one considers the amount of time it takes to
transmit an entire track, as compared to the amount of time it takes to
transmit a few sectors. Since hashing almost always involves retrieving
only one record per search, any extra transmission time resulting from
the use of extra large buckets is essentially wasted.

In many cases a single cluster is the best bucket size. For example,
suppose that a file with 200-byte records is to be stored on a disk system
that uses 1024-byte clusters. One could consider each cluster as a
bucket, store five records per cluster, and let the remaining 24 bytes go
unused. Since it is no more expensive, in terms of seek time, to access
a five-record cluster than it is to access a single record, the only losses
from the use of buckets is the extra transmission time and the 24 unused bytes.

The obvious question now is, "How do improvements in the number of collisions affect the average search time?" The answer depends
in large measure on characteristics of the drive on which the file is

loaded. If there are a large number of tracks in each cylinder, there will be very little seek time because overflow records will be unlikely to spill over from one cylinder to another. If, on the other hand, there is only one track per cylinder, seek time could be a major consumer of search time.

A less exact measure of the amount of time required to retrieve a record is average search length, which we introduced earlier. In the case of buckets, average search length represents the average number of buckets that must be accessed to retrieve a record. Table 11.5 shows the expected average search lengths for files with different packing densities and bucket sizes, given that progressive overflow is used to handle collisions. Clearly the use of buckets seems to help a great deal in decreasing the average search length. The bigger the bucket, the shorter the search length.

11.6.2 IMPLEMENTATION ISSUES

In the early chapters of the text, we pay quite a bit of attention to issues involved in producing, using, and maintaining random access files with fixed length records that are accessed by relative record number (RRN). Since a hashed file is a fixed length record file whose records are ac-

---

TABLE 11.5

Average number of accesses required in a successful search by progressive overflow

Packing density (%)	Bucket sizes				
	1	2	5	10	50
10	1.06	1.01	1.00	1.00	1.00
30	1.21	1.06	1.00	1.00	1.00
40	1.33	1.10	1.01	1.00	1.00
50	1.50	1.18	1.03	1.00	1.00
60	1.75	1.29	1.07	1.01	1.00
70	2.17	1.49	1.14	1.04	1.00
80	3.00	1.90	1.29	1.11	1.01
90	5.50	3.15	1.78	1.35	1.04
95	10.50	5.6	2.7	1.8	1.1

(Adapted from Donald Knuth, *The Art of Computer Programming*, ©1973, Addison-Wesley, Reading, Mass. Page 536. Reprinted with permission.)

cessed by RRN, you should already know much about implementing hashed files. Hashed files differ from the files we discuss earlier in two important respects, however:

1. Since a hash function depends on there being a fixed number of available addresses, the logical size of a hashed file must be fixed before the file can be populated with records, and it must remain fixed as long as the same hash function is used. (We use the phrase *logical size* to leave open the possibility that physical space be allocated as needed.)
2. Since the home RRN of a record in a hashed file is uniquely related to its key, any procedures that add, delete, or change a record must do so without breaking the bond between a record and its home address. If this bond is broken, the record is no longer accessible by hashing.

We must keep these special needs in mind when we write programs to work with hashed files.

BUCKET STRUCTURE.   The only difference between a file with buckets and one in which each address can hold only one key is that with a bucket file each address has enough space to hold more than one logical record. All records that are housed in the same bucket share the same address. Suppose, for example, that we want to store as many as *five* names in one bucket. Here are three such buckets with different numbers of records.

An empty bucket:	0	/ / / / /	/ / / / /	/ / / / /	/ / / / /	/ / / / /

Two entries:	2	JONES	ARNSWORTH	/ / / / /	/ / / / /	/ / / / /

A full bucket:	5	JONES	ARNSWORTH	STOCKTON	BRICE	THROOP

Each bucket contains a *counter* that keeps track of how many records it has stored in it. Collisions can occur only when the addition of a new record causes the counter to exceed the number of records a bucket can hold.

The counter tells us how many data records are stored in a bucket, but it does not tell us which slots are used and which are not. We need a way to tell whether or not a record slot is empty. One simple way to do this is to use a special marker to indicate an empty record, just as we did with deleted records earlier. We use the key value ///// to mark empty records in the preceding illustration.

INITIALIZING A FILE FOR HASHING. Since the *logical* size of a hashed file must be remain fixed, it makes sense in most case to allocate physical space for the file before we begin storing data records in it. This is generally done by creating a file of empty spaces for all records, then filling the slots as they are needed with the data records. (It is not necessary to construct a file of empty records before putting data in it, but doing so increases the likelihood that records will be stored close to one another on the disk, avoids the error that occurs when an attempt is made to read a missing record, and makes it easy to process the file sequentially, without having to treat the empty records in any special way.)

LOADING A HASH FILE. A program that loads a hash file is similar in many ways to earlier programs we use for populating fixed length record files, with two differences. First, the program uses the function *hash()* to produce a home address for each key. Second, the program looks for a free space for the record by starting with the bucket stored at its home address and then, if the home bucket is full, continuing to look at successive buckets until one is found that is not full. The new record is inserted in this bucket, which is rewritten to the file at the location from which it is loaded.

If, as it searches for an empty bucket, a loading program passes the maximum allowable address, it must wrap around to the beginning address. A potential problem occurs in loading a hash file when so many records have been loaded into the file that there are no empty spaces left. A naive search for an open slot can easily result in an infinite loop. Obviously, we want to prevent this from occurring by having the program make sure that there is space available for each new record somewhere in the file.

Another problem that often arises when adding records to files occurs when an attempt is made to add a record that is already stored in the file. If there is a danger of duplicate keys occurring, and duplicate keys are not allowed in the file, some mechanism must be found for dealing with this problem.

11.7
MAKING DELETIONS

Deleting a record from a hashed file is more complicated than adding a record for two reasons:

☐ The slot freed by the deletion must not be allowed to hinder later searches; and
☐ It should be possible to reuse the freed slot for later additions.

When progressive overflow is used, a search for a record terminates if an open address is encountered. Because of this, we do not want to leave open addresses that break overflow searches improperly. The following example illustrates the problem.

Adams, Jones, Morris and Smith are stored in a hash file in which each address can hold one record. Adams and Smith both are hashed to address 5, and Jones and Morris are hashed to address 6. If they are loaded in alphabetical order using progressive overflow for collisions, they are stored in the locations shown in Fig. 11.9.

A search for Smith starts at address 5 (Smith's home address), successively looks for Smith at addresses 6, 7, and 8, then finds Smith at 8. Now suppose Morris is deleted, leaving an empty space, as illustrated in Fig. 11.10. A search for Smith again starts at address 5, then looks at addresses 6 and 7. Since address 7 is now empty, it is reasonable for the program to conclude that Smith's record is not in the file.

Record	Home address	Actual address		
			4	
Adams	5	5	5	Adams . . .
Jones	6	6	6	Jones . . .
Morris	6	7	7	Morris . . .
Smith	5	8	8	Smith . . .

FIGURE 11.9 ▪ **File organization before deletions.**

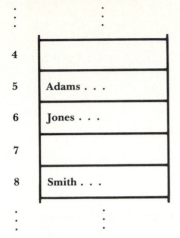

FIGURE 11.10 ▪ The same organization as in Fig. 11.9, with Morris deleted.

11.7.1 TOMBSTONES FOR HANDLING DELETIONS

In Chapter 5 we discuss techniques for dealing with the deletion problem. One simple technique we use for identifying deleted records involves replacing the deleted record (or just its key) with a marker indicating that a record once lived there but no longer does. Such a marker is sometimes referred to as a *tombstone* (Wiederhold 1983). The nice thing about the use of tombstones is that it solves both of the problems described previously:

☐ The freed space does not break a sequence of searches for a record; and
☐ The freed space is obviously available and may be reclaimed for later additions.

Figure 11.11 illustrates how the sample file might look after the tombstone ###### is inserted for the deleted record. Now a search for Smith does *not* halt at the empty record number 7. Instead, it uses the ###### as an indication that it should continue the search.

It is not necessary to insert tombstones every time a deletion occurs. For example, suppose in the preceding example that the record for Smith is to be deleted. Since the slot following the Smith record is empty, nothing is lost by marking Smith's slot as empty rather than inserting a tombstone. Indeed, it is actually unwise to insert a tomb-

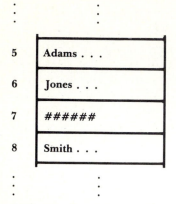

FIGURE 11.11 ▪ The same file as in Fig. 11.9 after the insertion of a tombstone for Morris.

stone where it is not needed. (If, after putting an unnecessary tombstone in Smith's slot, a new record is added at address 9, how would a subsequent unsuccessful search for Smith be affected?)

11.7.2 IMPLICATIONS OF TOMBSTONES FOR INSERTIONS

With the introduction of the use of tombstones, the *insertion* of records becomes slightly more difficult than our earlier discussions imply. Whereas programs that perform initial loading simply search for the first occurrence of an empty record slot (signified by the presence of the key /////), it is now permissible to insert a record where either ///// or ###### occur as the key.

This new feature, which is desirable because it yields a shorter average search length, brings with it a certain danger. Consider, for example, the earlier example in which Morris is deleted, giving the file organization shown in Fig. 11.11. Now suppose you want a program to insert Smith into the file. If the program simply searches until it encounters a ###### it never notices that Smith is already in the file. We almost certainly don't want to put a second Smith record into the file, since doing so means that later searches would never find the older Smith record. To prevent this from occurring, the program must examine the entire cluster of contiguous keys and tombstones to ensure that no duplicate key exists, and then go back and insert the record in the first available tombstone, if there is one.

11.7.3 EFFECTS OF DELETIONS AND ADDITIONS ON PERFORMANCE

The use of tombstones enables our search algorithms to work and helps in storage recovery, but one can still expect some deterioration in performance after a number of deletions and additions occur within a file.

Consider, for example, our little four-record file of Adams, Jones, Smith, and Morris. After deleting Morris, Smith is one slot further from its home address than it needs to be. If the tombstone is never to be used to store another record, every retrieval of Smith requires one more access than is absolutely necessary. More generally, after a large number of additions and deletions, one can expect to find many tombstones occupying places that could be occupied by records whose home records precede them but that are stored after them. In effect, each tombstone represents an unexploited opportunity to reduce by one the number of locations that must be scanned while searching for these records.

Some experimental studies show that after a 50 percent to 150 percent turnover of records, a hashed file reaches a point of equilibrium, so that average search length is as likely to get better as it is to get worse. (Bradley, 1982; Peterson, 1957) By this time, however, search performance has deteriorated to the point that the average record is three times as far (in terms of accesses) from its home address as it would be after initial loading. This means, for example, that if after original loading the average search length is 1.2, it will be about 1.6 after the point of equilibrium is reached.

There are three types of solutions to the problem of deteriorating average search lengths. One involves doing a bit of local reorganizing every time a deletion occurs. For example, the deletion algorithm might examine the records that follow a tombstone to see if the search length can be shortened by moving the record backward toward its home address. Another solution involves completely reorganizing the file after the average search length reaches an unacceptable value. A third type of solution involves using an altogether different collision resolution algorithm.

11.8
OTHER COLLISION RESOLUTION TECHNIQUES

Despite its simplicity, randomized hashing using progressive overflow with reasonably sized buckets generally performs well. If it does not perform well enough, however, there are a number of variations that may perform even better. In this section we discuss some refinements that can often improve hashing performance when using external storage.

11.8.1 DOUBLE HASHING

One of the problems with progressive overflow is that if many records hash to buckets in the same vicinity, clusters of records can form. As the packing density approaches one, this clustering tends to lead to extremely long searches for some records. One method for avoiding clustering is to store overflow records a long way from their home addresses by *double hashing*. With double hashing, when a collision occurs, a second hash function is applied to the key to produce a number c that is relatively prime to the number of addresses.† The value c is added to the home address to produce the overflow address. If the overflow address is already occupied, c is added to it to produce another overflow address. This procedure continues until a free overflow address is found.

Double hashing does tend to spread out the records in a file, but it suffers from a potential problem that is encountered in several improved overflow methods: it violates locality by deliberately moving overflow records some distance from their home addresses, increasing the likelihood that the disk will need extra time to get to the new overflow address. If the file covers more than one cylinder, this could require an expensive extra head movement. Double hashing programs can solve this problem if they are able to generate overflow addresses in such a way that overflow records are kept on the same cylinder as home records.

11.8.2 CHAINED PROGRESSIVE OVERFLOW

Chained progressive overflow is another technique designed to avoid the problems caused by clustering. It works in the same manner as progressive overflow, except that synonyms are linked together with pointers. That is, each home address contains a number indicating the location of the next record with the same home address. The next record in turn contains a pointer to the following record with the same home address, and so forth. The net effect of this is that for each set of syn-

---

†If N is the number of addresses, then c and N are relatively prime if they have no common divisors.

Key	Home address	Actual address	Search length
Adams	20	20	1
Bates	21	21	1
Cole	20	22	3
Dean	21	23	3
Evans	24	24	1
Flint	20	25	6

Average search length = (1 + 1 + 3 + 3 + 1 + 6)/6 = 2.5

FIGURE 11.12 ▪ Hashing with progressive overflow.

onyms there is a linked list connecting their records, and it is this list that is searched when a record is sought.

The advantage of chained progressive overflow over simple progressive overflow is that only records with keys that are synonyms need to be accessed in any given search. Suppose, for example, that the set of keys shown in Fig. 11.12 is to be loaded in the order shown into a hash file with bucket size one, and progressive overflow is used. A search for Cole involves an access to Adams (a synonym) and Bates (not a synonym). Flint, the worst case, requires six accesses, only two of which involve synonyms.

Since Adams, Cole, and Flint are synonyms, a chaining algorithm forms a linked list connecting these three names, with Adams at the head of the list. Since Bates and Dean are also synonyms, they form a second list. This arrangement is illustrated in Fig. 11.13. The average search length decreases from 2.5 to

$$(1 + 1 + 2 + 2 + 1 + 3)/6 = 1.7.$$

The use of chained progressive overflow requires that we attend to some details that are not required for simple progressive overflow. First, a *link field* must be added to each record, requiring the use of a little more storage. Second, a chaining algorithm must guarantee that it is possible to get to any synonym by starting at its home address. This second requirement is not a trivial one, as the following example shows.

Suppose that in the example Dean's home address is 22 instead of 21. Since, by the time Dean is loaded, address 22 is already occupied by Cole, Dean still ends up at address 23. Does this mean that Cole's pointer should point to 23 (Dean's actual address) or to 25 (the address of Cole's synonym Flint)? If the pointer is 25, the linked list joining Adams, Cole, and Flint is kept intact, but Dean is lost. If the pointer is 23, Flint is lost.

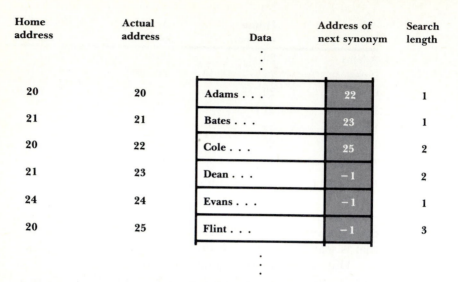

Home address	Actual address	Data	Address of next synonym	Search length
		$\vdots$		
20	20	Adams . . .	22	1
21	21	Bates . . .	23	1
20	22	Cole . . .	25	2
21	23	Dean . . .	−1	2
24	24	Evans . . .	−1	1
20	25	Flint . . .	−1	3
		$\vdots$		

FIGURE 11.13 ▪ Hashing with chained progressive overflow. Adams, Cole, and Flint are synonyms; Bates and Dean are synonyms.

The problem here is that a certain address (22) that *should* be occupied by a home record (Dean) is occupied by a different record. One solution to the problem is to require that every address that qualifies as a home address for some record in the file actually hold a home record. The problem can be handled easily when a file is first loaded by using a technique called two-pass loading.

Two-pass loading, as the name implies, involves loading a hash file in two passes. On the first pass, only home records are loaded. All records that are not home records are kept in a separate file. This guarantees that no potential home addresses are occupied by overflow records. On the second pass, each overflow record is loaded and stored in one of the free addresses according to whatever collision resolution technique is being used.

Two-pass loading guarantees that every potential home address actually is a home address, so it solves the problem in the example. It does not guarantee that later deletions and additions will not recreate the same problem, however. As long as the file is used to store both home records and overflow records, there remains the problem of overflow records displacing new records that hash to an address occupied by an overflow record.

The methods used for handling these problems after initial loading are somewhat complicated and can, in a very volatile file, require many extra disk accesses. (For more information on techniques for maintaining pointers, see Knuth [1973b] and Bradley [1982].) It would be nice if we could somehow altogether avoid this problem of overflow lists bumping into one another, and that is what the next method does.

11.8.3 CHAINING WITH A SEPARATE OVERFLOW AREA

One way to keep overflow records from occupying home addresses where they should not be is to move them all to a separate overflow area. Many hashing schemes are variations of this basic approach. The set of home addresses is called the *prime data area*, and the set of overflow addresses is called the *overflow area*. The advantage of this approach is that it keeps all unused but potential home addresses free for later additions.

In terms of the file we examined in the preceding section, the records for Cole, Dean, and Flint could have been stored in a separate overflow area rather than potential home addresses for later-arriving records (Fig. 11.14). Now no problem occurs when a new record is added. If its home address has room, it is stored there. If not, it is moved to the overflow file, where it is added to the linked list that starts at the home address.

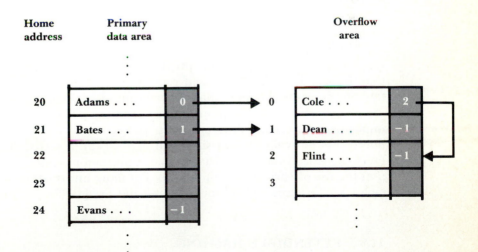

FIGURE 11.14 ▪ Chaining to a separate overflow area. Adams, Cole, and Flint are synonyms; Bates and Dean are synonyms.

If the bucket size for the primary file is large enough to prevent excessive numbers of overflow records, the overflow file can be a simple entry sequenced file with a bucket size of one. Space can be allocated for overflow records only when it is needed.

The use of a separate overflow area simplifies processing somewhat, and would seem to improve performance, especially when many additions and deletions occur. However, this is not always the case. If the separate overflow area is on a different cylinder than is the home address, every search for an overflow record will involve a very costly head movement. Studies show that actual access time is generally worse when overflow records are stored in a separate overflow area than when they are stored in the prime overflow area (Lum, 1971).

One situation in which a separate overflow area is *required* occurs when the packing density is greater than one—there are more records than home addresses. If, for example, it is anticipated that a file will grow beyond the capacity of the initial set of home addresses and that rehashing the file with a larger address space is not reasonable, then a separate overflow area must be used.

11.8.4 SCATTER TABLES— INDEXING REVISITED

Suppose you have a hash file that contains no records, only pointers to records. The file is obviously just an index that is searched by hashing rather than by some other method. The term *scatter table* (Severance, 1974) is often applied to this approach to file organization. Figure 11.15 illustrates the organization of a file using a scatter table.

The scatter table organization provides many of the same advantages simple indexing generally provides, with the additional advantage that the search of the index itself requires only one access. (Of course, that one access is one more than other forms of hashing require, unless the scatter table can be kept in primary memory.) The data file can be implemented in many different ways. For example, it can be a set of linked lists of synonyms (as shown in Fig. 11.15), a sorted file, or an entry sequenced file. Also, scatter table organizations conveniently support the use of variable length records. For more information on scatter tables, see Severance [1974] and Teorey and Fry [1982].

11.8.5 EXTENDIBLE HASHING

All of the techniques reviewed at so far are based on the idea that the original number of possible hash addresses must remain constant. If the file becomes so full, or overflow chains become so long, that re-

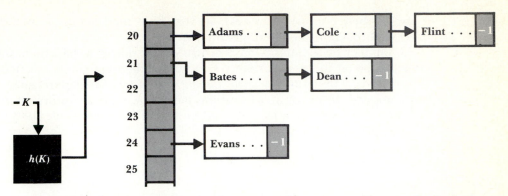

FIGURE 11.15 ▪ Example of a scatter table structure. Because the hashed part is an index, the data file may be organized in any way that is appropriate.

sponse becomes unacceptable, we have to increase the address space and, using a new hash function, rehash the entire file. Rehashing can be very costly since it involves randomly moving every record in the file. When we encountered the high costs of random file reorganization in Chapter 6, we looked for a way to move records without actually moving them. Ultimately, we built an index. We could reorganize the index while leaving the records in place.

Can we apply the same idea to hashing? With scatter tables, we already have our index, so all we need is an efficient way to reorganize a scatter table without moving the data records too much. A number of schemes have been proposed for organizing and reorganizing scatter tables. One relatively simple technique (Ullman, 1982) involves doubling the size of the scatter table when it becomes necessary to *rehash* the file. If the following restrictions are met, the technique works reasonably efficiently.

☐ The hash function must generate an integer that is much larger than the maximum number of addresses that will ever be used, then divide this number by the current address size and take the remainder.

☐ When the table is reorganized, the number of addresses must be multiplied by a fixed integer, commonly 2 (the scatter table doubles in size).

If the table is rehashed by doubling its size from, for example, n to $2n$, records that originally hash to address i now hash to either i or $i+n$, and no records from other buckets hash to i or $i+n$. We need to split only those buckets that contain overflow records (all others can be found at their original addresses), so very little time is wasted in the process of reorganizing the original table.

A number of techniques have grown out of this idea that the hash table can be an index with pointers to buckets that contain the actual data records. The terms *extendible hashing* and *virtual hashing* are sometimes applied to this genre of hashing technique. Further information on aspects of extendible hashing can be found in Fagin et al. [1979], Faloutsos [1985], and Scholl [1981].

11.9 PATTERNS OF RECORD ACCESS

> Twenty percent of the fishermen catch 80 percent of the fish.
> Twenty percent of the burglars steal 80 percent of the loot.
>
> *L. M. Boyd*

The use of different collision resolution techniques is not the only nor necessarily the best way of improving performance in a hashed file. If we know something about the patterns of record access, for example, then it is often possible to use simple progressive overflow techniques and still achieve very good performance.

Suppose you have a grocery story with 10,000 different categories of grocery items, and you have on your computer a hashed inventory file with a record for each of the 10,000 items that your company handles. Every time an item is purchased, the record that corresponds to that item must be accessed. Since the file is hashed, it is reasonable to assume that the 10,000 records are distributed randomly among the available addresses that make up the file. Is it equally reasonable to assume that the distribution of *accesses* to the records in the inventory are randomly distributed? Probably not. Milk, for example, will be retrieved very frequently, brie seldom.

There is a principle used by economists called the Pareto Principle, or The Concept of the Vital Few and the Trivial Many, which in file terms says that a small percentage of the records in a file account for a large percentage of the accesses. A popular version of the Pareto Principle is the 80/20 Rule of Thumb: 80 percent of the accesses are performed on 20 percent of the records. In our groceries file, milk would be among the 20 percent high activity items, brie among the rest.

We cannot take advantage of the 80/20 principle in a file structure unless we know something about the probable distribution of record accesses. Once we have this information, we need to find a way to place the high activity items where they can be found with as few accesses as possible. If, when items are loaded into a file, they can be loaded in such a way that the 20 percent (more or less) that are most likely to be accessed are loaded at or near their home addresses, then most of the transactions will access records that have short search lengths, so the *effective* average search length will be shorter than the nominal average search length that we defined earlier.

For example, suppose our grocery store's file handling program keeps track of the number of times each item is accessed during a one-month period. It might do this by storing with each record a counter that starts at zero and is incremented every time the item is accessed. At the end of the month the records for all the items in the inventory are dumped onto a file that is sorted in descending order according to the number of times they have been accessed. When the sorted file is rehashed and reloaded, the first records to be loaded are the ones that, according to the previous month's experience, are most likely to be accessed. Since they are the first ones loaded, they are also the ones most likely to be loaded into their home addresses. If reasonably sized buckets are used, there will be *very few*, if any, high-activity items that are not in their home addresses and therefore retrievable in one access.

SUMMARY

There are three major modes of accessing files: sequentially, through an index, and directly. Hashing represents the major form of file organization for permitting *direct access*.

Hashing can provide faster access than most of the other organizations we study, usually with very little storage overhead, and it is adaptable to most types of primary keys. Ideally, hashing makes it possible to find any record with only one disk access, but this ideal is rarely achieved. The primary disadvantage of hashing is that hashed files may not be sorted by key.

Hashing involves the application of a hash function $h(K)$ to a record key K to produce an address. The address is taken to be the *home address* of the record whose key is K, and it forms the basis for searching for the record. The addresses produced by hash functions generally appear to be random.

When two or more keys hash to the same address, they are called *synonyms*. If an address cannot accommodate all of its synonyms, *collisions* result. When collisions occur, some of the synonyms cannot be stored in the home address and must be stored elsewhere. Since searches for records begin with home addresses, searches for records that are not stored at their home addresses generally involve extra disk accesses. The term *average search length* is used to describe the average number of disk accesses that are required to retrieve a record. An average search length of 1 is ideal.

Much of the study of hashing deals with techniques for decreasing the number and effects of collisions. In this chapter we look at three general approaches to reducing the number of collisions:

- Spreading out the records;
- Using extra memory; and
- Using buckets.

Spreading out the records involves choosing a hashing function that distributes the records at least randomly over the address space. A *uniform distribution* spreads out records evenly, resulting in no collisions. A *random* or nearly random distribution is much easier to achieve and is usually considered acceptable.

In this chapter a simple hashing algorithm is developed to demonstrate the kinds of operations that take place in a hashing algorithm. The three steps in the algorithm are:

1. Represent the key in numerical form.
2. Fold and add.
3. Divide by the size of the address space, producing a valid address.

When we examine several different types of hashing algorithms, we see that sometimes algorithms can be found that produce *better-than-random* distributions. Failing this, we suggest some algorithms that generally produce distributions which are approximately random.

The *Poisson distribution* provides a mathematical tool for examining in detail the effects of a random distribution. Poisson functions can be used to predict the numbers of addresses likely to be assigned 0, 1, 2, and so on, records, given the number of records to be hashed and the number of available addresses. This allows us to predict the number of collisions likely to occur when a file is hashed, the number of overflow records likely to occur, and sometimes the average search length.

Using extra memory is another way to avoid collisions. When a fixed number of keys is hashed, the likelihood of synonyms occurring decreases as the number of possible addresses increases. Hence, a file organization that allocates many more addresses than are likely to be used has fewer synonyms than one that allocates few extra addresses. The term *packing density* describes the proportion of available address space that actually holds records. The Poisson function is used to determine how differences in packing density influence the percentage of records that are likely to be synonyms.

Using buckets is the third method for avoiding collisions. File addresses can hold one or more records, depending on how the file is organized by the file designer. The number of records that can be stored at a given address, called *bucket size*, determines the point at which records assigned to the address will overflow. The Poisson function can be used to explore the effects of variations in bucket sizes and packing densities. Large buckets, combined with a low packing density, can result in very small average search lengths.

Although we can reduce the number of collisions, we need some means to deal with collisions when they do occur. We examined one simple collision resolution technique in detail—*progressive overflow*. If an attempt to store a new record results in a collision, progressive overflow involves searching through the addresses that follow the record's home address in order until one is found to hold the new record. If a record is sought and is not found in its home address, successive addresses are searched until either the record is found or an empty address is encountered.

Progressive overflow is simple and sometimes works very well. Progressive overflow creates long search lengths, however, when the packing density is high and the bucket size is low. It also sometimes produces clusters of records, creating very long search lengths for new records whose home addresses are in the clusters.

Three problems associated with record deletion in hashed files are

1. The possibility that empty slots created by deletions will hinder later searches for overflow records.
2. The need to recover space made available when records are deleted.
3. The deterioration of average search lengths caused by empty spaces keeping records further from home than they need be.

The first two problems can be solved by using *tombstones* to mark spaces that are empty (and can be reused for new records) but should not halt a search for a record. Solutions to the deterioration problem include local reorganization, complete file reorganization, and the choice of a collision resolving algorithm that does not cause deterioration to occur.

Because overflow records have a major influence on performance, many different overflow handling techniques have been proposed. Five such techniques that are appropriate for file applications are discussed briefly.:

1. *Double hashing* reduces local clustering, but may place some overflow records so far from home that they require extra seeks.
2. *Chained progressive overflow* reduces search lengths by requiring that only synonyms be examined when a record is being sought. For chained overflow to work, every address that qualifies as a home record for some record in the file must hold a home record. Mechanisms for making sure that this occurs are discussed.
3. *Chaining with a separate overflow area* simplifies chaining substantially, and has the advantage that the overflow area may be organized in ways more appropriate to handling overflow records. A danger of this approach is that it might lose locality.
4. *Scatter tables* combine indexing with hashing. This approach provides much more flexibility in organizing the data file. A disadvantage of using scatter tables is that, unless the index can be held in RAM, it requires one extra disk access for every search.
5. *Extendible hashing* also combines indexing with hashing, but allows the size of the address space to grow dynamically as the file gets full and performance begins to deteriorate.

Since in many cases certain records are accessed more frequently than others (the *80/20 rule of thumb*), it is often worthwhile to take access patterns into account. If we can identify those records that are most likely to be accessed, we can take measures to make sure that they are stored closer to home than less frequently accessed records, thus decreasing the *effective* average search length. One such measure is to load the most frequently accessed records before the others.

KEY TERMS

Average search length. We define average search length as the *sum of the number of accesses required for each record in the file* divided by *the number of records in the file*. This definition does not take into account the number of accesses required for unsuccessful searches, nor does it account for the fact that some records are likely to be accessed more often than others. See *80/20 rule of thumb*.

Better-than-random. This term is applied to distributions in which the records are spread out more uniformly than they would be if the hash function distributed them randomly. Normally, the distribution produced by a hash function is a little bit better than random.

Bucket. An area of space on the file that is treated as a physical record for storage and retrieval purposes, but that is capable of storing several *logical* records. By storing and retrieving logical records in buckets rather than individually, access times can in many cases be improved substantially.

Collision. Situation in which a record is hashed to an address that does not have sufficient room to store the record. When a collision occurs, some means has to be found to resolve the collision.

Double hashing. A collision resolution scheme in which collisions are handled by applying a second hash function to the key to produce a number c, which is added to the original address (modulo the number of addresses) as many times as necessary until either the desired record is located or an empty space is found. Double hashing helps avoid some of the clustering that occurs with progressive overflow.

The 80/20 rule of thumb. An assumption that a large percentage (e.g., 80 percent) of the accesses are performed on a small percentage (e.g., 20 percent) of the records in a file. When the 80/20 rule applies, the *effective* average search length is determined largely by the search lengths of the more active records, so attempts to make *these* search lengths short can result in substantially improved performance.

Extendible hashing. A type of hashing that allows the size of a hash table to grow dynamically without having to reorganize the entire table every time it grows.

Fold and add. A method of hashing in which the encodings of fixed sized parts of a key are extracted (e.g., every two bytes) and are added. The resulting sum can be used to produce an address.

Hashing. A technique for generating a unique home address for a given key. Hashing is used when rapid access to a key (or its corresponding record) is required. In this chapter applications of hashing involve direct access to records in a file, but hashing is also often used to access items in arrays in RAM. In indexing, for example, an index might be organized for hashing rather than for binary search if extremely fast searching of the index is desired.

Home address. The address generated by a hash function for a given key. If a record is stored at its home address, then the search length for the record is one because only one access is required to retrieve the record. A record not at its home address requires more than one access to retrieve or store.

Indexed hash. Instead of using the results of a hash to produce the address of a record, the hash can be used to identify a location in an index that in turn points to the address of the record. Although this approach requires one extra access for every search, it makes it possible to organize the actual data records in a way that facilitates other types of processing, such as sequential processing.

Mid-square method. A hashing method in which a representation of the key is squared and some digits from the middle of the result are used to produce the address.

Minimum hashing. Hashing scheme in which the number of addresses is exactly equal to the number of records. No storage space is wasted.

Open addressing. See *Progressive overflow.*

Overflow. The situation that occurs when a record cannot be stored in its home address.

Packing density. The proportion of allocated file space that actually holds records. (Sometimes referred to as *load factor.*) If a file is half full, its packing density is 50 percent. The packing density and bucket size are the two most important measures in determining the likelihood of a collision occurring when searching for a record in a file.

Perfect hashing function. A hashing function that distributes records uniformly, minimizing the number of collisions. Perfect hashing functions are very desirable, but they are extremely difficult to find for large sets of keys.

Poisson distribution. Distribution generated by the Poisson function, which can be used to approximate the distribution of records among addresses if the distribution is random. A particular Poisson distribution depends on the ratio of the number of records to the number of available addresses. A particular instance of the Poisson function, $p(x)$, gives the proportion of addresses that will have x keys assigned to them. See *Better than random.*

Prime division. Division of a number by a prime number and use of the remainder as an address. If the address size is taken to be a prime number p, a large number can be transformed into a valid address by dividing it by p. In hashing, division by primes is often preferred to division by nonprimes because primes tend to produce more random remainders.

Progressive overflow. An overflow handling technique in which collisions are resolved by storing a record in the next available address after its home address. Progressive overflow is not the most efficient overflow handling technique, but it is one of the simplest and is adequate for many applications.

Randomize. To produce a number (e.g., by hashing) that appears to be random.

Synonyms. Two or more different keys that hash to the same address. When each file address can hold only one record, synonyms always result in collisions. If buckets are used, several records whose keys are synonyms may be stored without collisions.

Tombstone. A special marker placed in the key field of a record to mark it as no longer valid. The use of tombstones solves two problems associated with the deletion of records: the freed space docs not break a sequential search for a record, and the freed space is easily recognized as available and may be reclaimed for later additions.

Uniform. Term applied to a distribution in which records are spread out evenly among addresses. Algorithms that produce uniform distributions are better than randomizing algorithms in that they tend to avoid the numbers of collisions that would occur by chance from a randomizing algorithm.

EXERCISES

1. Use the function *hash(KEY, MAXAD)* described in the text to answer the following questions.

a) What is the value of *hash("Browns",101)*?

b) Find two different words of more than four characters that are synonyms.

c) It is assumed in the text that the function *hash()* does not need to generate an integer greater than 20,000. This could present a problem if we have a file with addresses larger than 20,000. Suggest some ways to get around this problem.

2. In understanding hashing, it is important to understand the relationships between the size of the available memory, the number of keys to be hashed, the range of possible keys, and the nature of the keys.

Let us give names to these quantities, as follows.

> M = the number of memory spaces available (each capable of holding one record);
>
> r = the number of records to be stored in the memory spaces;
>
> n = the number of unique home addresses produced by hashing the r record keys; and
>
> K = a key, which may be any combination of exactly five uppercase characters.

Suppose $h(K)$ is a hash function that generates addresses between 0 and $M-1$.

a) How many unique keys are possible? (Hint: If K were one uppercase letter, rather than five, there would be 26 possible unique keys.)

b) How are n and r related?

c) How are r and M related?

d) If the function h were a minimum perfect hashing function, how would n, r, and M be related?

3. The following table shows distributions of keys resulting from three different hash functions on a file with 6000 records and 6000 addresses.

	Function A	Function B	Function C
$d(0)$	0.71	0.25	0.40
$d(1)$	0.05	0.50	0.36
$d(2)$	0.05	0.25	0.15
$d(3)$	0.05	0.00	0.05
$d(4)$	0.05	0.00	0.02
$d(5)$	0.04	0.00	0.01
$d(6)$	0.05	0.00	0.01
$d(7)$	0.00	0.00	0.00

a) Which of the three functions (if any) generates a distribution of records that is approximately random?

b) Which generates a distribution that is nearest to uniform?

c) Which (if any) generates a distribution that is worse than random?

d) Which function should be chosen?

4. There is a surprising mathematical result called *the birthday paradox* that says that if there are more than 23 people in a room, then there is a better than 50-50 chance that two of them have the same birthday.

How is the birthday paradox illustrative of a major problem associated with hashing?

5. Suppose that 10,000 addresses are allocated to hold 8,000 records in a randomly hashed file and that each address can hold one record. Compute the following values.
a) The packing density for the file.
b) The expected number of addresses with no records assigned to them by the hash function.
c) The expected number of addresses with one record assigned (no synonyms).
d) The expected number of addresses with one record *plus* one or more synonyms.
e) The expected number of overflow records.
f) The expected percentage of overflow records.

6. Consider the file described in the preceding exercise. What is the expected number of overflow records if the 10,000 locations are reorganized as
a) 5000 two-record buckets; and
b) 1000 ten-record buckets?

7. Make a table showing Poisson function values for $r/N = 0.1, 0.5, 0.8, 1, 2, 5$, and, 10. Examine the table and discuss any features and patterns that provide useful information about hashing.

8. There is an overflow handling technique called *count-key progressive overflow* (Bradley, 1982) that works on block-addressable disks as follows. Instead of generating a relative record number from a key, the hash function generates an address consisting of three values: a cylinder, a track, and a block number. The corresponding three numbers constitute the home address of the record.

Since block-organized drives (see Chapter 3) can often scan a track to find a record with a given key, there is no need to load a block into memory to find out whether or not it contains a particular record. The I/O processor can direct the disk drive to search a track for the desired record. It can even direct the disk to search for an empty record slot if a record is not found in its home position, effectively implementing progressive overflow.
a) What is it about this technique that makes it superior to progressive overflow techniques that might be implemented on sector-organized drives.
b) The main disadvantage of this technique is that it can be used only with a bucket size of 1. Why is this the case, and why is it a disadvantage?

9. In discussing implementation issues, we suggest initializing the data file by creating real records that are marked empty before loading the file with actual data. There are some good reasons for doing this. However, there might be some reasons not to do it this way. For example, suppose you want a hash file with a very low packing density and cannot afford to have the unused space allocated. How might a file management system be designed to work with a very large *logical* file, but allocate space only for those blocks in the file that actually contain data.

10. This exercise (inspired by an example in Wiederhold, 1983, p. 136) has to do with the problem of deterioration. A number of additions and deletions are to be made to a file. Tombstones are to be used where necessary to preserve search paths to overflow records.
  a) Show what the file looks like after the following operations, and compute the average search length.

Operation	Home address
Add Alan	0
Add Bates	2
Add Cole	4
Add Dean	0
Add Evans	1
Del Bates	
Del Cole	
Add Finch	0
Add Gates	2
Del Alan	
Add Hart	3

  How has the use of tombstones caused the file to deteriorate? What would be the effect of reloading the remaining items in the file in the order Dean, Evans, Finch, Gates, Hart?
  b) What would be the effect of reloading the remaining items using two-pass loading?

11. Suppose you have a file in which 20 percent of the records account for 80 percent of the accesses, and that you want to store the file with a packing density of 0.8 and a bucket size of 5. When the file is loaded, you load the active 20 percent of the records first. After the active 20 percent of the records are loaded, and before the other records are loaded, what is the packing density of the partially filled file? Using this packing density, compute the percentage of the active 20 percent which would be overflow records. Comment on the results.

12. In our computations of average search lengths, we consider only the times it takes for *successful* searches. If our hashed file were to be used in such a way that searches were often made for items that are not in the file, it would be useful to have statistics on average search length for an *unsuccessful* search. If a large percentage of searches to a hashed file are unsuccessful, how do you expect this to affect overall performance if overflow is handled by
 a) progressive overflow; or
 b) chaining to a separate overflow area?
(See Knuth, 1973b, pp. 535–539 for a treatment of these differences.)

13. Although hashed files are not generally designed to support access to records in any sorted order, there may be times when batches of transactions need to be performed on a hashed data file. If the data file is sorted (rather than hashed), these transactions are normally carried out by some sort of cosequential process, which means that the transaction file also has to be sorted. If the data file is hashed, the transaction file might also be presorted, but on the basis of the home addresses of its records rather than some more '"natural" criterion.

   Suppose you have a file whose records are usually accessed directly, but that is periodically updated from a transaction file. List the factors you would have to consider in deciding between using an indexed sequential organization and hashing. (See Hanson, 1982, pp. 280–285, for a discussion of these issues.)

14. We assume throughout this chapter that a hashing program should be able to tell correctly whether a given key is located at a certain address. If this were not so, there would be times when we would assume that a record exists when in fact it does not, a seemingly disastrous result. But consider what Doug McIlroy did in 1978 when he was designing a spelling checker program. He found that by letting his program allow one out of every 4,000 misspelled words to sneak by as valid (and using a few other tricks), he could fit a 75,000 word spelling dictionary into 64K of RAM, thereby improving performance enormously.

   McIlroy was willing to tolerate one undetected misspelled word out of every 4,000 because he observed that drafts of papers rarely contained more than 20 errors, so one could expect at most one out of every 200 runs of the program to fail to detect a misspelled word. Can you think of some other cases where it might be reasonable to report that a key exists when in fact it does not?

Jon Bentley [1985] provides an excellent account of McIlroy's program, plus several insights on the process of solving problems of this nature. D.J. Dodd [1982] discusses this general approach to hashing, called *check-hashing*. Read Bentley's and Dodd's articles, and report on them to your class. Perhaps they will inspire you to write a spelling checker.

PROGRAMMING EXERCISES

15. Implement and test a version of the function *hash()*.

16. Create a hashed file with one record for every city in California. The key in each record is to be the name of the corresponding city. (For the purposes of this exercise, there need be no fields other than the key field.) Begin by creating a sorted list of the names of all of the cities and towns in California. (If time or space is limited, just make a list of names starting with the letter 'S'.)

a) Examine the sorted list. What patterns do you notice that might affect your choice of a hash function?

b) Implement the function *hash()* in such a way that you can alter the number of characters that are folded. Assuming a packing density of 1, hash the entire file several times, each time folding a different number of characters, and producing the following statistics for each run.

- The number of collisions; and
- The number of addresses assigned 0, 1, 2, . . . , 10, and ten-or-more records.

Discuss the results of your experiment in terms of the effects of folding different numbers of characters, and how they compare to the results you might expect from a random distribution.

c) Implement and test one or more of the other hashing methods described in the text, or use a method of your own invention.

17. Using some set of keys, such as the names of California towns, do the following.

a) Write and test a program for loading the keys into three different hash files using bucket sizes of 1, 2, and 5, respectively, and a packing density of 0.8. Use progressive overflow for handling collisions.

b) Have your program maintain statistics on the average search length, the maximum search length, and the percentage of records that are overflow records.

c) Assuming a Poisson distribution, compare your results with the expected values for average search length and the percentage of records that are overflow records.

18. Repeat Exercise 17, but use double hashing to handle overflow.

19. Repeat Exercise 17, but handle overflow using chained overflow into a separate overflow area. Assume that the packing density is the ratio of number of keys to available *home* addresses.

20. Write a program that can perform insertions and deletions in the file created in the previous problem using a bucket size of 5. Have the program keep running statistics on average search length. (You might also implement a mechanism to indicate when search length has deteriorated to a point where the file should be reorganized.) Discuss in detail the issues you have to confront in deciding how to handle insertions and deletions.

FURTHER READINGS

There are a number of good surveys of hashing and issues related to hashing generally, including Knuth [1973b], Severance [1974], Maurer [1975], and Sorenson, Tremblay, and Deutscher [1978]. Textbooks concerned with file design generally contain substantial amounts of material on hashing, and they often provide extensive references for further study. Each of the following can be useful:

- Hanson [1982] is filled with analytical and experimental results exploring all of the issues we introduce, and many more, and also contains a good chapter on comparing different file organizations.
- Bradley [1982] covers file hashing generally, but also includes much information on programming for hashed files using IBM PL/I.
- Loomis [1983], also covers hashing generally, with additional emphasis on programming for hashed files in COBOL.
- Teorey and Fry [1982] and Wiederhold [1983] will be useful to practitioners interested in analyses of trade-offs among the basic hashing methods.

One of the applications of hashing that has stimulated a great deal of interest recently is the development of *spelling checkers*. Because of special characteristics of spelling checkers, the types of hashing involved are quite different from the approaches we describe in this text. Papers by Bentley [1985] and Dodds [1982] provide entry into the literature on this topic. (See also Exercise 14.)

Extendible hashing schemes have recently generated much interest in connection with database applications because they permit the use of files that can grow larger or smaller without complete reorganization. Scholl [1981] provides an introduction to the literature on these approaches.

APPENDIXES

APPENDIX A

ASCII TABLE

	Dec.	Oct.	Hex.		Dec.	Oct.	Hex.		Dec.	Oct.	Hex.		Dec.	Oct.	Hex.
nul	0	0	0	sp	32	40	20	@	64	100	40	`	96	140	60
sol	1	1	1	!	33	41	21	A	65	101	41	a	97	141	61
stx	2	2	2	"	34	42	22	B	66	102	42	b	98	142	62
etx	3	3	3	#	35	43	23	C	67	103	43	c	99	143	63
eot	4	4	4	$	36	44	24	D	68	104	44	d	100	144	64
enq	5	5	5	%	37	45	25	E	69	105	45	e	101	145	65
ack	6	6	6	&	38	46	26	F	70	106	46	f	102	146	66
bel	7	7	7	'	39	47	27	G	71	107	47	g	103	147	67
bs	8	10	8	(	40	50	28	H	72	110	48	h	104	150	68
ht	9	11	9	)	41	51	29	I	73	111	49	i	105	151	69
nl	10	12	A	*	42	52	2A	J	74	112	4A	j	106	152	6A
vt	11	13	B	+	43	53	2B	K	75	113	4B	k	107	153	6B
np	12	14	C	,	44	54	2C	L	76	114	4C	l	108	154	6C
cr	13	15	D	−	45	55	2D	M	77	115	4D	m	109	155	6D
so	14	16	E	.	46	56	2E	N	78	116	4E	n	110	156	6E
si	15	17	F	/	47	57	2F	O	79	117	4F	o	111	157	6F
dle	16	20	10	0	48	60	30	P	80	120	50	p	112	160	70
dc1	17	21	11	1	49	61	31	Q	81	121	51	q	113	161	71
dc2	18	22	12	2	50	62	32	R	82	122	52	r	114	162	72
dc3	19	23	13	3	51	63	33	S	83	123	53	s	115	163	73
dc4	20	24	14	4	52	64	34	T	84	124	54	t	116	164	74
nak	21	25	15	5	53	65	35	U	85	125	55	u	117	165	75
syn	22	26	16	6	54	66	36	V	86	126	56	v	118	166	76
etb	23	27	17	7	55	67	37	W	87	127	57	w	119	167	77
can	24	30	18	8	56	70	38	X	88	130	58	x	120	170	78
em	25	31	19	9	57	71	39	Y	89	131	59	y	121	171	79
sub	26	32	1A	:	58	72	3A	Z	90	132	5A	z	122	172	7A
esc	27	33	1B	;	59	73	3B	[	91	133	5B	{	123	173	7B
fs	28	34	1C	<	60	74	3C	\	92	134	5C	¦	124	174	7C
gs	29	35	1D	=	61	75	3D	]	93	135	5D	}	125	175	7D
rs	30	36	1E	>	62	76	3E	^	94	136	5E	~	126	176	7E
us	31	37	1F	?	63	77	3F	_	95	137	5F	del	127	177	7F

B STRING FUNCTIONS IN PASCAL: *tools.prc*

FUNCTIONS AND PROCEDURES USED TO OPERATE ON *strng*

The following functions and procedures make up the tools for operating on variables that are declared as:

```
TYPE
    strng = packed array [0..MAX_REC_LGTH] of char;
```

The length of the *strng* is stored in the zeroth byte of the array as a character representative of the length. Note that the Pascal functions CHR() and ORD() are used to convert integers to characters and vice versa.

Functions include:

len_str(str)	Returns the length of *str*.
clear_str(str)	Clears *str* by setting its length to 0.
copy_str(str1,str2)	Copies contents of *str2* to *str1*.
cat_str(str1,str2)	Concatenates *str2* to end of *str1*.
	Puts result in *str1*.
read_str(str)	Reads *str* as input from the keyboard.
write_str(str)	Writes contents of *str* to the screen.
fread_str(fd,str,lgth)	Reads a *str* with length *lgth* from file *fd*.

fwrite_str(fd,str)	Writes contents of *str* to file *fd*.
trim_str(str)	Trims trailing blanks from *str*.
	Returns length of *str*.
ucase(str1,str2)	Converts *str1* to uppercase, storing result in *str2*.
makekey(last, first, key)	Combines *last* and *first* into key in canonical form, storing result in *key*.
min(int1,int2)	Returns the minimum of two integers.
cmp_str(str1,str2)	Compares *str1* to *str2*:
	If *str1* = *str2*, *cmp_str* returns 0.
	If *str1* < *str2*, returns a negative number.
	If *str1* > *str2*, returns a positive number.

```
FUNCTION len_str (str: strng): integer;
{ len_str() returns the length of str }
BEGIN
    len_str := ORD(str[0])
END;


PROCEDURE clear_str(VAR str: strng);
{ A procedure that clears str by setting its length to 0 }
BEGIN
    str[0] := CHR(0)
END;


PROCEDURE copy_str(VAR str1: strng; str2: strng);
{ A procedure to copy str2 into str1 }
VAR
    i    : integer;
BEGIN
    for i := 1 to len_str(str2) DO
        str1[i] := str2[i];
    str1[0] := str2[0]
END;


PROCEDURE cat_str (VAR str1: strng; str2: strng);
{ cat_str() concatenates str2 to the end of str1 and stores
  the result in str1  }
VAR .
    i    : integer;
BEGIN
    for i := 1 to len_str(str2) DO
        str1[(len_str(str1)+i)] := str2[i];
    str1[0] := CHR(len_str(str1) + len_str(str2))
END;
```

```pascal
PROCEDURE read_str (VAR str: strng);
{ A procedure that reads str as input from the keyboard }
VAR
    lgth   : integer;
BEGIN
    lgth := 0;
    while (not EOLN) and (lgth <= MAX_REC_SIZE) DO
    BEGIN
        lgth   := lgth + 1;
        read (str[lgth])
    END;
    readln;
    str[0] := CHR(lgth)
END;


PROCEDURE write_str (VAR str: strng);
{ write_str() writes str to the screen }
VAR
    i  : integer;
BEGIN
    for i := 1 to len_str(str) DO
        write(str[i]);
    writeln
END;


PROCEDURE fread_str (VAR fd: text; VAR str: strng; lgth: integer);
{ fread_str() reads a str with length lgth from fd }
VAR
    i   : integer;
BEGIN
    for i := 1 to lgth DO
        read(fd,str[i]);
    str[0] := CHR(lgth)
END;


PROCEDURE fwrite_str (VAR fd: text; str : strng);
{ fwrite_str() writes str to file fd }
VAR
    i : integer;
BEGIN
    for i := 1 to len_str(str) DO
        write(fd,str[i])
END;
```

```
FUNCTION trim_str (VAR str: strng): integer;
{ trim_str() trims the blanks off the end of str and
 returns its new length }
VAR
    lgth  : integer;
BEGIN
    lgth := len_str(str);
    while str[lgth] = ' ' DO
        lgth := lgth - 1;
    str[0] := CHR(lgth);
    trim_str := lgth
END;



PROCEDURE ucase (str1: strng; VAR str2: strng);
{ ucase() converts str1 to uppercase letters and stores the
   capitalized string in str2 }
VAR
    i   :  integer;
BEGIN
for i := 1 to len_str(str1) DO
    BEGIN
    if (ORD(str1[i]) >= ORD('a')) AND (ORD(str1[i]) <= ORD('z')) then
        str2[i] := CHR(ORD(str1[i])- 32)
    else
        str2[i] := str1[i];
    END;
str2[0] := str1[0]
END;



PROCEDURE makekey (last: strng; first: strng; VAR key: strng);
{ makekey() trims the blanks off the ends of the strngs last and first,
   concatenates last and first together with a space separating them,
   and converts the letters to uppercase }
VAR
    lenl     : integer;
    lenf     : integer;
    blank_str: strng;
BEGIN
    lenl := trim_str(last);
    copy_str (key,last);
    blank_str[0] := CHR(1);
    blank_str[1] := ' ';
    cat_str(key,blank_str);
    lenf := trim_str(first);
```

```
        cat_str (key,first);
        ucase(key,key)
END;


FUNCTION min (int1,int2: integer): integer;
{ min() returns the minimum of two integers }
BEGIN
        if int1 <= int2 then
             min := int1
        else
             min := int2
END;


FUNCTION cmp_str (str1: strng; str2: strng): integer;

{ A function that compares str1 to str2.  If str1 = str2, then
  cmp_str returns 0.  If str1 < str2, then cmp_str returns a
  negative number.  Or if str1 > str2, then cmp_str returns a
  positive number. }

VAR
     i       : integer;
     length  : integer;
BEGIN
        if len_str(str1) = len_str(str2) then
             BEGIN
             i := 1;
             while str1[i] = str2[i] DO
                  i := i + 1;
             if (i - 1) = len_str(str1) then
                  cmp_str := 0
             else
                  cmp_str := (ORD(str1[i])) - (ORD(str2[i]))
             END
        else  BEGIN
               length := min(len_str(str1),len_str(str2));
               i := 1;
               while (stri[i] = str2[i]) and (i <= length) DO
                    i := i + 1;
               if i > length then
                    cmp_str := len_str(str1) - len_str(str2)
               else
                    cmp_str := (ORD(str1[i])) - (ORD(str2[i]))
               END
END;
```

C

AN INTRODUCTION TO C

INTRODUCTION
C.1

HISTORY AND DISTINGUISHING FEATURES

C is a general purpose programming language that is especially well suited for systems programming. The language was designed during the early 1970s by Dennis Ritchie at Bell Laboratories. Its most famous application is its use in writing the UNIX operating system.

C is a relatively small language, making it suitable for implementation on small computers. C compilers are now available for most large computers as well as many small ones. It comes with a standard library of functions that provide it with the capabilities of much larger languages, while keeping the machine-dependent features out of the language itself. Most implementations of C adhere quite closely to a definition of the language given in the text *The C Programming Language* by Brian Kernighan and Dennis Ritchie [1978], so that *Kernighan and Ritchie C* is often taken as the standard. One effect of C's high degree of standardization is that C programs are more portable than those of most languages with similar capabilities.

If you are familiar with a modern programming language, such as Pascal, PL/I, or Fortran 77, you can recognize most of C's data types, operators and control structures, and you should be able to read most simple C programs with little difficulty. There are, however, some important differences between C's data types and operators and those of other languages. For example, C provides data types and operators that are very close to those provided in a machine's hardware. One result of this is that C programs can be made very efficient. Another is that in C you can perform low-level operations (such as bit manipulation and file I/O) with much less fuss than in other languages.

A potentially negative result of C's low-level operations is that C does not protect you from yourself the way other languages do. You must be more careful about what you do because the compiler and runtime environment do not look after you the way other languages do.

You should expect your programming style when using C to be different from your style when programming in other languages. C programs tend to rely heavily on user-defined and library functions. C functions tend to be short. The heavy use of unusual data types (such as pointers) and operators (such as *increment*) gives C programs an appearance that is substantially different from that of programs written in other languages. Your programs should be very readable, and they should also have a succinctness that demands that they be read and written with care.

C.2

THE C ENVIRONMENT

The C compiler is only one part of the C programming environment. Many of the features you use when programming in C are not, strictly speaking, part of C, but are features provided from somewhere else in C's programming environment. For example, there is no print command in C as there is in most languages, but there is a printing *function* that is always available in C's *standard I/O library*.

C.2.1 LIBRARIES

C's *standard libraries* consist of groups of *precompiled functions* that must be linked to any C program that calls them before the C program can be executed. The functions in the libraries are standard in the sense that they are specified as being standard in Kernighan and Ritchie [1978] or elsewhere. (If you have UNIX, the definition of what is available in the standard library is spelled out precisely in the UNIX manual. If you have another operating system, the standard library available to you should be spelled out in the documentation that comes with your compiler.)

If you want to have available precompiled functions that are not available in the standard libraries, you can make your own. Functions in these libraries must also be linked to your compiled program before execution. Taking the use of libraries into account, we can think of a program as going through the stages shown in Fig. C.1 before it can be executed.

You probably recognize these as the steps that are carried out on most programs before they can be executed. We give them special stress here because the use of libraries is extremely important in C and because understanding our next topic depends on your having a clear understanding of the compile-link-execute steps.

C.2.2 THE *#include* FILES

In addition to *pre*compiled function libraries, C source programs commonly make use of program files that have *not* been compiled. Suppose, for example, that you have a file containing definitions of constants and data structures, and that these definitions are ones that are used commonly by a lot of different programs you write. It would be nice if you could conveniently include the definitions file with any source program that might need it.

The use of extra source files of this sort is very common in C. There are, for example, a number of data structures and other objects

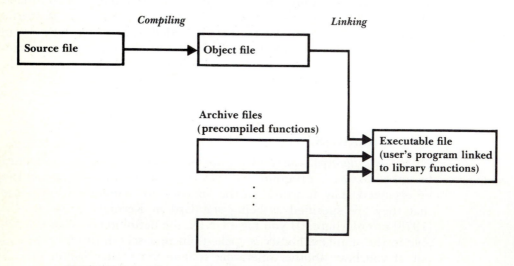

FIGURE C.1 ▪ The pre-execution stages of a program.

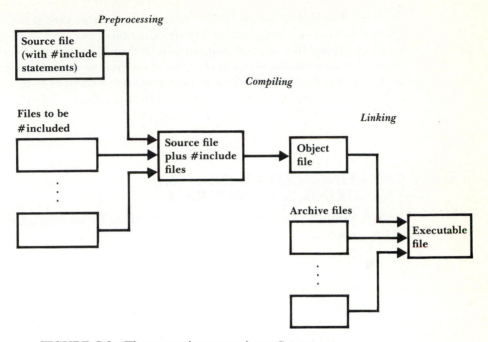

FIGURE C.2 ▪ The stages in processing a C program.

related to I/O that are useful to virtually every source program. A complete set of suitable definitions of these objects is kept in a file called *stdio.h*. (The *h* stands for *header* file—it is inserted at the head of the source file.) Before compiling the code in a program's main source file, the extra file *stdio.h* has to be *included* with the source file.

The C command *#include* lets you include files with your main source file. These files are inserted into the main source file prior to compilation so that, from the compiler's point of view, the contents of the included files appear to be part of the main source file. The program that inserts *#include* files is called the C *preprocessor*. Taking the use of *#include* files into account, we need to alter slightly the stages involved in processing a C program, as shown in Fig. C.2.

C.2.3 TOOLKITS

We stress the various ways files can be brought together to make up an executable program because it is much more common to do this sort of thing in C than in other languages. It is a rare C source program that does not *#include* at least a header file or two. Just as rare is a C program that does not make use of library functions. The idea of keeping special purpose files around that contain definitions and functions that are useful in a variety of contexts is fundamental to most C programming. Such collections of files are sometimes referred to as *toolkits* since they provide tools that can be used for different jobs.

C.3

CREATING, COMPILING, AND EXECUTING A C PROGRAM

Here is a simple program that shows it is working by sending a message to the screen.

```
main( )
{
printf("I work!\n");
}
```

If we want to run this program, the first thing we must do is create a file containing the program. The file can have any valid file name, but some systems require that the name end with the extension *.c,* as in *work.c.*

The next step is to compile the program.† The precise format for invoking the C compiler varies from compiler to compiler, so you should look this up in your documentation. It may not be precisely like the following, but it will be similar.

```
cc work.c
```

Invocation of *cc* typically causes the following tasks to be performed.

Compiling:

☐   Performs preprocessing functions, such as the inclusion of
    #include files;
☐   Checks the program for syntax errors (missing brackets,
    misspelled words, and so on) and prints error messages when it
    finds them;
☐   Translates individual parts of the program into assembler code;
    and

---

†If you have access to a C interpreter, the steps are slightly different. Consult the literature on your system for details.

☐   Translates the assembler code into object code—machine instructions that are equivalent to your C code. These instructions are put into the *object code file*.

Linking:

☐   *Links* your program to any other programs in a *library* that it needs to perform its work. (In the sample program, the library has a program called *printf()* that is used by your program.)

☐   Places the resulting executable program in an executable file.

In many environments the last two steps are not automatic. You may have to make a specific request that the program be linked. Check your system documentation.

Now you are ready to run the program. This is usually done by typing the name of the executable file. The name given to the executable file varies from system to system. On UNIX systems, you can give it a special name (see the following list) or you can type the default name

     `a.out`

whereupon (in our sample program)

     `I work!`

is written on the screen.

There are many options that can be invoked with the *cc* command. Unfortunately, they vary from one operating system to another. Two important options available on UNIX and UNIX-like systems are −*o* and −*c*. Here are some examples of their uses.

cc −*o work work.c*	Causes the executable code to be stored in a file called *work*, rather than *a.out*.
cc −*c work.c*	Tells the compiler to compile, but not link, the code in *work.c*. The resulting object file is automatically named *work.o* and may be linked at a later time (see the following).
cc −*o totprog work.c filea.c fileb.c*	Assumes that you have three files named *work.c*, *filea.c*, and *fileb.c*, and that these three files must all be compiled and linked to produce a working program. File *work.c* might contain the main program, whereas the other two files contain supporting functions. (Once compiled, they would be the user-defined archive files described earlier.)
	The result of executing the command is the creation of three object files called *work.o, filea.o,* and *fileb.o,* plus an executable file (*totprog*) created

by linking the three object files and the necessary standard libraries.

cc −o totprog work.c filea.o fileb.o

Takes advantage of the fact that two of the three input files do not need to be recompiled. It compiles *work.c* (producing *work.o*), but it does not recompile the other two files. Instead, it assumes from the fact that they have *.o* extensions that they are proper object files and it simply links them to *work.o* to produce the executable file *totprog*.

This option can be very handy when a bug needs to be corrected in one source file, but the other files need no changing. It saves compilation time, which can be substantial when the different files become large or numerous.

If you did not enter, compile, and execute the *work.c* program, you should do so now.

C.4
ERRORS

As you are no doubt aware, the process of compiling, linking, and executing does not always go smoothly. Your program might have errors that cause either the compilation or the execution of your program to misbehave. We should warn you that it is quite easy to make mistakes in C, especially in the early stages of learning the language. The best advice we can give you on this matter is to program as carefully and defensively as possible while you are mastering C.

For example, suppose we introduce an error into the *work.c* program by taking out the semicolon at the end of the *printf* statement. When we try to compile the erroneous program we most likely get an error message that does not give a lot of helpful information, something like: "It even gives the wrong line because it does not detect the error until it gets to the closing bracket and sees that it has a statement that does not end in a semicolon."

Throughout the text, we try to help you deal with error frustrations by pointing out areas where you need to be particularly careful and by discussing some of the more mystifying error situations you are likely to encounter. Be warned, however, that as a C programmer, you are expected to be more careful than you might be with other languages. C gives you power to do things that other languages shield you from. It is a power you will use to great advantage, but one that must be handled with care.

COMMON LANGUAGE FEATURES

Most algorithmic languages have the same basic building blocks: a clearly defined program structure, special symbols and key words, data types, operators, statements for controlling the flow of a program's execution, subroutines, and rules defining the scope of variables and subroutines. Since we assume that you already know a programming language, we do not spend time explaining why most of these features exist or how they should be used. Rather, we focus primarily on how they are realized syntactically in C, and ways in which C's implementation is unusual.

C.5 STRUCTURE AND SPECIAL SYMBOLS

In C, every program consists of a set of functions, one of which has to be called *main*. Consider the following simple C program.

```
main()

{
        printf("To C or not to C...\n");
}
```

When you execute a C program, the function called *main()* is executed first. Hence, all other functions that make up your program must be invoked, directly or indirectly, by *main()*. In the example, *main()* calls the function *printf()*, which happens to be in a library whose functions are available to all C programs.

We look in detail later at other features of functions (such as how parameters are passed), but for now we stick with *main()* functions, which have the general form:

```
main()

{
        <statements>
}
```

where

main()	Declares the function called *main*. In defining a function, the name must be followed by parentheses. We see later that the parentheses can include parameters.
{...}	Are a pair of braces, which must bracket the body of the function. When a C compiler sees a closing brace to

match the opening brace, it assumes that the function is completely defined. If it never finds the closing brace, it indicates an error.

<statements>   Are C statements that make up the body of the function. These statements may be as simple or as complex as necessary. Every simple C statement must end in a semicolon.

C.6
DATA TYPES

Most languages give us two ways to refer to data: constants and variables. Some, including C, allow us to use a third type of reference: pointers. We cover the use of pointers in later sections. Constants and variables are represented in much the same ways in C as they are in most other languages.

In C, every variable must be declared to have a certain data type. Use of an undeclared variable results in a compilation error. Declaration of a variable in C does not have the same implications it has in many other languages, however, because C is not a strongly typed language. We need to discuss the implications of this now.

C.6.1 C IS NOT A STRONGLY TYPED LANGUAGE

Some languages, such as Pascal, have *strong typing*. This means that for a given data type only certain operations can be performed. You cannot treat a character as an integer in Pascal, for example. Since C is not strongly typed, you can perform just about any type of operation you like on any type of data.

The implications of this are substantial. For a large part of the work we need our programs to do, it is essential that they be able to treat certain pieces of data in a variety of ways. Our programs would be larger, less likely to be correct, and less easy to maintain if we were forced to use complex procedures for getting around the restrictions of strong data typing.

On the other hand, there are certain dangers inherent in not having strong data typing. When there is no strong typing, it is easy unknowingly to treat data in ways in which they are not meant to be treated. As you program in C, you must learn to be very careful about how you mix data types to avoid unnecessarily tricky treatment of data and to document necessarily tricky treatment of data.

C.6.2 INTEGERS AND CHARACTERS

In C there are four and one half types of integers: *int, short, long, unsigned,* and *char*. The reason there are so many is to provide flexibility in programming.

int	Corresponds to the integer data type you see in most languages. It refers to a signed whole number (no fractional parts) stored in one computer word. The size of an *int* depends on the most common word size used by your computer. An *int* may range in size from 16 to 36 bits. An *int* constant is represented by one or more digits, possibly preceded by a sign, as in 1285 and -137.
short and *long*	Provide different sizes of integers, and their sizes are less variable from machine to machine. A *short* is usually two bytes (16 bits), and a *long* is usually four bytes (32 bits). Because their sizes vary less from machine to machine, and because we often find it important to be precise about the amount of storage a particular piece of data uses, we often use *short* and *long* in place of the less precise *int*. A *long* constant is represented in the same way as an *int* except that it must be followed by an L or *l*, as in 608L or 608*l*.
unsigned	Refers to integers that cannot be negative. They obey the laws of arithmetic modulo 2^n, where n is the number of bits in an *int*. *Unsigned shorts, longs,* and *chars* exist in many implementations of C as well.
char	Refers to one-byte integers capable of holding one character in a machine's character set. Since it is an integer, you can do arithmetic with a character. Because C does not have strong data typing, you can also treat it as a character. A *char* constant is represented by a single character enclosed in apostrophes, such as 'a'. The integer value associated with a *char* constant is the numeric value of the character in the machine's character set. For example, the ASCII code for 'a' (lowercase) is the decimal value 97.
	It is important in C to be able to represent certain character codes that have no graphic representation. Codes for *newline* and *tab*, for example, need to be represented. This is done by preceding certain key letters with a backslash, as in

`'\n'`	Newline
`'\t'`	Tab (corresponding to the tab typewriter key)
`'\0'`	Null (the *value* 0, not the character 0)
`'\b'`	Backspace
`'\r'`	Carriage return

`'\f'`	Formfeed (new page)
`'\\'`	Backslash
`'\''`	Single quote
`'\ddd'`	An octal constant

The following program illustrates some uses of integers as well as other familiar programming features. You can learn a great deal about the syntax of C by studying the program carefully. The program does not perform any useful function.

```
/* examples.c...
    Program to illustrate uses of integers in C.
*/
main()
{
    /* --- Declarations (next seven statements) ---             */
    int    a;
    int    b = 3;           /* Assignment during a declaration.  */
    int    x;
    int    funny_name;      /* Variable names may be long, but often for
                               internal names only the first eight characters
                               count. There is some variation from machine to
                               machine. The only special character allowed
                               is the underscore "_".            */

    short sh, Sh;           /* Upper- and lowercases are different.  More
                               than one variable can be declared at a time.  */
    long  l;
    char  c, d;             /* c is commonly used to hold a char.  */

    /* --- Expressions using integers (next nine statements) ---  */

    a = b + 3;              /* Assignment statement.             */

    funny_name = 'f';       /* Lack of strong typing allows this.  When
                               a char is assigned to an int,  it is
                               automatically converted to an int.  */
    x = 'A' - 65;           /* Same for arithmetic expressions.  */

    sh = a;                 /* int assigned to short.  This is fine if
                               a is small enough.  Otherwise, it causes
                               a nasty (i.e., hard to detect) bug.  */

    Sh = 40000;             /* WON'T WORK!! 40,000 is too big for a short.
                               32,767 is the biggest allowable short.  */

    l = b + 1000000L;       /* Shorter data types are converted to
                               longer ones.                      */
```

```
b       =                     /* Blanks, newlines, and comments may be        */
          25                  /* embedded anywhere in statements.             */
          -2                  /* Can you find the semicolon?                  */

;c = 'r' + 1;                 /* Adding 1 to a character gives the next
                                 character.                                   */

d = '\007';                   /* The octal constant 7. If your terminal has
                                 a bell, d will probably ring it.             */

/* --- Printing the results (next nine statements) ---                        */

printf("a=%d\n",a); /* printf is a library function for formatting
                       output.  This one sends the following to
                       your terminal:
                                     a=6
                       followed by a newline. Details follow.                 */

printf("b = %d\t%o\t%x.\n",b,b,b); /* Print value of b in decimal,
                                      octal, and hexadecimal.  Note
                                      uses of the tab ('\t').                 */

printf("funny_name = %c or %d.\n",   /* Print funny_name as a                 */
          funny_name,funny_name);    /* char and as a decimal int.            */

printf("x = %d.\n",x);        /* What would you expect here?  Hint:           */
                              /* ASCII for 'A' is 65.                         */
printf("sh = %d.\n",sh);

printf("Sh = %d.\n",Sh);      /* Should have been 40,000, but Sh is           */
                              /* too short to hold it.                        */

printf("l = %ld.\n",l);       /* Long integers need an  l  (ell) in           */
                              /* their format specifications.                 */
printf("c = %c\n",c);
printf("%c",d);
```

The output produced when this program is run appears as follows:

```
a=6
b = 23        27        17.
funny_name = f or 102.
x = 0.
sh = 6.
Sh = -25536.          (Note the erroneous result.)
l = 1000003.
c = s
^G                    ("Control-G," which usually causes a beep. The
                         "^G" probably does not appear on your screen.)
```

C.6.3 FLOATING POINT NUMBERS

C programmers do not use floating point numbers very much, but occasionally they come in handy. A floating point constant in C has an integer part, a decimal point, a fraction part, and an *e* or *E* followed by a signed integer exponent. Some of these are optional. Examples: 2.718 and 2.3E-6.

Floating point variables come in two sizes, *float* and *double*. The actual representation and precision of floating point variables and constants vary from machine to machine. A *float* generally occupies 32 bits and provides about six decimal digits of precision. A *double* generally occupies 64 bits and provides about 15 decimal digits of precision. Both provide exponents of at least $10^{\pm 38}$.

Floating point constants are always stored in *double* format. Conversions of floating point values to integers are machine dependent. Sometimes they truncate; sometimes they round. Conversions of integers to floating point are better behaved. Of course, some precision can be lost if an integer is too large.

C.6.4 HEXADECIMAL AND OCTAL CONSTANTS

Hexadecimal and octal representations are especially useful when you want to get a true picture of what data really looks like, or when there is no other convenient representation of a value you want to store somewhere. In C, an octal integer constant consists of the digit 0 followed by a sequence of octal digits (0–7). A hexadecimal integer constant consists of *0x* or *0X* followed by a sequence of hexadecimal digits (0–9, *A* or *a–F* or *f*). Examples:

Octal	Hexadecimal	Decimal
05	0x5	5
037	0x1*f*	31

A hexadecimal or octal constant is assumed to be of type *int* unless it is too large, or it is followed by the letter 'l' or 'L' (which makes it *long*.)

C.7
FUNCTION *printf()* FOR SCREEN OUTPUT

Function *printf()* is C's general-purpose function for sending output to a screen. Since in this text we are not interested in designing elegant screen output, we need not go into detail on all of the variations of formats for *printf()*. The general form of a *printf()* statement is

printf(<format>,<argument list>);

The *<format>* is enclosed in quotes and contains characters that are to be sent to the screen, plus format codes. The format codes tell how the values referred to in the *<argument list>* are to be formatted. The following format codes are available, among others.

%c	Character
%d	Decimal integer
%f	Floating point number
%o	Octal integer
%s	String
%x	Hexadecimal integer
%%	The % character

Long integers may be formatted by including "l", as in: %ld.

Note that the format used to print an item need not have anything to do with the item's data type. C lets you tell it to interpret the contents of a memory location any way you like, even if it makes no sense.

Exercise 1. Write a program to make the following assignments to *character* variables: $x = 7$ (octal), $y = 44$ (octal), $a = 3c$ (hex), and $b = 3a$ (hex). Have the program then print the *hex* and *character* representations of these values.

Exercise 2. Write a program to assign the values 100 and 200 to the variables x and y, respectively, then store the sum of x and y in the variable *sum,* and then print the results so that the output appears as follows.

```
The sum of 100 and 200 is 300 (decimal), 454 (octal), and 12c (hex).
            ^        ^     ^                                    ^
```

Numbers marked with a carat (^) should be printed from the corresponding variable values (e.g., the 100 is printed from x using the %d format.) The carats need not appear in the output.

Exercise 3. Write a program to show the results of printing the special character constants '\t', '\b', '\r', '\f', '\\' and '\" (e.g., the statement *printf("\tx\n\t\tx");* demonstrates how the tab character works.)

C.8

ARRAYS

There are important differences between the ways arrays are handled in C and the ways they are handled in most other languages. Since most of these differences depend on the fact that many array operations involve the use of pointers, our coverage of those differences has to be deferred until the section on pointers. In this section, we discuss those features of arrays that you are probably familiar with from your knowledge of some other language. An array

□   Is an aggregate of a single data type (including array);
□   Can have any number of dimensions;
□   Must be declared before use;
□   Is subscripted beginning with 0; and
□   Uses integer subscripts (constants or expressions).

The declaration

```
int a[16];
```

creates an aggregate of the 16 integer variables *a[0], a[1],* . . . *a[15]*. Since subscripting starts at 0, there is no *a*[16].

Multidimensional arrays are declared and referenced using separate brackets for every dimension, as in

```
short      table[20][30];
char       names[100][15];
```

which allocate 600 two-byte spaces for short integers, and 1500 bytes for characters. Array elements are stored row-wise (last subscript varies fastest).

C does no run-time bounds checking on array references. Hence, it is perfectly legal in C to write

```
j = 20;
a[j] = 7;
```

referring to the array *a[]* declared previously. The results of such an assignment are hard to predict. They could be disastrous.

One common mistake is to forget that the number that gives the length of an array cannot be used as a subscript. For example, *a[16]* refers to an element that is beyond the bounds of *a[]* as it is declared above.

C has no special operators for handling arrays, such as assignments that transfer entire arrays. If you want such operators in C, you must create them yourself in the form of C functions.

Exercise 4. Examine the following program and predict what will be printed when it is executed. Enter the program and see what actually is printed. Explain the results. What is wrong with using a value of 10 for *j*?

```
main()
{
    int  a[10], b[10], j = 10;

    a[0] = 33;
    b[0] = 44;
    a[j] = 55;
    b[j] = 66;
    printf(" a[0] = %d\n b[0] = %d\n",a[0],b[0]);
}
```

C.9
STRINGS

C has no declarable data type called *string*. Instead, a string is an array of characters that, by convention, ends with the null character '\0'. For example, the following code shows a crude way to store the string "Who?" in the character array *str[]*.

```
char    s[10];       /* Declare array of characters     */

s[0] = 'W';          /* Assignment of a string to s[],  */
s[1] = 'h';          /* one character at a time.         */
s[2] = 'o';
s[3] = '?';
s[4] = '\0';         /* Note that the null character     */
                     /* takes up space in the array.     */
```

We can think of this string as being represented internally as

s[0]	s[1]	s[2]	s[3]	s[4]	s[5]	. . .
'W'	'h'	'o'	'?'	'\0'		(Garbage from here on)

We cannot emphasize too much the importance of the null byte at the end of every string. If it is left off, many string functions will not know when they have arrived at the end of a string. Or, if it doesn't account for the extra byte required for the null character, a program could end up accidentally storing a null byte one position beyond the end of the array. In both cases a program would probably play havoc with data that should have been left alone.

There are *string constants* in C. A string constant is represented by enclosing the desired string in quotation marks, as in "Who?". When string constants are given in a program, they are allocated space internally and stored in just the same way we store strings in character arrays. Hence, the string "Who?" is represented internally just as it is in the preceding string illustration, except that it does not have a name. We use string constants frequently, as in

```
printf("Who?");
```

There are no predefined operations on strings. Instead, there are a number of *functions* available to perform operations on strings. These functions all assume that they are working with a group of consecutive bytes ending with '\0'. For example, there is a function called *strcpy()* to copy a string into an array. To assign the string "Who?" to *s[]* you write

```
strcpy(s, "Who?");
```

Other useful string-handling functions are discussed in the section on operators.

Exercise 5. Write a program to copy the string "Who's on first?" to an array *a*, then print the string from the array using the *%s* format.

C.10 ≡ STRUCTURES

In this section, we look briefly at what a structure is, and at a few simple operations on structures. We must defer full treatment of structures until we cover pointers because pointers are fundamental to working with structures.

A structure is an aggregate, like an array, but with an important difference. Unlike an array, the different elements of a structure may have different data types. Structures are especially useful in file processing because it is often necessary to collect different types of data from a file in one place and to refer to them collectively rather than as individual items.

Consider, for example, a record from a personnel file that contains a person's name, age, employee number, and gross pay. Structures allow us to aggregate all of this information under one name so that, when we want to, we can refer to the entire aggregate. Here is a declaration of a C structure for the employee record. It is called *emp_rec*.

```
struct {
    char    name[20];
    short   age;
    char    employee_number[8];
    long    gross_pay;
} emp_rec;
```

There are a number of variations on this form. For example, it is possible to define a structure type without actually declaring a corresponding structure. This is done by following the keyword *struct* by an identifier, or *structure tag*. Here the structure tag is *A*:

```
struct A {
    char    name[20];
    short   age;
    char    employee_number[8];
    long    gross_pay;
};
```

Later, the block describing the parts of the structure may be replaced by the structure tag, as in

```
struct A emp_rec;
```

Individual items in a structure are referred to by giving the name of the structure, followed by a period, followed by the name of the member, as in

```
emp_rec.age = 37;
printf("Name: %s\n",emp_rec.name);
if (emp_rec.gross_pay > 3000) tax = emp_rec.gross_pay * .35;
```

Exercise 6. Devise a structure to contain the following information about a member of a bowling league: *bowler's name* **(not more than 20 characters),** *team name* **(not more than 12 characters),** *high score* **(integer less than 301), and** *average score* **(floating point number).**

Sally Spare belongs to the Alley Cats bowling team. She has a high score of 214 and an average score of 183.7. Write a program that assigns Sally's statistics to your structure and prints out the elements of the structure in a nice format.

C.10.1 UNIONS

Unions allow different variables to share the same storage space. Unions can be used to save storage by allowing the same storage to be used for different purposes at different times. They can also be used to create data structures that adapt easily to different combinations of data.

Unions use a notation very similar to that of structures. For example, the following statement defines a four-byte union to store either a *long* or a four-byte character array.

```
union whichever {    /* "whichever" is the union tag  */
    long number;
    char letters[4];
} ;
```

In the following code, the first statement declares a union variable by the name of *sharer*. The second statement stores a string at the location in memory attached to *sharer*, and the third stores a long integer there, wiping out the string that was just stored there.

```
union whichever sharer;
strcpy(sharer.letters, "foo");
sharer.number = 15L;
```

Exercise 7. Write a program that declares a union to contain an array of 22 characters and an array of six long integers. Have the program store the string *First part* at the beginning of the character array, then have it store the two integers 255 and 4095 in the last two positions of the array of longs. Print the union out as a series of hex characters.

C.11
FUNCTION *scanf()* FOR KEYBOARD INPUT

C's general-purpose function *scanf()* gets keyboard input. The general form of a *scanf()* statement is

```
scanf(<format>,<argument list>);
```

The *<format>* is enclosed in quotes and contains the format codes of the expected input. The *argument list* contains the addresses of the variables that will be assigned the input. The address of a simple variable or structure is indicated by putting an & before its name; the address of an array is indicated simply by giving the array name. (The uses of addresses are discussed in more detail in later sections.)

The following call to *scanf()* reads characters from the standard input device (usually the keyboard), interprets them as a decimal integer, translates them into binary, and stores the result in the *int* variable *r*.

```
scanf("%d", &r);
```

When several values are to be read in, they may be separated by any number or combination of blanks, newlines, or tabs. For example, consider the following code.

```
short a; float b; char title[30];
scanf("%d %f %s", &a, &b, title);
```

If the input from the keyboard is

```
10                    654.3E-2
          assistant
```

then the values 10, 6.543, and the string *assistant* (null terminated) are assigned to *a, b,* and *title,* respectively.

As with *printf()*, we do not discuss some of the finer features of *scanf()*, such as the use of field widths and right and left justification of input.

Exercise 8. Write a program that uses *scanf()* to read in three numbers in decimal, then prints them out as hex values.

C.12

OPERATORS

Operators in C are different from those in many familiar languages in two ways. First, some common ones (such as string operators) are conspicuously absent. C makes up for this by providing a run-time library containing useful functions that effectively provide these operators and many more. Second, C classifies as operators some things (such as assignment and functions) that other languages do not call operators.

We discuss most of the C operators in this section, but some require special treatment and are deferred until later sections. These include *address of (&), indirection (*), structure pointer (→),* and the conditional operator *(?:).*

C.12.1 OPERATORS + − * / % && ¦¦ ! > <=, ETC.

Arithmetic operators include the familiar binary operators +, −, *, /, and % (modulus, for integers only). Division (/) between integers produces a truncated integer quotient.

Relational operators include < (less than), > (greater than), <= (less than or equal), >= (greater than or equal), = = (equal), and != (not equal). Failure to distinguish between = = (equal) and = (assignment) is a common source of errors among beginning C programmers. We discuss the difference between = = and = in the section on flow of control.

Relational operators return 1 for *true* and 0 for *false*. (In general, 0 means *false* and *nonzero* means *true*.)

Logical operators include && (AND), ¦¦ (OR) and ! (NOT). They have the usual meanings.

Bitwise operators allow for bit manipulation. The bitwise operators are & (AND), ¦ (OR), ^ (exclusive OR), and ~ (NOT). Don't confuse the bitwise operators with the corresponding logical operators. Whereas logical operators treat an entire operand as a *true* or *false* value, the bitwise operators are applied in parallel to the individual bit positions in an operand. Bitwise operators may be used only with integer data types.

The bitwise AND operator (&) can be used to mask off bits. For example, if *n* is a short integer

```
a = n & 0xFFF0;
```

sets the lower four bits of *n* to zero.

Two other bitwise operators are << (left shift), and >> (right shift). $x << n$ shifts the value of *x* to the left by *n* bit positions, filling the vacated positions with 0. For example,

```
a = x << 2;
```

shifts *x* two positions, effectively multiplying *x* by 4.

The operation $x >> n$ shifts *x* by *n* bit positions to the right. If *x* is unsigned, the vacated positions are filled with 0. If *x* is another type of integer, the value that fills the vacated positions is machine dependent.

Exercise 9. Predict the results of executing the following program. Enter the program and run it to check your results.

```
main()
{
    printf("Arithmetic: \n\t%d \n\t%d \n\t%d \n\t%d \n",
            17/5, -17/5, 17%5, -17%5);
    printf("Relational: \n\t%d \n\t%d \n\t%d \n\t%d \n",
            5 > 3,  5 < 3,  7 == 7,  8 == 7);
    printf("Logical: \n\t%d \n\t%d \n\t%d \n",
            (3>2) ¦¦ (2>3),  (3>2) && (2>3), !(3>2) );
    printf("Bitwise: \n\t%d \n\t%d \n\t%x \n\t%c \n",
            3 & 2,  3 ¦ 2,  ~0xfff8,  'a' & 0137);
    printf("Bitwise shift: \n\t%d \n\t%d \n", 37 << 2, 37 >> 2);
}
```

C.12.2 ASSIGNMENT

In most languages, assignment simply involves the placement of data in a location identified by a variable name. As we have seen, this is done in C using the $=$ operator, as in $a = b + c$;. Assignment in C goes beyond this simple form in two ways, however.

First, there are a variety of forms of assignment that cause operations to be performed before an actual assignment is made. These assignments take the general form

<variable> <op>= <expression>

which means the same as:

<variable> = <variable> <op> (<expression>)

Think of *<expression>* as an expression such as $b + c$ that returns a value. The *<op>* can be any of the arithmetic operators or the bitwise operators. For example,

```
x += y;          is equivalent to    x = x + y;
a *= b + c;      is equivalent to    a = a * (b + c);
```

The reasons for using these shorthand notations is that they can produce shorter and faster assembler code, and they improve readability.

The second difference between C assignments and those of many common languages is that in C an assignment operator (= or *<op>*=) is a true operator in the sense that it returns a value. This value can in turn be operated on. Hence, it is possible in C to say

```
d = (a *= b + c);      which is equivalent to    a *= b + c;
                                                 d = a;
```

This feature can be exploited to produce very tight code. It can also be used to produce obscure and error-prone code, as you will probably discover.

Exercise 10. Predict the results of executing the following program. Enter the program and run it to check your results.

```
main()
{
    int a=2, b=3, c=5, d, e=6;

    a += 17;
    e *= (d = b + c);
    printf(" a = %d\n b = %d\n c = %d\n d = %d\n e = %d\n", a, b, c, d, e);
}
```

C.12.3 INCREMENT AND DECREMENT

Incrementing (adding 1) and decrementing (subtracting 1) are so common in programming that the designers of C have given us special operators for them. The increment operator is $++$; the decrement operator is $--$. For example,

$$++a; \quad \text{is equivalent to} \quad a = a + 1;$$
$$--a; \quad \text{is equivalent to} \quad a = a - 1;$$

As with the other forms of assignment, the results of an increment or a decrement operation may be used, so

$$b = ++a; \quad \text{is equivalent to} \quad ++a;$$
$$b = a;$$

The $++$ and $--$ may be used before or after a variable, but when used after a variable they have a slightly different meaning. If it is part of some larger expression, $a++$ causes a to be incremented only *after* its value has been used. Hence,

$$b = a++; \quad \text{is equivalent to} \quad b = a;$$
$$a++;$$

Exercise 11. Predict the results of executing the following program. Enter the program and run it to check your results.

```
main(){
     int a, b, c, d, u, v, w, x;

     a = b = c = d = 2;
     u = ++a;
     v = b++;
     w = 3 + --c;
     x = 3 + d--;
     printf(" a = %d\n b = %d\n c = %d\n d = %d\n", a, b, c, d);
     printf(" u = %d\n v = %d\n w = %d\n x = %d\n", u, v, w, x);

}
```

C.12.4 STRING PROCESSING FUNCTIONS AS OPERATORS

Recall that a string in C is an array of characters with a null ('\0') terminator. Here is a list of some of the string processing functions that are particularly important when programming in C. They can all be found in the standard library.

strcat(s1,s2) Appends *s2* to *s1*. After *strcat* is executed, *s1* consists of all of the characters from the original *s1* except the '\0' at the end, followed by all of *s2*.

strcmp(s1,s2) Compares *s1* with *s2*, then returns an *int* value that is less than 0 if *s1* is lexically less than *s2*, equal to 0 if *s1* equals *s2*, and greater than 0 if *s1* is greater than *s2*.

strcpy(s1,s2) Copies the contents of *s2* to *s1*, overwriting the original contents of *s1*.

strlen(s1) Returns an *int* that is the number of characters in *s1*, excluding the null terminator.

Exercise 12. Predict the results of executing the following program. Enter the program and run it to check your results.

```
main()
{
        char sl[40], s2[40];

        strcpy(sl, "April is the cruelest month.");
        strcpy(s2, "April");

        if (strcmp(sl, s2) < 0)
            printf("s2 is bigger.\n");
        else if (strcmp(sl, s2) == 0)
            printf("sl and s2 are equal.\n");
        else
            printf("sl is bigger.\n");

        strcat(sl,s2);
        printf("\nsl and s2 together: %s\n", sl);
        printf("\nNew length of sl: %d", strlen(sl));
}
```

C.12.5 THE OPERATOR *sizeof()*

A handy special operator in C is *sizeof()*, which computes at compile time the size, in bytes, of a type or data object. You can use *sizeof* with actual data objects (simple variables, arrays, structures), data types (*int, short, float,* and so forth), and expressions.

For example:

```
struct vehicle {          /*  vehicle  is a structure tag          */
    char    name[10];
    int           weight;
    short   year;
};
```

```
struct vehicle truck;     /*  truck  is a vehicle                    */

v = sizeof(struct vehicle); /* Computes the total number of bytes
                               used by this type of structure.     */

w = sizeof(truck);        /* Computes the number of bytes used
                             by this specific structure.           */

x = sizeof(short);        /* On most machines assigns 2 to x.      */

y = sizeof(int);          /* Depends on machine's most convenient
                             word size.                            */

z = sizeof(x + 3.2);      /* Returns size of result that would be
                             returned if  x + 3.2  were evaluated.
                             Doesn't actually evaluate x + 3.2.    */
```

Three particularly useful applications of *sizeof()* occur when

☐ The type or data object is defined a long way from where its size
is needed, such as in an *#include* file;
☐ It is difficult for a programmer to compute an object's actual size,
as in the case of a structure; or
☐ The actual size of an object could change when the program
is implemented on a different system, as in the case of *int*
variables.

**Exercise 13. Write a program to determine the results of the
sizeof operators shown previously.**

C.12.6 CASTS

Sometimes it is important to convert a value from one data type to
another. For example, consider the following expression, in which *a*
and *b* are *int* variables and *x* is a *float* variable.

```
    x = a / b;   /* fractional part of quotient is lost */
```

Suppose you want to retain the fractional part of the quotient. One
way to do this is to *cast,* or convert, *a* or *b* to *float,* and then do the division:

```
    x = (float) a / b
```

Casts have the general form

(<type>)

In other words, a cast is simply a data type enclosed in parentheses. When it precedes an expression, the results of the expression are converted to the data type enclosed in parentheses before being used. Since the cast operator has higher precedence than any binary operators, it performs the conversion before any further operation is performed on the variable.

C.12.7 SUMMARY, WITH PRECEDENCE AND ASSOCIATIVITY

In Table C.1† operators within a group have the same precedence. Higher precedence operators occur higher in the table. Left-to-right associativity means that when several operators used in an expression have the same precedence, they are evaluated in order from left to right. For example, in *a * b / c*, the * and / have the same precedence, so the expression is interpreted as *(a * b) / c*.

C.13 FLOW OF CONTROL

Virtually all languages have several ways of altering the order in which statements are executed. Commonly, they include unconditional branching, conditional branching, looping, and procedure calls. Procedures are covered in the next section. We cover the others here.

C.13.1 STATEMENT BLOCKS

A group of statements (including declarations) can be treated as a single statement by including them in a *block*, or *compound statement*. Any group of statements surrounded by braces is considered a block. For example, the body of a main program is a block. From now on, when we say *<statement>*, we mean that either a simple statement or a block of statements may be used.

---

†Adapted from *The C Programmer's Handbook*, by M.I. Bolski, Prentice-Hall, 1985, p. 18.

TABLE C.1

Precedence and associativity in C operators

Operator	Function	Evaluation order
()	Function call	LEFT-TO-RIGHT
[]	Array element	
.	Structure or union member	
→	Pointer to structure or union member	
!	Logical not	RIGHT-TO-LEFT
~	One's complement	
−	Unary minus	
+ +	Increment	
− −	Decrement	
&	Address of	
*	Indirection	
(type)	Cast	
sizeof	Size in bytes	
*	Multiply	LEFT-TO-RIGHT
/	Divide	
%	Modulo (or remainder)	
+	Add	LEFT-TO-RIGHT
−	Subtract	
<<	Left shift	LEFT-TO-RIGHT
>>	Right shift	
<	Less than	LEFT-TO-RIGHT
<=	Less than or equal	
>	Greater than	
>=	Greater than or equal	
= =	Equal	LEFT-TO-RIGHT
!=	Not equal	
&	Bitwise and	LEFT-TO-RIGHT
¦	Bitwise or	LEFT-TO-RIGHT
&&	Logical and	LEFT-TO-RIGHT
¦ ¦	Logical or	LEFT-TO-RIGHT
?:	Conditional	RIGHT-TO-LEFT
=	Assignment (also *= /= %= etc.)	RIGHT-TO-LEFT

C.13.2 THE *if* STATEMENT

The *if* statement has several forms. The simplest has the form

```
if (<expression>) <statement>
```

as in

```
if (a == 7) ++a;
```

and

```
if (b >= 3) {
    d++;
    printf("d was incremented.\n);
}
```

When an *if* is executed, the expression in parentheses is evaluated. If its value is not 0, it is considered *true,* and <statement> is executed. If <expression> is 0 (false), <statement> is ignored. (This interpretation for true and false is exploited heavily in C programming.) Hence, in the first example, the expression

$$a == 7$$

returns a 0 if *a* is not equal to 7, and the $++a$ is not executed. If *a* equals 7, it returns a 1 and the $++a$ is done.

In the second example, if b >= 3, the two statements that make up the block are executed. Otherwise, the block is ignored.

It is important to point out that <expression> can be any valid expression—anything that returns a value. It could even be an assignment statement. Consider the following example.

```
main()
{
        int r = 4,
            p = 8,
            a = 0;

        if (r = p - 6) {        /* Examine this line carefully. */
            a++;
            printf("a was just incremented.\n");
        }
        printf("r = %d\na = %d\n", r, a);
}
```

If you are not used to C, there is a good chance you will interpret this example incorrectly. The expression $r = p - 6$ does *not* compare the value of *r* with that of $p - 6$, as it does in most other languages. (Remember, $==$ is used for comparison; $=$ is used for assignment.) Instead, $r = p - 6$ assigns the value 2 to r and, since 2 is not 0, the *if* thinks true and executes the following block. (What value is printed for r in the second *printf*?)

C.13.3 THE *if...else* STATEMENT

The *if...else* statement has the expected form and interpretation. For example, in

```
if (j > n)
    t = 7;
else {
    a++;
    t = 3;
}
```

If $j > 1$, the statement $t = 7$; is executed; otherwise, the statements $a + +$; and $t = 3$; are executed.

C.13.4 CONDITIONAL EXPRESSIONS

C has an operator that can be used to represent an *if...else...* conditional. The trick to understanding the usefulness of this operator is to think about a conditional as returning a value rather than simply choosing among one or more statements to be executed. For example, suppose you want to assign to a the maximum of the two values of x and y. Here is one way to do it.

```
if (x > y) a = x; else a = y;
```

But C provides a convenient shorthand for such a conditional expression. The statement

```
<e1> ? <e2> : <e3>
```

means

> if <e1> is true then return the value of <e2>
> else return the value of <e3>.

Hence, this also assigns the maximum of x and y to a:

```
a = (x > y) ? x : y;
```

This construction can be used to good effect in making code shorter and in expressing the intent of code more clearly than *if...else...* might. It can also be used in some places where *if...else...* cannot be used, such as in macro definitions.

Exercise 14. If the variable *n* is an integer, what does the following statement cause to be printed?

```
n = -1;
printf("%s\n", (n > 0) ? "greater than zero" : "less than zero");
```

C.13.5 THE *if...else if...else if...* NESTED STATEMENT

Nested *if* statements are often used to select one among many options. In the following example, the code on the right is used to determine a value for *tax* based on the table on the left.

Table:

w	Tax
w < 1000	50
1000 ≤ w < 3000	300
3000 ≤ w < 5000	650
5000 ≤ w	800

Code:

```
if      (w < 1000) tax =  50;
else if (w < 3000) tax = 300;
else if (w < 5000) tax = 650;
else               tax = 800;
```

C.13.6 THE *switch* STATEMENT

The *switch* statement tests whether the value of an <expression> matches one of a number of mutually exclusive constant values, then acts accordingly.

The general form of *switch* is†

```
switch (<expression>) {
    case <c-exp>: <0 or more statements>
    case <c-exp>: <0 or more statements>
        .
        .
        .
    case <c-exp>: <0 or more statements>
    default: <0 or more statements>        ⟵ Optional
```

The cases are examined sequentially until a <c−exp> that has the same value as <expression> is found. Then all subsequent <statements>

---

†Think of <*expression*> as any expression that returns an *int* value. Think of <*c-exp*> as any expression that contains only integer constants, character constants, and/or *sizeof* operations.

are executed until either the end of the *switch* is encountered or the statement

```
break;
```

is encountered. If no case is matched, the optional *default* case is selected, and its statements are executed. If no case is matched and there is no *default* statement, the *switch* is left with no statement executed.

Let's look at an example. Suppose that in response to a menu a user types in one character (*A, C, D,* or *E*) indicating a choice of one of four operations to be performed on a file. Suppose each choice involves one or two function calls as shown in the table. (Never mind what the functions do or how they work.) The variable *c* is an *int* variable that holds the character typed in by the user.

Value of *c*	Meaning	Function(s) to be called
A	Add a record	*add_rec( )*
C	Change a record	*lookup( ), display( )*
D	Delete a record	*delete_rec( )*
E	Examine a record	*lookup( ), display( )*

Note that choices '*C*' and '*E*' require the same initial action. Here is a switch statement that carries out the calls.

```
switch (c) {
case 'A':              /* If c == 'A' perform all statements  */
    add_rec();         /* that follow until a break is        */
    break;             /* encountered.                        */

case 'C':              /* Since 'C' and 'E' require the same   */
case 'E':              /* actions, they are grouped together.  */
    lookup();          /* If 'C' is matched, all subsequent    */
    display();         /* statements are executed until break  */
    break;             /* is encountered.                      */

case 'D':
    delete_rec();
    break;

default:               /* This is optional, but recommended.   */
    printf("\nUnrecognized command.\n");
    break;
}
```

If you are used to using a *case, select,* or similar construct in some other language, be sure that you understand how C's *switch* is different. In particular, be aware of the need for the *break* when you do not want execution to fall through to subsequent cases.

The *break* statement can be used in places other than *switch* statements. A *break* causes control to leave whatever *while, do, for,* or *switch* statement it happens to be immediately inside of.

C.13.7 THE *while* LOOP

C's *while* loop looks and behaves about the same as most *while* loops:

> while (<expression>)
>   <statement>

The <expression> is evaluated prior to each iteration. If it is nonzero (true), <statement> is executed. Otherwise the loop is terminated. For example:

```
i = 0;
while (i < 10) {
    printf("%d\n",i);
    ++i;
}
```

C.13.8 THE *for* LOOP

C's equivalent to the counting loop is more general than most counting loops. It is actually a special form of the *while* loop with a convenient format for initializing, testing, and altering the variables that control execution of the loop. The general form

```
for (<exprl>; <expr2>; <expr3>)
    <statement>
```

is equivalent to

```
<exprl>;
while (expr2) {
    <statement>
    <expr3>;
}
```

Here is a *for* loop that is equivalent to the *while* loop in the previous section.

```
for (i = 0; i < 10; i++)
    printf("%d\n",i);
```

The *for* loop is preferable to the *while* loop when the initialization, testing, and alteration of the loop control variable are simple because it displays them together at the top of the loop.

One difference between C's *for* loop and counting loops in some other languages is that the control variable always retains its value after loop termination. Also, there are no restrictions on altering any of the control variables within the body of the loop.

Each of <expr1>, <expr2>, and <expr3> can consist of more than one expression, provided the expressions they contain are separated by commas. For example, here is a *for* loop that counts the number of blanks in a string *s* whose length cannot exceed 100:

```
for (count = 0, j = 0; s[j] != '\0'  &&  j<100; j++)
        if (s[j] == ' ') count++;
```

C.13.9 THE *do...while* LOOP

The *do...while* loop is similar to the *while* loop, except that it performs the termination test at the bottom of the loop rather than at the top. Hence, its form is

```
do
     <statement>
while (<expression>);
```

Exercise 15. Write three programs to initialize every integer in an array of 100 integers to 7. Use *while*, *for* and *do...while*, respectively, in the three programs.

Exercise 16. The following program is supposed to search the string *str* for the first occurrence of a blank, then print its position. Some of the code is missing. You are to insert the missing code. Do it once using a *for* loop and once using a *while* loop. Test your code with the string "Hold the phone.", then with the string "Never. " (blank at the end only), then with " Hello." (blank at the beginning), and then with "Hello." (no blanks).

```
static char *strs[] = { "Hold the phone.",   /* This handy data structure   */
                        "Never. ",           /* will make more sense after  */
                        " Hello.",           /* you learn about pointers.   */
                        "Hello.",
                        "" };
main()
{
    char str[20];
    int  n, j;
```

```
for (j = 0; strs[j][0] != '\0'; j++) {
    strcpy(str, strs[j]);

    /* YOUR for or while loop code goes here */

    if (str[n] == ' ')
        printf("Blank is at position %d\n", n);
    else
        printf("Blank was not found.\n");

} /* end of outer for loop */
}
```

C.14 FUNCTIONS

Few languages encourage the development of a large library of functions as much as C does. The idea of building a toolkit of functions to be used in building higher-level programs is basic to the philosophy of C.

C.14.1 BASICS

C makes no distinction between subroutines and functions. Every C subprogram is a function in the sense that every subprogram returns a value. This is consistent with the idea that every expression, including assignment, returns a value.

The general form of a function definition is

```
<name> (<argument list, if any>)
<argument declarations, if any>
{
        <declarations and statements, if any>)
}
```

The function <name> must be preceded by a type if the function returns a value whose type is not *int*.

There are two ways to return values from functions: via the argument list, and via a *return* statement. We discuss the use of the argument list for returning values later, since it involves the use of pointers. The *return* statement has the form

```
return (<expression>);
```

and can appear anywhere within the body of the function, as often as needed. The *return* statement does two things. It returns the value of <expression>, and it returns control to the calling function.

Here is a function called *max3()*, which returns the maximum of three *int* arguments.

```
max3 (al, a2, a3)
int     al,a2,a3;
{
        int     m;
        m = (al > a2) ? al : a2;
        return ((m > a3) ? m : a3);
}
```

Functions are invoked by naming them and giving their actual arguments. For example, *max3()* can be invoked with a statement such as

```
x = max3(x,y,100);
```

To print the maximum of *x*, *y*, and 100, you can say:

```
printf("%d\n", max3(x, y, 100));
```

Since some functions do not need to return values, it is not neccessary to follow the word *return* with anything. In fact, the return statement may be omitted altogether if no value is to be returned. If the statements in the body of a function do not include a *return*, control is returned when execution reaches the closing right bracket. Here is a function that does not return a value.

```
greet(n)
int n;
{
    if (n == 0) return;
    if (n > 0)
        printf("Well, hello there!!!\n");
    else
        printf("Oh...it's you.\n");
}
```

Here is a definition of a function that fills the first 79 columns on the screen with a given symbol, together with a *main()* program that calls the function.

```
main()
{
        fill_screen('+');
}
```

```
fill_screen(symbol)
char    symbol;
{
        int r,c;
        for (r = 0; r < 25; r++) {
                for (c = 0; c < 79; c++) printf("%c",symbol);
                printf("\n");
        }
}
```

The statement *fill_screen* ('+'); causes the screen to be filled with the '+' symbol. The two functions *main()* and *fill_screen()* can be typed into a single file, which can then be compiled and executed.

Note that *fill_screen()* is separate from *main()*. It is not included within the block that defines *main*. Functions in C cannot be defined within other functions, even within *main*.

> **Exercise 17. Rewrite *fill_screen()* so that it fills only a certain number of columns on the left of the screen with the symbol, where the number of columns is given in the argument list.**

> **Exercise 18. Write and test a function that takes a character as its only argument, and returns the integer 0 if the character is '0', 1 if the character is '1', 2 if the character is '2', and so on. If the argument is not a character representation of a digit, the function should return -1.**

C.14.2 FUNCTION ARGUMENTS (FIRST PASS) AND OTHER MATTERS

Function arguments are passed by value. This means that when a function is invoked, each argument is evaluated and a copy of the result is passed to the function. This copy is used by the function. The function arguments are local to the function and are not accessible outside of the function. When control is returned, no change is made to the original arguments.

This would seem to imply that it is not possible to return values from a function via the argument list. In fact it is possible, but it requires the use of pointers, which we discuss in a later section. The use of external variables provides another (usually less desirable) way for functions to alter values of variables. External variables are discussed in the section on accessibility of variables.

C does not check to ensure that the types of the formal and actual arguments are the same. It is your responsibility to make sure that the declared types of function arguments are the same as the types of the arguments used when invoking the function. The lack of argument type checking is a major source of errors in C. (This is particularly true when porting programs between machines that use different sized *int* variables.)

Functions can be used recursively in C. No extra declarations have to be made when writing recursive functions.

Function definitions cannot be nested. In practice this means that all functions are external and that, with one exception, any function can have access to any other function. (The exception occurs when functions are declared *static*. We discuss *static* functions in the next section.)

C.15 ACCESSIBILITY OF VARIABLES

When you write a large program it is useful to be able to prescribe the times and places when variables are accessible. Accessibility of variables is determined in two ways in C: specification of *storage classes* for variables, and *scope rules*. The storage class of a variable is a specifiable attribute of the variable that indicates when and where it can be used— its *scope*. Scope rules determine the accessibility of a variable based on where it is declared. Clearly storage classes and scope rules are closely related.

C.15.1 STORAGE CLASSES

We said earlier that function arguments are local variables. Any variables declared in the body of a function are also local. By default, local variables have the storage class *automatic*, which means that they are created when the function is entered, and eliminated when the function is exited. You can declare a variable to have the storage class *static* if you want it to retain its value from one call of a function to another.

C functions can have access to variables that are not local. Variables that are defined outside of any function have the storage class *external*. Normally, external variables are available to all functions. (The exception to this is static external variables, which are available only within the file in which they are declared.)

The following is a summary of the storage classes used in C.

Automatic   These variables are local to a block and are discarded when the block is left. Unless otherwise specified, variables declared within a function or block are automatic. This includes formal function arguments.

Static   These variables retain their values throughout the execution of a program. Static variables must be declared specifically with the *static* attribute.

    Static variables that are declared inside a block or function are internal (like automatic variables) in the sense that they are accessible only within the block or function in which they are declared. When a block is exited and later reentered, static variables can be reused without reinitializing them. They will have the same value they had when they were last used.

    Static variables that are declared outside of any function are accessible to any function within the source file in which they are declared, but nowhere else. This type of static variable is useful when you want to have variables that are global to a certain file of functions, but inaccessible to others.

External   These variables are global. That is, they retain their values and are accessible to many functions. A variable defined outside of any function is external.

    External variables declared *static* are accessible only within the file in which they are declared. Other external variables are accessible to functions in other files only if they are declared *extern* within those other files. (This situation is explained in Section C.15.2.)

Register   These variables are automatic variables whose values are stored in fast registers. We do not concern ourselves with the use of register variables.

Typedef   This is not really a storage class, but it is often included in descriptions of storage classes. You can use *typedef* to define identifiers that can be used later as if they are data type keywords. A complex structure definition can be defined as a type, for instance, as the following example shows.

```
typedef struct {
    char    key[30];
    long rrn;
} KEYNODE;
```

Henceforth, *KEYNODE* can be treated as if it is a data type, as in the declarations

```
KEYNODE  node;          /* single node of type KEYNODE */
KEYNODE  node_array[100]; /* 100 nodes of type KEYNODE   */
```

The use of *typedef* can significantly improve readability of code in some circumstances, particularly code that involves complicated uses of pointers.

C.15.2 DEFINING DECLARATIONS VERSUS REFERENCING DECLARATIONS OF VARIABLES

There are two things a C compiler must do before a variable becomes available for use. First, it must associate the variable name with a block of storage that it sets aside. This is called variable *definition*. Then it must associate with the storage certain attributes that govern the way the bits in the storage are to be treated. This permits the program to *reference* the variable in a meaningful way.

When we use the term *declaration* we mean to imply that both of these things are being done. For example, when we declare a variable to be of type *short* within a function, as in

```
short sum;
```

the compiler allocates two bytes of storage with the name *sum* (the defining declaration), and associates with the name *sum* information about how the data stored in the two bytes are to be interpreted (the referencing declaration).

Under normal circumstances, defining declaration and referencing declaration occur at the time of declaration. There is one exception to this, however. When a variable is declared externally (outside of any function) in a certain file the variable is defined (has storage allocated), but can only be referenced from within the file. It is not available for referencing from another file. To make the variable available to functions in other files, it must be redeclared within those files. Such redeclarations begin with the keyword *extern,* as in

```
extern short sum;
```

This declaration does not **define** *sum*. It is assumed that *sum* has already been defined. In general, an external variable can be defined only once. All other declarations must begin with the keyword *extern* to assure that they not be redefined.

C.15.3 SCOPE RULES

C's scope rules parallel those of most block-structured languages:

1. If a variable is declared outside of any function, then it is accessible from the point at which it is declared through the rest of the source file in which it is declared.
2. A formal parameter is accessible only within the function in which it is declared.

3. A variable declared within a block is accessible in the block in which it is declared and in any blocks that are nested within the block.

4. If a block contains a declaration of a variable with the same name as that of a variable declared in a surrounding block (including an external declaration), the variable declared in the outer block is not accessible until the inner block is left.

5. If a function has an *extern* declaration of a variable, there must be a corresponding external *defining* declaration somewhere among the libraries and files constituting the complete program. The defining declaration does *not* contain the keyword *extern*.

C.16

SCOPE RULES FOR FUNCTIONS

Since function definitions cannot be nested, all C functions have the storage class external. This means that, generally speaking, every function is accessible from anywhere in a program.

The one exception to this is functions that are declared *static* in their definition. Static functions can be accessed only from within the file in which they are defined. This feature of static functions makes it possible to write C functions that have the same private, local nature as does an internal procedure in a language such as PL/I.

All C programs must have at least one function: *main()*. Execution of a C program always begins with the function *main()*. All other functions are subordinate to *main()* and are called directly or indirectly from *main()*.

Two other categories of functions in C are the standard C library functions and user-defined functions.

C.16.1 LIBRARIES AND OTHER FILES CONTAINING FUNCTIONS

Virtually every C implementation comes with one or more files containing commonly needed C functions. One such file contains the standard I/O library described earlier. A typical implementation of C also has other libraries with functions for performing other important programming tasks, such as common mathematical functions. Consult your system documentation for information on the libraries that your C system makes available for you.

Some libraries, such as the standard I/O library, are automatically available. Others, including those created by programmers for their own special purposes, are not automatically available. They must be either included with a source file before compilation using the *#include* preprocessor command, or linked to the object file after compilation. Consult your system documentation for information on how to create and link library object files.

THE PREPROCESSOR

Before a C source file is compiled, a preprocessor examines the source text for certain *preprocessor commands*. Preprocessor commands provide convenient facilities for defining constants and macros, for including other files with the source file, and for conditional compilation. Many languages provide preprocessing facilities, but few languages incorporate them as integrally in the program development process as does C. The effective use of toolkits relies heavily on the use of preprocessing.

All preprocessor commands begin with the character '#'. (Most compilers require that the # be in column 1.)

C.17 THE *#define* COMMAND

A command of the form

```
#define <name>   <token-string>
```

causes <token-string> to be substituted for <name> wherever <name> occurs in the source file after the definition. Such a substitution is called a *macro substitution*. In its simplest form <token-string> is just a constant, but it can be any string of characters that the programmer wants to have substituted in the code. It can also contain arguments of a sort. Here are some examples.

```
#define MAX_LENGTH    350                       /* a numeric constant     */
#define PROMPT        "\nEnter two numbers\n"   /* a string constant      */
#define PRINT_A       printf("a = %d\n", a)     /* a specific function call */
#define MAX(a,b)      ((a) > (b) ? (a) : (b))   /* use of arguments       */
```

Frequently *#define* statements precede *main()*, but they can appear anywhere. Here is an example of how some of our *#defines* can be used.

```
#define PROMPT            "\nEnter two numbers\n"
#define MAX(a,b)          ((a) > (b) ? (a) : (b))
main()
{
        int x, y;

        printf(PROMPT);
        scanf("%d %d", x, y);
        printf("The winner is...%s\n", MAX(x,y));
}
```

Macro arguments (e.g., *a* and *b* in the definition of *MAX*) are not to be confused with function arguments. When a variable name is used as an argument in a function, its **value** is passed to the function. When an argument is used in a macro substitution, there is no value involved. Instead, the symbols that are used in place of the arguments (*x* and *y* in the example) simply replace the arguments themselves.

Here are some reasons for using *#define*.

☐   A frequently used constant can be defined to have a certain value in one application of a program, then changed in another application merely by changing one *#define* statement.

☐   Complex code can be hidden by using simple expressions in place of the corresponding code, as in the *MAX(a,b)* macro in the preceding example.

☐   A macro executes faster than a corresponding function would, since a macro does not involve call-and-return overhead.

☐   Macro arguments can be *generic:* since they are not declared, they can be constructed to have data of any type substituted for them.

C.18

THE *#include* COMMAND

The *#include* command makes it easy to bring into a file a toolkit of functions, *#defines*, and global variable declarations. We discussed the very important role of *#include* in the introduction. A command of the form

```
#include "filename"
```

causes the contents of the indicated file to be processed as if they appeared in the same place as the *#include* command.

The preprocessor looks for the indicated file first in the directory holding the original C program. If it does not find the file there, the preprocessor searches the standard system directories. If you want the preprocessor to search only the standard system directories, replace the quotation marks with < and >, respectively, as in

```
#include <filename>
```

C.19
CONDITIONAL COMPILATION

Among the preprocessor statements are some that allow part of a program to be compiled or not compiled depending on some condition. Conditional compilation can be handy when debugging or when the choice of which statements to compile depends on which machine is being used. We do not cover conditional compilation here.

Exercise 19. To make sure you know how *#include* works, create a file with the *#define*s that are illustrated in the text and create a *second* file with the main program that uses the definitions. Use an *#include* statement in the second file to include the definitions from the first file.

POINTERS

All the data types we have discussed have meaning outside of their uses in computing. Integers and characters, for example, have been around since people began to count and write. Pointers are different—pointers are specific to computing. Pointers give us a way to refer to the location in a computer's memory where the bit pattern that represents a certain piece of data is stored. Pointers are memory addresses. Most computer languages do not encourage programmers to make use of pointers. C *demands* that pointers be used.

Normally when we work with simple variables there is no need for us to be aware of the address of a particular value, let alone manipulate that address. There are times, however, when it is very convenient to be able to manipulate addresses. Kernighan and Ritchie [1978] explain:

"Pointers are very much used in C, partly because they are sometimes the only way to express a computation, and partly because they usually lead to more compact and efficient code than can be obtained in other ways."

C.20

BASICS

To talk about pointers, we need to revise our usual concept of a variable. A variable in C has associated with it the following four objects:

☐ A name;
☐ A value in the form of a bit pattern that is stored somewhere in computer memory;
☐ A size, which indicates how many bytes of memory it requires; and
☐ A pointer, which identifies the place in memory where the value is stored.

When you use a simple variable name in a program, the computer must determine where in memory the value associated with the name is located. For every variable name, then, there must be a pointer. Suppose, for example, we have the declaration and assignment

```
short  sum;
sum = 463;
```

The value of *sum* is stored somewhere in memory (for example, location 1036) and takes up two bytes. Schematically:

<name>	<pointer> ⟶ <value>
sum	location 1036 ⟶ 463

If you want to work with a pointer explicitly, you must give it a name. There are two ways to do this in C. One is to use the *address-of* operator & as in

```
&sum
```

In the example, *&sum* refers to location 1036. A more general way to refer to a pointer is to use a *pointer variable,* which can be declared as follows.

```
short  *psum;     /* pointer of type short-pointer */
```

The * tells the compiler that *psum* can be assigned an address of a *short.* Note that a pointer type is described in terms of the type of data to which it points, so *psum* is a *short-pointer*. We see the importance of this shortly. To assign to *psum* the address of *sum,* you write

```
psum = &sum;                    /* assignment of an address  */
```

The unary operator *, when not used in a declaration, means *the contents of the location pointed to.* Hence, in the following code the two print statements do the same thing.

```
psum = &sum;
printf("The sum is %d\n",sum);
printf("The sum is %d\n",*psum);
```

C.21

ARRAY NAMES AS POINTERS

In C an array name is a pointer to the first element of the array named. Individual array elements are identified by giving the array name followed by a subscript. Consider the declaration

```
long     a[100];
long     *pa;
```

The first declaration causes the computer to allocate space to hold 100 long integers (four bytes each). The variable *a* is a long-pointer to the first element of the array. It gives the address of the first element of the array (which is a *long*). The subscripted name *a[0]* gives the value of the first element of the array.

Since *pa* is a *long-pointer* it has the same data type as *a,* and *pa* can be assigned the value of *a,* as in

```
pa = a;
```

Since *&a[0]* also points to the first element of *a,* the same thing can be accomplished with

```
pa = &a[0];
```

This diagram illustrates the result:

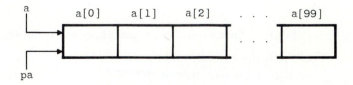

The statement

```
pa = &a[2];
```

changes the picture to

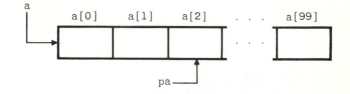

C.22
POINTER ARITHMETIC AND ARRAYS

Some very convenient kinds of arithmetic can be performed on pointers. If an integer i is added to the pointer *pa,* the result is a pointer to the ith element beyond the one pointed to by *pa.* For example, the following code sums the even-numbered elements in the array pointed to by *a.*

```
long    a[100], *pa, sum = 0;

for (pa = a; pa < &a[100]; pa += 2)
        sum += *pa;
```

Note that in the expression *pa* $+= 2$, the computer does not simply add the value 2 to the address *pa.* It has to consider the size of the data type pointed to by *pa.* Since *pa* is a long-pointer, it probably adds 8 ($2 \times 4 = 8$) to get each new address.

In general, when an integer i is added to a pointer, i is multiplied by the size of the object to which the pointer points, then added to the pointer value. The result is a pointer that points to an element in the array that is offset i elements from the original element.

The increment and decrement operators work similarly: *pa*++ adds to *pa* the size of the object pointed to by *pa* (four in the example). Hence, if *pa* points to the first element in the array *a,* the following are equivalent expressions.

```
pa + 3     a + 3      &a[0] + 3      &a[3]
```

Subtraction of an integer from a pointer works similarly. However, if a **pointer** is subtracted from another pointer, the result is an integer corresponding to the number of elements between them.

Exercise 20. Write a program to assign the string

"All rice on doves don t make as is sad goner."

to an array, then print every third character, starting with the first character (A). Use a pointer to scan the array. Do not use subscripts.

C.23
POINTERS AND FUNCTION ARGUMENTS

In C, function arguments are passed *by value*. This means that a function does not know the location of a variable whose value it receives via an argument. As a result, functions are not able to change arguments. In other words, a function may *receive* a value via its argument list, but it may not *change* a value via its argument list. That's the bad news.

The good news is that it is possible, using pointers, to change the value *pointed to* by a function argument. When a function argument is a *pointer* to a variable's address, the function knows where the variable's value is stored. It can then change the value of the variable by changing the value stored at the location pointed to.

C.23.1 CHANGING PARAMETERS THAT ARE SIMPLE VARIABLES

Let's develop a function to determine the position in a string where a particular character first occurs, and also where it last occurs. If the character does not occur at all, we want the function to return 0.

Our function returns three separate values. The first two we call *first* and *last,* and they will be parameters. The third value is returned via the *return* statement. Here is a function that does the job.

```
find_fl(str, chr, first, last)
char str[];          /* the string to be scanned           */
char chr;            /* the character to look for           */
int  *first, *last;  /* first and last are addresses. *first and *last will
                        be int values stored at addresses first and last  */

    len = strlen(str);
    for (i = 0; str[i] != chr && i < len; i++) /* scan for *first */
        ;
    if (i == len)    /* if not found, return */
        return(0);
```

```
else                    /* otherwise, assign i to the place   */
  *first = i;           /* in memory pointed to by first       */

for (i = len - 1; str[i] != chr; i--)  /* scan backwards for *last  */
    ;
  *last = i;
  return(1);
}
```

When *find_fl()* is called, its arguments must, of course, conform to the formal arguments given in the definition. In particular, *first* and *last* must be pointers. We know that we can refer to the pointer to a variable by using the *address-of* operator &, so a call to *find_fl()* might look something like this:

```
int   x, y;     /* actual parameters, to be bound to first and last */

r = first_fl("one#two#three#four#five", '#', &x, &y);
printf("first = %d and last = %d\n", x, y);
```

Exercise 21. Write a function *classify(s, u, l, d, o)* **that examines the string in array** *s* **to determine how many uppercase letters, lowercase letters, digits, and other characters there are, and returns the numbers in** *u, l, d* **and** *o,* **respectively.**

C.23.2 CHANGING PARAMETERS THAT ARE ARRAYS

In C an *array name* is a pointer that points to the first element in an array. Therefore, when an array is passed to a function as a parameter, there is no need to use the & operator. In declaring a parameter in a function that is to correspond to an array, you have two choices. You can declare it as a pointer, as in

```
char  *str;    /* pointer to value of type char    */
```

or you can declare it as an array (which makes its name a pointer), as in

```
char  str[];   /* this is how we did it in find_fl()  */
```

The two versions are equivalent. The version you choose should depend on which you find most readable in the context of what you are doing.

The following is a function that copies the contents of one array of type short into another.

```
copyshort(a1, a2, size)    /* Copy  all elements of a2 into a1.
                              size gives size of a2.     */
short    a1[], a2[];
int      size;
{
        int i;
        for (i = 0; i < size; i++)
            a1[i] = a2[i];
}
```

An invocation of *copyshort* is also uncomplicated, as in

```
short x[20], y[20], j;

for (j = 0; j < 20; j++)       /*  Load y[] so that there */
    y[j] = j*j;                /*  is something to copy.  */

copyshort(x, y, 20);
```

Note that no & operator is required with the *x* and *y* parameters since they are already pointers. If the & operator were used in this case, the result would not be the desired one.

It is common in C to exploit the fact that pointer **variables** are bound to array names. Consider, for example, the following function, which does the same thing as *copyshort()*.

```
new_copyshort(a1, a2, size)
short    *a1, *a2;               /* same as short  a1[], a2[];} */
int      size;
{
        int i;
        for (i = 0; i < size; i++)
            *a1++ = *a2++;       /* not quite the  same as
                                    a1[i] = a2[i];       */
}
```

The declaration *short *a1, *a2;* in the new version is exactly the same as the declaration *short a1[], a2[];* in the previous version. But the statements that transmit the numbers from *a2* to *a1* behave a little differently in the two versions.

In *new_copyshort()* the statement **a1++ = *a2++;* makes the value pointed to by *a1* the same as the value pointed to by *a2*, and *then* increments the pointers *a2* and *a1* so that they point to the next positions in their corresponding arrays. The effect is the same as if *a1* and *a2* were subscripted (as they are in the first version). One advantage of doing it the second way is that it takes much less time to increment a pointer than it does to subscript an array.

Exercise 22. Write a function *substr(s1, s2, start, n)* **that copies** *n* **characters from** *s1* **to** *s2*, **beginning with the position indicated by** *start*, **and puts a null at the end of the characters moved into** *s2* **(to make it a valid string). Function** *substr()* **should return 0 if the string in** *s1* **is not long enough.**

Exercise 23. Recall that the function *strcpy(s1, s2)* **copies the contents of** *s2* **to** *s1*. **If a programmer enters the following code, an error results.**

```
char   str[30];
strcpy(str, 'Do not move me!');
```

It is hard to predict what actual error message would be printed. (The system might just silently go away without printing a message.) The reason for the error is that the statement is trying to access a part of storage that is not available. Explain.

C.24

POINTERS AND STRUCTURES

There are only three operations you can perform on a C structure— take its address, access one of its members, and take its size. One implication of this is that you can't simply pass an entire structure to a function, as you would a simple variable.† There are two ways that a structure can be accessed by a function:

☐ Make the structure *external* to the function; and
☐ Pass the structure's *address* (which is a simple variable) to the function, so that the function can operate on the structure through its address.

In both cases, the original version of the structure, not a copy, is being operated on by the function. In this sense, structures and arrays are handled similarly. Section C.15 discusses the use of external variables. Here we cover the implications of passing a structure's address.

Suppose you want to pass an entire structure to a function *print-vals()*, which prints the values of its members. The following code shows how a certain structure address is passed to the function. The shape of

---

†If a *member* of a structure, such as *emp_rec.name*, is a simple variable, it can be passed to a function just like any other simple variable. The problem we are dealing with in this section applies to the passing of *entire* structures.

the structure is defined outside the main procedure so that the definition can be referred to conveniently where needed.

```
typedef struct {                /* This is a definition of a     */
    char    id_number[8];       /* type of structure.  When      */
    short   quantity;           /* PART_REC is used later in a    */
    char    name[20];           /* declaration, space will be     */
} PART_REC;                     /* allocated for a structure of */
                                /* this particular shape.        */
main()
{
PART_REC truck_part;            /* truck_part is declared to     */
                                /* have the shape defined by     */
                .               /* PART_REC.                     */

        printvals(&truck_part); /* Send the address of record    */
                .               /* truck_part to printvals().    */
                .
}
```

If *printvals()* is to operate correctly on the members of *truck_part,* it must know more than just the address of *truck_part.* It must know the sizes and shapes of *truck_part*'s members. In other words, *printvals()* must have within its definition a definition of a structure that is equivalent to that of *truck_part.* Thanks to the *typedef* of *PART_REC,* this is easily done:

```
        printvals(inv_rec)

        PART_REC *inv_rec;    /* inv_rec is a local pointer    */
        {                     /* to a structure with the shape */
                .             /* defined by PART_REC.          */
                .

        }
```

Our next problem is to figure out how *printvals()* accesses individual members of the structure pointed to by *inv_rec.* For example, suppose we want to print the value of the *quantity* member of the structure. Recall that the "thing pointed to" by *inv_rec* is denoted in C by **inv_rec.* To denote "the *quantity* member of the thing pointed to by *inv_rec,*" we can write

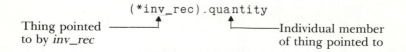

Thing pointed ————⌐   ⌐——————Individual member
to by *inv_rec*   (*inv_rec).quantity   of thing pointed to

Since this is an awkward and rather inexpressive notation for what is being referred to, the designers of C have provided an operator that means the same thing but expresses the meaning better. It is the $->$ operator:

```
inv_rec->quantity
```
means the same thing as `(*inv_rec).quantity`

Now we can put a statement in *printvals()* that actually prints the value of the *quantity* member of the structure:

```
printvals(inv_rec)

PART_REC *inv_rec;
{
        .
        .
    printf("quantity = %d\n",inv_rec->quantity);
        .
        .
}
```

PART_REC, truck_part, inv_part are three names that seem to refer to the same thing, but actually don't quite refer to the same thing. Let's review:

PART_REC	The name of the *definition* of a data type that happens to be a structure. It does not set aside storage. It does not refer to actual data. It merely says what a thing of type *PART_REC* will look like, *if* such a thing is ever declared.
truck_part	The name of the actual structure that can hold real data, and for which actual memory space is allocated. When *truck_part* is declared in *main()*, it is declared to have the shape defined by *PART_REC*.
inv_part	A pointer variable that contains the address of *truck_part*. It is a simple pointer variable, so it can be used as a function argument. When the function call *printval(&truck_part)* is made, the address *&truck_part* is assigned to *inv_part*.

Exercise 24. Complete the function *printvals()* so that it prints all parts of the structure.

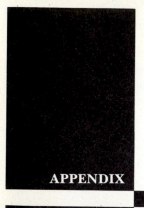

D COMPARING DISK DRIVES

There are enormous differences among different types of drives in terms of the amount of data they hold, the time it takes them to access data, overall cost, cost per bit, and intelligence. Furthermore, disk devices and media are evolving so rapidly that the figures on speed, capacity, and intelligence that apply one month may very well be out of date the next month.

Access time, you will recall, is composed of seek time, rotational delay, and transfer time.

Seek times are usually described in two ways: *minimum seek time* and *average seek time*. Usually, but not always, minimum seek time includes the time it takes for the head to accelerate from a standstill, move one track, and settle to a stop. Sometimes the track-to-track seek time is given, with a separate figure for head settling time. One has to be careful with figures such as these since their meanings are not always stated clearly.

Average seek time is the average time it takes for a seek if the desired sector is as likely to be on any one cylinder as it is on any other. In a completely random accessing environment, it can be shown that the number of cylinders covered in an average seek is approximately one-third of the total number of cylinders (Pechura and Schoeffler, 1983). Estimates of average seek time are commonly based on this result.

Certain disk drives, called *fixed head disk drives*, require no seek time. Fixed head drives provide one or more read/write heads per track, so there is no need to move the heads from track to track. Fixed head disk drives are very fast, but also considerably more expensive than movable head drives.

There are generally no significant differences in *rotational delay* among similar drives. Most floppy disk drives rotate between 300 and 600 rpm, and most hard disk drives rotate at 3600 rpm. Floppy disks usually do not spin continuously, so intermittent accessing of floppy drives might involve an extra delay due to startup of a second or more. Strategies such as sector interleaving can mitigate the effects of rotational delay in some circumstances.

Data *transfer rate* is constrained by two things: rotation speed and recording density. Since rotation speeds vary little, the main differences among drives are due to differences in recording density. In recent years there have been tremendous advances in improving recording densities on disks of all types. Differences in recording densities are usually expressed in terms of the number of *tracks per surface,* and the number of *bytes per track.* If data are organized by sector on a disk, and more than one sector is transferred at a time, the effective data transfer rate depends also on the method of sector interleaving used. The effect of interleaving can be substantial, of course, since logically adjacent sectors are often widely separated physically.

Although it is very possible that most of the figures in Table D.1 will be superseded during the time between the writing and the publi-

TABLE D.1

Comparisons of disk drives

	5¼ inch floppy (IBM PC/AT)	5¼ inch Winchester (QUBIE PC20)	Small removable (DEC RM03)	Large fixed sectored (DEC RP07)	Large fixed blocked (IBM 3380)
Seek times					
Minimum (msec)	*	3	6	5	*
Average (msec)	95	105	30	23	16
Rotational delay (msec)	100	8.5	8.3	8.3	8.3
Transfer rate (KB/sec)	23	484	1,200	2,200	3,000
Capacities					
Bytes/track	4,608	8,192	16,384	25,600	47,476
Tracks/cylinder	2	4	5	16	15
Cylinders/drive	40	611	823	1,260	1,770
Megabytes/drive	0.36	20	67	516	1,260

*Not available.

cation of this text, they should serve to give you a basic idea of the magnitude and range of performance characteristics for disks. The fact that they *are* changing so rapidly should also serve to emphasize the importance of being aware of disk drive performance characteristics when you are in a position to choose among different drives.

Of course, in addition to the quantitative differences among drives, there are other important differences. The IBM 3380 drive, for example, has many built-in features, including separate actuator arms that allow it to perform two accesses simultaneously. It also has large local buffers and a great deal of local intelligence, enabling it to optimize many operations that, with less sophisticated drives, have to be monitored by the central computer.

Bohl [1981] and Hanson [1982] provide very thorough coverage of large, sophisticated disk drives. These drives are evolving much more gradually than are the relatively inexpensive drives used with microcomputers.

BIBLIOGRAPHY

Baase, S. *Computer Algorithms: Introduction to Design and Analysis*. Reading, Mass.: Addison-Wesley, 1978.

Batory, D.S. "B$^+$ trees and indexed sequential files: A performance comparison." *ACM SIGMOD* (1981): 30–39.

Bayer, R., and E. McCreight. "Organization and maintenance of large ordered indexes." *Acta Informatica* 1, no. 3 (1972): 173–189.

Bayer, R., and K. Unterauer. "Prefix B-trees." *ACM Transactions on Database Systems* 2, no. 1 (March 1977): 11–26.

Bentley, J. "Programming pearls: A spelling checker." *Communications of the ACM* 28, no. 5 (May 1985): 456–462.

Bohl, M. *Introduction to IBM Direct Access Storage Devices*. Chicago: Science Research Associates, Inc., 1981.

Borland. *Turbo Toolbox Reference Manual*. Scott's Valley, Calif.: Borland International, Inc., 1984.

Bourne, S.R. *The Unix System*. Reading, Mass.: Addison-Wesley, 1984.

Bradley, J. *File and Data Base Techniques*. New York: Holt, Rinehart, and Winston, 1982.

Chaney, R., and B. Johnson. "Maximizing hard-disk performance." *Byte* 9, no. 5 (May 1984): 307–334.

Chang, C.C. "The study of an ordered minimal perfect hashing scheme." *Communications of the ACM* 27, no. 4 (April 1984): 384–387.

Chichelli, R.J. "Minimal perfect hash functions made simple." *Communications of the ACM* 23, no. 1 (January 1980): 17–19.

Claybrook, B.G. *File Management Techniques*. New York: John Wiley & Sons, 1983.

Comer, D. "The ubiquitous B-tree." *ACM Computing Surveys* 11, no. 2 (June 1979): 121–137.

Cooper, D. *Standard Pascal User Reference Manual.* New York: W.W. Norton & Co., 1983.

Crotzer, A.D. "Efficacy of B-trees in an information storage and retrieval environment." Unpublished Master's thesis, Oklahoma State University, 1975.

Davis, W.S. "Empirical behavior of B-trees." Unpublished Master's thesis, Oklahoma State University, 1974.

Deitel, H. *An Introduction to Operating Systems.* Revised 1st Ed. Reading, Mass.: Addison-Wesley, 1984.

Digital. *Introduction to VAX-11 Record Management Services.* Order No. AA-DO24A-TE. Digital Equipment Corporation, 1978.

Digital. *Peripherals Handbook.* Digital Equipment Corporation, 1981.

Digital. *RMS-11 User's Guide.* Digital Equipment Corporation, 1979.

Digital. *VAX-11 SORT/MERGE User's Guide.* Digital Equipment Corporation, 1984.

Digital. *VAX Software Handbook.* Digital Equipment Corporation, 1982.

Dodds, D.J. *"Pracnique:* Reducing dictionary size by using a hashing technique." *Communications of the ACM* 25, no. 6 (June 1982): 368–370.

Dwyer, B. "One more time—how to update a master file." *Communications of the ACM* 24, no. 1 (January 1981): 3–8.

Fagin, R., J. Nievergelt, N. Pippenger, and H.R. Strong. "Extendible hashing—a fast access method for dynamic files." *ACM Transactions on Database Systems* 4, no. 3 (September 1979): 315–344.

Faloutsos, C. "Access methods for text." *ACM Computing Surveys* 17, no. 1 (March 1985): 49–74.

Flores, I. *Peripheral Devices.* Englewood Cliffs, N.J.: Prentice-Hall, 1973.

Gonnet, G.H. *Handbook of Algorithms and Data Structures.* Reading, Mass.: Addison-Wesley, 1984.

Hanson, O. *Design of Computer Data Files.* Rockville, Md.: Computer Science Press, 1982.

Held, G., and M. Stonebraker. "B-trees reexamined." *Communications of the ACM* 21, no. 2 (February 1978): 139–143.

Hoare, C.A.R. "The emperor's old clothes." The C.A.R. Turing Award address. *Communications of the ACM* 24, no. 2 (February 1981): 75–83.

IBM. *DFSORT General Information.* IBM Order No. GC33-4033-11.

IBM. *OS/VS Virtual Storage Access Method (VSAM) Planning Guide.* IBM Order No. GC26-3799.

Jensen, K., and N. Wirth. *Pascal User Manual and Report,* 2d Ed. Springer Verlag, 1974.

Keehn, D.G., and J.O. Lacy. "VSAM data set design parameters." *IBM Systems Journal* 13, no. 3 (1974): 186–212.

Kelly, A., and I. Pohl. *A Book on C.* Menlo Park, Calif.: Benjamin/Cummings, 1984.

Kernighan, B., and R. Pike. *The UNIX Programming Environment.* Englewood Cliffs, N.J.: Prentice-Hall, 1984.

Kernighan, B., and D. Ritchie. *The C Programming Language.* Englewood Cliffs, N.J.: Prentice-Hall, 1978.

Knuth, D. *The Art of Computer Programming.* Vol. 1, *Fundamental Algorithms.* 2d Ed. Reading, Mass.: Addison-Wesley, 1973a.

Knuth, D. *The Art of Computer Programming.* Vol. 3, *Searching and Sorting.* Reading, Mass.: Addison-Wesley, 1973b.

Lang, S.D., J.R. Driscoll, and J.H. Jou. "Batch insertion for tree structured file organizations—improving differential database representation." CS-TR-85, Department of Computer Science, University of Central Florida, Orlando, Flor.

Levy, M.R. "Modularity and the sequential file update problem." *Communications of the ACM* 25, no. 6 (June 1982): 362–367.

Loomis, M. *Data Management and File Processing.* Englewood Cliffs, N.J.: Prentice-Hall, 1983.

Lorin, H. *Sorting and Sort Systems.* Reading, Mass.: Addison-Wesley, 1975.

Madnick, S.E., and J.J. Donovan. *Operating Systems.* Englewood Cliffs, N.J.: Prentice-Hall, 1974.

McCreight, E. "Pagination of B* trees with variable length records." *Communications of the ACM* 20, no. 9 (September 1977): 670–674.

McKusick, M.K., W.M. Joy, S.J. Leffler, and R.S. Fabry. "A fast file system for UNIX." *ACM Transactions on Computer Systems* 2, no. 3 (August 1984): 181–197.

Maurer, W.D., and T.G. Lewis. "Hash table methods." *ACM Computing Surveys* 7, no. 1 (March 1975): 5–19.

Microsoft, Inc. *Disk Operating System. Version 2.00.* IBM Personal Computer Language Series. IBM, 1983.

Murayama, K., and S.E. Smith. "Analysis of design alternatives for virtual memory indexes." *Communications of the ACM* 20, no. 4 (April 1977): 245–254.

Nievergelt, J., H. Hinterberger, and K. Sevcik. "The grid file: an adaptive symmetric, multikey file structure." *ACM Transactions on Database Systems* 9, no. 1 (March 1984): 38–71.

Ouskel, M., and P. Scheuermann. "Multidimensional B-trees: Analysis of dynamic behavior." *BIT* 21 (1981):401–418.

Pechura, M.A., and J.D. Schoeffler. "Estimating file access of floppy disks." *Communications of the ACM* 26, no. 10 (October 1983): 754–763.

Peterson, J.L., and A. Silberschatz. *Operating System Concepts,* 2nd Ed. Reading, Mass.: Addison-Wesley, 1985.

Peterson, W.W. "Addressing for random access storage." *IBM Journal of Research and Development* 1, no. 2(1957):130–146.

Pollack, S., and T. Sterling. *A Guide to Structured Programming and PL/I.* 3rd Ed. New York: Holt, Rinehart, and Winston, 1980.

Ritchie, B., and K. Thompson. "The UNIX time-sharing system." *Communications of the ACM* 17, no. 7 (July 1974): 365–375.

Robinson, J.T. "The *K-d* B-tree: A search structure for large multidimensional dynamic indexes." *ACM SIGMOD 1981 International Conference on Management of Data.* April 29–May 1, 1981.

Rosenberg, A.L., and L. Snyder. "Time and space optimality in B-trees." *ACM Transactions on Database Systems* 6, no. 1 (March 1981): 174–183.

Sager, T.J. "A polynomial time generator for minimal perfect hash functions." *Communications of the ACM* 28, no. 5 (May 1985): 523–532.

Salton, G., and M. McGill. *Introduction to Modern Information Retrieval*. McGraw-Hill, 1983.

Scholl, M. "New file organizations based on dynamic hashing." *ACM Transactions on Database Systems* 6, no. 1 (March 1981): 194–211.

Severance, D.G. "Identifier search mechanisms: A survey and generalized model." *ACM Computing Surveys* 6, no. 3 (September 1974): 175–194.

Snyder, L. "On B-trees reexamined." *Communications of the ACM* 21, no. 7 (July 1978): 594.

Spector, A., and D. Gifford. "Case study: The space shuttle primary computer system." *Communications of the ACM* 27, no. 9 (September 1984): 872–900.

Standish, T.A. *Data Structure Techniques*. Reading, Mass.: Addison-Wesley, 1980.

Sussenguth, E.H. "The use of tree structures for processing files." *Communications of the ACM* 6, no. 5 (May 1963): 272–279.

Sweet, F. "Keyfield design." *Datamation* (October 1, 1985): 119–120.

Teory, T.J., and J.P. Fry. *Design of Database Structures*. Englewood Cliffs, N.J.: Prentice-Hall, 1982.

The Joint ANSI/IEEE Pascal Standards Committee. "Pascal: Forward to the candidate extension library." *SIGPLAN Notices* 19, no. 7 (July 1984): 28–44.

Tremblay, J.P., and P.G. Sorenson. *An Introduction to Data Structures with Applications*. New York: McGraw-Hill, 1984.

Ullman, J. *Principles of Database Systems,* 2d Ed. Rockville, Md.: Computer Science Press, 1980.

VanDoren, J. "Some empirical results on generalized AVL trees." *Proceedings of the NSF-CBMS Regional Research Conference on Automatic Information Organization and Retrieval*. University of Missouri at Columbia (July 1973): 46–62.

VanDoren, J., and J. Gray. "An algorithm for maintaining dynamic AVL trees." In *Information Systems, COINS IV,* New York: Plenum Press, 1974: 161–180.

Wagner, R.E. "Indexing design considerations." *IBM Systems Journal* 12, no. 4 (1973): 351–367.

Webster, R.E. "B$^+$ trees." Unpublished Master's thesis, Oklahoma State University, 1980.

Wiederhold, G. *Database Design,* 2d Ed. New York: McGraw-Hill, 1983.

Wirth, N. "An assessment of the programming language Pascal." *IEEE Transactions on Software Engineering* SE-1, no. 2 (June 1975).

Yao, A. Chi-Chih. "On random 2-3 trees." *Acta Informatica* 9, no. 2 (1978): 159–170.

Zoellick, B. "CD-ROM software development." *Byte* 11, no. 5 (May 1986):173–188.

INDEX